Southern Unionist Pamphlets and the Civil War

*

Shades of Blue and Gray Series
Edited by Herman Hattaway and Jon L. Wakelyn

*

THE SHADES OF BLUE AND GRAY SERIES will offer Civil War studies for the modern reader—Civil War buff and scholar alike. Military history today addresses the relationship between society and warfare. Thus biographies and thematic studies that deal with civilians, soldiers, and political leaders are increasingly important to a larger public. This series will include books that will appeal to Civil War Roundtable groups, individuals, libraries, and academics with a special interest in this era of American history.

Southern Unionist Pamphlets and the Civil War

EDITED BY JON L. WAKELYN

University of Missouri Press
Columbia and London

Copyright © 1999 by

The Curators of the University of Missouri

University of Missouri Press, Columbia, Missouri 65201

Printed and bound in the United States of America

All rights reserved

5 4 3 2 1   03 02 01 00 99

Library of Congress Cataloging-in-Publication Data

Southern unionist pamphlets and the Civil War / edited by Jon L. Wakelyn.

  p. cm.—(Shades of blue and gray series)

Includes index.

ISBN 0-8262-1264-6 (alk. paper)

  1. Confederate States of America—Politics and government—Sources.   2. United

States—History—Civil War, 1861–1865—Pamphlets.   3. Unionists (United States Civil

War).   4. United States. Army—Southern unionists.   5. Secession—Southern

States—Sources.   I. Series.   II. Wakelyn, Jon L.

E487.S75 1999

973.7 21—dc21   99-044234

㊏™ This paper meets the requirements of the

American National Standard for Permanence of Paper

for Printed Library Materials, Z39.48, 1984.

Designer: Stephanie Foley

Typesetter: BOOKCOMP, Inc.

Printer and binder: Thomson-Shore, Inc.

Typefaces: Adobe Jenson and Caslon Antique

To my adult children,

David J. Wakelyn of Chicago, Illinois, and
Meredith E. Wakelyn of Denver, Colorado

CONTENTS

PREFACE

WITHIN THE SOUTHERN CONFEDERACY and among the border slave states lived a number of people who openly supported the Union during the Civil War. Some of those unionists played an active part in opposing the Confederacy, both in the dangerous home front of the Confederacy and on its periphery. Others were forced to flee their homes and the South itself for a time. A few held seats in the Federal Congress or served as governors in exile from their home states. Those exiles, before they returned home, lectured in northern cities and in the border slave states that remained loyal to the Union. The southern unionist leaders, from inside and outside the South, used their powers of oral and written persuasion to oppose the Confederacy, often publishing their speeches and writings in the form of pamphlets that they circulated in the North, in the slave border states, and even into the heart of the Confederacy itself. The contents of those pamphlets shed much light on the southern unionists' motivations to remain loyal, their personal activities as loyalists, the actions of their friends and enemies, the perilous lives of unionists behind the military lines, their continued support for the Federal government despite much adversity, and their hopes for the restored Union.

Pamphlets, as I have written on other occasions, were quite useful political instruments for a number of reasons.[1] They allowed speeches, newspaper accounts, articles, and personal memoirs to be reproduced in an easily readable form. They were cheap to print and could be obtained in large quantities. Small in size, they were easily sent through the mails or delivered by hand. If need be, they could be smuggled behind the Confederate lines.

1. Jon L. Wakelyn, ed., *Southern Pamphlets on Secession, November 1860–April 1861* (Chapel Hill: University of North Carolina Press, 1996); Jon L. Wakelyn, "The Politics of Violence: Unionist Pamphleteers in Virginia's Inner Civil War," in Daniel Sutherland, ed., *Violence, Unionism, and Guerrilla Warfare in the Confederate States of America* (Fayetteville: University of Arkansas Press, 1999).

They often targeted specific constituents, fellow leaders, and other opinion makers. Recipients often made use of them in their own speeches and writings. Thus, the unionist pamphlets may well have been the best form of communication among slave state supporters of the Federal cause in those perilous war times.

The eighteen pamphlets included in this volume have been selected from some sixty written throughout the war that I have surveyed. Three of the eighteen are from 1861. Two only were published in 1862, a year of special turmoil for southern unionists. Five were printed in the crucial year of 1863, which included the declaration of abolition of slavery, the Union occupation of large parts of the Confederacy, and perhaps the military turning point of the war. The largest number, seven, were written and published in 1864, just as presidential reconstruction heated up. The one from 1865 reveals southern unionists' hopes for a reunited nation without slavery.

The pamphlets selected for inclusion are representative of the works of wartime unionist leaders and important private citizens from most of the slaveholding states. One each came from the border slave states of Maryland and Kentucky, and two were written and published in Missouri, where a vicious internal war divided the people. Ten came out of Federal-occupied Confederate states. Four of those are from Virginia, of which the army controlled only the border regions, although one of the pamphleteers later represented West Virginia in the wartime U.S. Congress. Two are from Tennessee, one written and published in Nashville, the other first delivered as a speech in Philadelphia and sent into east Tennessee. One was given as a speech in Arkansas but printed elsewhere and sent into that state in pamphlet form only late in the war. And three came from inside Union-occupied New Orleans. Of the lower South states, the last to yield to Federal army incursion, one pamphlet each came from Mississippi, Alabama, North Carolina, and Texas. Of the four from the lower South, only the one from Mississippi was written at home, although it was published in Memphis. Two of the other three pamphleteers returned from exile and personally delivered their pamphlets to allies. I have been unable to find any pamphlets written by unionists from Florida, South Carolina, or Georgia.

All of the pamphleteers lived in the slave states before the war started, but only nine were born in the states for which they fought. Five were born in other slave states but spent their formative years in the states they represented during the Civil War. One was born in a northern border state, had family ties to a slave state, and only later moved to the state he represented. Two others were born in northern states but had long lived in the slave states. One was born abroad and moved as a youth to the slave

South. Thus, all had years of experience in the slave states before the war, even if their upbringing in the North or on the border south may have given some of them the perspective to oppose a separate Confederacy and argue for a restored Union.

The pamphleteers came from the ranks of local and national political leaders, as well as concerned private citizens, military, and clergy. One woman journalist-activist pamphleteer is included. Two were preachers, one a former Confederate general, and one a well-known novelist and former politician. Three were private citizens, all of whom in their own way had spoken out before the war in support of the Union. Five held office as governor of their respective states. Three of them served as military or provisional governors, one became a governor in exile who spent little time in his state, and one gained election as a governor from a border slave state. One of those military governors, Andrew Johnson, had served in the wartime U.S. Senate and became President Abraham Lincoln's vice president in 1864. The governor in exile, Andrew Jackson Hamilton, before the war had been a member of the U.S. Congress. Three others served in the wartime Federal Congress but were kept under careful scrutiny by their so-called northern friends.

The topics they discussed and the events they described covered a range of topics of interest to themselves and to their fellow unionists at home. The authors were aware that their northern allies would read their pamphlets. Thus, they also wrote to solicit northern aid, to renew efforts to defeat the Confederacy, and to gain sympathy for the plight of their people behind the lines, a plight at times caused by the activities of their northern allies. All of the pamphleteers personalized their efforts by including threats to their own well-being in their descriptions of life behind the lines. Mostly they discussed the issues of the war and vividly depicted events caused by an internal war made worse by the lawlessness of the times.

In this edition, the punctuation and spelling of the originals have been retained, except in the case of obvious typographical errors, which have been silently corrected. Except for the insertion of [sic] in a few cases, material in brackets is in the original. A few of the pamphlets have been edited to cut out needless repetition and excessive quotes. The deletions are indicated by ellipses and are summarized in the notes.

To supplement the views of the eighteen pamphleteers chosen for this volume, I have listed and discussed twenty-two other pamphlets. This is necessary in part because this rich lode of information has seldom been used in the many books written about the Confederacy or about southern unionism. The exception is the splendid effort of William C. Harris, which only whets the appetite for further analysis.[2] These twenty-two additional pamphlets, some written by authors represented in this volume, add to our understanding of the issues that preoccupied those southern unionists. That the meaning and the function of governance during wartime was of prime interest to them should surprise no one. Like many other southern unionists, they were forced by the overpowering Confederate military might and the government encouragement of guerrilla hostilities against them to flee the South or to remain silent. Everywhere they saw the failure of government to protect the people, and all attempted to communicate their concerns about ineffectual political organization to those back home. Those who wrote from within the slave states, too, remarked often on the faults of civil governance.

I have also summarized ten unionist pamphlets published during the early years of reconstruction, some of whose authors at last were free to speak their minds openly. All of them addressed the role of former wartime southern unionists in the South's reconstruction. All to some extent chronicled the decline of power among the unionist leadership, in part because of the failure of the Federal government to keep the unionist movement alive. Perhaps the fact that so many of them faded quickly from public view explains why those pamphleteers who gave such vivid descriptions of internal disruption and wrote so much about their plans for a new South have largely gone unstudied.

Combined, these works reveal a great deal about southern resistance to the Confederacy, the plight of southern unionists during the war, and their relations with their northern allies. It is hoped that the printing of and commentary on these seldom-used sources will encourage others to study the writings and other activities of those southern unionists who so ardently favored the defeat of the Confederacy and the restoration of the Union.

2. William C. Harris, *With Charity for All: Lincoln and the Restoration of the Union* (Lexington: University Press of Kentucky, 1997); William C. Harris, "The Southern Unionist Critique of the Civil War," *Civil War History* 31 (March 1985): 39–56.

ACKNOWLEDGMENTS

T HESE PAMPHLETS HAVE BEEN obtained from a number of archives and libraries. Of course, anyone in search of a comprehensive collection of the pamphlets and books cited should begin with the Rare Book Room of the Library of Congress. Even so, that splendid repository contains only some of the pamphlets studied and represented in this volume. Persistent searchers should also visit the Barker Center at the University of Texas, Austin; the Virginia State Historical Society in Richmond (which has a large collection of bound pamphlets that, alas, remain uncataloged); the Alderman Rare Book Room at the University of Virginia, Charlottesville; and the gold mine called the Southern Historical Collection at the University of North Carolina, Chapel Hill.

For assistance in finding some of these pamphlets I must thank my former students John Allen and Clayton Jewett, both part bloodhound. A current student, Stephen Carney, has provided able computer assistance. Also, David Kelly of the Reference Division, Library of Congress, again provided much help, especially since scholars no longer have access to the stacks. William C. Harris of North Carolina State University not only revealed himself to me as one of the University of Missouri Press's outside readers but also provided me with much assistance from his large knowledge of those oppressed southern unionists. Dan Sutherland of the University of Arkansas gave me the opportunity to write on the Virginia unionists, and his comments on those border leaders have been most helpful in this project. Last, I want to thank Joyce Walker, who offered no scholarly advice, but put up with my insistence that southern unionists offer a major wrinkle on the complexity of life in the beleaguered Confederacy.

Southern Unionist Pamphlets and the Civil War

Southern Unionist Pamphleteers on Governance during the Civil War

T HAT A NUMBER OF CITIZENS of the slave states opposed the southern Confederacy during the war has long been known. There is a body of literature on yeoman discontent, including soldiers who deserted, and one recent study of a non-slave-owner rebellion in North Carolina. Slaves rebelled in many ways, and the efforts of the Freedman and Southern Society Project have borne fruit on that subject. In addition, the indomitable Richard Current recently has analyzed the lives of southern men who fought for the Union. Another historian has suggested, tantalizingly, that even some of the Confederacy's military and civilian leaders, by action or inaction, harmed the war effort. Yet another points out that the Confederate government never managed to unite its citizenry, including some people of importance, and thus faced internal opposition from the beginning.[1] But how those committed unionist leaders attempted to undermine the authority of the Confederacy has not been studied in full.

A few of those loyalists did take up both sword and pen to resist the Confederacy and to restore the Union. Some of them came from the border slave states that had not seceded and led precarious lives in their own regions, which had many pro-Confederates. Others who resided in the Confederacy itself for a time had to flee their homes and go underground or

---

1. Ella Lonn, *Desertion during the Civil War* (New York: Century Co., 1928); Georgia Lee Tatum, *Disloyalty in the Confederacy* (Chapel Hill: University of North Carolina Press, 1934); Wayne K. Durrill, *War of Another Kind: A Southern Community in the Great Rebellion* (New York: Oxford University Press, 1990); Ira Berlin et al., eds., *Slaves No More: Three Essays on Emancipation and the Civil War* (New York: Cambridge University Press, 1992); Richard N. Current, *Lincoln's Loyalists: Union Soldiers from the Confederate States* (Boston: Northeastern University Press, 1992); William W. Freehling, *The Reintegration of American History* (New York: Oxford University Press, 1994), 220–52.

to the North. The border slave states became points of entry for the Federal army into the Confederacy, and the unionist supporters in those states aided that invasion. The Federal army of occupation, it has recently been shown, then gave unionist supporters within the Confederate lines the opportunity to reemerge and speak out, and encouraged those who had fled to return and foment further resistance to the southern cause.[2] Thus, the southern unionists who came from eastern and northwestern Virginia, coastal North Carolina, the Nashville basin, the lower Mississippi River from Arkansas to New Orleans, and even the interior Confederacy mounted a vigorous external and internal written opposition to the Confederate authorities.

One of their most effective means of resistance was through the publication and wide dissemination of pamphlets. In their pamphlets, those southern unionists discussed a number of issues related to their support for the Federal cause. Many of them criticized secessionist promises to the southern people, highlighting the failure of the Confederate government to create a nation able to protect its people. Because the southern unionist leaders so identified with their own followers' plight, they often combined descriptions of scenes of domestic horror with comments on how Confederate threats on their lives had forced them to flee their homeland. But if the Confederate government behaved badly and failed the people, the southern unionists also had much to say about their allies, the Federal government and its army. The pamphleteers expected to gain power from the Federal victory, and they said so often. The pamphlets of the southern unionists thus address the conduct of the war from many aspects.

The slave state unionist pamphleteers necessarily maintained a delicate balance between being seen by their allies as too pro-Yankee and being seen by their northern friends as too soft on the South. They created rhetorical flourishes and wrote lurid tales of persecution and disruption of lives to appeal to all loyal unionists. They waved Old Glory until it became tattered. Eyes filled with tears at its sight. Liberty burst forth on every page. Rebellion, they wailed, had to be crushed. The old Ship of State wore well. Reunion became the "ardent desire" of every patriot. They demanded unconditional loyalty. Often they invoked historic heroism and sacrifice. In fact, great heroes were mentioned so often in these works that one wonders if the southern unionists were refighting the American Revolution. Depiction of the deeds of past heroes united southerners and northerners, so that George Washington and Patrick Henry were linked with John Adams and

2. Stephen V. Ash, *When the Yankees Came* (Chapel Hill: University of North Carolina Press, 1995).

John Hancock. Loyal citizens, present and past, sacrificed, bled, and lost their lives because all unionists loved the United States flag and the "great" democratic republic.[3]

Tales of contemporary heroics add to the unionist pamphleteers' images of loyalty. One who had served in his state's secession convention described his campaign for election to that convention. He demonstrated his own loyalty by invoking the loyalties of the people in his county. Thus he told eloquently the story of the old men who, though under threat by secessionists, came to hear him speak. They seated themselves near him and listened intently. All had served in the American Revolution, and all came to the speech grounds clad in uniforms from that war. One almost can imagine the tears rolling down their faces when the pamphleteer proclaimed that to a man those patriots voted the Union ticket.[4]

Another pamphleteer, in an attempt to convince the Federal Congress to seat him, told his own personal history of loyalty to the Union cause. He stated that enemies had circulated vicious rumors about his loyalty throughout the Federal Congress. All these attacks, he proclaimed, were because his son fought for the Confederacy. The unionist would-be congressman described with strong emotion how he had seen both his own beautiful daughter and her husband and child and his handsome and healthy son depart for the war's front. But then he claimed that he had sacrificed that family by fighting for the union cause. Humiliated, he declared: "I loved the stars and stripes better than my own flesh and blood!"[5]

All of these loyal words and stories at first blush seem only to capture devotion to the Union cause. But careful study of their meaning shows a pattern of special interest to the pamphleteers. All reflected issues of governance, especially faith in the Federal government to end the crisis and to make peace. The loyal southern leaders at home, the exiles and their governments, and the escapees who returned to lead, all linked their cause to patriotism. A few pamphleteers even announced that a counterrevolution

3. Waitman T. Willey, *Speech on the Object of the War* (Washington, D.C.: Congressional Globe Office, 1862), 4; John W. Wood, *Union and Secession in Mississippi* (Memphis: Saunders, Parrish and Whitmore, 1863), 54; Thomas C. Fletcher, *Speech on the Occasion of the Reception by the Legislature of the News of the Passage of the Convention Ordinance Abolishing Slavery in Missouri* (Jefferson City: W. A. Curry, 1865), 6; Jeremiah Clemens, *Letter* (Philadelphia: J. B. Lippencott and Co., 1864), 16; Andrew Jackson Hamilton, *Address to the People of Texas* (New Orleans: Printed at the Era Office, 1864), 8. Also see Freehling, *Reintegration*, 216.

4. Wood, *Union and Secession in Mississippi*, 20, 21.

5. Joseph Segar, *Speech . . . in Defence of His Claim to a Seat in That Body* (Baltimore: John Murphy and Co., 1864), 23–24.

in the South against Confederate authorities had been launched to save the flag, or to redeem national government.[6]

Those writers thus combined patriotic rhetoric with comments on what they expected from the U.S. government. Anna Ella Carroll's diatribe against John C. Breckinridge's traitorous behavior led her to assert that "he who is not with the Government is against it." She used this argument as an excuse to urge the president to assume rigorous command of the war effort and pursue it vigorously. Congressman Waitman Willey of Virginia opined that only an active Federal government could protect the southern loyalists. Robert J. Breckinridge insisted that the United States could exist only in a single government. The way to win, he said, was for the U.S. government to assume a position of supreme authority. John Wood of Mississippi insisted that "a re-union in feeling among the people of the United States, should be the ardent desire of every patriot." The Alabama novelist-politician Jeremiah Clemens best summed up this linkage when he insisted that southern unionists had "proved to the world" that they were capable of "still higher heroism" as they fought to save the nation.[7]

If the pamphleteers made hyperbolic and excessive effusions of national patriotism and called for Federal military support, they commented also about the failure of secessionists to fulfill their promises to the southern people. Of course, those political pamphleteers knew full well that to link the causes of the war to secessionist claims for the future allowed them to contrast Confederate government promises with wartime reality.

This fiction of secession, said one, "strikes at the fundamental idea of a national government" and leads to anarchy and confusion. A number of other pamphleteers agreed as they rejected Confederate claims for secession as the only way to protect slavery, and they insisted instead that the Federal government itself best defended slavery. Others asserted that secessionists were the slave-owning elites who wanted to destroy republican institutions

---

6. Francis Harrison Pierpont, *Letter to His Excellency the President . . .* (Washington, D.C.: McGill and Witherow, 1864), 55; Robert J. Breckinridge, "The Civil War: Its Nature and End," *Danville Quarterly Review* 1 (December 1861): 655 (this article was later printed as a pamphlet; citations are to pages in the *Review*). For a view of this patriotic language see Andrew W. Robertson, *The Language of Democracy: Political Rhetoric in the United States and Britain, 1790–1900* (Ithaca: Cornell University Press, 1995).

7. Carroll, *Reply to the Speech of Hon. J. C. Breckinridge* (Washington, D.C.: Henry Polkinhorn, 1861), 3; Willey, *Object of the War,* 4; Breckinridge, "The Civil War: Its Nature and End," 652; Wood, *Union and Secession in Mississippi,* 54; Clemens, *Letter,* 16. Also see Jeremiah Clemens, *Tobias Wilson: A Tale of the Great Rebellion* (Philadelphia: J. B. Lippincott and Co., 1865).

and even enslave poorer whites.[8] More sinisterly, Robert J. Breckinridge claimed the secessionists planned to destroy the Federal government and conquer the nation. For William G. Brownlow, and a number of other unionists who had been marginalized or made to feel as outsiders in their own communities, the rebellion was the culmination of a gigantic conspiracy.[9] Indeed, said they, the secessionists tricked the good people of the slave states into believing that their interests lay outside the Federal union. In time, the southern unionist pamphleteers insisted, the citizenry would understand this deception, and then unite with them to break the Confederate government's hold on the lives of the southern people.

To support the case of a people deceived, the southern unionist leaders linked the arguments for secession to promises the radical separationists had made. The secessionists, the unionists asserted, claimed that there would be no war because the northerners and their government were soft and too materialistic to resist. Because "cotton was king," European powers, resisting disruption of the precious flow of that commodity, would tell the North that they would defend the Confederacy. But, even if war came and blood was shed, secessionists insisted, the U.S. government was too weak to defeat the South. In addition they said that southern soldiers, determined to protect their homeland at any cost, were much too strong for Union troops. During the war, secessionists proclaimed, the southern people would thrive. Not only would markets for foreign trade remain open, but southern finances would grow stronger. A free press also would comment truthfully about the government's activities. A benevolent government would feed, shelter, and clothe the people behind the lines, especially women and children.[10] In short, insisted the unionists, the Confederates made all those false promises to enlist the support of the people in a fateful attempt to overthrow the Federal government.

The unionist pamphleteers wrote about those promises to remind their constituents of what the Confederacy could not deliver, and thus also to evaluate that government's performance. Promises, they claimed, were far from the reality. In the first place, as the war wore on and more and more lives were wasted, it became apparent that cotton was not king. European powers not only did not try to protect their economic investment, they got

8. Willey, *Object of the War*, 7, 11. Also see Harry Eckstein, "On the Etiology of Internal War," *History and Theory* 4, no. 2 (1965): 133–63.

9. Breckinridge, "The Civil War: Its Nature and End," 644; Brownlow, *Speech against the Great Rebellion* (Washington, D.C.: Scammell and Bros., 1862).

10. Clemens, *Letter*, 3; Wood, *Union and Secession in Mississippi*, 6.

by without cotton. Neither arms, calls for the war to cease, nor any other aid came from Europe. Even attempts to finance the war through European loans came to naught.[11]

Next, though the southern fighting man proved to be resourceful and brave, the flawed government and mediocre generals let down the troops. In battle after battle, said the unionists, the Confederacy failed to take advantage of successes. As the war ground on and as Confederates gave way to superior Union numbers, they became desperate. A former Confederate general turned unionist charged that corrupt government officials colluded with Arkansas political-military bosses to shelve the talented general Albert Pike, because they did not want to compete with that popular man for the people's favor. Corruption like that in the high command, claimed Edward W. Gantt, resulted in excessive loss of life and an ever encroaching Union army.[12]

Behind the ever dwindling Confederate lines, said the pamphleteers, matters grew worse for the civilians. Unionists appeared to take delight in revealing how Confederate authorities were unable to protect their own. Plans to stabilize finances, they gloated, failed completely. Instead, hyper-inflation wrecked the economy and left people in desperate straits. Some could not even feed themselves because of rising prices. The Confederate government, in short, was so poorly run that it could not help the people in any way. Only the state governors, some of whom developed real hatred toward Confederate authorities, managed a bare assistance plan. Then, in desperate attempts to continue the failing war effort, the government turned on its own people. Horror stories of sons ripped from their mother's arms and fathers taken from the fields abounded. Confiscations of goods—horses, crops, even money—were the acts of a desperate government, the unionists said.[13]

To make matters worse, failed generals ofttimes took out their own grievances on the troops themselves. The name Braxton Bragg became synonymous with the horrors of war. When troops were shot summarily for slacking or desertion the unionists called the generals criminals. A

11. Edward W. Gantt, *Address in Favor of Reunion in 1863* (New York: Loyal Publication Society, 1865).

12. Ibid., 3, 7. For more on the treatment of Albert Pike see Robert E. Shalhope, *Sterling Price: Portrait of a Southerner* (Columbia: University of Missouri Press, 1973), 200–205. The most recent biography of Pike is Walter Lee Brown, *A Life of Albert Pike* (Fayetteville: University of Arkansas Press, 1997).

13. The best discussions of these atrocities are in Wood, *Union and Secession in Mississippi*, 46; Clemens, *Letter*, 7; and Hamilton, *Address to the People of Texas*, 8.

wrenching story of twin sons of nineteen accused of desertion especially agitated one southern unionist. Those boys, claimed the author, had only gone to visit nearby relatives. For their "crime" the general sentenced them to be hanged. The pamphleteer described in detail the pitiful scene in which the youths' aged father pleaded for clemency, was refused, and then was forced to watch them die.[14]

The pamphleteers also discussed how the Confederate government and its soldiers treated those civilians behind the lines who tried to remain neutral or who supported the Union cause. They often used attacks on their own persons to stir up their readers. Leaders like "Parson" Brownlow, Jeremiah Clemens, and Bryan Tyson wrote vividly of being imprisoned in cold dungeons and then forced to flee their homeland.[15] But mostly they wrote about the brutalization and even murder of innocent people who had spoken out, and they insisted that the Confederate government neither believed in freedom of speech nor had the power to stop irregular troops or guerrillas who preyed on innocent unionist civilians. Lawlessness, paying back old grudges, disrupting loyal leaders, they remonstrated, all led to extralegal bandit activity.[16]

Thus, the pamphleteers described the slave states' political failure to stem the horrible treatment of innocent southerners. In doing so, they demonstrated to the people trapped behind the lines that they identified with their plight and wanted to do something about it. Their descriptions of personal escape often were linked to the promise to return and restore good government. The unionist pamphleteers also spoke to their northern allies, especially the Federal government, from which they expected relief for their fellow unionists. This discussion of the South's failure to protect civilians was designed not to chastise ordinary southern citizens but to attack the elites who ran the Confederate army and the civilian government leaders who unleashed them on the people. In all cases, the pamphleteers who wrote about Confederate lies commented on that government's inability to defend its own.

14. Gantt, *Address in Favor of Reunion*, 5.

15. Brownlow, *Speech against the Great Rebellion*, 4; Clemens, *Letter*, 9–10; Tyson, *A Ray of Light: or, Treatise on the Sectional Troubles, Religious and Morally Considered* (Brower's Mills, N.C.: Published by the Author, 1862). Also see William G. Brownlow, *Sketches of the Rise, Progress, and Decline of Secession; with a Narrative of Personal Adventures among the Rebels* (Philadelphia: George W. Childs, 1862).

16. Gantt, *Address in Favor of Reunion*, 16; Eckstein, "On the Etiology of Internal War," 148. Perhaps some of these stories of atrocities perpetrated on unionist civilians were exaggerated. But much corroboration exists of these tales in the official reports of Federal military officers.

But if the Confederate government failed the southern people, how did the northern government perform? How did the escaped unionists who desired to return, and often did, interact with their northern friends? On one level, certainly, the southern unionists had much good to say about those who allowed them to return home. For example, the return theme almost always invoked the Federal government's role in aiding its southern unionist allies. Governors such as Francis Pierpont of the restored state of Virginia and Andrew Johnson of Tennessee told stories of how the Union military advance relieved the plight of southern loyalists.[17] The pamphleteers also analyzed Federal policies in hopes of influencing them, as well as justifying them to the people back home.

The unionist pamphleteers always began the policy sections of their works by combining loyalty to the cause, their own role in the war, and their gratitude for the armies and politics of liberation. Even those who became quite critical of Federal policies and activities thanked the Union for coming to their rescue. No doubt these required encomiums served multiple purposes. Some told northerners of southern unionist's sacrifices in behalf of the troops and asked for materiel support for the cause. They also claimed a camaraderie with their liberators. Others wanted to stir their own people to further sacrifices. Still others directed their efforts to their northern civilian friends, especially the various lecture societies that supported the war, to get them to sustain the fight through to a favorable reunion. With the northern peace movement growing, those southern pamphleteers who knew that only total victory could help their cause seemed almost frantic in their insistence on their love for the Union.[18] Those southern unionists who had direct dealings with the Federal government, Congress, the military, and civilian loyalists made certain their obsequies and gratitude were heard in those political circles.

But, if the pamphleteers were quick to praise their allies, they criticized them, too. The Federal government's antislavery policy concerned them the most. Even before the preliminary emancipation proclamation of September 1862, the unionists, many of whom held or formally owned slaves, warned that slavery was a volatile issue that could disrupt southern

17. Pierpont, *Letter to the President,* 4; Johnson, *Speech on the Restoration of State Government* (Nashville: Dispatch Printing Co., 1864), 3. See also the excellent collection of Johnson letters in Leroy P. Graf and Ralph W. Haskins, eds., *The Papers of Andrew Johnson,* vol. 6, *1862–1864* (Knoxville: University of Tennessee Press, 1983).

18. Hamilton, *Address to the People of Texas,* 9, 11. This idea of nationalism has been explored in Ernest Gellner, *Encounters with Nationalism* (Oxford: Blackwell, 1994), esp. xi, 192, 200.

unionist support. Even loyal border-state slave owners, they warned, might give their support to the Confederates, or at least refuse to join the ranks of the unionists. If slaves were freed, some of them said, competition with free labor could sour relations with small farmers and urban workers. Besides, who would pay them for their slaves, and how would the states be rid of the ex-slaves?[19]

No southern unionist proslavery advocate spoke more bitterly about the Lincoln government's abolition of slavery than did the North Carolina Democrat and escapee Bryan Tyson, who wrote his pamphlet from the safe confines of Washington City. That pamphlet, published in late 1863, before the presidential campaign of 1864, circulated among northern Democrats and southern unionists. In it, Tyson supported ex-general George B. McClellan in the hopes a conservative peace would restore slavery. Its venomous racism reveals the dilemma of combining southern unionist support for the nation's policies with loyalty to one's home, and the real dangers of coupling southern unionist activities with the desire to end slavery. It bears careful explication.

Tyson began by stating baldly that slavery caused the war, and he wanted his northern audience to understand what slavery was like and his southern friends to know that he was a unionist but loyal to their interests. Claiming to take both sides—to be arguing both for abolition and for retention of slavery—Tyson did nothing of the kind. He mainly described how well slaves had been treated in the South and the life of a society committed to that system of labor. Tyson then warned that ex-slaves would be unable to care for themselves and, worse, that a race war would ensue.[20]

But that argument for the harmony of slave society was indeed old hat, and Tyson himself even seemed too bored to promulgate it. What he really wanted to do was link slavery to the way the war was fought and to the future peace where ex-unionists would make North Carolina a viable part of the Federal Union. Tyson warned that Confederate leaders would fight harder and prolong the war in hopes of saving slavery. Slyly he said that, if abolition would end the war sooner, then he was for it. But he believed that it would not. His real point was that "a reunion, to be worth anything,

19. John S. Carlile, *Speech on the Bill to Confiscate the Property and Free the Slaves of Rebels* (Washington, D.C.: Congressional Globe Office, 1862), 5, 8. For the best analysis of this southern unionist view of the North see William C. Harris, "The Southern Unionist Critique of the Civil War," *Civil War History* 31 (March 1985): 39–56.

20. Tyson, *The Institution of Slavery in the Southern States, Religiously and Morally Considered* (Washington, D.C.: H. Polkinhorn, 1863), esp. 14, 36; also see Carlile, *Speech on the Bill to Confiscate the Property*, 8.

must be based upon the will of the people governed, and that, therefore, to have a good and permanent Government the extremists North and South must yield, and let the question at issue be decided by a popular vote of the people."[21] Tyson obviously believed that many northerners opposed abolition, and that unionists could gain power in restored North Carolina if they too opposed abolition.

Most of the southern unionist pamphleteers, however, seized on the issue raised by leaders like Tyson to claim that if ending slavery meant the defeat of the Confederacy and the restoration of a united nation, then they advocated abolition as a war aim. Ex-Confederate general Edward Gantt perhaps best captured that feeling when he stated forthrightly that slavery had become "incompatible with the existence of the Government."[22] Still others turned Tyson's view on its head to proclaim that southerners were coming to understand that slavery was incompatible with their future economy. In a restored Union, they claimed, a South without slavery not only would welcome to power the committed unionists but also would live without the specter of slave revolts and even the fear of unworkable race relations. That is, many southern unionists told their constituents that the Federal government planned to free slaves and to colonize them.[23]

A number of southern unionists used the cover of the Federal government's abolition of slavery to assert that they had never really supported slavery. They wrote that a slave-owner elite had treated ordinary white nonslaveholders like peasants, and the end of slavery would allow those people to vie for power. Andrew J. Hamilton of Texas, for one, insisted that the end of slavery would end the southern elite's control of government.[24] Military governor Andrew Johnson of Tennessee, formally a slaveholder and a defender of slavery until after his return home in 1862, sought to rally his fellow unionists to support a new Tennessee constitution that abolished slavery and forever disestablished the slave owners who had been treasonous to the Federal government.[25] Although Louisiana's unionists equivocated over abolition policy, they too linked slave ownership with political power and saw the abolition of slavery as the end to that rule.[26] Border unionists,

21. Tyson, *The Institution of Slavery in the Southern States*, 51.
22. Gantt, *Address in Favor of Reunion*, 20.
23. Johnson, *Speech on the Restoration of State Government*, 8. Johnson said he hoped the ex-slaves would go to Mexico.
24. Hamilton, *Address to the People of Texas*, 12–14.
25. Johnson, *Speech on the Restoration of State Government*, 6.
26. Michael Hahn, *What Is Unconditional Unionism?* (New Orleans: Printed at the Era Office, 1863), 7, 8; Anthony P. Dostie, *The Political Position of Thomas J. Durant* (New Orleans: Printed at the Office of the True Delta, 1865), 4.

such as Charles D. Drake of Missouri, had for years believed slavery stood in the way of the state's commercial and population growth and thus welcomed abolition. Drake, too, joined the demise of slavery with his fellow steadfast unionists' rise to power. With a free government, he concluded, the ex-slave states would never again be prey to tyrants.[27]

If almost all these southern unionist pamphleteers eventually supported the policy of abolition, they had mixed feelings about other wartime policies and practices of the Federal government. Louisiana's wartime unionist leaders felt unappreciated by the Congress and too much under the control of their liberators, the Union generals.[28] The pamphleteers commented in their works about poor treatment by Congress and the generals to influence northern public opinion and to show their constituents their independence. But they also knew that by allowing northerners to question their leadership power they damaged the Union cause in the South.

No one better grasped this view than Joseph Segar, unionist representative from Virginia's eastern shore. He had been deprived of his seat for a short time in 1862, and again in 1864, and he wrote a pamphlet to beg Congress to seat him and to remind his constituents of his faithfulness to their interests. Of course, Segar pointed out that when he and many fellow unionists had been forced to flee their homes, the unionist vote necessarily had diminished, which cost him critical numbers of supporters. But he finally returned home to learn about the plight of his followers so that he could do something for them in Washington. To northerners he connected his own situation with that of his constituents and asked Congress how it expected them to remain loyal if they did not have a voice in the Federal government. You want us to pay taxes, and to bleed for the Union, but you give us no representation, he complained. You are delegitimizing those who support the Restored government of Virginia, he charged. If the only representatives Virginians have are the Confederates, he admonished, then perhaps even loyalists will go over to that side. For the sake of reunion and

27. Drake, *The Wrongs to Missouri's Loyal People* (Jefferson City: privately printed, 1863), 13. It is difficult to understand just when these unionists turned against slavery. Some, like Drake and Breckinridge, had opposed slavery before the war. Others, perhaps most of these pamphleteers, had owned slaves and still defended slavery in 1861. This may explain why so many of them coupled the end of slavery with war policies to alleviate the plight of their unionist constituents and allies. Others linked slavery to southern elite control of the common people, and thus related slavery to planter antidemocratic tendencies.

28. Thomas J. Durant, *Letter to the Hon. Henry Winter Davis* (New Orleans: H. P. Lathrop, 1864), 30. See William C. Harris, *With Charity for All: Lincoln and the Restoration of the Union* (Lexington: University Press of Kentucky, 1997).

of fairness, and the hope for a viable southern unionist government, Segar had written his pamphlet.[29]

Another comment on the viability of governance came from Francis H. Pierpont, governor of the Restored state of Virginia. He felt that the Federal government had increasingly marginalized the state's Restored government after the formation of the state of West Virginia. Pierpont became even more agitated when the occupying general, Benjamin Butler, virtually ostracized him from political power and ignored his pleas for fair treatment of eastern coastal Virginia's beleaguered unionists. His pamphlet, addressed to President Lincoln and forwarded to Congress, also circulated among Virginia's unionists. In it he attempted to protect his people with his pen because he had no real power as governor.

Pierpont began his pamphlet with discussion of how Butler had personally insulted him, his office, and his people. He then described Butler's treatment of the state's loyalists in agonizing detail. He depicted one constituent's loss of his newspaper and how others had their stores and shops closed, their china and other goods stolen, were deprived from importing goods into the coastal region, and had been forced to pay bribes for any government services. Pierpont used references to "the provost marshal's fund"— a euphemism for bribery—as a rhetorical device throughout. Of course, he gave the usual warning that such behavior by the Federal army would drive Virginia's unionists into the arms of the Confederates. His major complaint, however, was that General Butler had begun to rehabilitate ex-Confederates and to give them civil and business power. What, he wondered, would this do to the unionists who hoped to lead a restored state?[30] If other unionists praised the propriety of the Federal government and the military sharing power, and protecting the lives of the people, Pierpont's charge against Butler made many southern unionists ask if the Federal sword actually had lowered unionist morale and caused real political harm.

What becomes obvious in the southern unionist pamphleteers' praise for and resentment of Federal authority are their worries about the kind of peace they would get and their own roles in the future state governments. As the Federal government lurched toward victory, its policies regarding a reconstructed nation began to take shape. Those policies, however, were in part a Federal war tactic, and the role the government planned for southern

---

29. Segar, *Speech in Defense of His Claim to a Seat.* I have written on these matters in my article "The Politics of Violence: Unionist Pamphleteers in Virginia's Inner Civil War," in Daniel Sutherland, ed., *Violence, Unionism, and Guerrilla Warfare in the Confederate States of America* (Fayetteville: University of Arkansas Press, 1999).

30. Pierpont, *Letter to the President.*

unionists must be seen in that light. Almost all of the pamphleteers who wrote after mid-1862 certainly were quite aware of the emerging Federal reconstruction policy. In their pamphlets, they commented on it at length, especially in regard to what they personally expected out of it.

Unionist pamphleteers requested their northern allies to allow loyal men to lead the restored democratic South. Gantt of Arkansas insisted that loyalists immediately gain places in the Federal Congress in order to take command of the state's political leadership. Segar, among others, worried that Congress's pattern of refusing to seat loyalists meant they would be excluded from a restored Union. What did that mean for loyalist government power, he wondered? Pierpont's diatribe against "Beast" Butler's favoritism toward ex-secessionists made him ask what role he and his fellow loyalists who had sacrificed so much to restore the Union would have in the new state governments.[31] Over and again, the southern unionists insisted that they should govern a reconstructed South.

Most of the unionist pamphleteers who wrote late in the war rejected any idea of a return to the antebellum status quo, which meant they opposed the rebirth of slavery, as they demanded that former Confederates be excluded from postwar leadership positions. Gantt, for one, believed Confederates plotted for postwar power, and he hoped that the abolition of slavery would deter their actions. Governor Hamilton of Texas, whose authority at best was fragile, insisted that Texans would thrive without slavery. New people would settle, and democratic values would be protected, he claimed. Obviously, Hamilton believed a democratic people would bestow power on him. Charles D. Drake of Missouri demanded that the U.S. government help preserve the power of devoted unionists in the border states. Since Missouri had not seceded, he said, it did not need to undergo reconstruction. But only the Federal authorities could guarantee that the unionist government would retain power. He "demanded the perpetual disfranchisement" of all the proslavery leaders who had supported "this damnable rebellion." Drake's governor, Thomas Fletcher, in his address on the Missouri day of Jubilee, coupled the end of slavery with the issue of governance. Fletcher called on all loyal Missourians to support the military authorities under Gen. Grenville M. Dodge, and he sought to keep from office any lawless individuals who threatened loyalists and wanted to restore slavery.[32] Thus southern unionists joined the final abolition of slavery to their inheritance of the fruits of victory.

31. Ibid., 11, 49; Wakelyn, "The Politics of Violence."
32. Gantt, *Address in Favor of Reunion*, 21; Hamilton, *Address to the People of Texas*, 19; Drake, *Wrongs to Missouri's Loyal People*, 13; Fletcher, *Speech on the Reception of the News*, 5, 6.

This linkage of worries about who would lead and the end of slavery perhaps is best seen in the Louisiana pamphleteers' discussion of their expectations for the restored state. (That Louisiana would have to wait some time before it could return to the Union does not take away from the importance of its unionists' squabbles over who would win the political victory.) Michael Hahn, for one, believed he had been slandered by his so-called friends because he wanted New Orleans's leaders to control the state constitutional convention. He insisted that a restored government under an abolitionist constitution meant that citizens from the city would retain power over the rural slaveholder elites.[33] Thomas Durant wanted to make certain the ex-Confederates were deprived of the vote and kept from office in the restored government. But when the constitutional convention hesitated over an abolition clause, Durant charged to his congressional allies in Washington that some unionists plotted to share power with the slaveocracy. Durant was willing to resist President Lincoln's proposal for restoring the state and to play up to Congress in order to gain power for himself. His former ally, Alexander Dostie, attacked him viciously in a letter to Congress that he circulated as a pamphlet to the state's unionists. Dostie believed Durant meant to undermine the Louisiana free state movement. The worst thing Dostie could say about Durant was that he was a secret secessionist.[34] Thus, over slavery's future and their own desire for power, did some southern unionists fall out.

If the southern unionists at times revealed a human side in their political and personal squabbles, a common thread of concern and interest runs through all these pamphlets. Not surprisingly, almost all of the pamphleteers dwelt on the wartime conduct of government. Perhaps because they were themselves refugees and fugitives, forced to practice politics away from their homeland, or as part of an occupying team of leaders under Federal authority, they all were aware of the problems of governance in a war-torn society. Those who wrote about the Confederate takeover of their local government recriminated against years of slaveholder control of their political rights. Others insisted the Confederate government had failed to protect the people's rights. Worse, the Confederate authorities had imposed

33. Hahn, *What Is Unconditional Unionism?* 10, 11. For study of the struggles in Louisiana see Ted Tunnell, *The Crucible of Reconstruction* (Baton Rouge: Louisiana State University Press, 1984), and Gerald Capers, *Occupied City: New Orleans under the Federals* (Lexington: University Press of Kentucky, 1965).

34. Durant, *Letter to Henry Winter Davis*; Dostie, *Political Position of Durant*, 5. Durant's best defender is Joseph G. Tregle Jr., "Thomas J. Durant, Utopian Socialism and the Failure of Presidential Reconstruction in Louisiana," *Journal of Southern History* 45 (November 1979): 485–512.

excessive hardships on the citizenry. In the view of the union leaders, the Confederacy had made little effort to save unionists from the horrors of guerrilla warfare. Indeed, some charged, the Confederate government had encouraged atrocities against the loyal citizenry. As for their own conduct, the southern unionists were proud of what little they had been able to do to protect their allies. They even admonished the Federal government, their ally, for failing to save the loyal people from Confederate counterinvasion, disrupting their lives, and even punishing them. When it came to what they expected from a restored Union, over and again the southern unionist pamphleteers agonized over just who would rule. Thus, for the escapee-returnees, the leaders sheltered under the Federal wing, and those on the periphery of power, the need for able governance, their authority as leaders, and their future power seemed the most important issues of that civil conflict.

One way, perhaps the only way, for the southern unionists to influence events was by giving speeches and writing articles, and turning them into pamphlets for circulation among northerners and their friends back home. All of those leaders wanted to inform their audiences of policies and activities in their favor, and most identified their own experiences with those of their constituents. They attempted to use the rhetorical devices of complaint and praise to persuade others to support their views. Thus, if the pamphleteers at times appeared unrealistic, argumentative, disappointed, and petty, it may have been because they were trying to influence policy and the war's conduct with little power of their own.

For example, look at the political behavior of escapee governor-in-exile Andrew Jackson Hamilton of Texas. He lectured to northerners about the horrible conditions of his constituents back home, met unsuccessfully for his personal ambitions with the president and members of Congress, lived frustrated in occupied New Orleans many miles from his Confederate-controlled home, and could only agonize over and identify from afar with the plight of his people. His pamphlet to the loyal citizens of Texas confirms the central theme in these pamphlets. Hamilton wrote: "How many owners of plantations and negroes have you heard, since the rebellion commenced, boldly asserting that Democracy is a failure, as evidenced by the weakness and inability of the United States Government to protect itself from dismemberment, and that a *stronger* government was necessary?"[35] Indeed, all of the southern unionist leaders who opposed the Confederacy expressed the desire to have a stronger government during the war and after.

---

35. Hamilton, *Address to the People of Texas*, 10. Also see John L. Waller, *Colossal Hamilton of Texas* (El Paso: Texas Western Press, 1968).

Reply to the Speech of Hon. J. C. Breckinridge, Delivered in the United States Senate, July 16th, 1861

(Washington, D.C.: Henry Polkinhorn, 1861)

Anna Ella Carroll (1815–1894) came from Maryland's eastern shore. Descended from an old planter family, she early turned against slavery and later settled in Baltimore and Washington, D.C. Carroll tangled with local leaders when she championed the writings of the nativist, anti-Catholic minister Robert J. Breckinridge of Kentucky. During the Civil War she sought to advise Federal military and political leaders. A fine writer and a newspaper reporter, she offered her services as a pamphleteer to the Federal government. Some of her efforts were widely circulated, and one, *The War Powers of the Federal Government* (Washington, D.C.: Polkinhorn, 1862), written in December 1861, received wide discussion in Congress. She also wrote *The Relation of the National Government to the Revolted Citizens Defined* (Washington, D.C.: Henry Polkinhorn, 1862). But Carroll was doomed to disappointment as her talents seemed unappreciated by the Lincoln administration. She spent the last years of her life in a vain quest for acknowledgment that she had supplied helpful plans for military victory on the western front.

The pamphlet included herein, her August 8, 1861, attack on Kentucky senator John C. Breckinridge for opposing federal laws and obstructing the Union war effort, revealed her support for presidential war policies. Carroll insisted that anyone who assisted the insurrectionary Confederacy was a traitor. So popular was this pamphlet that ten thousand copies of it were sent into the border and upper South slave states.

For more on Carroll see Janet L. Coryell, *Neither Heroine Nor Fool: Anna Ella Carroll of Maryland* (Kent, Ohio: Kent State University Press, 1990); Sarah Ellen Blackwell, *Life and Writings of Anna Ella Carroll* (Washington,

D.C.: Judd and Detweiler, 1895); and Winifred E. Wise, *Lincoln's Secret Weapon* (New York: Chilton, 1961).

* * *

I had read with pain the speech of the Hon. John C. Breckinridge, delivered recently in the United States Senate, and with still deeper pain, I now see him descending from his high position as a Senator and come to Maryland, to use the fallacies of that speech, for the purpose of stimulating and strengthening the Confederate rebellion. I see him addressing the passions of the crowd, as they cheer "Davis and Beauregard," and evidently his purpose is, to incite the military uprising of the people in this State against the Government, in aid of Southern Treason, and to prepare them for action whenever the leaders shall give the signal.

I have in the spirit of friendship, repeatedly repelled by my pen, the charge of disunion heretofore made against him. I could not bring myself to believe that one belonging to a family so illustrious in our annals as his own, could now be willing to alienate our blessed political heritage. When I also witness the devoted patriotism of his great and gifted uncle, (Rev. Dr. R. J. Breckinridge,) in the present struggle for Constitutional liberty; I cannot but feel sorrow, that one who has enjoyed under this Government every degree of elevation but the Presidency, and to whom so large a portion of the American people have hitherto looked with confidence and hope, should at last prove himself recreant to the Union's cause.

In his senatorial speech, to which he refers so vauntingly, he charges that the "President, in violation of the Constitution, made war on the Southern States for subjugation and conquest, has increased the army and navy, called forth the militia, blockaded the Southern ports, suspended the writ of *Habeas Corpus*; and, without warrant, arrested private persons, searched private houses, seized private papers and effects, &c., &c." And now, in his Baltimore speech, he asserts that the State of Maryland is abolished, and that her people are "under the shadow of a broad-spreading military despotism." With splenetic acerbity and the skill of the demagogue, he reiterates the charge of arrest without warrant of citizens in this State.

These are grave charges, and if true, the President should be made to suffer the extreme penalty of the law.

I shall not refer to the "small band," including Messrs. Powell, Polk, Kennedy, *id genus omne*, whom he says "*would* be heard in the Senate on the personal and political rights of the people," but confine my remarks to Mr. Breckinridge himself.

The argument turns wholly on the question of *fact*, whether the overt act of treason which the Constitution defines to be levying war against the United States, has been committed? Whether the Confederate States of the South commenced the war?

But, granting his main proposition, that the President has been guilty of making the war, (the sad realities of which are before us,) it is not less the duty of every American citizen to stand by his country and sustain the Government until the war is terminated by an honorable peace.

There can be no equivocal position in this crisis; and he who is not with the Government is against it, and an enemy to his country.

But the major premise of the Senator, namely, that the President made the war upon the South, is *untrue*, and I proceed to show that no one in America knows this better than that gentleman. So far, then, as his position as a Senator of the United States can serve, he has assumed the awful responsibility of conspiring for the overthrow of *his* Government— defending accomplices in their labors to dissolve it, and proclaiming the President a usurper for his efforts to preserve it.

Secret but powerful efforts to dissolve this Union have been made in the cotton States, since 1831; but, on the 7th of May, 1849, under the instigation of Calhoun, then the chief conspirator, a meeting was held at Jackson, Mississippi, when the secession party formally organized, to form a *Southern Confederacy* upon the first act of the General Government on which they could base a pretext. They there laid down their programme, which the conspirators of '60 and '61 have faithfully acted out.

After the death of Calhoun, in 1850, Senator Davis and his confederates in both branches of Congress agreed upon a provisional government and sketched a constitution for a Southern Confederacy! He managed, by intrigue, to have himself named as its President! This document and the proceedings of the conspirators found its way into the hands of Mr. Clay; but under such circumstances as forbade any public use of it.[1]

In the running debate in the United States Senate, Mr. Clay made frequent and pointed personal allusions to Davis, in order to draw forth some remark, which would justify its public use; but Davis, undoubtedly suspecting the motive, studiously avoided giving him the opportunity. That constitution was similar to the one the traitors have now adopted; except

1. See Jesse T. Carpenter, *The South as a Conscious Minority* (New York: New York University Press, 1930), chap. 4.

that it specially provided for the acquisition of Cuba, Mexico, and all Tropical America.

General Quitman, however, was the recognized leader of the disunion party, and his correspondence, as Governor of Mississippi, with the prominent conspirators, especially in South Carolina, fully illustrates that programme, and develops the treason movement of this day. . . . [2]

Here we have every idea on which the conspirators are now acting. The calling of conventions; the withdrawal of South Carolina to *force the issue*; the assembling of the cotton States at Montgomery, Alabama; the organization of a Southern Confederacy; the forcing the border slave States to choose between a Northern and Southern Confederacy; the proposition even of the Crittenden Compromise; the arming of the Southern States; the firing on Fort Sumter, with the hope of *drawing blood to cement the Southern States.*

Unfortunately, through Mr. Breckinridge, the original programme of tendering a compromise to the Northern States *"before parting with them"* was incorporated into the Crittenden Compromise. Abusing the confidence reposed in him by Mr. Crittenden, he being in the entire interest of the traitors, artfully introduced into it the very platform on which the secessionists had supported him for the Presidency. This was done to make its passage through Congress an impossible thing.

This was an audacious insult to every party but the supporters of Mr. Breckinridge, *per se*, because each of these parties had expressly repudiated the doctrine by an overwhelming vote of the American people at the Presidential election. But the *people* were clamorous for the salvation of the Union, and without reference to this objectionable feature, they at once committed themselves to the proposition, and when it was rejected, thousands at the South went over to secession! Men who, in voting for Bell or Douglas, had planted themselves defiantly against that doctrine, were unwittingly cheated and captured by the dastardly secession *manœuvre!*

An illustration of the use made of the Crittenden compromise may be proper. The State of Georgia passed an ordinance of secession in Convention, but agreed to refer it to the people. During the canvass it became apparent that the people would *defeat* it; and the secessionists resorted to the strategy of *agreeing to abide by the Crittenden Compromise*, in order to commit the Union party to the measure; and Toombs returned

2. Carroll quotes at length that 1850–1851 correspondence between Gen. John A. Quitman of Mississippi, Gov. Whitemarsh Seabrook of South Carolina, U.S. senator John J. McRae of Mississippi, Gen. Maxcy Gregg of South Carolina, and state senator John S. Preston of South Carolina on plots to call state secession conventions.

to the Senate for the purpose of *defeating* that Compromise, while ostensibly favoring it!

There was a majority in the Senate committee of thirteen in favor of its passage, had *the secessionists voted for it*. They went into that Committee with the express design (as they afterwards boasted) of entrapping the Opposition into a vote rejecting the proposition. They assumed in committee that as the Compromise was a tender to the South, the North should make the terms, and thereby declined to vote with such a supercilious bearing as to constrain Northern men to reject it *in toto*. One of the conspirators then jesuitically *suggested* that they had better adopt the "Chicago platform," when some of the Republicans most unwisely assented; whereupon the secessionists hurried off telegrams to all parts of Georgia, that *"all hope of compromise is gone. The Crittenden proposition has been rejected, and the Chicago platform adopted as the ultimatum!"* The people were thus deceived by these lying dispatches and the Union party was silenced and subdued.

The doctrine found in Seabrook's letter is the doctrine of the conspirators to-day—that *the Government cannot use force against a State*; and if so, it is an act of war! This fatal idea was introduced by Buchanan in his message in December and, whether by his own treachery or by the traitorous advisers who controlled his Administration, it thrust a knife into the ribs of the Constitution which is now pouring out its life's blood. Had he been true to his oath and exercised his constitutional authority he would have sent a military force to South Carolina, as General Jackson did in 1833, to suppress the rebellion, and enabled men to rally to the flag of the Union throughout the South.[3]

It was on this heretical idea that the General Government cannot use force in a State to execute *its* laws, that Virginia, Tennessee, North Carolina, and Arkansas seceded. Mr. Breckinridge, in connection with Magoffin, used the doctrine in his State; Jackson did so in Missouri; and the secession party in Maryland.

The Southern people in 1851 would not sustain the leaders in sufficient strength to enable them to carry out their treasonable designs at that period. These men, therefore, went into the Democratic party to expedite their ambitious and wicked designs against the Union. They were in the Baltimore Convention in 1852, and forced the Virginia and Kentucky resolutions into the Democratic platform, in order to commit the party stealthily to the doctrine of secession. They then secured the nomination

---

3. Of course, President Andrew Jackson did not send a "military force" to South Carolina.

of Franklin Pierce, and thereby controlled his Administration. The same party procured the nomination of Buchanan, and took the stand that they never would surrender the power. They openly proclaimed that if Fremont was elected they would dissolve the Union. That opportunity having been lost, it is not necessary to say here how the administration of Buchanan was improved to their advantage![4] It is also a matter of too recent occurrence to adduce the proof that the delegations from the cotton States were instructed to go into the Charleston Conventions to plant their right to the protection of slave property in the Territories, and failing in that to secede, and nominate a candidate representing their peculiar views. *They failed,* and adjourned to Richmond; but finding only the delegates of the cotton States in attendance, they feared to risk a nomination, and adjourned temporarily, sending a portion of their members to Baltimore, under the jesuitical pretense of harmonizing the Democratic party! Their real purpose was to draw recruits from the border slave States, which being accomplished they again seceded, and nominated Mr. Breckinridge. Then, returning with his name in Richmond, they *renominated* him; and he thus became the disunion candidate *per se*—formally accepting the same!

The object of that nomination was, if they should fail in the election, *to prevent by armed force* the inauguration of a Republican President. They had planned to inaugurate Breckinridge. I have the avowal of one of the conspirators, who, when asked if Breckinridge assented, replied, we have not asked him; but he accepted our nomination, and of course will carry out our views.

In fact, they addressed to the ambition of the Vice President the exciting language of Max[c]y Gregg to Gen. Quitman, in 1851:

> "In this great struggle the South wants a great leader; with the mind and the name to impel and guide revolution. *Be that leader,* and your place in history will remain conspicuous for the admiration of all ages to come."

The chiefs of the conspirators went to Washington after the election and assumed the direction of the entire treason movement, and proceeded to organize a military force for the purpose of seizing the Government, expelling Lincoln, and inaugurating Breckinridge. But failing to secure Maryland and Virginia, by ordinances of secession, they fell back in January upon their original programme; and they directed the seceded

---

4. Recent work on President James Buchanan casts his activities in a better light. See Michael J. Birkner, ed., *James Buchanan and the Political Crisis of the 1850s* (Cranbury, N.J.: Associated University Presses, 1996).

States to assemble in Convention at Montgomery, Alabama, on the 4th of February, for the purpose of installing the provisional government organized at Washington, with Senator Davis at its head. They resolved to seize the entire property belonging to the General Government in the Southern States; and to retain in their seats a sufficient number of Senators from the seceded States to embarrass any legislation of Congress which might be inimical to their movements, and to act as spies upon the Government.

They improvised armies, and continued to exercise all the functions of the provisional government until its formal installation at Montgomery on the 4th of February.

I have it upon the authority of a Senator who was present, that Mr. Breckinridge united with the conspirators in their consultations, and gave to them the influence and sanction of his high position. It is a phenomenon in the history of governments, without a parallel, and will be an everlasting disgrace upon our civilization, that Cabinet Ministers, the Vice President, Senators, and members of Congress should for weeks and months, by the apparent sanction of the President of the United States, have wielded the powers of an organized rebellion, for the overthrow of the Constitution and Government they had sworn to support! Our fathers never could have anticipated this catastrophe. They never dreamed of this parricidal assault upon the Constitution! They wisely provided for the alteration, change, or amendment of our Government, whenever a majority of the people in the Whole United States willed it, or that two-thirds of the States demanded it. But they never foresaw that a few atrociously corrupt men would rise, without regard to the will of the majorities in their several States, and perpetrate the crime of DOUBLE TREACHERY against their State and Federal Governments!

After the formal meeting of the Confederate Government and the inauguration of Mr. Davis at its head, they continued the augmentation of the army by recruits from all the Southern States, including Maryland and the District of Columbia. They invested Fort Pickens, stormed Fort Sumter, and put in motion a formidable army for the capture of Washington and the overthrow of the Government.

In the sight of these astounding facts, the President issues his Proclamation, appealing to the patriotism of the nation for the salvation of the Union, and Mr. Breckinridge grossly insults the intelligence of the country by charging that the President made war against the South!

The facts adduced establish beyond controversy that the President *did not* make the war as charged, but that the traitors made the war, which now threatens the subversion of the Government, and endangers our national existence.

Under this fearful exigency, I proceed to inquire what are the duties imposed upon the President by the Constitution?

I maintain that the Government of the United States is a Government of limited powers; that the President of the United States can exert no power that is not granted in express terms, or clearly implied, as necessary to carry into effect the powers which are expressed. I should be the last person to defend any usurpation of power, or unconstitutional act of any one in authority, much less a President of the United States. . . . [5]

"The executive power is vested in the President," and he is required "to take care" that each government, State and Federal, and the several authorities are maintained in their respective spheres.

In the event of the rebellion or insurrection assuming such proportions as to overthrow the *"republican form of government guaranteed to every State in the Union,"* so that the officers can no longer execute the supreme law, the President is required by his oath of office, "to preserve, protect, and defend" this supreme law. For this purpose the sword, by the Constitution, is placed in his hands. "He is the Commander-in-Chief of the Army and Navy, and of the militia of the several States when called into the service of the United States." He needs, therefore no statute law to enable him, in the absence of Congress, to defend the assault on the nation's life; because his right rests on the supreme or universal law of self-defense, common to nations as individuals—that everything that has life, every being that has existence, has the right to resist, and slay the assailant when an attack is made upon that life.

Our fathers presumed not to foresee all the dangers which in time might beset the Constitution, or to prescribe the mode of its defense, but in making the President its defender, it was wisely left to him to resist the sword raised against the nation's heart, by the sword. The express grant of the *war-conducting power* conferred upon the President carries with it the implied power to use every belligerent right known to the law of war.

Now, an atrociously wicked war is waged against the Government, and its formidable armies have overwhelmed every civil right, from the Potomac to the Rio Grande, and threatens the annihilation of the Government and the nation itself. By virtue of the express and implied powers of the Constitution just indicated, it is impossible to question the duty of the President to use

5. Here Carroll quotes from the second article of the Constitution of the United States, which delineates presidential powers as commander-in-chief of the army and navy.

every belligerent right, every instrument known to the law of war:—To annoy, to weaken, to destroy the enemy, until its armies are overthrown and the civil authority is re-established. If there was no statute law, or no act of Congress authorizing an army and navy, and even if the act of 1795 did not apply to this exigency, still the act of the President in improvising an army for the defense of the government was strictly in accordance with the principles of the Constitution. And if Congress had failed to perform its duties, it was still the right and duty of every American citizen to rally under the flag in its defense.

It is a maxim at common law, "when a known felony is about to be committed upon any one, not only the party assaulted may repel force by force, *but his servant attending him, or any other person present* may interpose to prevent the mischief, and if *death ensue*, the party so interposing *will be justified.*"

Upon this principle of common law, which justified a servant or by-stander in slaying the felon who attempts the life of a friend, *a fortiori*, is a citizen of the United States justified, who rises at the call of the President, and slays the enemy endeavoring to kill, not one man only, or a generation of men, but the nation itself!

According to Rutherford, "no action can be unlawful, if it is not possible for a man to have done otherwise. Whatever is unavoidable is not unlawful. An act done from compulsion or necessity, is not a crime, is not unlawful. To this proposition the law makes no exception."[6]

Mr. Breckinridge cites the authority of Webster and Douglas against the blockade of the Southern ports. Their opinions have no application whatever to a state of war. Blockade is a *belligerent* right, and can be exercised only by the President as Commander-in-Chief in time of war, and against the enemy. . . . [7]

Mr. Breckinridge was careful to refrain from referring to the authority of General Jackson. The suspension of the writ of *habeas corpus* in 1815, and the imprisonment of the Judge, as well as the arrest and execution of Arbuthnot

6. She is probably referring to William J. Rutherford, a lawyer from Richmond, Virginia.

7. Carroll quotes from a long letter of Gen. George Washington in 1776 to various state committees of safety in order to show that Senator Breckinridge is incorrect on the powers to repeal a writ of habeas corpus. In order to make her point about those who turn against their country she talks about "instances where Tories were shot and hung, and their property confiscated without the form of law, during the American revolution. In fact, martial law transcended all civil authority while our ancestors were struggling to establish our national existence."

and Ambrister without trial, have received the unanimous sanction of the American people. . . . [8]

If there had been no express grant in the Constitution to suspend the writ of *habeas corpus*, still the power to suspend all civil authority when necessary to maintain our national existence would have been complete. It stands upon *"the unwritten laws of necessity, of self-preservation, and of the public safety."*

The Senator charges that the blood-bought rights of the people secured by the 4th article of the Constitution, have been wantonly violated by the President. This has no foundation in fact. On the contrary, the enemy which commands all the sympathies of the distinguished Senator are themselves the violaters of these sacred rights.

The fourth article of the Constitution which secures the right of the people to their persons, houses, papers, and effects, against searches or seizures without warrant of law, does not apply to the public enemy in time of war. This article does not conflict with or control the constitutional principles which have been adduced, but strictly harmonizes with them. Should a spy be found within the American camp, or the chances of war throw Davis or Beauregard in the hands of our army, no one would think their arrest and imprisonment unconstitutional, or doubt the duty of the commander to disregard any writ of *habeas corpus* issued for their liberation. Should a commander capture a cargo of provisions or a wagon load of Enfield rifles *in transitu* to the enemy, no one could pretend to believe that he had violated this article of the Constitution! . . . [9]

Finally, Mr. Breckinridge charges that the Constitution was violated by the suppression of a St. Louis press![10]

This is a grave charge. The freedom of speech and the press are especially guarded by constitutional provisions. I hold the right as inalienable to citizen and Christian. It has a priceless value to our civil liberty; and as an independent member of the press I will never consent to see its powers trammeled or its freedom abridged by President or ruler.

It is unquestionably true that the press seized in St. Louis was in the service of the Southern rebellion, and engaged in the destruction of *these very rights*, and of the entire Constitution and Government.

8. Carroll is referring to Alexander Arbuthnot and Robert Chrystie Ambrister. She also quotes from a letter of Thomas Jefferson to J. B. Colvin of December 1810, in which the former president talks of a higher law of duty to one's country.

9. Carroll then quotes President Thomas Jefferson on the Aaron Burr conspiracy to support her position on military arrests in Maryland and Missouri.

10. See Mark E. Neeley Jr., *The Fate of Liberty: Abraham Lincoln and Civil Liberties* (New York: Oxford University Press, 1991), 38–39.

Upon the principles of the Constitution, which I have heretofore cited in this article, it necessarily follows that any one who is aiding the rebellion by treasonable utterances, whether spoken or written, is as amenable to martial law as though enrolled in the Confederate army; and by the same authority it is as much the duty of the commander-in-chief to arrest and hold subject to martial law any one found aiding the rebellion by treasonable utterances, spoken or written; as it is his duty to arrest any one found sending into the enemy's camp intelligence, provisions or arms.

In the progress of events the rebellion may assume such formidable proportion as to override both the judicial and legislative powers, leaving the military as the only visible power in the land. It would then be the clear duty of the President, as commander-in-chief, to maintain the military authority over every foot of territory of the United States until the judicial and legislative power could be restored. In such an exigency it may be his duty to call several millions of men into the service. It may be necessary to arrest traitorous Senators and members of Congress, Judges of Courts, who are in complicity with the rebellion, and treat them as public enemies. Instead of arresting a few traitors he may arrest all traitors, and deprive them of the means of warring on the Government.

This Government relies on individual duty and obligation. It has the power to tax *individuals* in any mode and to any extent to maintain it; and to call out citizens, as individuals, for military service to defend it.

In this supreme struggle for its existence men of all sections should adhere to it. They should not only sustain it, but, if necessary, meet death to preserve it until the roar of the final fire, and the Judgment of the quick and the dead.

Better that Washington had perished like Hampden. That Jefferson had never drafted the Declaration of Independence. That Lee, Hancock, Adams, Franklin, Sherman, Livingston, &c., had died like Sydney and Russell upon the block, than that this Union, created to be the *day-light* to break the night of ages, should finally collapse, and *traitors* be permitted to write the epitaph, "it lived and died."

The Civil War: Its Nature and End

(Cincinnati: Office of the Danville Review, 1861)

R obert Jefferson Breckinridge (1800–1871) was born into the powerful Breckinridge family of Lexington, Kentucky. He attended Jefferson College and later Union College in New York and prepared for the bar. Breckinridge followed many members of his family into law and politics, but a personal tragedy turned him toward the church. He became a Presbyterian clergyman in 1832, took a church in Baltimore, and in 1845 was elected president of Jefferson College in Pennsylvania. He later returned to Lexington to the First Presbyterian Church, wrote a number of books, and in the 1850s became a professor at the Danville Theological Seminary, a position he held until 1869. A temperance advocate and a nativist, Breckinridge also opposed slavery. His most famous work, *The Knowledge of God, Considered* (1855), revealed his antislavery views. Breckinridge ardently defended the Union during the Civil War, becoming a leader in the Kentucky cause. He also edited the important journal the *Danville Quarterly Review* from 1861 to 1865 and made it a leading unionist voice in the border slave states. Breckinridge reprinted articles from that journal and fast-day and other sermons as pamphlets that he circulated widely throughout the border slave states, and he even filtered some of them into Tennessee and North Carolina.

One of Breckinridge's most important wartime pamphlets, *The Civil War: Its Nature and End* showed his contempt for the Confederacy and his support for the Union. In it he also argued that it was in the interests of the border slave states to support the Union. But, like others in the border slave states, he worried that Federal mistakes could drive Kentuckians into the hands of the Confederacy. Nevertheless, Breckinridge's vehement attack on Jefferson Davis and other radical Confederates certainly helped to warn the border states of the risk of flirting with the lower South cotton states.

No full biography of this extraordinary man exists. For details of his life see William Hutchinson Vaughan, *Robert J. Breckinridge as an Educational Administrator* (Nashville: George Peabody College for Teachers, 1937); E. Merton Coulter, *The Civil War and Readjustment in Kentucky* (Chapel Hill: University of North Carolina Press, 1926); and, especially, Thomas J. Klotter, *The Breckinridges of Kentucky, 1760–1981* (Lexington: University Press of Kentucky, 1986). There are Breckinridge papers at the Library of Congress.

* * *

I. For what are we fighting, on one side, and on the other? What are the interests at stake, so immense and so opposite, that justify either party to this war in embarking in it at first, or in prosecuting it with the terrible earnestness everywhere manifest? What is the present aspect of it, generally considered—what is its probable future course—what the conclusion that must be reached, at last? What are to be its probable effects—directly upon ourselves, indirectly upon the other nations of the earth, and in both ways upon the immediate future of the human race, and possibly upon generations to come? How much of what either party is fighting for is really attainable, and of that which is attainable, how much is worth what it will cost? These are questions which every enlightened man—every free citizen—is bound to ask himself. The answer to them involves our lives and fortunes and liberties; nay more than even these, our *duty* as citizens, as patriots, and as Christians. It is to render such aid as we may be able, to all who will accept our aid, in deciding these vast questions, that we now attempt to develop still further the great truths we have discussed several times heretofore, and to apply them to the posture of public affairs now existing.

There are considerations of various kinds, and of the most decisive force, which render it impossible for peace to be restored to the country, except upon the condition of a single National Government, common to the whole American people, and embracing every loyal and every revolted State. As a question of national strength in the presence of all foreign nations—and therefore of national independence; as a question of permanent national life struggling against anarchy in the form of secession; as a question of law, and government, and constitutional freedom, measuring its strength against an immense and utterly profligate political conspiracy; as a question of personal freedom, and popular institutions, in conflict with a class minority possessed of vast wealth, and reckless of everything but its own aggrandizement; as a question of the universal domination of this daring class, not only in the Slave States, so many of which it had temporarily subjugated, but over the nation itself, which it betrayed, plundered, insulted, and to which it claimed to dictate ignoble terms of composition, at the head of a military force threatening the capitol; as a question of the duty of the nation to its loyal citizens, constituting at that time the actual majority in the fifteen Slave States—but suddenly and by fraud and violence reduced to a state of helpless degradation: we attempted, from the beginning, to show that there was no course, either of honor, or duty, or safety left to the nation, except to meet force by force, and to maintain the institutions of the country, and enforce the laws of the land, by the whole power of the American people. Nor do we suppose there is a single loyal person on this continent, who does not now look with contempt, or with execration, upon the conduct of Mr. Buchanan and his Cabinet, during the last year of his administration: nor a single one who does not applaud the vigor and determination which the Congress of the United States, under the lead of Mr. Lincoln, have manifested in maintaining the integrity of the Union. But what we have now to urge goes beyond the state of the question heretofore discussed, and briefly recapitulated above. Influenced by such considerations as these, the nation accepted the war as unavoidable. What we maintain is, not merely that those considerations forbid the nation to terminate the war forced upon her, except in its complete success, but that in the very nature of the case, of the country, of all our institutions, and of the war itself, permanent peace is impossible, except upon the condition of a single national government. We will endeavor to illustrate this idea.

Whoever will look at a map of the United States will observe that Louisiana lies on both sides of the Mississippi river, and that the States of Arkansas and Mississippi lie on the right and left banks of this great stream—eight hundred miles of whose lower course is thus controlled by these three States, unitedly inhabited by hardly as many white people as inhabit the city of New York. Observe then the country drained by this river, and its affluents, commencing with Missouri on its west bank, and Kentucky on its east bank. There are nine or ten powerful States—large portions of three or four others—several large Territories, in all a country as large as all Europe, as fine as any under the sun, already holding many more people than all the revolted States—and destined to be one of the most populous and powerful regions of the earth. Does any one suppose that these powerful States—this great and energetic population—will ever make a peace that shall put the lower course of this single and mighty natural outlet to the sea, in the hands of a foreign government far weaker than themselves? If there is any such person, he knows little of the past history of mankind; and will, perhaps, excuse us for reminding him that the people of Kentucky, before they were constituted a State, gave formal notice to the Federal Government, when General Washington was President, that if the United States did not acquire Louisiana, they would themselves conquer it. The mouths of the Mississippi belong, by the gift of God, to the inhabitants of its great Valley. Nothing but irresistible force can disinherit them.[1]

Try another territorial aspect of the case. There is a bed of mountains abutting on the left bank of the Ohio, which covers all Western Virginia, and all Eastern Kentucky, to the width, from east to west, in those two States, of three or four hundred miles. These mountains stretching southwestwardly, pass entirely through Tennessee—cover the back parts of North Carolina and Georgia—heavily invade the northern part of Alabama—and make a figure even in the back parts of South Carolina and the eastern parts of Mississippi; having a course of, perhaps, seven or eight hundred miles, and running far south of the northern limit of profitable cotton culture. It is a region of 300,000 square miles—trenching upon eight or nine Slave States, though nearly destitute of slaves itself—trenching upon at least five cotton States, though raising no cotton itself. The western part of Maryland and two-thirds of Pennsylvania, are embraced in the northeastern continuation of this remarkable region. Can anything that passes under the name of statesmanship, be more preposterous, than the notion of permanent peace on this continent, founded on the abnegation of a common and paramount government, and the idea of the supercilious domination of the cotton interest and the slave trade, over such a mountain empire, so located, and so peopled?

As a further proof of the utter impossibility of peace, except under a common government, and at once an illustration of the import of what has just been stated, and the suggestion of a new and insuperable difficulty; let it be remembered that this great mountain region, throughout its general course, is more loyal to the Union than any other portion of the Slave States. It is the mountain counties of Maryland that have held treason in check in that State; it is forty mountain counties in Western Virginia that have laid the foundation of a new and loyal commonwealth; it is the

1. For Breckinridge's comments on the importance of the Mississippi River to the nation see Jon L. Wakelyn, ed., *Southern Pamphlets on Secession, November 1860–April 1861* (Chapel Hill: University of North Carolina Press, 1996), 247–61.

mountain counties of Kentucky that first and most eagerly took up arms for the Union; it is the mountain region of Tennessee that alone, in that dishonored State, furnished martyrs in the sacred cause of freedom; it is the mountain people of Alabama, that boldly stood out against the Confederate Government, till their own leaders deserted and betrayed them. Now, is the nation prepared, under any imaginable circumstances, to sacrifice these heroic men, as a condition of peace conquered from them by traitors? Will the nation sell the blood—we will not say of a race of patriots—but of even a single one of them? The Representatives of these men sit in Congress; their Senators are in the Capitol. Will the rebel States dismember themselves, that cotton may have peace? Will the nation turn its back on the five Border Slave States—deliver over Western Virginia to the sword—and cover its own infamy under the ruins of the Constitution? Never—never! Our sole alternative—is victory. To know this, is to render victory certain.

Again: Consider the question of boundary, as preliminary to peace. We have shown, on a former occasion, that the States of Maryland and Missouri stand in such relations, geographical and otherwise, to the nation, that they must necessarily share its fate. Since we gave expression to that opinion, much has happened to strengthen it, and increase the difficulties of any peaceful division of the country. Amongst other things, Congress has openly recognized the revolutionary Government in Western Virginia— and received Senators and Representatives from States in open rebellion: the armies of the Confederate States have invaded Western Virginia, Missouri, and Kentucky: and *to conquer a boundary* extending to the Chesapeake, the Ohio, and the Missouri, is one of the avowed objects of those invasions. Whatever may have been the state of public opinion in any of the five Border Slave States, at an early stage of our national difficulties, at present there is not, probably, a single loyal citizen in either of them, who would entertain, for a moment, the idea of being attached to the Southern Confederacy— or who would not denounce as atrocious, on the part of the General Government, any suggestion that looked toward the surrender of those five States of the Southern Confederacy, as a condition of peace. On the opposite side, it is most probable that every secessionist in those five States would greatly prefer the continuance of the war, to peace, accompanied by such a division of the nation as would attach the Border Slave States to the Northern portion; while the more violent portion of them would, probably, prefer the continuance of the war, to the complete restoration of the Union on any terms. But these Border Slave States are, and must continue to be the chief theater of the war, so long as the issue of the war hangs in the least suspense. We say nothing, here, of the absolute necessity of the conquest of the secession party, and the restoration of the Union and the power of the National Government, as the solitary condition upon which the peace or safety of the whole country is possible. What we say is, that in the actual condition of the country, of the war, and of the avowed aims and recognized obligations of both parties, the question of boundary renders peace impossible, even if both parties desired peace upon every other ground. We readily admit that there is hardly an imaginable contingency, in which the Confederate Government can ever conquer, or the nation ever concede, any boundary—that ought to be an allowable basis of peace. But this only shows how clear it is that the nation can contemplate no alternative but triumph or ruin; and that the conspirators against its peace and glory have madly plunged into a wicked rebellion, which could have no result but the subjugation of the whole nation, or their own destruction. At first, their pretext was—the *right* of each State to secede. Now, they seek to *conquer* States that refuse to secede. Perfidious, at first, to all the States; perfidious, now to each separate State.

There are difficulties of a kind different from any of those yet suggested; and so aggravated by the conduct and principles of the secessionists, that there seems to be no possibility of even so much as finding a basis on which to negotiate. Take, as an example, their conduct toward the Indian Tribes which occupy, thinly, at least one-half of the whole area within our national boundaries—and some of the most civilized of which are settled upon the finest lands adjoining our inhabited borders, and were bound, by treaties highly advantageous to them, to the United States. As far as the public has information, it appears that the Confederate Government has made diligent efforts to excite these savages to war against us, along the whole Indian frontier, and along all the emigrant routes to the Pacific States. This much is certain, that the Tribes of the Southwest have taken up arms, that many thousands of them are boastfully declared by the Confederates to be ready to join their armies, and that a considerable force of their warriors is now with the troops invading Kentucky. We do not say they are unfit allies for the refugee Kentuckians who are leading them to the slaughter of their kindred, and the devastation of their country. Nor do we say that either the savages or the refugee marauders are unfit instruments of traitors, who first subvert every principle which holds society together in installing their rebellion—and then subvert every pretext on which they revolted, by banding with savages and parricides in an atrocious attack upon the only sovereignty they pretended to revere. We leave to others to depict these enormities as they deserve, and confide to a just posterity the retribution of such crimes. What we demand now is, what figure are these savage allies of traitors to cut, in the preliminaries of peace? What stipulations are the Confederate States to demand—what guarantees are the American people to give, as the price of peace—concerning its future Indian policy, and concerning recompense for past Indian perfidy and outrage?

The question of slavery offers us another example, in the same category with the preceding one, of the madness of the whole secession conspiracy; and another proof that the restoration of permanent peace to the country by means of its division into two confederacies, or by any other means except the restoration of the Union and the maintenance of a single national government coextensive with the whole nation, is totally impossible. Upon the supposition that all parties were willing to divide the nation on the slave line, *provided* the new confederacies could make mutually satisfactory agreements, and could be mutually made to keep them in regard to negro slavery; such a basis of peace would rest on this childish absurdity—that the obligations of a treaty between hostile States are more effectual than the obligations of a government over the different portions of its own citizens—notwithstanding governments have the sanction of force in a hundred-fold greater degree than treaties can have, and have, in addition, ten thousand sanctions which no treaty can have. We think we have demonstrated, on a former occasion, that the profitable continuance of negro slavery anywhere on this continent, and its continuance at all in the Border Slave States, depends absolutely upon the existence of a common national government embracing both the Free States and the Slave States; and it seems to us that the developments of the war add continually to the force of what we then said. The preservation of the Union and the Constitution preserves at the same time, in all its integrity, the national settlement of the question of slavery made at the adoption of the Constitution itself; which was effectual for all the purposes intended, through more than seventy years of unparalleled prosperity; and is competent still through all coming time to give peace and security, if anything under heaven is competent to do so. On the contrary, forfeiting that settlement as soon as we subvert the Constitution and destroy the Union—it may be confidently asserted that the new confederacies which are to arise will find themselves incompetent to settle even the preliminary basis of a treaty concerning their mutual rights and obligations touching the negro race on this continent; and that, even if they should be able to come to some uncertain and temporary understanding on the subject, stable peace between the parties, much less stable security to slave property, would be impossible. Our political system, made up of sovereign commonwealths united under a supreme Federal Government, affords not only the highest, but the only effectual protection for interests that are local and exceptional—and at the same time out of sympathy with the general judgment of mankind. And of all possible interests, that of the owners of slaves, in a free country, stands most in need of the protection of such a system. It is extremely difficult to say what effect, precisely, this war and its possible results may have upon the institution of slavery in America. So much at least is certain—that the total suppression of the present revolt, is hardly more important to any class of American citizens, than to the slaveholders of the country: and that the obstinate continuance of the war, by the South, will do nothing more surely than drain the slaves, owned by secessionists in the Border States, farther south—and leave the slave interest in the restored Union, a far weaker political element than it was when they sought to strengthen it by revolution.

We need not press any further the proof of the great truth we are asserting. The service we are doing is not so much to disclose new truths, as to make a clear statement of the grounds of a common and fixed conviction, which the public mind has widely and instinctively adopted. It is a conviction just in itself, and noble both in its origin and impulses. We will not agree to the ruin of our glorious country; and so we are not grieved to see that we cannot do it with any hope of peace thereby. We will not allow the Constitution to be subverted, the Union to be destroyed, and the nation to be divided; and so we are glad that in the order of God's Providence, the alternative to which the nation is shut up—is victory. If the people in the States which have taken up arms against our national life, will rise up in their might, recover their liberty, and put an end to the traitorous dominion of the cruel and perfidious class minority which is degrading and oppressing them, the nation has no further cause of war with them. If they will not do this, or if they cannot do it in their present miserable condition, it must be done for them—and it will be. The American people have not sought this war; they were led to the brink, not only of ruin, but of infamy, in the attempt to avoid it. The American people have neither approved nor participated in the injuries or the insults, inflicted on any portion of the nation by any other portion of it. On the contrary, their whole national history attests that, whatever factions and sections may have done or attempted, the nation has been faithful in its lot, and true to its sublime mission. And now, in this great crisis, if God will own our efforts we will retrieve our destiny—and teach mankind a lesson which after ages will be slow to forget.

II. The *Art of War*—for even those who are the most devoted to it as a pursuit, hardly venture to call it a *science*—has probably produced a smaller proportion of individuals who have, in the settled judgment of mankind, deserved supreme eminence, than any other reputable calling to which the human race has addicted itself, or to which its progress has given rise.[2] And notwithstanding the perpetual slaughter of the battle-field, during the whole life of the world, it would probably be impossible to designate as many as twenty pitched battles, in the whole history of mankind— concerning which it can be made apparent that the destiny of our race would have been materially changed, if they had never been fought, or if they had resulted differently. There is no adequate evidence that any man now lives, who is competent to wield, with the highest efficiency, an army of the largest class; and we are free to risk public ridicule, by expressing the opinion that if Napoleon, or Wellington, or Marlborough, or Cromwell— not to mention a few more ancient names—had been placed in a day's march of Manassas, ten days before the bloody and resultless battle, with a force equal to the smallest, and provided no better than the worst, of the two armies that fought there; he would probably have cut both of them to pieces within the ten days. From generation to generation, the art of war progresses slowly, and gradually establishes itself upon certain axioms and certain results: and then some great genius suddenly appears, and, despising the axioms and setting at nought the results, creates by his conquests new ideas and a new school of the art. And then the old process of codifying his campaigns into the body of the art of war, is renewed, till another great genius appears. And so on,—till our own day: in which, if God shall be pleased to point out the man—and the nation shall have sense to recognize him—the end will have come. Till such a captain appears—one of God's most uncommon gifts—we must content ourselves with such judgments as can be formed, from the common causes and the common course of events. Or if he should appear on the side of our rebellious countrymen—and no match for him on ours—we must put forth as much additional force and courage, as will counteract the excess of skill against us. It seems to us to be plain—upon any supposition that can be made short of the effectual interposition of God for the total change of the course and destiny of this great country, and as a necessary consequence of the whole order and result of human affairs—that this nation is not only perfectly competent to crush this rebellion, and extinguish the doctrine and practice of secession; but that there is no ordinary possibility of any other result. It is this which we now desire to illustrate.

2. After his opening discussion on how to put the Union back together, Breckinridge turns to what powers the Federal government must use to "crush" the rebellion. His major concern was where the war was being fought and its costs to the border unionists.

If the five Border Slave States (Delaware, Maryland, Virginia, Kentucky, and Missouri) had stood firmly by the Union—the ten remaining Slave States could hardly have made a show of military resistance to the overwhelming power of the nation, even if they had all seceded, and been unanimous. The white population of the whole ten may be stated, in round numbers, at about four millions, against twenty-four millions in the remaining twenty-four States. In fact, however, but for the treasonable conduct of the secession minorities in the Border States, and especially but for the outrage perpetrated in Virginia, by means of which the secessionists usurped the control of that State, and suddenly threw it into a condition of war with the Federal Government; it is in the highest degree probable, that neither North Carolina, Tennessee, nor Arkansas would have seceded. Moreover, if the State Governments in Virginia, Kentucky, and Tennessee, had been loyal, their influence—backed, as it undoubtedly would have been, by the mass of the people in those States—would, at the very least, have placed the loyal population in North Carolina, Tennessee, and Arkansas in such a position as to have kept the traitors in check in all those States— even if they ventured to secede. The very worst that can happen, has already occurred: four of the Border States are the chief theater of the war; three at least, if not four, of those States, are for the Union; one, possibly two of them, may be considered against it. For the purposes before us let all five be omitted, in reckoning the strength of either party. Let it be supposed that their whole white population, which may be stated at about four millions, is equally divided—and will add as much, taking the five States, to the military force on one side as on the other side. What follows is, that the war is to be decided by the relative force of the nineteen Free States, and the ten most southerly Slave States. But the case is far stronger, in favor of the General Government, than this statement would make it appear. For by making these Border States the theater of war, however much the ten southern States may gain, the nineteen Northern States gain far more, in every way. They gain physically, by gradually drawing, as the war progresses, a greater and greater proportion of Union men into the Federal army; while to the whole extent that these States are occupied by Federal troops, the secession element is greatest at the first violent military movement, and becomes relatively less and less available afterwards. They gain morally, by the whole effect produced upon the Union people of the Border Slave States, fighting side by side with the Northern soldiers, in a common and glorious cause; and by the whole effect produced on the Northern troops, by seeing for themselves, who and what the loyal people of the South are. But they gain also, in a military point of view. To menace

Nashville, is a very different thing from being menaced at Cincinnati. A victory at Springfield in southern Missouri is widely a different thing from a victory at Springfield in Central Illinois. When the theater of war passes out of Virginia and Kentucky to the South—the beginning of the end to rebellion is reached. If it were to pass out of Virginia and Kentucky to the North, it would only mean the annihilation of whatever Confederate troops might venture across the Ohio River. The Confederate armies will find their attempt to invade Kentucky a very serious matter before all is over; though there is only an air line in their rear, and a million of people—one-third of whom are disloyal—immediately before them. What could they expect, north of the Ohio River—with that broad and generally difficult stream in their rear, and six or seven millions of loyal and warlike people, in Ohio, Indiana, Illinois, Michigan, and Wisconsin, in point blank range of them? The secession gasconade about wintering in Cincinnati—with which the air of the West has been laden for some months—when last heard of was making good time, with a strong force, through the north-eastern mountains of Kentucky, hurrying toward Virginia, out of the way of a small column of raw troops, under a navy Lieutenant, who has lately become an amateur General.[3]

Upon the whole, therefore, the case against the nation is not quite so bad as we before admitted—when, counting out the Border Slave States, it seemed to stand about twenty millions in the nineteen Free States, against about four millions in the ten secession States of the South. In both clusters of States, we leave out all but the white population; and every one will judge for himself how far the leaving out of a few hundred thousand free negroes may be unjust to the stronger side, and the leaving out of some three millions of slaves, several hundred thousand free negroes, and an indeterminate quantity of Indian savages, may be unjust to the weaker side. There certainly are conditions in which this vast body of slaves may be considered a very powerful element in the military strength of the South: the chief of which conditions are—*first*, that the military force of the United States should not be able to penetrate the heart of the disloyal slave region,—and—, *secondly*, that after penetrating that region, the General Government should be weak enough to treat slave property, in the hands of rebels and traitors, as if it were sacred. On the other hand, there are conditions in which this Indian and slave population may become fatal to the weaker party; as, for example, if the Indian savages who have been

3. William Nelson (1824–1862), a midshipman in the Mexican War and head of the Kentucky Horse Guard.

enlisted against us were required, as the condition of peace and protection to their tribes, to ravage those who have engaged their scalping knives against our women and children; and if the slaves were supported from the estates of their disloyal owners, and made to labor upon every species of military work—the number, variety, and extent of which needed by a hostile force, in such a country as the South, and in the present state of the military art, are so great. Still, however, omitting these populations altogether—as neither a weakness nor a strength—there remain the abiding elements, face to face, twenty millions against four millions. It is certainly true, that no one can tell beforehand how a particular battle may eventuate—or how a particular campaign may end. No one can guess how many cowards a few brave men may conquer—how many fools a man of genius may set at nought—how many advantages may be gained over numbers, by superior activity, intelligence and daring. Oliver Cromwell conquered Great Britain, Ireland, and Scotland, with a handful of men: Bonaparte annihilated three Austrian armies, each greater than his own, in one of his brief Italian campaigns: Alexander the Great conquered the whole known world with thirty thousand men. And to come to our own times—*somebody*, we don't exactly know who, has held Manassas, and menaced Washington City, during this whole war, in defiance of the whole power of the nation: and, what seems to us really a marvelous achievement—*somebody* has virtually blockaded the Potomac River from one of its shores, in defiance of our whole naval power, and in the face of probably a hundred and fifty thousand good troops, in his front, and upon his flanks. Still, however, here are our twenty millions against four millions—any four millions of the former, equal to the latter four millions—and we having every possible advantage which they can possess, and many besides of the greatest importance, which they do not possess. This is the undeniable state of the case, considered as a whole. Upon it, there is no ordinary possibility of but one final result. Concerning it, whatever is known to be out of the ordinary course of human affairs, is, in the aggregate, more for us than against us. With regard to it, no motive that can operate upon a rational mind or a patriotic heart, is wanting to impel us to do with our might, what has been now shown to be completely in our power;—what, it was before shown, involves our national ruin if we fail; and what, we must add, covers us with ignominy if we omit.

In one of our former papers, published in the month of March last, we endeavored to point out the method in which the national peril at that dark period could be averted, and to designate the elements, few but immense and decisive, in which the triumphant deliverance of the country lay. Nine or ten months of herculean efforts on the part both of the nation and of the rebels, have passed since that paper was published. The whole field lies far more clearly open before us now than it did then. Public opinion, everywhere, has been consolidated in one direction or another, and is far more comprehensible. The whole continent has passed into a state of war, military operations have been conducted on the most gigantic scale, and the nation and the rebels have reached a position in which their relative strength must be fairly and speedily measured. It seems very clear to us, that all the indications, taken together, are in a high degree favorable to the country; and that this can be made apparent in the shortest manner, by a slight recapitulation of the points in which our national safety seemed to us to lay at the darkest period, and a general view of the tendency and present state of public affairs, with reference to them.

It seemed to us, in the *first* place, that the salvation of the country depended upon the Federal Government's recognizing and assuming its great position as the true and only representative of the nation, and as the supreme authority in these United States: that so acting, its highest mission was to save the nation—to that end putting forth the whole strength of the country—rallying every loyal citizen to its support—and crushing treason everywhere. Whoever will compare the state of the national administration and of the country, as left by Mr. Buchanan and as found by Mr. Lincoln on the 4th of March, with the present aspect of both; will not need any detail by us, to be convinced that what we then declared to be the first condition of our deliverance, has been completely realized, and has produced all the effects that we anticipated. The nation was betrayed by the Federal Government, and was virtually lost on the 4th of March, 1861. The Congress of the United States, under the lead of Mr. Lincoln, and by means of a sublime outburst of national patriotism, has retrieved the ruin elaborately prepared for us, through long years of perfidy, conspiracy, and treason. The whole difference between the two positions of the country may be clearly estimated, by picturing to ourselves, on one hand, five hundred thousand brave and loyal men under arms; and by picturing to ourselves, on the other hand, a traitorous faction everywhere shouting "*no coercion,*" to a betrayed and stupefied people.

In the *second* place, the deliverance of the country seemed to us to depend upon a vigorous, and, as far as possible, successful effort, to arrest the spread of secession, at the cotton line—and if that failed, then at the Southern boundary of the Border Slave States. It was always our opinion, frequently expressed, that a national movement of the whole fifteen Slave States, against the Union, could not be defeated. It was our opinion for thirty years, that a growing school of Southern politicians, had no other object but the production of this result—an opinion, the truth of which no one, we suppose, now doubts; and we have personal knowledge that the support of Major Breckinridge for the Presidency, in Kentucky, was largely given to him under the delusion—countenanced, at least, by himself—that the designation of himself as the candidate of the Southern wing of the Democracy, meant that they had definitely abandoned this conspiracy and all schemes of disunion, and would risk their fate as a party and as a people, in the Union. Yes, we perfectly well know that under this delusion, and because of the decisive influence of this pretended change in the South upon the perpetuity of the Union, multitudes of men—who never saw a moment in which they would not willingly have laid down their lives for the Union—supported him for the Presidency who, in effect, was the representative of disunion. Such is treason. The effects which have been produced by the course of events in Virginia, plainly show what might have been expected, if all the Slave States had cordially united in the revolt: while the effects that have been produced by the course of the intrepid Union men of Kentucky, under the most difficult circumstances, as plainly show what might have been expected, if all the Border Slave States had cordially espoused the cause of the Union. The pestilence was not arrested at the cotton line—nor even fully stayed at the Southern boundary of the Border States. But enough has been done to show how just and important the opinion we expressed in March was; to show how fatally the vacillation and timidity of the nominal Union party in most of the Border States, has operated; and to show how certainly these five States will be preserved to the Union, and how decisive that fact must be, upon the fate of the revolt.

In the *third* place: About the time of Mr. Lincoln's inauguration, and in full apprehension, on one side, of the terrible fact that Mr. Buchanan's Cabinet had sold the nation to the Southern conspirators, and that they were preparing to seize it; and, on the other side, with the profound conviction that the state of public feeling and opinion throughout the North was incompatible, in the existing temper of the times, with the continuance of the Union, or the steadfast loyalty to it of a single Slave State—we did not hesitate to declare that a revolution in opinion and feeling at the North must promptly occur, or all was lost. We ventured to predict that it would occur;—that the extreme principles of the party which had carried the Presidential election, would not be, could not be carried out; that new, better, and more exalted ideas, would supersede the vehement and exaggerated principles of the newly triumphant party; and that the people of the North would stand by the Union, and by every man, everywhere, that was loyal to the country. And now we confidently assert, that no more illustrious instance of patriotic ardor, no more striking proof of the warlike spirit of a free people devoted to the pursuits of peace, has been exhibited in modern times—than is to be found in the conduct of the people of the North, at this terrible crisis of their country. We have felt obliged, many times in the course of many years, to condemn certain tendencies in the Northern mind, and various acts which seemed to be approved by the mass of the Northern people, hostile to the rights of the Southern States, and incompatible with their own duty as citizens of the United States. In the same spirit of fearless justice, we now give expression to our grateful and confiding admiration of conduct on the part of the North, full of high and multiplied proofs of wisdom, magnanimity and heroism. We solemnly believe, this day, that the North is willing to do for the loyal States of the South, more, in every way, than any magnanimous Southern man would have the heart to ask. What a shame—what a burning shame—that men should be betrayed by villains, to seek each other's lives—who, if they did but know one another, would rush into each other's arms.

The *fourth* necessity asserted by us, was such a counter revolution—throughout the more southerly States that had then seceded, or were then deeply agitated on the subject—as would put down the secession movement, and bring the loyal party of the South into power, everywhere. Our hope, at first, was that this counter revolution would manifest itself in the most powerful of those States—as for example, in Georgia, North Carolina, and Tennessee—by means of popular elections, and other ordinary peaceful means; and that the weight of an irresistible public opinion—the comparative weakness of the disloyal States—and the effectual but forbearing interposition of the Federal Power, would deter the leaders of the conspiracy, and give the patriotism and common sense of the people space and opportunity for reaction, concert and triumph. Under any but the most extraordinary circumstances, that would have been the course and result of affairs. To state and explain these circumstances fully, appertains to the historian of these eventful times: we have heretofore given a brief and general account of them. We still await, still confidently expect, the counter revolution throughout the South—which, under ordinarily wise and courageous treatment, would have crushed the secession conspiracy as soon as it had developed its nature, spirit and designs—but which must now extinguish it when its course is run. The grounds upon which we expect it, instead of being removed, are every way confirmed by the progress of events. It is more certain now than it was at first, that the conspirators have reason to dread, and that loyal persons may confidently rely on, the resolute purpose of the American people to uphold the Union, the Constitution and the laws: so that the assurance of unavoidable failure to the one, and of speedy and complete deliverance to the other, becomes day by day the very nourishment of the reaction which is inevitable in its set time. That which is thus unavoidable, in the nature of the case as it exists, cannot be called in question, by any one who believes that there are such human endowments as patriotism and common sense; by any one who confides in the capacity of mankind for self-government; by any one who knows that to deceive a people, and then betray them, and then oppress them, and then impoverish them, are crimes which no people ever forgive; by any one who understands that the indignation of mankind is relentless, in proportion as the sacrifices have been costly and bitter which the folly of corrupt rulers forced them to make, to no end but ruin and ignominy; by any one who accepts the assurance of God, that civil society is an ordinance from heaven, and is compatible with the permanent reign of anarchy. Nor do the innumerable facts, which, in a thousand ways, reach us from the whole area covered by the usurped power of the Confederate Government, fail to confirm, in the public mind, the conviction already stated. On the one hand, there comes up a subdued but incessant wail of a loyal people groaning for deliverance; on the other, a fierce cry for blood and plunder, mixed with a wild clamor about cordial unanimity. The nation pities and heeds that wail of our brethren, and, by God's help, will make it audible throughout the earth, as a lesson to all conspirators. And so far is it from being credible that their deliverance cannot be accomplished except by the slaughter of vast populations—nor maintained afterward except by immense standing armies; all the facts of this sad case show, that what has happened in all ages and countries, will happen again here; and *the mass of the people* speedily and joyfully return to their allegiance, as soon as the military force of the rebels is broken, and society is allowed to return to its ordinary condition. These are terrible episodes in the history of nations. No people has escaped them: it is the feeble only that perish by means of them: the great survive them, and become greater.

III. Supposing what has been said to be worthy of serious consideration, as pointing out the single condition on which the restoration of peace is possible—and as showing the complete ability, and the clear duty, of the American people to enforce that condition, and conquer peace: it becomes all the more important to observe with candor, the actual state of the country, as that is influenced by the war, or as it may, in turn, influence its progress and end; because, according to our apprehension, the indefinite continuance of the war can be arrested only by the triumph of the nation. Classified in an orderly way, the Civil and Military condition of the country is sufficiently though incidentally brought to light, for our present design, in the course of the two preceding divisions of this paper. What remains, related, therefore, more particularly to the Moral, Political, Financial, and Industrial condition of the country—considered with relation to the war. It is to some general consideration of this aspect of the case, in relation to our general course of thought, that we now proceed.

When we speak of the Moral condition of the country, we do not intend, especially, its spiritual state, as in the sight of God. We mean that moral state which is the sum of all the good and all the evil, presented in our mixed and confused probationary state—and presented to us now and amongst ourselves, as characteristic of our condition, and as decisively influential upon the future. This rebellion begins in an outrage upon many of the clearest obligations of Natural Religion—loyalty, love of country, fidelity to public trusts, gratitude for honors bestowed, truth and manhood in the discharge of obligations voluntarily assumed, nay, eagerly sought. How many of the leaders of this rebellion are free from the stain on their personal honor, of deliberately transgressing some or all of those natural obligations, which no contingency under heaven can justify any one in violating! We speak not of the mere fact of treason, as defined by human laws. What we speak of is the perfidy, in every revolting form, which has marked this treason, in its birth, in its growth, and in its present frantic struggle: man seeking to overthrow monuments, demented by the blood of their immediate ancestors; man dishonoring names, illustrious through many generations; men betraying their friends, their neighbors, their kindred; men seducing children to take up arms against their parents—and then banding them with savages to desolate their own homes with fire and sword. It is a madness—a fearful madness. No madness can be greater, except the madness that could induce this great nation to suppose that God allows it to let this go unpunished.

Perhaps the most dangerous, as well as the most universal form, in which this characteristic perfidy has made itself manifest, is the suddenness with which thousands of *spies and informers* have appeared throughout the nation, the tenacity with which they have everywhere followed their degrading employment, and the alacrity with which honors and rewards, almost to the very highest, have been lavished upon them by the rebel government and people. In the States which have seceded, the mass of the loyal people, overwhelmed by force, have quietly acquiesced. In the loyal States, the mass of the disloyal people—wherever opportunity offered—seem to have given themselves up to a regular system of espionage, by means of which the rebel authorities, civil and military, have been kept perfectly informed of all they desire to know. All ranks of society, persons in private life and those in every kind of public employment from the lowest to the highest, persons of every age and of both sexes; appear to make it the chief business of their lives to obtain secret and dangerous information for the benefit of the rebel authorities. Betraying their country, they break with indifference every tie that binds human beings to each other. The humiliated parent doubts whether his own disloyal child will not betray him; the husband may not safely confide in his disloyal wife; and as for the obligation of civil or military oaths, or the honor which should bind every one in whom trust is reposed, no loyal man in America any longer believes that the mass of secessionists scattered through the loyal States, recognize the validity of these sacred bonds. It is, we suppose, certain, past doubt, that every important military movement since the war began has been betrayed to the enemy before it was made; and nine-tenths of the evils and miscarriages we have suffered have been occasioned by *spies and informers* in our midst.

Such a state of affairs as this cannot be endured. The danger of it renders it intolerable. The enormity of it justifies any remedy its extirpation may require. And they who are innocent of such turpitude themselves, instead of raising a clamor at the use of any means by which society seeks to protect itself, ought to be thankful for any opportunity to clear themselves from the suspicion under which they may have fallen. And they who are guilty, and expect to silence public justice by clamor about irregular proceedings against them, ought to bear in mind, that a people outraged past endurance, has much shorter processes than any that imply infallibility in corrupt judges, or writs out of chancery. It does not appertain to us to argue and determine nice and doubtful points of criminal law—concerning which men who ought to be competent to decide, are pleased to differ and to dispute; and which the present Chief Justice of the United States is alleged to have decided in two exactly opposite ways. The boundaries between the civil and military authorities, in time of war, under the Constitution and laws of the United States—may be sufficiently obscure, to serve the turn of those who habitually transgress both. And the boundaries between those powers which can be exercised, in war, by the President alone, and those which must be exercised jointly by the power both of Congress and the President, may be liable to grave questioning by persons, amongst others, who are not very desirous to have their career of mischief cut short. Spies, and other persons who may be justly considered liable to military punishment, can look, we suppose, with very small hope to honest civil tribunals, for deliverance from military authority; and it is very certain that all the prisons in the United States would not hold the tenth part of those, who have made themselves liable to punishment for such offenses. As for offenses of other kinds, especially for the highest offense known to the laws of all civilized countries, *Treason*—these, when added to the highest military offense, that of being a *Spy*, (and no one can be a *spy* in *this* war without being a *traitor* also)—the public authorities are certainly inexcusable if they punish innocent men, when so many are flagrantly guilty—and are hardly excusable when they punish insignificant men, when so many of great distinction have been allowed to escape, or are still unquestioned. The legality of particular modes of arrest, the proper legal treatment after arrest, and the whole doctrine about the writ of *habeas corpus;* are matters, no doubt, of great importance in their place. As for us, we are ready to stand by the chief law officer of the Government, the Attorney General of the United States, who, as we understand the matter, has given explicit sanction of his high professional standing, and that of his great office, to the course which the President has taken. And we suppose all loyal men will agree with us, that—if the American people can endure the pretended violations of law, which their enemies say are daily perpetrated in the arrest and detention of suspected, and indicted, Spies and Traitors—it is no great thing to ask of those who declare the Constitution to be already a nullity, and all lawful government at an end, that they will bear with composure irregularities which loyal men do not complain of. And, perhaps, all earnest patriots would agree, that, at the worst, the salvation of the country from the reign of anarchy and the despotism of traitors, is worth all the human laws and constitutions in the world. We can make governments; for society is supreme over them. But we have only this one country. And it is audacious hypocrisy, for those who are seeking alike the overthrow of our government, and the degradation of our country—to revile us about some pretended irregularity, in our attempt to subject them to punishment, for their crimes against the existence of society.[4]

The financial condition and prospects of the country—the cost of the war in money, the questions of public credit, taxes, currency, public debt, and the like—are of great importance in themselves; and the use which is made of the popular ignorance on such subjects—by exaggerating whatever is evil and suppressing whatever is favorable, and by both means shaking the public constancy in pushing the war to a complete triumph—adds greatly to that importance. They who are familiar with such topics can do no greater service to the country than to remove all mystery from them, and

---

4. See Mark E. Neeley Jr., *The Fate of Liberty: Abraham Lincoln and Civil Liberties* (New York: Oxford University Press, 1991).

disclose with precision our condition and prospects with reference to them. For ourselves, we readily admit that, in our judgment, the end demanded—namely, the independence of the nation, the freedom of the people, the security of society, and the glory of the country—ought to be achieved, let the pecuniary cost and the financial result be what they may. After our triumph, the country will remain, and it will belong to our posterity; and no one need doubt that the triumphant people will make the glorious country worth all it cost us to save both; nor that posterity will venerate, as they should, the heroic generation that sacrificed all, to save all. There is, however, no ordinary possibility that very great pecuniary sacrifices will be required of the loyal portion of the nation; and it is not out of the reach of probability that they may, as a whole, derive considerable pecuniary advantage from the aggregate result of this unnatural war. We will explain ourselves in as few words as possible.

So far as the great losses, if not the total ruin, of large numbers of people in a nation, are necessarily pecuniary misfortunes to the whole population; we do not see how the restored nation is to escape very great loss by this war. For it seems to us impossible for the Southern States, even if the war could be arrested at once, to extricate themselves from their deplorable financial condition, without extreme sacrifice; just as it seems to us certain that the main source of their affluence, in their own opinion—their virtual monopoly of cotton in the market of the world—is forever ended. If they protract this war to their utmost power, the Confederate Government, and every State government connected with it, will come out of the war utterly bankrupt. The creditors of all those Governments will be so far ruined, as the loss of some thousand millions of dollars due to them by those Governments, can ruin their creditors. Some thousand millions more will be sunk in individual losses, unconnected with the Governments. Every species of property will fall, say one-half or more, in its merchantable value. The whole paper currency, after falling gradually till it ceases to be competent for any payment at all—will fall as an entire loss on the holders of it; the precious metals having long ago ceased to circulate. In the meantime, if the country is not speedily conquered, it passes over from the hands of the present usurpers, into the hands of three or four hundred thousand armed men—whose only means of existence is their arms. This, in every item of it, means desolation. In the aggregate, it presents a condition, which all the statesmen in the world have not the wisdom to unravel into prosperity, without first passing through multiplied evils, the least of which is infinitely greater than the greatest of those for which they took up arms against the Union. No such revolution as that attempted in the South can succeed;

and its inevitable failure draws after it, always, a revolution in property. The present disloyal race of cotton and sugar and rice planters of the South—its great property holders, who ought, above all men, to have put down this rebellion—will, as a class, disappear, beggared, perhaps in large proportion extinct, when the war is over. It is a fearful retribution; but we do not see how they can escape it.

In effect, therefore, the Federal Government and the loyal States of America have no alternative but, besides maintaining their own financial solvency and credit during the war, to retrieve the ruin of the Southern States, as a part of the nation, after the war is done. No enlightened man ought to have any doubt of their ability to do both. At the present moment, we will enter no farther into the question of the national ability to do the latter, after the war is over; than to desire the reader to make, for himself, a full and just comparison of the present financial conditions of the United States, and the Confederate States—and satisfy himself of the true causes of the immeasurable difference between them. It is, just now, the other point— our financial ability to carry the war triumphantly through, without great pecuniary sacrifices to the loyal people of the nation—that interests the public mind; and about which we have a few words to add.

A nation, like an individual, can spend its entire annual accumulations, within the year, without being a cent the poorer, or a cent in debt. It can do this forever; and it can do it in carrying on war, as well as in any other way. If all the people of the United States would put the whole of their annual accumulations in the hands of the Government, *as a gift*, their boundless wealth might be spent on war, forever, and nobody be any poorer—and the Government owe no debt. If they will not let the Government have it *as a gift*, there are two other modes by which the Government may obtain the whole of it—and still no one be any poorer. It can be done by taxation;— limiting the taxes—at the highest—to the available annual accumulations; and distributing the taxes so that they shall fall only on the accumulations: both very nice operations, which few public men have ever understood, and few nations have willingly endured. It can be done also, by means of *Public Credit*; which is at once the highest product of civilization, and its greatest safeguard. There is a third method by which, emphatically, in wars like this, conquering nations are accustomed to relieve themselves: *first* by making the conquered party pay, in whole or in part, the expenses of the war; and *secondly*, by confiscating the property of enemies, and especially of rebels. The equity of these latter methods cannot be questioned; and they have this high justification, that they discountenance all rash, needless, and criminal wars. It was a madness in the Confederate States—as the weaker and the aggressive party—to set us the example of the most sweeping confiscations; for it pointed to a fund, in the hands of traitors, too large to be stated with even approximate truth; out of which we might conquer them without costing any loyal man a farthing.

The Congress of the United States has resorted to both of the two expedients first stated above: Taxation and Loans to the Government. To state the matter in other words, this generation agrees to take on itself its fair share of preserving the country; and this share is expressed in the form of taxes and interest upon money borrowed by the Government. It justly proposes to cast on future generations, some portion of the cost of that which concerns them as deeply as it does us; and this share is expressed in whatever amount of debt and interest this generation may leave unpaid. Let us observe, however, that the nature of wealth is such, in the present state of human civilization, that the surplus capital of the world, to an almost boundless extent, is constantly seeking for safe and easily convertible investments; amongst the most eagerly desired of which, are such as are the most likely to be perpetual. The debt we may leave to posterity, therefore, may be truly said to be no more than the interest in perpetuity, on the amount unpaid, and which posterity may prefer not to pay, when it shall enter upon the most glorious inheritance in the world, charged with a very small comparative annuity, created in defence of the inheritance itself. If this war should last five years, at a cost of five hundred millions a year, over and above the income from direct and indirect taxes, we should make our children the foremost nation on earth; and oblige them to pay, therefore, one hundred and fifty millions a year. This is less, a good deal, than the yearly interest paid on the present national debt of Great Britain: and it is extremely probable it could be raised, in a prosperous condition of the country, by indirect taxes, without detriment to a single one of its great interests, and with great advantage to many of them. But, in truth, we may say, the war will not cost so much as five hundred millions a year, over and above the ordinary income; nor will the war last five years; nor will there be any difficulty, under a wise and economical administration of public affairs, for the same generation that makes the war debt, to pay its interest, and gradually redeem the debt itself. Nay; a previous limitation stated by us, is theoretically true, only in a certain sense. For any man, or any nation, in good credit, can borrow, from other men and other nations, and do so borrow continually, immense sums of money, on the credit not of surplus accumulation, nor even of gross income—but of the capital itself;—nay, often to the value of an enormous credit beyond the value of the capital itself. We were originally a thrifty people, economical in paying salaries, averse to high taxes, and shy of public debts; some indulgence in which latter, in later years, has not made us more favorable to them. But of all absurdities, none can be more palpable than the idea of any inherent pecuniary difficulty on the part of the American people, in carrying out this war to complete triumph. Undoubtedly, this is on the supposition of competent skill, in the raising and disbursement of such immense sums of money. And, so far as we are informed and are competent to judge, there is much reason to ascribe the highest capacity to the present Secretary of the Treasury. Undoubtedly, also, it is on the further supposition that this vast fund is neither stolen, nor perverted, nor used wastefully and fraudulently; but that it is skillfully, faithfully, and economically applied to its right use, by the agents of the Government, through whose hands it passes. To this end, it is probable, further legislation by Congress is needed—as well as a sleepless vigilance on the part of the public—and the condign punishment, without respect to persons, of all official corruption.

There are some other topics of much interest, touching which we had designed to say something—as, for example, the question of paper currency, whether furnished by the Government or the Banks, in its relation to the circulation of the precious metals and the possible drain of them from the country—and the bearing of the actual management of the public finances upon these questions, and upon the internal trade of the country, by means of the substitution of cash payments, instead of credits, both in public and private transactions. But great as the bearing of these topics is, upon the general questions we are discussing, the topics themselves are too much beside the common knowledge of mankind, to be very clearly stated in the remaining space allotted to this portion of this paper. We content ourselves, therefore, with saying that, in our opinion, an incompetent Secretary of the Treasury had it completely in his power to have placed the public finances in a condition out of which immediate and ruinous discredit to the Government would have sprung—and, as a consequence, the general circulation of a depreciated paper currency, the disappearance of the precious metals, a ruinous fall in the value of property, the impossibility of active trade, and the gradual impoverishment of the country, in the midst of the war. Instead of calamities so untimely and dreadful, it seems to us perfectly clear that the course taken by Mr. Chase has had a most powerful influence in maintaining the public credit at a very high point; in opening to the Government, as a favored borrower, the whole unfixed wealth of the nation; and in aiding, in a very high degree, the rapid development of that prosperity which the industrial condition of the country exhibits in all the loyal States.[5] There are, no doubt, other causes—some of them greater than was foreseen by most persons, others which were not foreseen by any one— to which we must attribute the chief influence in producing the universal industrial activity, and the substantial industrial prosperity, which the loyal States enjoy; instead of the starvation to which the mad conspirators of the South, expected to reduce those States. It is a great lesson—this unexpected working of this civil war upon the industrial condition of the two sections of the Union. We would willingly enter into some exposition of the causes, which have warded off so many heavy calamities from one section, and hurled them with such crushing force upon the other. But we content our-selves, as in several previous instances, with suggesting the great fact to the reader, and urging him to verify it for himself. Its bearing is most decisive on the course and end of this war. And its just exposition throws great light on the true interests of the whole country, and on the real sources of its power.

IV. The secessionists would have mankind believe, that their conduct is prompted by the most elevated principles, and directed by the noblest instincts. In illustration of these pretensions, those who were in the highest civil stations, plundered the Government under which they were Senators, Members of Congress, and Cabinet officers: those who were in the naval and military service, betrayed the flag of their country, and delivered up, not only strong places, but the troops confided to them: those who had the opportunity, robbed the Government of money: those who were on foreign diplomatic service, used their positions to the greatest possible injury of the nation: and if there were any exceptions of honorable conduct amongst them they occurred amongst those of subordinate rank, and have been concealed by their comrades, as marks of weakness. All these degrading evidences of the total demoralization of the party, occurred in that stage of the conspiracy, immediately preparatory to the commencement of open hostilities by them. At first, they seemed to have supposed that the nation would make no serious attempt to reduce them by force, and that a great people, betrayed and sold, would accept the ignominious fate prepared for it. When they awoke from this stupid dream, their first resort was, very naturally, to an exhibition of the quality of their heroism; and their wail of "No coercion" resounded through the land—echoed back by the concerted cry of their secret allies in the loyal States, "Peace, on any terms, with our brethren." Their next resort, just as naturally, was a manifestation of the reality of their boasted confidence in themselves, in their resources, and in

5. For comments on Chase's policies see John Nivins, *Salmon P. Chase* (New York: Oxford University Press, 1996).

their cause. This, also, they exhibited in a manner perfectly characteristic. Emissaries were despatched to all foreign nations, embracing even the distracted Governments south of us, and not forgetting even our Indian tribes, or the Mormon kingdom. Everywhere, under the sun, where the least help seemed attainable, by whatever means they supposed might be effectual, they eagerly sought it. Sometimes by menaces, sometimes by solicitations, sometimes seeking alliance, sometimes protection, sometimes offering everything, sometimes begging for anything—even for a King, if they could get nothing better. But always, and everywhere, help was what they wanted! Help, against their own country, which they had betrayed. Oh! patriots! Help, against their own people, whom they professed to have terrified, and to be able to subdue. Oh! heroes! A more shameful record does not disfigure the history of sedition.

The United States have had three foreign wars, in eighty-six years; two with Great Britain, one with Mexico; the whole three occupying less than one-seventh part of their national existence. Peace is emphatically the desire and policy of the nation; for peace offers to it conquests, well understood by it, far greater than any nation ever obtained by war. To treat all nations as friends, to treat them all alike, to have alliances with none, to have treaties of peace and commerce with all, to demand nothing that is not just and equal, to submit to nothing that is wrong: this is the simple, wise, and upright foreign policy of this great country. Seated, so to speak, on the outer margin of the world, as the world's civilization stood at the birth of this great nation, the fathers of the Republic understood and accepted the peculiar lot which God had assigned to their country; and their descendants, to the fourth and fifth generation, had steadily developed the noble and fruitful policy of their ancestors, beholding continually the increasing power and glory, in the fruition of which, in our day, they constituted one of the chief empires of the world. Whatever else the nation may have learned, or left unlearned, in a career so astonishing; it has learned at least that the career itself is not yet accomplished, and that it must not be cut short. It must not be; for we dare not allow it, as we would answer to God, to the human race, to the shades of our ancestors, and to the reproaches of our posterity. The very idea of forcing us, by means of foreign intervention, besides the indignation it begets, shows us how indispensable it is to our independence as a nation, that we must preserve the power by which to defy all such atrocious attempts. The true interpretation for a wise nation to put on such a menace, is that it already behooves it to become more powerful. In the present condition of the chief nations of the earth, invincible strength is the first condition of national independence. And we, who are out of the European community of States, and out of the scope of their fixed ideas of European balance of power, which has, for so long a period, regulated that continent; are, beyond all other nations, pressed with the necessity of augmenting, instead of diminishing our power, if we would preserve our freedom. Two nations of moderate force made out of ours—and the continent is at the mercy of every powerful European combination: and this is the idea of freedom and glory, that characterizes the Confederate Government. One mighty nation—and the United States may defy all Europe combined; and this is the American idea of American independence. Let the fact, therefore, be taken as final, that any foreign attempt to support the secession rebellion, is not merely tantamount to a declaration of war—but to war against the future independence of the United States. And let the Federal Government clearly understand, that this is the deliberate sense of the American people. And let all foreign governments be made fully aware that this is the sense in which such an attempt will be taken.

We do not ourselves believe that any foreign Government will interfere in our unhappy civil war. The doctrine of non-intervention in the domestic affairs of nations, is not only the settled international law of Europe; but it has been of late thoroughly and generally enforced, and its present breach would completely tear in pieces the web of diplomacy that involves the European system of peace. Nor do we see what any European nation could gain by assailing us, comparable to the risk it would run. They certainly would get but little *cotton* by it, if that is what they seek—for some years to come, if ever. Cotton is a product of the plow and the hoe—not of the sword and the gun; and commerce means peace, not war. We do see, moreover, how any serious injury to the United States, might fatally affect one and another European nation; and we can hardly imagine the overthrow of our national power to be attempted by any European combination, under existing circumstances, without producing a general European war—if not immense European revolutions. France, it is clear, has the highest interest in preventing the destruction of the only maritime power in the world, besides herself, that can even keep in check the dominion of England over the sea; a dominion which, for seventy years, France has been diligently preparing to dispute. England, whatever may be the wishes and feelings of certain classes, is still more thoroughly restrained. For—to say nothing of the probable loss of her American possessions, nothing of the ruin of her commerce throughout the world—her fierce population, educated for a whole generation to a fanatical hatred of slavery, and having hardly finished paying a hundred millions of dollars to extinguish it in their own cotton and sugar colonies; would be slow to indulge in the spending of two or three thousand millions more, in a war which they would understand to be for the maintenance of the very cotton and sugar slavery in foreign States, which they have so lately bought out, at home. They are a people, besides, that when driven to extremity, have small faith in royal dynasties—and have, before now, despatched kings in the closet, on the battle-field, and upon the scaffold. Spain is hardly worth speaking about in this connection, except as the owner of some desirable islands in the Gulf of Mexico; *mare nostrum* (*our sea*) as the Romans proudly called the Mediterranean. And these are the chief maritime powers of Europe—certainly the only ones we need take into this account. We will add nothing concerning the friendly dispositions of all other European Governments; nothing concerning the public opinion of Europe, before which even Governments must bow; nothing concerning the traditional and vehement sympathy of those masses of European population who make revolutions, whose hearts are with the United States even against their own sovereigns, and so many thousands of whose near kindred and friends are to-day amongst the best officers and most effective troops in our armies. Enough, it seems to us, has been said to direct the thoughts of the reader toward these considerations, which ought to satisfy the public mind on this particular topic. With ordinary prudence, courage, and fair dealing, on the part of our Government, with foreign States, it does not appear to us that there is any ordinary possibility of a serious rupture with any of them, growing out of this war.

If, however, contrary to our judgment of the facts, war should be forced upon us by any foreign nation—or should occur from any untoward accident; there is no reason to doubt our ability to put down the rebellion in the South, and maintain the Union, notwithstanding the utmost aid the greatest foreign nation could give to the rebels. We will not now discuss the subject, in that aspect. Such a war as we have said, will, probably, not occur in our day. If it ever does occur, either it will wholly fail in its avowed object— or its effects will be far greater and more lasting, than they who bring it on expect or intend. Let mankind, at length, receive the sublime truth, that great nations do not die; that great peoples do not perish. Let them accept, at last, the astonishing fact—more palpable in the developments of our age, than ever before—that nationalities once established, are, according to any measure of time known to history, really immortal. And then let them remember, that this is, in truth, a great nation, and that the nationality shared by the American people, is not only thoroughly established, but one of the most distinct and powerful that ever existed.

It seems proper, in this connection, to make some general allusion to the Naval arm of the public service, and to the Naval power of the United

States. Proper in some part of this paper; because that element of our national power, must be considered decisive of the contest with the rebel States, even if they were in other respects as strong as the nation itself. Proper in this place; because it is the supremacy of the Navies both of France and Great Britain over ours—that exposes us to the degradation even of a menace, from either of those powers—and that begets the wild hope in the Confederate Government, that either of them will interfere in this war, on its behalf. If the Navy of the United States bore any fair comparison with that of either of the two powers that rank with us, as the great maritime States of the world; no one ever would have heard a whisper about the armed intervention of either of them, in our domestic troubles. And if, at the commencement of this rebellion, the military marine of the United States, even such as it then was, had been promptly and skillfully used, the revolt could have been suppressed at the tenth part—perhaps the hundredth part—of the treasure and the blood it may cost. It is, unhappily, true that the conspiracy against the country embraced a large number of the officers of the Navy, as well as of the army; and that the ships and Navy Yards, as well as the Forts and Regiments, had been carefully disposed, by a corrupt administration, in such a manner as to render them as little serviceable as possible. But, besides this, both arms of the service, and especially the Navy, were shamefully inadequate to the safety, the power, and the dignity of the nation; and both arms, but especially the Navy, came utterly short, at first, of what might have been justly expected of them. It is to be hoped that the time has fully come, to retrieve errors which have cost us so much.

From the remotest antiquity, the maritime powers of the world have exerted an influence over human affairs, altogether disproportionate to their relative strength, as compared with other nations. The Phoenicians, the maritime cities of Greece, the Greek cities of Asia Minor, the Carthagenians, the Italian Free Cities of the Middle Ages, more recently Holland, and, for nearly two centuries past, Great Britain: everywhere, in all ages, the same truths are palpable—commerce is the parent of national wealth—and a military marine is, relatively to all other means of national power and security, by far the cheapest, the most effective, and the least dangerous to public freedom. The United States are fitted, in every way, to become the first maritime power in the world. And some of the best fruits of the terrible lesson we are now learning, will be lost; unless our statesmen of the present age, and of future generations, comprehend more clearly than hitherto, that the mission set before the American people cannot be accomplished, either in its internal completeness, or its external force, except by means of a military marine equal, at the very least, to the greatest in the world.

The liberty and glory of the Greeks were altogether personal. The freedom and power of the Roman Republic were altogether public. The great problem yet to be solved, is the transcendent union of both. It belongs to the American people, if they see fit, to give and enjoy this sublime illustration of human grandeur. The indispensable elements of success, are, *internally*, the perfect preservation of our political system, in its whole purity, its whole force, and its whole extent: and, *externally*, the complete independence of the nation, of all foreign powers. In maintaining the former, our immediate necessity is—to extinguish, at whatever cost, this civil war. In preserving the latter, our immediate necessity is—to repel, amicably if we can, with arms if need be, and at every hazard, all foreign interference in support of this rebellion. We are able, if God requires it at our hands, to do both, by His help. Our star is set, when we fail of doing either. With nations, there is a great choice in the way of dissolution—the choice between the contempt, and the veneration, of the human race.

Speech on the Object of the War

(Washington, D.C.: Congressional Globe Office, 1862)

W aitman Thomas Willey (1811–1901) came from Monongalia County, Virginia (later West Virginia). He graduated from Madison College in Pennsylvania, later studied law, and then practiced in Morgantown, Virginia. A Whig, he held various prewar political posts, including clerk of the county court and member of the state constitutional convention of 1850, in which he advocated white manhood suffrage; but he lost in his race for lieutenant governor in 1860. A delegate to the 1861 Virginian secession convention, he voted against secession. Elected to the U.S. Senate in 1861 as a member from the Restored government, Virginia's unionist government in exile, Willey became an ardent antislave supporter and a leader of the West Virginia statehood movement. In 1863 he gained election as a Republican to the U.S. Senate from West Virginia; he was reelected in 1865 and served in that body until 1871.

Willey's pamphlet of December 19 and 20, 1861, concerns his support for the Union and the dangers of internal war to the loyal citizenry of the Virginia border. Personal threats to his own life in April 1861 had sharpened his worries about the safety of others. Willey thus described early in the Civil War the value of loyalty to the Union for western Virginians and the vicious treatment of border unionists. He also pointed out that slaveholding aristocrats controlled the Confederacy and were determined to undermine the democratic practices of the border state citizens. Thus, his ringing call for immediate Federal military invasion of western Virginia had special meaning for the home folk.

For further comment on his career see Charles Henry Ambler, *Waitman Thomas Willey: Orator, Churchman, Humanitarian* (Huntington, W.Va.: Standard Printing and Publishing Co., 1954), and William Willey, *An Inside*

View of the Formation of West Virginia (Wheeling, W.Va.: News Publishing Co., 1901).

* * *

"*Resolved*, That the existing war, forced upon the country by the States in rebellion, without justifiable cause or provocation, was, and is, designed by them to destroy the Union and the Constitution; and their purpose, moreover, was at first, and is now, to disavow and repudiate the fundamental principles of republican government on which our fathers established the Union and the Constitution."[1]

The resolution offered a few days ago enunciates, as I think very properly, what are the purpose and motives of the United States in prosecuting this war. The resolution that I now submit enunciates what I conceive to be the motive and purpose of the States in rebellion in precipitating this war upon the country, and in prosecuting it. As I remarked just now, we have in the States in rebellion, in the State which I have the honor to represent, not only the conflict of the sword, but we have also the war of opinion. I think it is appropriate that the Senate and the country should understand what were and are the real motives and purposes of the South in instigating this rebellion; and I propose to submit my views somewhat at length upon this proposition.

Our forefathers, when they threw off their allegiance to the British crown, admitted that a "decent respect to the opinions of mankind required that they should declare the causes which impelled them to the separation."

They also acknowledged that "Governments long established should not be changed for light and transient causes;" that revolution was justifiable only when government "became destructive of the ends for which it was instituted among men," such as "the inalienable rights of life, liberty, and the pursuit of happiness."

Having secured the recognition of our national independence, they proceeded to organize a government; and in order "to form a more perfect union, establish justice, insure domestic tranquillity, provide for the common defense, promote the general welfare, and secure the blessings of liberty to themselves and their posterity, they ordained and established the Constitution" under which we have since lived so happily, and prospered so well.

1. Willey begins with a resolution from Sen. John C. TenEyck of New Jersey.

If this "respect to the opinions of mankind" is still to be recognized as obligatory, may we not properly inquire what justification is offered by the insurgents against the Government of the United States for their recent and existing terrible efforts to subvert and overthrow it? What essential right has been infringed or withheld? What intolerable wrong has been threatened or inflicted? In what respect has there been a failure to secure to the citizen the enjoyment of his life, his liberty, or the pursuit of his happiness? When or how has the General Government failed to accomplish any of the great purposes of its organization?

"To err is human." It were idle to claim that either of the two parties now in conflict, or that any of the great parties which have distracted the councils of the country, were wholly inculpable. But the question now is, has anything occurred in the administration of the national Government to justify this rebellion? Has the Federal Government become so destructive of the ends of its institution as to create the right in the people, or any portion of the people, "to alter or to abolish it, and to institute a new government?" Respectfully appealing to the "opinions of mankind," and inviting the most rigid scrutiny and criticism, I confidently declare that this rebellion is wholly inexcusable.

In what I shall have to say I shall avoid all theoretical and speculative examination of the fitness and adaptation of our system of government for the accomplishment of the purposes for which it was ordained. It has been tried for three fourths of a century, and now there is no necessity or room for speculation. We have the results of actual experiment. And what do they teach? What is the testimony which they bear to the security of the great inalienable right of life in this country? Where has life been more secure than in the United States? I respectfully challenge an answer to this question from the apologists of this rebellion, here or elsewhere. Spread out the map of the world, and designate the nation where the life of the citizen or subject or serf is more thoroughly protected than was the life of the American citizen prior to this rebellion. Unfold the volume of universal history, and show me the page which records the existence of greater personal security than was enjoyed by the people of the United States. How many millions of our people, twelve months ago, in village and hamlet and cottage, slept with doors unbarred, in calm and conscious security, both of life and estate; and when either life or estate was assailed, where and when did there exist a Government more prompt and efficient to avenge the injury?

And as to liberty, what unwarrantable restraint has ever been imposed upon the enjoyment of it? The American citizen worships God everywhere according to the dictates of his own conscience. His religious liberty is incomparable. As a citizen, his rights are equally well defined and secured. His civil liberties were incomparable; and what political franchise or privilege has ever been denied or infringed by the Federal Government? Who, in all these respects, was so happy as the American citizen? Wheresoever the flag of the Republic floated; on every ocean and sea under the whole heavens; wheresoever it marked the residence of the American minister or American consulate; in every city and seaport and town beneath the sun; in the palaces of kings and the cottages of peasants, to earth's remotest boundary, the name of American citizen had become a guarantee of personal and political security and privilege as high and as assured as ever attached to the national character of any human being.

I am touching upon an inspiring theme; but I will not allow myself to be betrayed into a further pursuit of it. I may be allowed to say, however, that while, like all our guilty race, the American citizen inherits the primal curse attaching to our first progenitor, yet no portion of the posterity of Adam ever came so near to the enjoyment of that wide and unrestricted freedom that in the fancy of the great poet fell to the lot of our federal father, as he turned his back upon the gates of Paradise, when

> "The world was all before him, where to choose
> His place of rest, and Providence his guide."

My purpose is more practical. It is to appeal to matters of fact known to every intelligent man. It is to challenge the production of an instance in the nomenclature of nations where liberty has been more perfectly secured and enjoyed than it was in the United States, and to demand specifications of those infractions of liberty by the Federal Government which may justify this great rebellion. But I shall challenge in vain. There will be no response to my just demand.

And what shall we say of the pursuit of happiness? Surely that people ought to be happy whose property, person, and life, and whose liberties, civil, religious, and political, are fully secured to them. But, apart from the enjoyment of these great rights, what has been the practical operation of the Government upon the physical condition of the people, and how has it affected the common weal in respect of the merely material interests of the country? Has there been any deficiency here? I again beg to appeal to the facts; I again challenge a parallel of progress and prosperity. Three quarters of a century have hardly passed away since we entered upon the arena of independent nations. We commenced the war of independence with a population of three million; now we number more than thirty million. In what age, in what clime, shall we find a parallel? We started in the race of national development with thirteen isolated, disconnected, impoverished colonies. When this rebellion broke out, it required the shores of the two oceans to circumscribe our enlarged and consolidated empire. Our commerce burdened every wave of the sea, and filled every port on the globe. We could have proudly defied the world in arms.

I am not dealing in pictures of fancy. I am not painting with the colors of an unbridled imagination. I am not indulging in figures of speech. I am quoting from the census. I am appealing to recorded facts. All the fancy belongs to the authors of the rebellion. It is they who are abnegating the results of experience, and are madly rushing after the phantoms of a disordered imagination; deserting the beaten paths of long-attested security and prosperity, to follow the *ignis fatuus* of a frenzied speculation. Nor can it be said that there were any indications of decline in our national prosperity. Down to the very day of the insurrection our growth in population and wealth and power was advancing with a constantly accelerated momentum and progress. And this remark is as applicable to the seceded States as to any other section of the Confederacy. It will be found that this rebellion was precipitated upon the country when the condition of the South exhibited incontestable evidence of greater prosperity than it had ever done in any previous period of our national existence.

What is the plain deduction from this unexampled national prosperity? Is it not that there could have been no real grievance justifying rebellion?

But we may, with equal confidence, challenge a more minute examination of the policy and administration of the General Government affecting the States in rebellion. And here I do but allege what the records of the country will amply attest, when I say that in the bestowment of official patronage and emolument, and position in every branch of the Government, the South has ever enjoyed an eminently liberal proportion of favor. The journals and acts of Congress will verify the assertion that every important measure of national policy has either originated with southern statesmen, or has been made, sooner or later, essentially to conform to the demands of southern sentiment. This is a broad assertion, but it is true. The South has always exercised a controlling influence in the councils of the Republic. She has had more than an equal share of Presidents; she has had more than a fair proportion of appointments in the Cabinet; the Supreme Court has been adorned with a full quota of her eminent jurists; the *corps diplomatique* has had no just cause of complaint for the want of representatives from south of Mason and Dixon's line; and the glorious annals of our Army and Navy attest on every page the valor and skill of southern chieftains.

But the great outcry of the South against the North has been predicated principally on alleged grievances respecting slavery. Now, I shall offer no apology for the unfriendly legislation of some of the free States in their distinct capacity. This legislation has sometimes been in direct conflict with the plainest provisions of constitutional law; but the judiciary in every instance, I believe, where a case has arisen under this species of State legislation has declared it to be unconstitutional, and thus rendered it nugatory. Nor will my sense of propriety allow me to do aught else than condemn and denounce the miserable misrepresentation and vituperation of the domestic institutions of the South, which have disgraced in too many instances the northern press and pulpit. But why should the General Government be made responsible for these things? What has it done unfriendly to the South? Look at the facts. The South has always prevailed in questions affecting slavery. For instance: was more efficient legislation required to secure the constitutional right of recovery of fugitives from labor, southern men prepared the law to suit themselves, and it was enacted accordingly. Did fanaticism interpose to rescue the fugitive from the custody of the law, the General Government, with a northern President in the chair of the Executive, enforced the law at the point of the bayonet. The South asked for the Missouri compromise, and got it; and then the South asked for its repeal, and got that. What reasonable demand of the South was ever denied? To the credit and honor of the North, I answer—none! none!

Thus may we speak of the past; but what of the future? The pretense was that the Republican party intended to abolish slavery in the States wherever it existed, or, in some manner, to assail it detrimentally. I am not a member of the Republican party. I opposed to the extent of my poor ability the election of Mr. Lincoln; and I have nothing to regret or to retract. But I never believed that it contemplated any interference with the domestic institutions of the slave States. Whatsoever else may be obnoxious in the avowed principles, or in the actual administration of the Government by this party, it is not, I think, justly liable to animadversion in this respect. Such a design has been expressly repudiated by every respectable exponent of the Republican party from the commencement of its organization. The fourth resolution in the Chicago platform, on which Mr. Lincoln is elected, explicitly declares:

"That the maintenance inviolate of the rights, and especially the right of each State, to order and control its own domestic institutions according to its own judgment exclusively, is essential to that balance of power on which the perfection and endurance of our political fabric depends."

I have seen nothing in the administration of the Government, as yet, which would warrant any just apprehension of a departure from this avowal of constitutional obligation, and there have not been wanting exigencies to test its fidelity. If anything could cause it to swerve from the right line of constitutional duty on this point, it would be the unholy rebellion of the slave States, which are waging a relentless war upon it. And yet I remember with what supreme satisfaction I read the proclamation issued to the people of Virginia by General McClellan, when he first entered that Commonwealth, declaring there should be no infringement of the rights of slaveholders, and that all attempts at servile insurrection should be summarily suppressed.[2] I refer with equal satisfaction to the entire unanimity with which Congress, at the last session, resolved that the war, brought upon the country by the South, should be prosecuted with the sole purpose of suppressing the rebellion, and restoring the Government to its legitimate constitutional supremacy, and that when these purposes were accomplished the war should cease.

In harmony with this avowal was the act of Congress for the confiscation of property employed in aiding and supporting the rebellion. The rights of the loyal slaveholder were sedulously guarded, and the determination of the Government not to interfere with the institution of slavery especially manifest. And so it was, when General Frémont, by his proclamation, proposed a different policy, he was promptly rebuked by the President, and commanded to revoke his unauthorized procedure. I might multiply proofs; I cannot forbear to mention another. When General Sherman disembarked his troops at Beaufort, in the very flush of a glorious victory, he does not, as the representative of the Government, forget his constitutional obligation as an officer or as a citizen, but by his proclamation to the people of South Carolina, doing equal credit to his head and his heart, assured even that rebellious State that "he had come among them with no feelings of personal animosity, no desire to harm her citizens, destroy their property, or interfere with any of their lawful rights, or their social and local institutions." And now, the President of the United States, in his late message, crowns these repeated demonstrations of fidelity to the Constitution, with his official sanction and authority. I honor him for it; and pledge to him the

2. See "To the Inhabitants of Western Virginia," in Stephens W. Sears, ed., *The Civil War Papers of George B. McClellan* (New York: Ticknor and Fields, 1989), 34–35.

support of the loyal citizens of Virginia, so long as he adheres to his present position.

This apprehension, real or assumed, of unconstitutional aggression upon slavery in the States where it exists, is without reasonable cause.

But it was alleged that there could be no misapprehension of the purpose of the Republican party, by congressional intervention, to exclude the South from carrying their slaves into the Federal Territories. I am sorry to be compelled to admit that this objection is well taken. Now, I am free to declare that by no active agency of mine shall the area of slavery ever be extended. I will never aid in its diffusion. As a slaveholder, believing that under existing circumstances the welfare—moral, physical, and religious—of the African race requires that they should be, for the present at least, kept in bondage, I say this. But sworn as I am to support the Constitution, I will concur in no act which shall deprive any citizen or any section of any constitutional right. Consulting my own opinion of the powers of Congress under the Constitution, I should have had little hesitation in saying that the recognition or the exclusion of slavery in the Territories was entirely a matter of legislative discretion; and in the exercise of such discretion, I repeat, that by no active agency of mine should slavery ever be established where it had not existed. The Territories are the common heritage of all the people; and I would leave them to be settled by any or all of the people, from every section, without restriction as to the character of the property which they might carry with them. If the slaveholder wanted to go there with his slaves, let him do so, and let him abide the result of the popular determination when the time arrived for the organization of the Territory into a State. Taking the responsibility of carrying his slaves into the Territory, let him encounter the risk of the character of the constitution which may be ordained. Such is my poor view of congressional power in the premises, and of the proper policy to be adopted in the exercise of it. But my opinion must yield to better authority. The Supreme Court of the United States is the constitutional exponent of disputed principles of constitutional law. As a citizen, and especially as an humble member of this august body, I bow with implicit submission and loyalty to the judgment of this great constitutional arbiter. In my estimation, any other course will be disastrous in the extreme—prolific of anarchy, and subversive of the foundations and security of all popular government. Submission, unqualified submission, to the arbitrament of the Supreme Court is the great sheet-anchor of our safety. Let it be understood that Congress is not bound by its decisions and interpretations of constitutional law, and what would be the result? The sense of the Constitution would vary with the political complexion of the party in power. To-day it would mean one thing; to-morrow it would mean another. The rights of the people would become the sport of party spirit, and the order and security of society would be convulsed and upheaved, and confusion becoming perpetually worse confounded would ensue, until the whole benefit of established government would be lost.[3]

What if the Supreme Court err in its judgment? This is possible—nay it is probable. But in such case we are not remediless. Let the error be corrected by an amendment of the Constitution in the mode prescribed in that instrument; and let the matter of dubious construction, and the errors of the Supreme Court, be obviated by terms which shall not admit of misconstruction. My Lord Coke, long ago, said in reference to this principle, "certainty is the mother of repose." We can have no certainty, no repose, no security, no liberty, no good government, unless we abide by the judgment of the judiciary in questions of constitutional law. But I find myself departing from my purpose not to be drawn into an argument upon abstract principles of government. I come back to the facts and legitimate deductions from facts proving that this rebellion is without justification.

And now, I inquire what has the Republican party done, since the avowal of its policy, to exclude slavery from the Territories? Why, with a decided majority in the other branch of Congress, it has allowed several territorial governments to be organized without intervention to exclude slavery. The South was at perfect liberty to emigrate there with their slaves if they thought proper. Will it be a sufficient reply to this fact to allege, as southern politicians have alleged, that this liberality on the part of the North would never have been manifested if it had not been known that the soil and climate of those Territories were of such a character as to practically prevent the existence of slavery there. Grant the fact; what wrong has the North done to the South? Was the North responsible for the climate and soil? This outcry against the North in regard to these Territories applies only to the God of nature; and, so far as secession is predicated upon the exclusion of slavery from any of the present Territories of the United States, it is a revolt against inexorable laws of nature and Providence. The spirit which dictated it is akin to the spirit which inspired the angelic revolt in Heaven. May its overthrow be as complete.

But the South itself being judge, I aver there was in the policy and administration of the General Government in reference to the Federal Territories no just cause of complaint. I need not remind the Senate that

---

3. Later in the war, Willey came out for the abolition of slavery in West Virginia. Here, early on, Willey seems to want to appease his border state allies.

this averment is authoritatively admitted in the official action of southern Senators on this floor. Senators all remember the resolution of Mr. Brown, of Mississippi, offered for the consideration of this body only a few months prior to Mr. Lincoln's election. I will read it:

> "*Resolved*, That experience having already shown that the Constitution and the common law, unaided by statutory provisions, do not afford adequate and sufficient protection to slave property, some of the Territories having failed, others having refused to pass such enactments, it has become the duty of Congress to interpose and pass such laws as will afford to slave property in the Territories that protection which is given to other kinds of property. . . ."[4]

Every southern Senator, excepting three only, voted against this resolution, thereby acknowledging that down to that day, at least, there was no territorial grievance requiring redress.

Indeed, the act of secession logically implies that the exclusion of slavery from the Territories was not considered to be an intolerable grievance; for secession is a voluntary and final abandonment and surrender to the North of all claim to them by the South.

How utterly absurd are all the pretexts of the insurgents for their rebellion. Granting, for the sake of argument, that the policy and purposes of the Republican party were justly obnoxious to the animadversion which has been heaped upon them, what had the South to fear? If the south had remained loyal to the Government, and its Representatives in this and the other house had remained in their seats, what could your President or your party have accomplished prejudicial or objectionable to the South? You were powerless to do us harm. Your President could not have appointed a member of his Cabinet without our concurrence. With a clear majority in both branches of Congress against you and your party, your hands were tied. No minister to a foreign court could have represented this Government against the consent of the South. No law could have been enacted which was not acceptable to the South. The finances, that omnipotent lever of political power, were under the control of the majority opposed to your party and your policy. You were completely dependent on us for the means of administering the Government. I am recounting facts. And yet, with all

4. Willey then lists the votes on Sen. Albert G. Brown's resolution. For comments on Brown's pamphlet on the subject see Jon L. Wakelyn, ed., *Southern Pamphlets on Secession, November 1860–April 1861* (Chapel Hill: University of North Carolina Press, 1996), 377–78.

the power and control of the Government and of the Republican party in the hands of the South, secession commences. South Carolina recalls her Senators and Representatives in Congress. Mississippi follows her example. Other States tread in their rebellious wake—all crying aloud as they go against the overshadowing power of the North, which was all the time in the minority; till at length by the defection of State after State, our majority here was destroyed, and we of the border States, hitherto secure in our conservative principles, alike aloof from the ultraism of the extremists North and South, and fortified by our majority here, were left in a helpless minority, standing as it were "between the devil and the deep sea." And to-day the so-called confederate States are appealing to the sympathies of the world to rescue them from the persistent oppression of the United States Government!

These subterfuges were so transparent that the more astute of the conspirators, seeing that they must be convicted by the verdict of reason, and the voice of mankind of duplicity, have boldly avowed that the election of Mr. Lincoln, and the triumph of the Republican party, were not the causes of their rebellion. It became convenient for them to make these things the occasion of it. The careful observer of events might have seen their shadows coming before, twenty-five years ago. The real course of this rebellion I hope to make apparent before I conclude. At present suffice it to say, that it was no sudden, unpremeditated insurrection—it was the result of a deliberate, long-concocted conspiracy; as has been virtually acknowledged by many of the principal conspirators.

We all remember the letter of William L. Yancey, urging the policy of "firing the southern heart," for the purpose of "precipitating" a dissolution of the Union.

In the late convention in South Carolina, most of the leading members expressed themselves in terms of exultation, that the event so long devoutly wished for had been consummated.

Mr. Keitt, a prominent member of the other branch of Congress, declared that he had "been engaged in this movement ever since he entered political life."

Mr. Rhett said:

> "It is nothing produced by Mr. Lincoln's election, or the non-execution of the fugitive slave law. It is a matter which has been gathering head for thirty years."

Mr. Inglis said:

"*Most of us* have had this matter under consideration for the last twenty years."

I might multiply the evidence; but the fact is now unquestionable.

It was necessary to apologize for their withdrawal under some pretense of justification. Hence the dogma of "peaceable accession"—the right of a State to peaceably secede at the pleasure and within the sole discretion of the State seceding! A new theory of our Government was thus propounded to cover the ignominy of the retreating parties. And what an idea of government! What a Union! A Government without authority to maintain itself, and a Union with no obligation or bond to perpetuate it! What a commentary on the wisdom of Washington and Franklin, of Madison and Jefferson! The Constitution which we have hitherto regarded and revered as the wisest and best plan of government ever devised, turns out, if this dogma of secession be true, to be a mere solecism, a miserable abortion. Under this theory we have a constitutional Government avowedly on its face claiming to form a more perfect Union, yet containing within itself a fundamental principle of its own destruction.

Our Federal Constitution is a farce if this right of secession be admitted. It is a mere caricature of government. It is less efficient than the old Articles of Confederation, which were acknowledged to be a failure. . . . [5]

And yet, if it be true that a State may secede at pleasure, Washington, with the sages who cooperated with him in the establishment of the Federal Constitution, and who professed in their preamble to it to desire and to have provided for a "more perfect union," utterly unconscious of the imbecility and of the true import of his own labors to remedy preexisting evils, succeeded only in furnishing to his countrymen a constitution of government less efficient and containing less force of national unity and power than the shackling and rickety articles of the old Confederation which were superseded. And this delusion and ignorance of the import of his labors must have followed and possessed the "Father of his Country" all through the eight years of his illustrious administration of the Federal Government. . . . [6]

5. Willey cites here letters from George Washington to Charles Warren, James Madison, and John Jay on the failings of the Articles of Confederation and the need for a strong central government.

6. Willey quotes George Washington's famous "Farewell Address" on obedience to the established government and refers readers again to his letter to Charles Warren. He also cites Andrew Jackson's presidential message of January 16, 1833, denying the right of a state to leave the Union.

Equally repugnant to this doctrine of secession are the powers vested in the General Government by the express terms of the Constitution. The Constitution expressly vests in the General Government all the fundamental functions of complete national sovereignty. By section eight of article one, among other attributes of sovereignty, power is conferred on Congress

"To levy and collect taxes, duties, imposts, and excises.
"To regulate commerce with foreign nations, and among the several States.
"To coin money, and regulate the value thereof.
"To declare war, and grant letters of marque and reprisal.
"To raise and support armies.
"To provide and maintain a navy.
"To make treaties."

And, as if the framers of the Constitution were apprehensive of future assumptions of authority upon the part of the States, incompatible with the exercise of this national sovereignty, they did not rest satisfied with conferring these positive powers on the General Government; but they also, by negation, expressly prohibited the exercise of such powers by the States. So, in article one, section ten, of the Constitution, it is provided, among other restrictions, that

"No State shall enter into any treaty, alliance, or confederation; grant letters of marque or reprisal; coin money; emit bills of credit," &c.

And finally, as if to exclude all controversy, it is ordained in the second section of article six, as follows:

"This Constitution, and the laws of the United States which shall be made in pursuance thereof, and all treaties made, or which shall be made, under the authority of the United States, shall be the supreme law of the land."

The advocates of this right of discretionary secession do not pretend that it is either expressly or impliedly reserved in any clause of the Constitution; but they allege the right is inferrible from the manner in which the Constitution was ratified by the States; that it was ratified by the States distinctively in their sovereign capacities as States; and that, therefore, the Constitution is a mere compact between sovereign States, and is in fact nothing more than the terms of a league between independent sovereignties, liable to be dissolved at the pleasure of any of the parties to it. All this is mere assumption. Not so did Mr. Madison, the great artificer of the Constitution, understand his own handiwork. He says:

> "It was formed by the States—that is, by the people in each of the States, acting in their highest sovereign capacity; and formed consequently by the same authority which formed the State constitutions. . . ."[7]

And the form and mode of submission of the Constitution for ratification are repugnant to the idea of a mere compact or league between the States in their distinctive sovereign capacity. Look at the preamble to it. It does not commence, we the States; nor, indeed, we the people of the States respectively do ordain and adopt the following compact or league. No, it speaks out honestly and to the purpose. It plainly and broadly declares: "We, the people of the United States, do ordain and establish this Constitution for the United States of America."

This device of anarchy and confusion was exploded in the very beginning. Some of the jealous devotees of State rights, apprehensive of the overshadowing power of the central Government, started the idea of a conditional adoption of the Constitution, reserving the right to withdraw if it should afterwards appear to be necessary. Hence, Mr. Hamilton wrote to Mr. Madison, inquiring if it would be competent to do so. What was Mr. Madison's answer? Mr. Madison then, just fresh from his labor of framing the Constitution, in 1788, replied as follows:

> "The Constitution requires an adoption in toto and forever. It has been so adopted by the other States. An adoption for a limited time would be as defective as an adoption of some of the articles only. In short, any condition whatever must vitiate the ratification. What the new Congress, by virtue of the power to admit new States, may be able and disposed to do in such a case, I do not inquire, as I suppose that is not the material point at present. I have not a moment to add more than my fervent wishes for your success and happiness. The idea—and these are the words to which I wish particularly to refer—of reserving the right to withdraw was started at Richmond, and considered as a conditional ratification, which was itself abandoned as worse than rejection."

Where, then, can this extraordinary right of secession find its predicate? Verily, it is said, in the resolutions of the Virginia and Kentucky Legislatures, passed 1798–99, and 1800. It would be more to the point to refer to the Constitution itself. The Legislatures of Virginia and Kentucky were, no

---

7. Madison goes on to mention specific powers of the Federal government.

doubt, very respectable bodies; but they were not the parties who made the Constitution; nor can their resolves supersede the Constitution. But it is alleged that Mr. Madison, who was in fact the father of the Constitution, was also the author of the resolutions of 1798–99; and that therefore these resolutions are, in fact, his exposition of State rights under the Constitution. Did Mr. Madison mean, by his enunciation, in these celebrated resolutions, of the right of State interposition in certain contingencies, that a State had a right to withdraw from the Union? I answer, no. If Mr. Madison, as the principal framer of the Constitution, is authority for the correct exposition of the Constitution, let the same rule apply to him as the author of the resolutions. And here I cite him as authority that he never designed by these resolutions to enunciate any such power in the States, both on the grounds of his intelligence as a statesman and his integrity as a man of truth. He has said he meant to enunciate no such principle. He has repeatedly so declared—in his letters to Mr. Everett, Mr. Cabell, Mr. Stephenson, and Mr. Trist. And yet his great name is persistently paraded before the public as sanctioning the pestilent principle of secession!

The truth is, the assumption of the right of a State to withdraw from the Union of its own accord, and without reference to the will or the wishes of any or of all of the other States in the Union, has only found champions bold enough to avow it within the last few years. Even Mr. Calhoun himself, so late as 1844, declared:

> "That each State has a right to act as it pleases in whatever relates to itself exclusively, no man will deny; but it is a perfectly novel doctrine that any State has such a right when she comes to act in concert with others in reference to whatever concerns the whole. In such cases, it is the plainest dictate of common sense, that whatever affects the whole should be regulated by the mutual consent of all, and not by the discretion of each."[8]

At the time of the passage of the resolutions of 1789–99, the construction now placed upon them was not dreamed of. Mr. Wirt, then in the vigor of youthful manhood, and the ardent admirer and personal and political friend of Mr. Madison and Mr. Jefferson, writes to Judge Carr, of Virginia, under date of January 6, 1833:

> "As to the right of a State to secede from the Union, I do not recollect to have ever heard it made the subject of discussion in the high times

8. This was taken from John C. Calhoun's letter to the Baltimore Democratic Convention of 1844, declining nomination for the presidency.

of 1798–99 and 1800, and consequently never heard the denial of the right to secede treated as a high Federal doctrine." "Mr. Madison's and Mr. Jefferson's resolutions were not for secession—they were appeals to the other States, and looked no further than the repeal of the laws," &c.[9]

That Mr. Wirt is entirely correct in this assertion there can be no doubt. Other contemporaries and contemporaneous events corroborate the statement of Mr. Wirt. For instance, at a festival held by the presidential electors of Mr. Jefferson, in 1800, at the city of Richmond, there were present some of the leading statesmen and exponents of Virginia policy and opinion, and most prominent among the sentiments offered on that occasion was, "secession is treason."

If any journal may be quoted as authority for the views of the State-rights party in Virginia at least, and as reflecting the opinions of Mr. Jefferson and Mr. Madison especially, the Richmond Enquirer was certainly worthy of that distinction. Now we find in the Richmond Enquirer of November 1, 1814, the following:

> "No man, no association of men, no State, or set of States, has a right to withdraw itself from this Union of its own account. The same formality which formed the links of the Union is necessary to dissolve it. The majority of States which formed the Union must consent to the withdrawal of any one branch of it. Until that consent has been obtained any attempt to dissolve the Union, or distract the efficacy of its constitutional laws, is treason—treason to all intents and purposes."

Thus, it seems to me that these celebrated resolutions afford no warranty for the "right of a State to withdraw itself from the Union of its own account;" and the pretense for peaceable, irresponsible secession, predicted upon them, dissolves from view, "like the baseless fabric of a vision;" and the secession of the States now in arms against the Government, stripped of its specious disguises and sophistries and garniture of falsehood, stands forth in its true character—"treason to all intents and purposes"—a willful, unprovoked, diabolical conspiracy against the best Government God ever vouchsafed to man, and against the last cherished hope of constitutional liberty in the world.

It will require the concentrated and accumulated indignation of centuries to denounce, in terms of commensurate severity, the monstrous sin and

9. Madison's reference here is to William Wirt, a prominent Virginia lawyer who served in President Monroe's cabinet.

turpitude of this rebellion. It is a crime against the human race. It has no shadow of apology. The false pretenses of its authors and abettors will not avail to shield them against the coming execration of mankind. Even Calhoun was constrained to admit, in his letter to General Hamilton in 1832, that—

> "With institutions every way so fortunate, possessed of means so well calculated to prevent disorders, and so admirable to correct them when they cannot be prevented, he who would prescribe for our political disease disunion on one side, or coercion of a State, in the assertion of its rights, on the other, would deserve, and will receive, the execrations of this and all future generations."

Truth will ere long strip these conspirators naked before the world, and the people whom they have so cruelly misled will rise up and curse them. History—impartial history—will arraign and condemn them to universal contempt. It will hold them responsible before man and God for the direful consequences already brought upon the country, and for the evils yet to come—for the desolations of war, its pillage, and rapine, and blood, and carnage, and crime, and widowhood, and orphanage, and all its sorrows and disasters. . . . [10]

It must remain for some future American Sallust to delineate in terms of adequate execration the causes, instrumentalities, and personages of this wicked rebellion. How far he may find parallels of treason and turpitude in the pages of his Roman prototype, I shall not now pause to inquire. It may not become his duty to portray the character of any American Catiline in colors of moral debasement, as dark and horrible as those which have justly consigned the name of the Roman conspirator to eternal infamy; but the cardinal offense—the treason itself—of the modern patricides will transcend the enormity of the ancient rebels by so much as the blessings and liberty of America excel those of Rome. For if Sallust properly presented, as the most astonishing and deplorable feature of the effort to subvert the Roman republic, the fact that it was instigated at a time when "every nation from the rising to the setting of the sun lay in subjection to her arms, and though peace and prosperity, which mankind think the greatest blessings, were hers in abundance, there were yet found among her citizens men who were bent with obstinate determination to plunge themselves and their country in ruin," what shall be said of those who, without pretense of provocation, have conspired to destroy the unexampled peace and prosperity

10. I have dropped a rather poor poem about a mad Satan.

of the United States, and to overthrow the wisest and best Government which the annals of history have ever presented to the admiration of mankind?—a Government of which one of the principal conspirators, now vice president of the organized rebellion, said a little more than a year ago—

> "That this Government of our fathers, with all its defects, comes nearer to the objects of all good governments than any other on the face of the earth, is my settled conviction."[11]

I come now to the inquiry, what has produced this rebellion? What is the design of the leaders of the rebellion in attempting to destroy the Government? We have seen that there has been no just cause of dissatisfaction with the Government. It has most successfully accomplished the end of its institution in securing "life, liberty, and the pursuit of happiness" for the citizen, and in "promoting the general welfare." We have seen that the policy of the Government has always been controlled by the South, and that at the time of the outbreak of the insurrection the administration of the Government was completely within the power of the South and its friends. We have seen that slavery and the rights of slaveholders were secure from any successful aggression by the Republican party or by the General Government. It was no dread of the abolitionists which precipitated the rebellion. Ex-Governor Adams was not singular in the sentiment to which he gave utterance at Columbia, when he declared:

> "The abolitionists were our best friends. Thank God for what they have already done." "If to-morrow morning they repealed every anti-slavery law, and said they would never whisper the word 'negro' again, he would still loose his connection with them."

We must, therefore, seek for the impelling causes in other considerations. Perhaps they were multifarious and somewhat complex. Perhaps disappointed political aspirations had something to do with the matter. Envy and chagrin at the prosperity of the other sections, the sole and legitimate result of industry, enterprise, and skill, and not the fruits of partial legislative policy, may have exerted their baleful influences; for the tenor of alleged grievances oft-times bore striking resemblance to the complaints which Catiline poured in the ears of his co-conspirators. . . . [12]

11. This is a quote from Alexander H. Stephen's unionist speech before the Georgia legislature in November 1860.
12. The Roman jurist Catiline here is quoted on why his government should be overthrown.

An ungenerous envy of northern thrift may have, in some instances, been productive of prejudice in the southern mind. But why should the South envy the prosperity of the North? Let us rather turn with joy and gratitude to the natural resources of the South, inviting development—a climate unrivaled; a soil as fat as the Delta of the Nile; mines of inexhaustible magnitude and incalculable value; rivers in which navies may ride secure; sea-ports where the commerce of the world may find harbor—all the elements of individual and national prosperity and happiness worthy of the Almighty hand that poured them in such infinite exuberance around us. Fostered and protected by the best Government man ever enjoyed, and proud of our name and position as American citizens, let us rather be stimulated by the prosperity and success of our neighbors to energy and industry, and show ourselves worthy of the rich gifts which God and nature have so munificently bestowed upon us.

But what was the primary inciting cause of this rebellion? I answer—dissatisfaction with the principles and operation of democratic government. It was hostility to the simplicity and equality of republican institutions. We may not find any direct and unequivocal avowal of this fact on the part of the conspirators. It would be strange if we should. Satan ever approaches his victims as an angel of light. Liberty has always been destroyed in the name of liberty. Despotism is strategic. It fights with masked batteries. All history will attest that encroachments on human rights have generally been made in the guise of freedom and friendship.

I am not before you either as the defender or the denouncer of slavery. Its friends, however, claim that it is necessary to the perfection of any high degree of civilization; that by exempting those who possess slaves from those menial and servile offices inseparably incident to the economy of any condition of society, it affords leisure and means for superior mental and social improvement, and imparts a dignity of character and polish of manners unattainable where slavery does not exist. If this assumption be confined in its application to the slaveholder, it may, to some extent, be true; but how small a proportion of the people of the South own slaves!

I dare not say, with George Mason of Virginia, that "every master of a slave is born a petty tyrant," for I am a slaveholder. I despise the vituperation so indiscriminately heaped upon slaveholders by the madness of fanatic abolitionists. They are the worst enemies of the slave in the world. They have already injured him much; and if their policy were carried out it would degrade the slave still below his present position, and entail miseries upon him exceeding the horrors of the slave-ship. It would beggar both master and slave, and demoralize the whole country. Let us leave slavery where the

Constitution and laws have placed it, and await the progressive influences of that blessed Christianity, which, in God's own time, shall redeem and regenerate the human race.

But, it may nevertheless be so that slavery does tend to foster in the feelings and mind of the slaveholder sentiments averse to the perfect level of natural and political equality upon which the system of American republican institutions is based. Labor is not so reputable in slaveholding as it is in non-slaveholding communities; and although the laws do not create or tolerate any distinctions predicated upon this fact, we find them existing with a power and influence as inexorable as if they were a part of the Constitution. I remember the startling effect of a passage in the speech which the eloquent Preston, sent as a commissioner from South Carolina to the later Virginia convention at Richmond, made before that body. Said he:

> "Southern civilization cannot exist without slavery. None but an equal race can labor at the South. Destroy involuntary labor, and the Anglo-Saxon civilization must be remitted to the latitudes from which it sprung."[13]

How I did wish that these remarkable sentences could have reached the ears of the five million laboring inhabitants in the South who own no slaves! Whatever may be the cause of this aristocratic sentiment in the South, and especially in the Gulf States, I shall leave the further discussion of it to philosophers and statesmen. It is the fact that I am at present considering; and that the fact exists is, I think, indisputable. It will not be denied that Judge Pratt, of South Carolina, is an eminently able man, and may justly claim to be considered an authoritative exponent of the views of a large portion of the people of his section. . . . [14]

Judge Pratt is by no means singular in his repudiation of the cardinal principle of democratic institutions—the right of the majority to govern. The constitution of his State confines the political power, in fact, to a comparatively small number; and the fundamental laws of several of the other southern States, including my own, have denied that population or suffrage is the true basis of political power, but secure to property a representation in the Legislature.

13. Reference here is to John C. Preston of South Carolina and his speech before the Virginia Convention in February 1861.

14. Thomas G. Pratt is quoted at length on slavery in the South as the major social distinction between the sections. Pratt also rejects democracy as being disorderly and prefers a hierarchical political system.

Mr. Jefferson enunciated the axiom that "absolute acquiescence in the decisions of the majority was the vital principle of republics." Thus he summed up the argument in favor of adhering to the General Government and preserving it:

> "The preservation of the General Government in its whole constitutional vigor as the sheet-anchor of our peace at home and safety abroad; a jealous care of the right or election by the people—a mild and safe corrective of abuses which are lopped by the sword of revolution where peaceable remedies are unprovided; and absolute acquiescence in the decisions of the majority—the vital principle of republics, from which there is no appeal but to force, the vital principle and immediate parent of despotism."

But Mr. Preston, the South Carolina commissioner, to whom I have already referred, delivered a very different message to us last spring, in the Virginia convention. He declared to us:

> "In the free States, the simple, isolated, exclusive, sole political principle is a pure democracy of mere numbers, save a scarcely discernible modification, by a vague and undefined form of representation. In these States there can be no departure from this principle in its extremest intensity. The admission of the slightest adverse element is forbidden by the whole genius of the people and their institutions. It is as delicate in its sensitiveness as personal right in England, or slavery in Carolina; it is the vitalizing principle, the breath of the life of northern socialism. The almighty power of numbers is the basis of all social agreement in the northern States. A fearful illustration of this is at this moment exhibiting its results in the Government under which you are consenting to live. That Government was 'instituted and appointed' to protect and secure equally the interest of the parts. By the agency of mere numbers, one section has been restricted and another expanded in territory; one section has been unduly and oppressively taxed, and one section has been brought to imminent peril; and in this hour the people of the North are consulting whether they can subjugate the people of the South by the right of number.
>
> "The 'government by the people' is equally the rule of the South, but the modification of the 'rule of numbers' is so essential in the slave States, that it cannot coexist with the same principle in its unrestricted form. In the South it is controlled, perhaps made absolutely subject, by the fact that the recognition of a specific property is essential to the vitalization of the social and political organisms. If, then, you attempt to institute the rule of either form into the organism of the other, you instantly destroy the section you invade. To proclaim to the North that numbers shall not be absolute, would be as offensive as to proclaim the extinction of slavery in

the South. The element of property would neutralize the entire political system at the North; its exclusion would subvert the whole organism of the South."

This is not the opinion of isolated individuals. It is wide spread in the South. It is already incorporated, in some form or other, in the organic laws of several of the States; and other States are seeking to give it constitutional authority. Thus, in the constitutional convention of Virginia, recently in session, Mr. Stuart, formerly Secretary of the Interior, as chairman of the committee having the subject in charge, made a report, from which I read the following extracts: . . . [15]

Great astonishment has been expressed at the hostility of southern statesmen to popular education. But we ought not to be surprised at all. Knowledge is power; and to keep the masses in ignorance is a necessary precaution to keep them in subjection. To maintain the oligarchy of the few owning the capital, it is necessary to bind down with the slavish chains of ignorance the many who perform the labor. Hence, Mr. Stuart connects with the recommendations which I have just read, the following:

> "This tendency to a conflict between labor and capital has already manifested itself in many forms, comparatively harmless, it is true, but nevertheless clearly indicative of a spirit of licentiousness which must, in the end, ripen into agrarianism. It may be seen in the system of free schools, by which the children of the poor are educated at the expense of the rich."

The true reason of this hostility to popular education is hostility to democratic institutions.

I need not remind many of the members of this body with what pertinacity Mr. Calhoun resisted the application of the majority principle to our system of national government, as subversive of the rights of the States. He warred upon this great principle from the time of his Fort Hill address, and before that time, down to the day of his death, in the Senate, in popular addresses, and in labored volumes of essays. Nor need I advert to the mighty influence which this great man exerted on southern opinion. There is a wide-spread hostility all through the Gulf States, more especially, to the great fundamental political right of the majority to rule.

It will be remembered, moreover, that the headspring of this rebellion was in the very State where, in the war of the Revolution, the attachment

---

15. Alexander H. H. Stuart here fulminates against the "despotism of king numbers."

of the people to the aristocratic institutions of the mother country was the hardest to subdue. This attachment was never wholly extinguished. Flashes of the old aristocratic flame have often gleamed out from the revolutionary ashes, as they did recently, when Mr. Russell was assured by many there that they longed to renew their allegiance to some descendant of the royal family of England. There is a wonderful "hankering" in South Carolina after the "flesh-pots of Egypt." By referring to the January (1850) number of the Democratic Review, I find an elaborately-written article, from which I have taken the following extract:

> "The formation of the cotton States, with Cuba, into a great cotton, tobacco, sugar and coffee-producing Union, calling forth the boundless fertility of Cuba, and renovating the West India Islands with the labor of the blacks of the southern States, in those hands in which their labor and numbers have thriven so well, and THIS EMPIRE ANNEXED TO BRITAIN, by treaties of perfect reciprocity, giving the latter the command of the eastern commerce by way of Nicaragua, and all the benefits of possession, without the responsibility of slave ownership, would be a magnificent exchange for the useless province of Canada. . . ."[16]

In an address which this gentleman made before the Virginia Legislature a year or two ago, he uttered sentiments as little in accord with the spirit and genius of our American democracy.

I recently cut from the National Intelligencer—a paper which, by its wise, conservative, and patriotic course through a long series of years, has placed the friends of constitutional liberty under the most lasting obligations—the following short article:

> "A Nascent Nobility.—In the number of DeBow's Review for July, 1860, is an elaborate article from the pen of George Fitzhugh, Esq., author of 'Sociology for the South,' and long a prominent advocate of disunion. In the article designated he gives expression to the following aspiration:
> "'England has once tried to dispense with nobility, and France twice, but each experiment was a failure. In America we have the aristocracy of wealth and talents, and that aristocracy is somewhat hereditary. The landed aristocracy of the South, who own slaves, approach somewhat to the English nobility. Time must determine whether the *quasi* aristocracy of the South has sufficient power, permanence, and privilege to give

16. Willey quotes more of the same from Christopher G. Memminger of South Carolina, the Confederate secretary of the treasury.

stability, durability, and good order to society. It is sufficiently patriotic and conservative in its feelings, but, we fear, wants the powers, privileges, and prerogatives that the experience of all other countries has shown to be necessary.'

"If such was Mr. Fitzhugh's fear while the South remained in the Union and under the Constitution, we presume his hopes have considerably risen since the outbreak of the present war, for in the same article he avows a preference for a military government, as being the 'most perfect' known to man, and imputes it as a fault to the Republican party that the more advanced of its number were averse to wars. Mr. Fitzhugh's language under this head is as follows: (It will be seen that he finds the perfection of military government in the fact that it allows 'the least liberty' to its subjects.)

" 'The most perfect system of government is to be found in armies, because in them there is least of liberty, and most of order, subordination, and obedience.' "[17]

It is but a short time since Governor Brown, of Georgia, charged upon the leaders of the secession movement in that State a design to establish

"A strong central government, probably preferring, if they did not fear to risk an avowal of their sentiments, a limited monarchy, similar to that of Great Britain, or other form of government, that will accomplish the same thing under a different name."

Only two or three days before the victory of our fleet at Port Royal, Governor Pickens, of South Carolina, closed his message to the Legislature of that State with the following significant intimations:

"As far as the northern States are concerned, their Government is hopelessly gone; and if we fail, with all our conservative elements to save us, then, indeed, there will be no hope for an independent and free Republic on this continent, and the public mind will despondingly turn to the stronger and more fixed forms of the Old World.

"In this point of view I most respectfully urge that you increase the power and dignity of the State, through all her administrative offices, and adhere firmly to all the conservative principles of our constitution."[18]

It were easy to multiply the evidence of hostility among the instigators of secession to what Judge Pratt calls the "horizontal plane of pure democracy."

17. For an analysis of George Fitzhugh's thoughts on the subject see Eugene D. Genovese, *The World the Slaveholders Made* (New York: Pantheon Books, 1969), chap. 3.
18. Gov. Francis W. Pickens.

The columns of most of the leading journals in the interest of the rebellion teem with assaults, direct or indirect, upon the great principles of political equality on which our republican institutions are based. I shall not weary the Senate by any detailed reference to them. I will give an extract from one as an example of many. I have taken the following extract from the Richmond Whig, of June 14, 1861. Speaking of the southern States:

> "This vast region, inhabited by a people who are bred from childhood to horsemanship and the use of arms, and who know what liberty is, and love and adore it, is portioned out for subjugation by the disgusting Yankee race, who don't know how to load a gun, and look contemptible on horseback. That they may be drilled into respectable military machines by the Virginian, who commands them, is likely enough; but without disjointing the eternal fitness of things and dislocating the order of nature, that they should become capable of empire, is simply absurd. Grant that mere brute force should enable them to overrun the land like a cloud of eastern locusts, their reign would pass with themselves. They possess not one quality that fits them for command. Since their beginning as a nation, and out of all their seething population, they have never yet produced a general or a statesman. That is an effort beyond their ability. But for organizing hotels, working machinery, and other base mechanical contrivances, they are without equals in the world. And the very law of nature which invests them with excellence in those inferior departments of humanity, condemns them to inferiority in those of a nobler and more exalted strain."

Senator Hammond is by no means alone in his conception of the dignity of labor. There are hundreds of thousands who concur in his estimate of laboring men as the mere "mudsills" of society, on which there should be erected an aristocracy, controlling the political power of the State.[19]

Do you ask me, do the masses of the people of the South understand the purpose of the advocates of this subversion of democratic government? I admit the proportion of the southern people holding these views was, and perhaps still is, greatly in the minority. They consist mostly of slaveholders and their immediate dependents. The number of actual slave-owners in the southern States does not, perhaps, exceed four hundred thousand, and the number of dependents and expectants in interest will not amount to above one million five hundred thousand more. But then it must be considered that these slaveholders are the principal men of wealth,

19. Reference here is to Sen. James H. Hammond of South Carolina and his "mudsill" speech that so outraged antislavery forces.

education, intelligence, and social influence. Besides, as I have already said, the aggressions of the few upon the rights of the many are always accomplished under false pretenses. The cry of "southern rights," "southern rights," "southern rights," has been rung in the ears of the people with such ceaseless, vehement importunity, as to create an honest impression on the public mind that grievous and outrageous wrong has been done to southern rights already, and that still further and greater outrages are imminent. Especially has the opinion been propagated that slavery is everywhere to be abolished in defiance of constitutional guarantees, and the rights of the States are to be sacrificed to the caprices of northern fanaticism. Thus has the "southern heart been fired." Still it may be asked, how could such a meager minority precipitate such a rebellion as now exists if the masses were not cooperating? I ask, what had the people to do in seceding the States out of the Union, and in the organization of the provisional confederate government? What had the people in my own once honored State to do in attaching Virginia to the southern confederacy? Nothing. Nothing.

Speech on the Bill to Confiscate
the Property and Free the Slaves of Rebels
(Washington, D.C.: Congressional Globe Office, 1862)

John Snyder Carlile (1817–1878) came from a Winchester, Virginia, family of modest circumstances and became a store clerk in Beverly. He read law at night and soon moved to Clarksburg, where he developed a Kanawha Valley law practice. Carlile ran as a Whig for the state senate in 1847, served in the Virginia constitutional convention of 1850, became a U.S. congressman from 1855 to 1857, and supported the nativist party. A member of the Virginia secession convention of 1861, he opposed secession and spoke out against the violent treatment of Virginia's unionists. Carlile led the Wheeling Convention of May 1861, where he called forcefully for a new state of West Virginia. Later he would for a time turn against the statehood movement. He served in the U.S. House in 1861 as a representative from Virginia, entered the U.S. Senate in late 1861 to replace Robert M. T. Hunter, and held office until 1865. He voted often with the border state contingent and published a number of important pamphlets that circulated in West Virginia and among Virginia's unionists. After the war he practiced law in West Virginia.

In this pamphlet of March 11, 1862, Carlile stood steadfast for the Union, attacked radical secession, and wrote stirringly of the Confederate wrongs to Virginia's unionists. He called for Federal troops to put down violent guerrilla war in his part of the state. Carlile also castigated the Lincoln administration for moving to abolish slavery. Specifically, he was referring to a bill Charles Sumner had introduced into the Senate to confiscate the property and free the slaves of the Confederates. He worried that loyal western Virginians who supported slavery would break with the Union. That that did not happen is in no way due to Carlile's effort, as his words reveal just how strongly some southern unionists defended the cause of slavery. But Carlile also insisted that the war was an insurrection and not a civil war and that the slave states had never left the Union. (This distinction would come back to haunt those southern unionists who lived in states that had to ask to return to the Union after the Civil War.)

Carlile unfortunately has no biographer. For information on his life see William P. Willey, *Inside View of the Formation of West Virginia* (Wheeling, W.Va.: News Publishing Co., 1901), and Richard O. Curry, *A House Divided: A Study of Statehood Politics and the Copperhead Movement in West Virginia* (Pittsburgh: University of Pittsburgh Press, 1964).

* * *

I do not propose to follow the example set us by my friend, the honorable Senator from Illinois,[1] who addressed the Senate yesterday, by saying what I may do in the future upon the happening of a contingency which, in my judgment, never can arise. I am content to deal with the present. If I can meet wisely the questions of the hour, I shall be satisfied; and in my opinion it would be well if we would, in this the day of our trial, act upon the maxim, "Sufficient unto the day is the evil thereof." The bill under consideration is entitled "A bill to confiscate the property and free the slaves of rebels." The objects of the bill, as stated in the title, are, in my opinion, beyond the power of accomplishment, if we regard our constitutional obligations. The Supreme Court would have to pronounce such a law unconstitutional in any case arising under it, if it could be brought before that tribunal for its decision. The founders of the Government intended to secure to every citizen, and to have so provided in the Constitution, the right to test the constitutionality of any congressional enactment before the Supreme Court; but here is a bill taking from more than one fourth of the entire population of this whole country all their property of every kind and description, reducing them to beggary and want, without judicial trial or legal investigation. The bill denies to the citizen the constitutional right of testing the constitutionality of the act before the tribunal created by the Constitution. It would seem as if the authors of the bill, conscious of the unconstitutionality of the proposed measure, purposely framed it so that its constitutionality could not be pronounced upon by the Supreme Court.

1. Orville Hickman Browning, an ally of President Lincoln.

The bill proposes to confiscate to the use of the Government all the property, real and personal, belonging to the citizens of the seceded States who are or may be in the service of the so-called confederate States, or who in any way give aid and comfort to the rebellion. When it is remembered that the authors of the rebellion were in possession of the various State governments, and used the power and machinery of their respective State governments to compel the people to acquiesce in their unconstitutional acts, and to recognize their usurped authority, it will be seen that all the property of each and every citizen in the seceded States would be forfeited under this bill. Such a sweeping proposition, so unjust and cruel a measure, one better calculated to continue the war forever and exhaust the whole country, never has been in the history of the world, and I predict never will be again, proposed to any legislative assembly representing a civilized community.

By the bill all the property, except slaves, is to be sold, and the proceeds put into the public Treasury. The slaves are to be emancipated in violation of the Constitution and in disregard of the acknowledged constitutional rights of the owners and of the States wherein they reside. The want of power in Congress to interfere with slavery in the States where it exists has always heretofore been admitted; the most ultra abolitionists admit that Congress cannot interfere with slavery in the States, and because this is so they denounce the Constitution as a covenant with death and a league with hell. The ablest speech made this session in Congress in favor of converting the struggle in which we are engaged into an anti-slavery war, was made by the Representative in the House from Kansas.[2] It is a speech that must challenge the admiration of those who differ with its author, for its boldness, frankness, and candor. The member from Kansas with directness meets the questions he discusses; there is no mistaking his position. Not a dollar or a man will he vote for the restoration of the Union. Millions for an anti-slavery war, not one cent to suppress insurrection and to restore the supremacy of the Constitution and the laws. Do I misrepresent him? Let him speak for himself:

> "For one, I shall not vote another dollar or man for the war until it assumes a different standing, and tends directly to an anti-slavery result. Millions for freedom, but not one cent for slavery!" . . . [3]

2. Martin Franklin Conway, Kansas member of the U.S. House, a leading western abolitionist.
3. Carlile quotes Conway further, this time on how the objects of the war have changed and how he would end slavery.

I have read from the speech of the member from Kansas, because, in my opinion, it is a representative speech, and because he has had the boldness to avow what I believe are the real views of his party, but what his party associates, less bold than himself, for prudential reasons do not avow. If a member from a slave State had uttered such sentiments as those I have read from the speech of the member from Kansas, the whole air would have been filled with the cry of disloyalty and his expulsion demanded. The press that clamored so loudly for the expulsion of the late Senator from Indiana and the rejection of the Senator from Oregon, is engaged in applauding the sentiments of the member from Kansas.[4] Those sentiments are, as I have shown you, that unless the confederate States are recognized as an independent Power and war is waged upon them for the abolition of slavery, not another man or dollar of money will the member from Kansas vote. Let a member from a slave State of either House declare that he would— unless the so-called confederate States are recognized and war allowed, not to conquer the northern States and hold them as subject provinces, but only to secure constitutional guarantees for slavery in the Union—not vote another man or another dollar; how long, think you, would he or ought he to retain his seat in Congress? And yet what would be the difference? Whose utterances would be most disloyal, or, if you please, most treasonable?

For more than twenty-five years, the representatives of the abolitionists and of the secessionists have pulled the same string at different ends, heretofore sitting together in the same Congress and acknowledging the same country. They are still pulling the same string at different ends of the string and each in his own end of the country. Both want the so-called confederate government recognized; both want the rebellion dignified by the name of war; both want their rights. The one wants you to acknowledge his right to take his slave into the Territories, not that he will ever take him there; the other wants you to acknowledge his right to liberate the slave in the slave States, not that he would do it, for he will not let the free negroes live in his State, and he knows that they will not be permitted to live in the slave States. The secessionist is fighting for his rights; the abolitionist would have you fight for his. Both contend that the Union is dissolved. *Par nobile fratum.* People of America look at them! Behold a pair of noble brothers—abolition and secession; twins they are; spawned at the same time in the same muddy stream.

4. Here he is referring to Sen. Jesse Bright of Indiana. (See my comments on Andrew Johnson's speech on Bright in "Comments on Southern Unionist Pamphlets Not Selected for Inclusion.")

The third section of this bill makes it the duty of the President to colonize the negroes at the cost of the Government, of course the Government to get the money by taxing the people. It is not enough to tax them for war purposes, but they must be taxed to pay overseers on Georgia and South Carolina plantations; taxed to the tune of ten dollars an acre, to buy implements of husbandry for all the land tilled by these overseers in Georgia and South Carolina; taxed to buy land in tropical climates; taxed to send negroes to tropical climates; in short, the people are to be taxed upon lying down and getting up, standing or walking, asleep or awake, all for the glorious privilege of evincing to the world that enlarged philanthropy that can view with complacency the sufferings and the groans of the white race, but is horrified at the sight of four millions of negroes comfortable, contented, and happy, unconscious of suffering until informed by some philanthropic Greeley; who was willing to permit their masters to withdraw them and the States in which they reside from the Government to which the labor of the one and the productions of the other has contributed more than any other portion of our country to make it what it was a little more than one year ago—the proudest, richest, and most prosperous on the globe.

I was about to call the attention of the Senate to the third section of the bill. This section makes it the duty of the President to provide for the transportation, colonization, and settlement of such emancipated negroes as may be willing to emigrate to some tropical climate, to be selected for them by the Executive. The bill fails to make provision for the negroes who shall be unwilling to leave the land of their birth and the home of their nativity. That this latter class will comprise at least ninety-nine hundredths of the slaves, is a fact known to all acquainted with the race, and I presume is known to the advocates of this measure in the Senate. I see from a speech reported in the Globe, made by a member of the House, concurring in opinion with the advocates of this measure, that the negro's attachment to his native land is well understood by the member. . . . [5]

Assuming that the attachment of the negro to his "native soil" is as Mr. Davis represents, and that all the free negroes in the non-slaveholding States are, as he intimates, to be colonized for settlement in the now slaveholding States, and that the advocates of this bill so understood their proposed schemes of emancipation, colonization, and settlement, the conclusion that it is their purpose to Africanize American society in the southern States is irresistible. If this be their purpose, I assure

---

5. Carlile quotes the comments of Henry Winter Davis of Maryland that northerners have nothing to fear because freed slaves will not move north.

them they are mistaken. Self-preservation would compel the States within which slavery now exists, if the slaves were emancipated, either to expel them from the State or reënslave them. If expelled, where would they go? The non-slave-holding States, many of them, exclude them by express constitutional provision; others would do so, for we are told by the advocates of emancipation that the negro is not to be permitted, when liberated, to come into their States. What follows? Extermination or reënslavement. Can it be possible that the Christian sentiment of the North, which it is said demands the abolition of slavery, desires the extermination of the negro race? Such, I trust, is not the sentiment of any considerable number of persons anywhere. The result would be that the States would do what they have the acknowledged constitutional right to do, reënslave them. The wellbeing, if not the existence, of the white race would demand their reënslavement, and it would be done. I ask then, what good to either race would be accomplished by the passage of this section of the bill?

The Senator from Illinois, the patron of this bill, as I understood him, admitted the want of power in Congress to forfeit real estate for a longer period that the life of the owner. If I am in error, I desire to be corrected. . . .[6]

I thank the Senator, because I desire to understand his position. I now understand him to say that, while it is not in the power of Congress, aided by the judicial department of the Government, upon trial and conviction for treason, to confiscate the real estate of the traitor beyond his life, Congress can yet of itself, without the intervention of the judicial department of the Government, inflict that punishment, not upon a convicted traitor, but upon one who in the eye of the law is presumed to be innocent until he is proven to be guilty. That is to say, you may without conviction impose a heavier penalty than can be imposed upon guilt being ascertained and judgment being pronounced. It is worse than I supposed. Such a proposition I shall not detain the Senate by discussing.

The Senator referred us, in his argument, to several decisions of the Supreme Court. I have examined those cases. Not one of them bears upon his proposition. In Brown's case the court seem to say that Congress can by legislation provide for the confiscation of enemy property. This is not authority for the confiscation of the private property of our own citizens, although they may be rebels. The Constitution provides against the confiscation or forfeiture of the estate of the latter in as plain language as it forbids the enactment of bills of attainder. That this bill is a bill of

6. Sen. Lyman Trumbull of Illinois offers a correction. He said "it is not a bill against persons who can be reached by judicial process."

attainder, as such bills have been defined by our own judges, is beyond the shadow of a doubt. The Supreme Court has said that "a bill of attainder may effect the life of an individual, or may confiscate his property, or both." Judge Tucker says a bill of pains and penalties is a bill of attainder. The true definition of a bill of attainder, is any bill providing for the infliction of punishment by Congress for political offenses, without the intervention of the judicial department of the Government—without legal trial. Such bills the Constitution prohibits and forbids, and takes care to secure to the citizen a jury trial, and to secure him from being deprived of his property without due process of law. Congress can as well pass a bill making it the duty of the President to order the seizure by such officers, military or civil, as he may designate, of all persons in the seceded States, and direct the officers so seizing them to hang them without the intervention of judge or jury, as they can pass this bill which makes it the duty of the President to order such officers as he may designate, military or civil, to seize the property of the citizens of the seceded States, and confiscate it.

But, say the advocates of confiscation, there ought to be such a power, and therefore we will enact such a law. How different such sentiments from those given us by the Father of his Country. Washington says:

> "If, in the opinion of the people, the distribution or modification of constitutional powers be wrong in any particular, let it be corrected by an amendment in the way which the Constitution designates. *But let there be no change by usurpation;* for though this in one instance may be the instrument of good, it is the customary weapon by which free governments are destroyed. The precedent must always greatly overbalance in permanent evil any partial or transient benefit which the use can at any time yield."

The advocates of this bill would have us believe that although in time of peace the Constitution is the paramount law of the land, in time of war it ceases to be of binding obligation, and therefore feeling the want of constitutional power they seek to show, by citations from Grotius and others, that such a measure is authorized by the law of nations, forgetting that the laws of war fix the rules by which separate and independent nations are to be governed when engaged in war with each other. Senators who contend for the power to enact this bill ignore the great fact which lies at the foundation of all our institutions, that this is a Government of limited powers, clearly defined in a written Constitution forbidding the exercise of any power not authorized by it, and denying to the legislative branch of the Government the authority to enact any law which is not authorized by a grant of power.

It is unnecessary to detain the Senate by a reference to authorities to show that this is a Government of limited powers, such as I have stated it to be. It is an admitted truth that no man, I take it, at this day will dispute. But I deny that the laws of war authorize any such measure as this bill proposes; and I go further, and deny that even if sanctioned by the laws of war Congress could enact any such law, unless the power were given in the Constitution. I deny, as Senators seem to suppose, that in time of rebellion the Constitution is a dead letter. I deny what the rebels assert, and what Senators seem to admit, that the act of rebellion has destroyed constitutional government, and left us at the mercy of the unrestrained will of Congress. Let us see what Vattel says of these confiscation propositions. In speaking of the ancient rules of war, he says: . . . [7]

Justice Story, in treating of the clause in the Constitution giving to Congress power to punish treason, but forbidding the forfeiture of the estate for a longer period than life, says:

> "Two motives probably concurred in introducing it as an express power. One was, not to leave it open to implication whether it was to be exclusively punishable with death, according to the known rule of the common law, and with the barbarous accompaniments pointed out by it, but to confide the punishment to the discretion of Congress. The other was, to impose some limitation upon the nature and extent of the punishment, so that it should not work corruption of blood or forfeiture beyond the life of the offender. . . ."[8]

This bill does not forfeit the private property of alien enemies, inhabitants of the enemy's country, but it proposes to take all the property belonging to our own citizens who have been compelled to submit to a power they could not resist, which claims to be both a *de facto* and a *de jure* government, and which does possess the physical force to compel obedience to it from those within its limits. This Government—the Federal Government—which claims the allegiance of these citizens has been unable to relieve them or to protect them in their assertion of that allegiance. Are not allegiance and protection mutual obligations, and when you fail to afford the one will you punish for the want of the other, when it was not in the power of the citizen to give it, and when, if proclaimed, it would have cost him his life?

7. Emmerich de Vattel is quoted from *Laws of Nations*, book 3, chap. 3, on the treatment by the victor of defeated nations.

8. Joseph Story, *On the Constitution*, book 3. Carlile further quotes Story on problems with bills of attainder.

It should never be forgotten, but always borne in mind, that the struggle in which we are engaged is not on our part, constitutionally speaking, a war. We are not engaged in war. Congress makes war, declares war. Congress has made no such declaration; nor has Congress declared, as in the case of the war with Mexico, that war exists. When we speak of war generally we mean public war. If we do not, we use some expression to define the kind of war of which we speak, as civil war, servile war, and the like. The war spoken of by the writers on the laws of war quoted in this debate is public war, that which takes place between nations or sovereigns, where one nation seeks to enforce its alleged rights against another and separate nation; where, in the language of Scripture, "nation lifts up the sword against nation." The struggle in which we are now engaged is not, strictly speaking, even a civil war; but is, on our part, an effort to suppress insurrection, as an extract from Vattel will show. The war of the Revolution was a civil war. Why? Because there was justice on the side of those who were in rebellion. They had right on their side; and whenever you speak of a civil war to a man who understands its definition, you admit that there is some justice for that war. I deny that there is any justice for this rebellion. It is an unholy and wicked effort on the part of ambitious men to enslave the people and make them subservient to their own wicked purposes. Senators will mark the distinction which Vattel makes, because I shall call their attention to the definition of insurrection presently:

> "The name of *rebels* is given to all subjects who unjustly take up arms against the ruler of the society, whether their view be to deprive him of the supreme authority, or to resist his commands in some particular instance, and to impose conditions on him."

Are not these people rebels?

> "A popular commotion in a concourse of people who assemble in a tumultuous manner, and refuse to listen to the voice of their superiors, whether the design of the assembled multitude be leveled against the superiors themselves, or only against some private individuals. Violent commotions of this kind take place when the people think themselves aggrieved, and there is no order of men who so frequently give rise to them as the tax-gatherers. If the rage of the malcontents be particularly leveled at the magistrates, or others vested with the public authority, and they proceed to a formal disobedience or acts of open violence, this is called a *sedition*. When the evil spreads, when it infects the majority of the inhabitants of a city or province, and gains such strength that even the

sovereign is no longer obeyed, it is usual more particularly to distinguish such a disorder by the name of *insurrection.*"

Now, what is the definition of civil war?

"When a party is formed in a State who no longer obey the sovereign, and are possessed of sufficient strength to oppose him—or when, in a republic, the nation is divided into two opposite factions, and both sides take up arms—this is called a *civil war.* Some writers confine this term to a just insurrection of the subjects against their sovereign, to distinguish that lawful resistance from *rebellion,* which is an open and unjust resistance. But what appellation will they give to a war which arises in a republic torn by two factions, or in a monarchy, between two competitors for the crown? Custom appropriates the term of '*civil war*' to every war between the members of one and the same political society. If it be between part of the citizens on one side, and the sovereign with those who continue in obedience to him on the other, provided the malcontents have any reason"—

mark—

"For taking up arms, nothing further is required to entitle such disturbance to the name of *civil war,* and not that of *rebellion.*"[9]

I deny that this is a civil war. I deny that there was anything to justify the men who inaugurated it. I pronounce it a rebellion, and those who are engaged in it are rebels.

I deny, therefore, that if Congress were not restrained by the Constitution the laws of war would authorize or justify the enactment of such a law as the bill proposes; but whether right or wrong in this proposition, I plant myself upon the Constitution, deny the power, and challenge contradiction. I assert what will not be denied, that, prior to the rebellion, the advocates of this bill themselves admitted the want of power in Congress to interfere with slavery, or to change the *status* of the slave in the slaveholding States. No Senator has shown, or can show, any grant of power in the Constitution to warrant the enactment of such a law, or from which the power to do so is deducible. The want of such a power is conclusive, and should end the discussion.

I will read, however, from the eighty-fourth number of the Federalist, written by Mr. Hamilton, who certainly is believed at this day to have

9. All quotes on rebellion and civil war are from Vattel, *Law of Nations,* book 3, chap. 18.

claimed as large powers as the most latitudinous construction could give to the Constitution. He is endeavoring to show why a bill of rights was not necessary:

> "I go further, and affirm that bills of rights, in the sense and to the extent they are contended for, are not only unnecessary in the proposed constitution, but would even be dangerous. They would contain various exceptions to powers not granted; and on this very account would afford a colorable pretext to claim more than were granted. For why declare that things shall not be done, which there is no power to do? Why, for instance, should it be said that the liberty of the press shall not be restrained, when no power is given by which restrictions may be imposed?"

Again, I call the attention of Senators to the very first section of the first article of the Constitution itself:

> "All legislative powers herein granted shall be vested in a Congress of the United States, which shall consist of a Senate and House of Representatives."

Then it is only the legislative power granted in the instrument that the Senate and House of Representatives can exercise, and none other. I go further, and show that not only is there no such power given in the Constitution, but the exercise of such a power is expressly forbidden; first by the clause declaring that

> "No bill of attainder or *ex post facto* law shall be passed. . . ."[10]

Where but twenty dollars is involved, the right of trial by jury is secured, and admitted to be secured by the Constitution; and yet under this bill all that the citizen may have is swept from him without even the first process known to our courts being served upon him.

It is incumbent upon Senators who, prior to the rebellion, admitted that Congress could not interfere with slavery in the States where it exists, but who are now the advocates of this bill, to show the clause in the Constitution conferring upon Congress the power claimed. Congress has the power to legislate for the suppression of insurrection, but the insurrection must be suppressed and the rebellion put down by constitutional means, and in a constitutional way, otherwise all that would be necessary to overthrow

---

10. Carlile, in support of this argument, cites the treason clause and the Fifth and Seventh Amendments.

the Constitution and destroy the Government under it, would be to incite insurrection. If Congress were not to suppress insurrection by constitutional means and in a constitutional way, there would be nothing for the loyal citizen to fight for. He readily obeys his country's call, and enrolls himself in its military service. Why, and for what? That the Constitution may be overthrown, that his fellow-citizens in the rebellious States may be deprived of their constitutional rights secured to them by the common bond? No, God forbid. He takes up arms for no such purpose; he enlists under the banner of his country to uphold it and all the rights of which it is the emblem. He spills his blood that the constitutional Government under which he has lived may be preserved, and all his constitutional rights maintained. It was for this, and this alone, as I know full well, that the brave Lander sacrificed his life. Patriot soldier he was. Long will his memory live in the hearts of the loyal people of my State.[11] He it was that led our troops to battle and to victory at Philippa and Rich Mountain. It is one of the proudest recollections of my life that I urged upon the President and his Cabinet his nomination as brigadier general. I reflect with satisfaction upon my agency in procuring his nomination. I will not now check the unbidden tear that fills my eyes while I recall before me his manly form and reflect upon his heroic courage. No man ever guarded more carefully the honor of his country, or more scrupulously protected the rights of private property.

Massachusetts's son was made a Virginia brigadier. Your records will show that it was Frederick W. Lander, of Virginia, that the President nominated and the Senate confirmed. Virginia adopted him as her son, and she claims the privilege to mingle her tears with those of his own native State. This is as it should be between States united as are the States of this Union, under one Constitution, having one country and one destiny. Let us remember that to the united efforts, in war and in peace, of Massachusetts and Virginia and their sister States we are indebted for our glorious Constitution. I would acknowledge our indebtedness to Massachusetts for loaning to us, through her Governor, in our darkest hour last spring, two thousand stand of arms. Such recollections are themes upon which I love to dwell. Would to God there had been in the past nothing inconsistent with the kind and friendly service to which I have referred. Let us bury forever all recollection of what has occurred to interrupt the kindly relations between the two old States or between the sections of our common country. Let us again be a united and a happy people, animated by that fraternal feeling so necessary to our peace and prosperity as a nation.

11. Frederick West Lander died of pneumonia on March 2, 1862.

God grant that again we may be bound together by the silken cord of brotherly love, never to be broken; each State vieing with the other in the kindly discharge of every constitutional obligation and all frowning indignantly upon the first dawning of any attempt to alienate the sections or to disturb the harmony of the whole.

The Senator from Maine the other day argued that we were engaged in a war, and contended that Congress had the power to do what he said the law of nations authorized sovereign and independent nations engaged in public war to do. Assuming his positions, he argued to prove what the rebels have been striving to make the world believe, that the so-called confederate States were a nation and an independent Power, entitled to be recognized as a belligerent Power, and therefore, according to his assumption, as we have the right to confiscate the property of a belligerent Power, we have the right to pass this bill and confiscate, not the property of the belligerent, but all the property, lands, and goods of private individuals inhabiting the domain over which the government of this belligerent Power extends. If the Senator be right, we should cease to complain of England for so far recognizing the so-called confederate States as a belligerent as to maintain a neutral position between us.[12]

The Senator from Maine follows the Representative from Kansas, from whose speech I have quoted, and contends that the conduct of the rebels invests this nation with the high prerogatives of war. In other words the unconstitutional acts of rebels confer upon Congress powers not delegated by the Constitution. I humbly submit to the Senator if he has not done what no foreign Government has yet done, and what we would be ready to resent if any foreign Government were to do—recognized by his speech the pretended confederate government. He has gratified the conspirators by dignifying their rebellious acts into acts of war. He would concede to them what they claim, that they are not engaged in rebellion, but in waging war against a foreign Government; for the Senator from Maine has arrived at the conclusion, to use his own language, that we are in a state of involuntary war with a belligerent Power, and therefore, he would confiscate the property, not of the belligerent, for the belligerent has none—the custom-houses, forts, dock-yards, mints, &c., are ours—but he would confiscate the property and free the slaves of private individuals. I confess I do not understand the Senator's logic. We are not at war with a belligerent Power, but with rebellious citizens. The Senator from Maine asks how shall it ever be known when we are in a state of war? I reply, Congress

12. Sen. William Pitt Fessenden of Maine.

will inform him. The Constitution confers upon Congress the power to declare war.

I object to this bill because it violates an express provision of the Constitution in this: the Constitution declares that no person shall be deprived of life, liberty, or property without due process of law, and that private property shall not be taken for public use without just compensation. This bill, without judicial accusation or trial, would sweep from the entire population of the seceded States the property of every person residing therein. It dispenses with the judicial tribunals of the country, condemns without a hearing, and punishes without a trial. In short, it does what the Constitution expressly forbids—executes itself. I inquire, was there ever before such a proposition submitted to any legislative assembly in any civilized country on the face of the earth?

In the same letter, to which I before referred, Mr. Hamilton quotes Justice Blackstone: . . . [13]

The friends of this measure contend that it is necessary to the suppression of the rebellion. How can this be? It can only be enforced where rebellion has never existed, or where it has been suppressed. How can you execute this law in those States and districts where all your laws are successfully resisted? Before you confiscate the property of rebels you must first be able to possess yourselves of it. You can only do this where your armies have preceded you, and where the rebels have been dispersed. This bill can only be enforced in the districts occupied by your Army or by loyal citizens who recognize their obligations to the Constitution and laws, and who will aid you in their enforcement. If the mere passage of an act would put down the rebellion, all you have to do is to pass an act confiscating all the powder in the seceded States, and the rebellion is ended at once. The absurdity of such an effect to be produced by the mere passage of a bill to operate in States where you are unable to enforce any law must be apparent to all. This bill, if it become a law, like all of your laws, will remain upon your statute-book, a dead letter in the seceded States until you shall have crushed out the rebellion and suppressed the insurrection. When that is done, this bill cannot aid in suppressing what is not in existence.

Is it expedient to beggar six millions of your people? Will the avowal of such a purpose have the effect to strengthen the loyal sentiment of the seceded States? Will it confirm and bring to your aid the hesitating and

13. The quote refers to confiscation of land without a trial. Carlile uses this quote to comment that the Constitution would not authorize such an action.

doubtful, or will it not rather, if that be possible, make more desperate those now arrayed against you, increase their power, and bring to them an active strength that has up to this time kept aloof from the struggle? What will be its effect upon the thousands that have been impressed into the rebel army who are now anxiously looking for an opportunity to rush to your standard? There is scarcely a family of any size in all the loyal portion of my State that has not one or more members of it, or some one connected with it in the rebel service, or who have not in some way aided the rebellion. It has divided parents from their children, brother from brother, and separated husband and wife. I will, with the permission of the Senate, read an extract from a letter I received yesterday from a highly respectable lady, a resident of northwestern Virginia, a daughter of a late judge of the United States, and a grand-daughter of a former Governor of the State of Ohio, and a member of the Cabinets of Mr. Madison and Mr. Monroe.

> "I have never had a line from my husband since last August, and am not in communication with him at all. It is only through Mrs. _____, who returned a fortnight ago, that I know his whereabouts. I do not and never have thought secession a practical or desirable move. I have been here with my children making every effort to send or to go to Dixie to induce him to return. You know that I was possessed of sufficient means to at least live comfortably before our marriage, but as it consisted of notes, bonds, and money, it has been almost all reconverted into other property, and can be all taken. I cannot believe it is the intention and desire of the wise and humane rulers of this country to throw upon the world without means of subsistence unoffending women and innocent children."

Is it expedient to deprive decrepid age and helpless infancy of the means of support? If we do this thing, the cry of the widow and the wail of the orphan will go up to heaven, and the God of the widow and the Father of the fatherless will say in the storm-cloud: "Vengeance is mine, and I will repay, saith the Lord."

The incendiary press of this country seize upon the hour that exhibits to the gaze of the world the heart-rending spectacle of the only Government on earth where man enjoys as much liberty as is consistent with his nature, struggling for existence, and would add to our difficulties by reviving sectional feuds by which we have been torn and distracted in order to secure the accomplishment of the wishes of those who have for years denounced the Constitution of Washington and his compatriots as a covenant with death and a league with hell. This, too, at a moment when the efforts of all should be directed to the single object of extinguishing the flames lighted by the fires of rebellion. The temple of liberty is on fire, and instead of an honest effort on the part of all to save the noble structure, the anti-slavery element is engaged in an unholy effort to destroy the southern wing, not seeming to know or care that the destruction of part involves the loss of the whole. The rebels have applied the torch, and the anti-slavery element say, let it go, unless the entire southern portion is shorn of its fair proportions, its dimensions narrowed and contracted, and its occupants made dependent upon our will and subservient to our views. These are they who attribute this wicked rebellion to the existence of slavery, and who, by misrepresentations, would lead the people they ought to honestly instruct to war upon the Constitution. From such teachings we are warned by the Father of his Country in his Farewell Address—

> "One of the expedients of party to acquire influence within particular districts is to misrepresent the opinions and aims of other districts."

These are they who say if there had been no slavery there would have been no rebellion. As well might they attribute the rebellion to the Union, for if there had been no Union there would have been no rebellion against it. Has the country forgotten that thirty years ago a similar attempt at rebellion was initiated, and would have grown to as great proportions, perhaps, as the present, if a Buchanan instead of a Jackson had been the Chief Magistrate? And do we not know that the tariff was then the pretext? Who, at that day, insisted that commerce should be destroyed, or said if there had been no commerce there would have been no attempt at rebellion? No, Mr. Yancey and his associates spoke the truth when they wrote to the British minister "that it was from no fear that the slaves would be liberated that secession took place." The true cause, the real motive, is the same that influences the men who now clamor that this shall be made an anti-slavery war. They would convert the holy struggle in which we are engaged for a restoration of the Union into a wicked crusade against slavery, bringing down upon us the just vengeance of a righteous God and the denunciations of the whole civilized world. So long as our efforts are confined to a vindication of the Constitution and a restoration of the Union, we have the sympathies of the good throughout the earth, and, I sincerely believe, the approval of Heaven; for are we not engaged in a struggle to maintain religious as well as civil liberty? The cause of the rebellion was a determination on the part of its authors to rule or ruin. The opposition to a restoration of the Union is to be attributed to the same cause. The restoration of the Union buries in the same grave abolitionists and secessionists. In life their labors have tended to the same end; it is fitting that they should be consigned to the same grave. May Heaven speed their demise.

It is for us to preserve the best Government on earth, and to keep inviolate our plighted faith. The passage of this bill would be a violation of the nation's faith as pledged through the Executive and Congress, and a fraud upon our people. What was the call of the President to which your citizen soldiers so promptly responded? Was it not to aid him in the enforcement of the laws, protect the nation's property, and to enable him to keep his oath of office, by which he swore to preserve, protect, and defend the Constitution, and to see that the laws were faithfully executed? Did not the President in his inaugural address declare:

> "I have no purpose, directly or indirectly, to interfere with the institution of slavery in the States where it exists. I believe I have no lawful right to do so, and I have no inclination to do so."

And did he not, in his annual message to Congress, in July last, say:

> "Lest there be some uneasiness in the minds of candid men as to what is the course of the Government towards the southern States, after the rebellion shall have been suppressed, the Executive deems it proper to say it will be his purpose then, as ever, to be guided by the Constitution and the laws; and that he will probably have no different understanding of the powers and duties of the Federal Government relating to the rights of the States and the people under the Constitution, than that expressed in the inaugural address."

Did not your present General-in-Chief, in May last, when he entered my State at the head of our brave friends from Ohio and Indiana who responded to the President's call, assure us that he came not to make war upon us or our institutions, but that he came to crush out treason and deliver us from the power of traitors. Hear him:

> "Notwithstanding all that has been said by the traitors to induce you to believe that our advent among you will be signalized by interference with your slaves, understand one thing clearly, not only will we abstain from all such interference, but we will, on the contrary, with an iron hand, crush any attempt at insurrection on their part."[14]

What was the mission of the brave Burnside, and the equally brave Goldsborough, as declared by them to the people of North Carolina? They shall speak for themselves: . . . [15]

14. Refers to George B. McClellan.
15. Carlile quotes Union general Ambrose Burnside and Adm. L. M. Goldsborough as saying they will not invade the rights of the people of eastern North Carolina.

What was the order of the accomplished officer, a gallant soldier, and I may add, enlightened statesman, General Halleck, as his troops were about to advance into Tennessee? . . . [16]

How did Congress speak in February, 1861, upon the motion, I believe, of my friend from Ohio,

> "*Resolved*, That neither the Federal Government nor the people or governments of the non-slaveholding States have a purpose or a constitutional right to legislate upon or interfere with slavery in any of the States of the Union.
>
> "*Resolved*, That those persons in the North who do not subscribe to the foregoing proposition, are too insignificant in numbers and influences to excite the serious attention or alarm of any portion of the people of the Republic, and that the increase of their numbers and influence does not keep pace with the increase of the aggregate population of the Union."[17]

How, again, did Congress speak in July last, in the House of Representatives, upon the motion of the hero, patriot, and sage, the venerable Crittenden:

> "*Resolved by the House of Representatives of the Congress of the United States,* That the present deplorable civil war has been forced upon the country by the disunionists of the southern States, now in arms against the constitutional Government, and in arms around the capital; that in this national emergency, Congress, banishing all feelings of mere passion or resentment, will recollect only its duty to the whole country; that this war is not waged on their part in any spirit of oppression, or for any purpose of conquest or subjugation, or purpose of overthrowing or interfering with the rights or established institutions of those States, but to defend and maintain the *supremacy* of the Constitution, and to preserve the Union with all the dignity, equality, and rights of the several States unimpaired; and that as soon as these objects are accomplished the war ought to cease."[18]

Shall it be said that this resolution was adopted under the fearful excitement growing out of the battle of the day before, at Bull Run? No; never will the nation allow any such intimation to be made against its honor. What said the Senate in July last upon the motion of the distinguished Senator from Tennessee,

---

16. Here Carlile quotes Gen. Henry Halleck's proclamation to the people of Tennessee that his troops have not come to oppress and plunder them.

17. Resolutions of John Sherman of Ohio.

18. Resolution of John J. Crittenden of Kentucky.

"*Resolved,* That the present deplorable civil war has been forced upon the country by the disunionists of the southern States, now in revolt against the constitutional Government and in arms around the capital; that in this national emergency Congress, banishing all feeling of mere passion or resentment, will recollect only its duty to the whole country; that this war is not prosecuted upon our part in any spirit of oppression, nor for any purpose of conquest or subjugation, nor purpose of overthrowing or interfering with the rights or established institutions of those States, but to defend and maintain the supremacy of the Constitution and all laws made in pursuance thereof, and to preserve the Union, with all the dignity, equality, and rights of the several States unimpaired; that as soon as these objects are accomplished the war ought to cease."[19]

Now, I call the attention of the Senate to the vote upon that resolution. Every Senator present and voting, save one, voted for that resolution. It is significant, and the country should know who it was that, on the 25th day of July, refused to vote for that resolution. Breckinridge, now an open traitor at the head of rebel forces, Johnson of Missouri, in the same position, Polk, in the same position, Powell, and Trumbull. I was about to do my friend from Illinois, the chairman of the Judiciary Committee, injustice. I find, what I did not notice before, that his name is recorded with the names of Breckinridge, Johnson of Missouri, Polk, and Powell, against the resolution. He is consistent, I must confess.

What did the distinguished gentleman at the head of the State Department, Mr. Seward, in his letter of instructions, in April last, to Mr. Dayton, our minister to Paris, say: . . . [20]

I respectfully call upon the Senator from Illinois, taking the position that he does, to read at his leisure this last paragraph quoted from our Secretary of State, a statesman who has spent the greater portion of his life in the service of his country.

Think you that these declarations had nothing to do with our successes at Roanoke, Fort Henry, and Fort Donelson? I would not detract in the slightest degree from the honor won by our brave soldiers, but I assert it as my honest belief that we owe much to the Union sentiment that was in the confederate service. If the rebel force had been animated by the spirit that inaugurated this rebellion, it would never have surrendered as it did, and it is the realization of this fact that made Jeff Davis admit in his message

19. Sen. Andrew Johnson.
20. William L. Dayton, U.S. minister to France. Seward said that the condition of slavery would remain the same.

that they had undertaken more than they could achieve. The same fact was pressing upon the rebel officer who wrote to the Richmond Examiner the extract I read:

> "The Roanoke affair is perfectly incomprehensible. The newspapers are filled with extravagant laudations of our valor; the annals of Greece and Rome offer no parallel; whole regiments were defeated by companies, and we yielded only to death. Our men finally surrendered 'with no blood on their bayonets,' and what is the loss? Richmond blues, two killed and five wounded; McCulloch Rangers, one killed and two wounded; the other four companies lost in all two killed and eleven wounded. Comment is needless. The whole army had better surrender at once, for it will eventually come to it."

I think so, too. I concur in opinion with him.

Let us never violate our faith. It has been well remarked by some writer that the chief of all powers is moral power, and I believe we owe more to-day to our moral position which we secured by the declarations I have read than we do to our armies, great as I know our obligations are to them, which obligations I take pleasure in acknowledging. Think you, if General Halleck and Commodore Foote had announced to the people of Tennessee that their purpose was to confiscate their property and turn them houseless and homeless upon the world, and to free their slaves, Nashville and Clarksville would have been ours? Would they not have been reduced to ashes, and would not their people have rushed with eagerness to the field and arrayed themselves under the standard of rebellion? Pass this bill, disregard the tears of widowhood and the cry of orphans, visit upon the children to the third and fourth generation the sins of the father, impoverish the wife and pauperize the child, as this bill proposes to do, and the mother, instead of taking upon her knee her lisping babe to instill into his infant mind sentiments of love for his country and gratitude for its beneficence, will cause her child to kneel by her side and swear undying hate and eternal hostility to the Government that took from her the means of support, and turned mother and child beggars upon the world. Pass this bill, and interminable, never-ending war will be the result.[21]

This bill proposes to do what the President forbid General Frémont from doing, and what, in the opinion of the President, would have thrown Kentucky against us, and alarmed the Union men of the South. So impressed was the President of the danger to the cause of the country

---

21. Carlile quotes a poem on the cruelty of war.

by the announcement of such a policy by a subordinate military officer, that he addressed to him the following letter:

> Washington, D. C., *September 2, 1861,*
>
> My Dear Sir: Two points in your proclamation of August 30 give me some anxiety.
>
> First: Should you shoot a man, according to the proclamation, the confederates would very certainly shoot our best men in their hands, in retaliation; and so, man for man, indefinitely. It is, therefore, my order that you allow no man to be shot, under the proclamation, without first having my approbation or consent.
>
> Second: I think there is great danger that the closing paragraph, in relation to the confiscation of property, and liberating slaves of traitorous owners, will alarm our southern Union friends, and turn them against us—perhaps ruin our rather fair prospect for Kentucky. Allow me, therefore, to ask that you will, as of your own motion, modify that paragraph so as to conform to the *first* and *fourth* sections of the act of Congress, entitled, 'An act to confiscate property used for insurrectionary purposes,' approved August 6, 1861, and a copy of which act I herewith send you. This letter is written in a spirit of caution, not of censure. I send it by a special messenger, in order that it may certainly and speedily reach you.
>
> Yours very truly,   A. Lincoln
>
> To Major General Frémont.

The path of duty is clear. Let us march steadily on observing the line of policy laid down by ourselves. Let us not violate our own solemn declarations by which we are bound not only to our own people but to the whole world. The declarations of our Chief Magistrate and our own solemn resolves have gone to the world, and have been read and approved of in Europe as well as upon this continent. We have a law for the punishment of treason; enforce it; try, convict, and hang by the neck the traitor leaders, the authors of this wicked conspiracy to destroy our Government. Grant to the rank and file who have been seduced and unwillingly and unwittingly forced into the rebellion a pardon for past offenses. Leave it to the loyal Legislatures of the States, which will have to bring back into the Union their respective States, to exclude from office all whose lives are spared, who willingly participated in this rebellion. In this way you will punish the guilty and protect the innocent. So impressed was I with the importance of a declaration of policy such as I have briefly alluded to that, after the capture of Fort Donelson, I called upon two gentlemen who I had reason to believe enjoyed the confidence of the President, and asked them to urge upon him the propriety of issuing a proclamation announcing such a policy as I have indicated. I believed that the hour of victory was the hour of magnanimity, and I now believe if this had been done, we should have had peace in less than ninety days. I may be mistaken, but I am glad to find that in this opinion I am not alone. Hon. James Guthrie, in a speech the other day, expressed similar views. I will read an extract or two from his address:

"This day"—

That was the 22nd of February, the anniversary of Washington's birthday . . . [22]

I invite the attention of Senators while I read an extract from the farewell address of General Jackson. I read it without comment. Senators will see the lesson which it teaches:

"The Constitution cannot be maintained nor the Union preserved in opposition to public feeling, by the mere exertion of the coercive powers confided to the Government. The foundations must be laid in the affections of the people; in the security it gives to life, liberty, character, and property in every sector of the country, and in the fraternal attachment that the citizens of the several States bear to each of the members of one political family, contributing to the welfare of each other."

The Senate will pardon me for a moment while I allude to myself. I am not in the habit of speaking of myself. I do not think it in good taste, and look upon it as a custom more honored in the breach than the observance; but there are occasions when it becomes necessary to do so. Intimations questioning my loyalty have been made by those who would impress upon the country that to be loyal it is necessary to be an abolitionist. The senate will, therefore, pardon me for saying that I have periled all, life itself, in defense of the Constitution and Union of my country. I have been engaged in this fight actively since December, 1859. I saw the storm coming, and sought to prepare the people of my own mountain home for it, so that when it did come we would be able to resist it. I stood in the capitol of my own State fighting the battles of the Constitution and the Union amid the jeers and taunts, hisses and threats of the mob. From the 7th day of March to the 18th day of April, in the city of Richmond, the assassins sought my life. On

22. Guthrie, a loyal Democrat from Kentucky, President Franklin Pierce's secretary of the treasury, and wartime unionist president of the Louisville and Nashville Railroad, spoke in favor of amnesty for all southerners.

Saturday the 13th day of April last, a crowd of not less than one hundred men, devils I will call them, came to my lodgings about midnight with drum and fife and rope to hang me. My colleague in the House witnessed the scene. For weeks after my return to my own home in my own town my life was threatened. When I would leave to go to a neighboring county to address the people, my friends would follow to guard me on the road without informing me of it. I led the movement, and drew the resolution adopted by the people of my own county of Harrison, to whom belongs the honor of inaugurating the movement which resulted in organizing and making effective the Union sentiment of northwestern Virginia. I stand here to-day in the nation's Capitol, as I stood in the capitol of my State, to defend from assault the Constitution and Union of my country, come from what quarter it may. In their defense I am prepared to sacrifice all—life itself. I stand upon the platform of the President as announced by himself in his inaugural, reiterated in his message to Congress in July last, and again in his message to Congress at the commencement of this session. I stand upon the solemn declarations of the last Congress and of this. I maintain, as the Union was formed so it should continue and endure forever an everlasting monument of the wisdom and patriotism of its founders.

Let us, in the language of a distinguished statesman and former Senator upon this floor, "cling to the Constitution as the mariner clings to the last plank when night and the tempest close around him."

Speech against the Great Rebellion

(Washington D.C.: Scammell and Bros, 1862)

William Gannaway Brownlow (1805–1877), born in Wythe County, Virginia, early moved with his parents to the Knoxville, Tennessee, region, where he was orphaned. He learned the trade of a carpenter, but the restless and ambitious youth soon pursued the life of a traveling Methodist minister. He gained fame as an outspoken opponent of slavery and an internal-improvement Whig in a heavily Democratic district. He became well known as the editor of a Knoxville Whig newspaper, supported Lincoln for president in 1860, and soon had to flee east Tennessee for his life after his paper was suppressed in October 1861. After arresting and imprisoning him, the Confederate authorities eventually set Brownlow free inside the union lines of Kentucky in March 1862. Although his story was not exactly one of escape, in his speeches, pamphlets, and autobiographical writings the minister often invoked the harrowing experience of a unionist fugitive. In aid of the border Union effort, Brownlow spoke often to urge northern support for the war. His famous *Sketches of the Life, Progress, and Decline of Secession* (Philadelphia, 1862) became a best-seller in the North, and he secreted copies of it to unionists throughout the middle South. A beadle-press biography of his life, *Parson Brownlow and the Unionists of East Tennessee* (1862), recounted the horrors perpetrated on southern unionists and also became a best-seller in the North, selling more than one hundred thousand copies. The impassioned unionist editor returned to east Tennessee with the Union army of occupation in the autumn of 1863 and reopened his newspaper and called for a return of Tennessee to the Union. He was elected governor in 1865 and entered the U.S. Senate in 1869.

Brownlow's pamphlet selected for this volume captures his pugnacious qualities and his real anger over the treatment of east Tennessee unionists. In May 1862, the parson regarded the Confederacy as an evil empire, soon to fail, and he kept up that drumbeat throughout the war. His pamphlet also is a fine example of how southern unionist writers identified their own plight with that of the persecuted people back home.

The best study of his life remains that of E. Merton Coulter, *William G. Brownlow: Fighting Parson of the Southern Highlands* (Chapel Hill: University of North Carolina Press, 1937). Coulter's life is critical, and there is need for a more objective appraisal of this extraordinary man's career. See William G. Brownlow, *Two Speeches on the State of the Country* (Cincinnati: Press of E. Morgan and Co., 1862), for Brownlow's view of his own life. See also Stephen V. Ash, *Secessionists and Other Scoundrels: Selections from Parson Brownlow's Book* (Baton Rouge: Louisiana State University Press, 1999).

* * *

I take occasion, in advance of anything and all I may say, to apprize you of what you will all have discovered before I take my seat—that is to say, in my public addresses, no matter what my theme may be, I do not present it to an audience with an eloquence that charms, or with that beauty of diction which captivates, fascinates and charms. This, I may be allowed to say, I most sincerely regret, because there is no power on earth—there is no power so great and of such influence upon the human mind as the power and influence of oratory, finished and high wrought. Caesar controlled men by exciting their fears; Cicero by captivating their affections. The one perished with its author; the other has continued throughout all time, and, with public speakers, will continue to the end of time. But there is one thing I am confident of this evening, and that is, I address an appreciative audience, an assemblage who have congregated on this occasion to hear some facts in reference to the great rebellion South—the gigantic conspiracy of the nineteenth century; and I shall therefore look more to what I shall say than to the manner of saying it—more, if you please, to the subject matter of what I shall say than to any studied effort at display or beauty and force of language. I will be allowed by you an additional remark or two personal in their nature to myself. For the last thirty-five years of my somewhat eventful life, I have been accustomed to speak in public upon all the subjects afloat in the land, for I have never been neutral on any subject that ever came up in that time. Independent in all things, and under all circumstances, I have never been entirely neutral, but have always taken a hand in what was afloat. About three years ago my voice entirely failed from a stubborn attack of bronchitis, and for two years of that time I was unable to speak above a whisper. During that period I performed a pilgrimage to New York and had an operation performed upon my throat, and was otherwise treated by an eminent physician of this city, who greatly benefited me, and who, when I parted with him, enjoined it upon me to go home and occasionally exercise my speaking machinery, and if I could do no better, to retire to the grove or village of the town where I live, and to make short speeches, to declaim upon stumps or logs, as the case might be. Instead of doing so, however, in the town in which I live I frequently addressed a temperance organization in favor of total abstinence; and you all know that is a good cause. At other times, as a regular ordained licensed Methodist preacher, I tried to tell short sermons to the audience. That is a good cause, you admit. And yet, both together failed to restore my voice—and when I left home for the North, by way of Cincinnati, I had no intention or expectation of making a speech; but as soon as I opened my batteries in Pike's Opera House, in Cincinnati, against this infinitely infernal rebellion, I found myself able to speak and to be heard half a mile. I attribute the partial restoration of my voice to the goodness, the glory and the Godlike cause in which I profess to be engaged—that of vindicating the Union.

We are in the midst of a revolution, and a most fearful one, as you all know it is. I shall, in the remarks I may make here, advance no sentiment, no idea, I shall employ no language, that I have not advanced and employed time and again at home, away down in Dixie. I should despise myself, and merit the scorn and contempt of every lady and gentleman under the sound of my voice, if I were to come here with one set of principles and opinions for the North, and another set for the South when I am there. I will utter no denunciation of the wretched, the corrupt, and the infamous men who inaugurated this revolution South here, that I would not utter in their hearing on the street where I reside. I therefore say to you, in the outset of the remarks I purpose to make, what I have time and again said through the columns of the most widely circulated paper they had in the South—a paper, by the way, they suppressed and crushed out on the 25th of October last—the last Union journal that floated over any portions of the Southern confederacy, and to this good hour the last and the only religious journal in the eleven seceded States. I say, then, to you, as I have said time and again, that *the people of the South, the demagogues and leaders of the South, are to blame for having brought about this state of things, and not the people of the North.* They have intended down South for thirty years to break up this Government. It has been our settled purpose and our sole aim down South to destroy the Union and break up the Government. We have had the Presidency in the South twice to your once, and five of our men were reelected to the Presidency, filling a period of forty years. In addition to that we had divers men elected for one term, and no man at the North ever was permitted to serve any but the one term; and in addition to having elected our men twice to your once, and occupied the chair twice as long as you ever did, we seized upon and appropriated two or three miscreants from the North that we elected to the Presidency, and ploughed with them as our heifers. We asked of you and obtained at your hands a fugitive slave law. You voted for and helped us to enact and to establish it. We asked of you and obtained the repeal of the Missouri compromise line, which never ought to have been repealed. I fought it to the bitter end, and denounced it and all concerned in repealing it, and I repeat it here again to-night. We asked and obtained the admission of Texas into the Union, that we might have slave territory enough to form some four or five more great States, and you granted it. You have granted us from first to last all we have asked, all we have desired; and hence I repeat that this thing of secession, this wicked attempt to dissolve the Union, has been brought about without the shadow of a cause. It is the work of the worst men that ever God permitted to live on the face of this earth. It is the work of a set of men down South who, in winding up this revolution, if our Administration and Government shall fail to hang them as high as Haman—hang every one of them—we will make an utter failure. I have confidence myself, and, thank God, I have always had faith and confidence, in the Government crushing out this rebellion. We have the men at the head of affairs who will do it—and that gallant and glorious man McClellan—a man in whose ability and integrity I have all the time had confidence and prophesied he would come right side up. My own distracted and oppressed section of the country, East Tennessee, falls now by the new arrangement into the military district of that hero, Fremont. We rejoiced in Tennessee when we heard that we had fallen into his division, and although I have always differed with him in politics, yet, in a word, he is my sort of man. He will either make a spoon or spoil a horn, in the attempt. When he gets ready to go down into East Tennessee I hope he will let me know. I want to go with him side by side, on a horse; and our friend Briggs, of New York, a former member of Congress, who is now on the platform, has promised me a large coil of rope, and I want the pleasure of showing them who to hang.[1]

We have had experiments in this thing of crushing out rebellion. We had a long time ago one on a small scale in Massachusetts, and the Government crushed it out. Afterwards we had the whiskey rebellion in the neighboring State of Pennsylvania, and the Government applied the screws and crushed

1. George Briggs served in the U.S. House as a Republican from 1859 to 1861.

it out. Still more recently we had a terrible rebellion in South Carolina, and, with Old Hickory at the helm, we crushed it out. And if my prayers and tears could have resurrected the Old Hero two years ago—though I never supported him in my life—and placed him in the chair, disgraced and occupied by that miserable mockery of a man from Wheatland, we would have had this rebellion crushed out; for, let General Jackson have been in politics what he was—I knew him well—he was a true patriot and a sincere lover of his country. When Floyd commenced stealing muskets and other implements of war, and his associates commenced plotting treason, had Old Hickory been President, rising about ten feet in his boots, and taking Floyd by the collar, he would have sworn by the God that made Moses, *this thing must stop.*[2] And when Andrew Jackson swore that a thing had to stop, it had to stop. More recently still, we had a rebellion in the neighboring State of Rhode Island, known as the Dorr rebellion, and the Government very efficiently and very properly put it down. But the great conspiracy of the nineteenth century and the great rebellion of the age is now in hand, and I believe that Abe Lincoln, with the people to back him, will crush it out. It will be done, it must be done, and it shall be done. And, having done that thing, if they will give us a few weeks' rest to recruit, we will lick England and France both, if they wish it. And I am not certain but we will have to do it—particularly old England. She has been playing a two-fisted game, and she was well represented by Russell, for he carried water on both shoulders.[3] I don't like the tone of her journals; and when this war is finished we shall have four or five hundred thousand well drilled soldiers, inured to the hardships of war, under the lead of experienced officers, and then we shall be ready for the rest of the world and the balance of mankind.

When the rebellion first opened—something like twelve months ago—I saw, as every observing man could see, where we were driving to, and what would be the state of things in a very short time. In the inauguration of the rebellion I took sides with the Union and with the Stars and Stripes of my country. How could it be otherwise? I had traveled the circuit as a Methodist preacher in the State of South Carolina in 1832, in Pickens and Anderson counties [Anderson county being the one where John C. Calhoun lived,] and I fought with all the ability I possessed, and all the energy I could muster, the heresy of nullification then. I even prepared a pamphlet in South Carolina, of seventy pages, backing up and sustaining

2. Brownlow here refers to John Floyd of Virginia, President Buchanan's secretary of war.

3. William Howard Russell, British war correspondent.

Old Hickory and denouncing the nullifiers—and they threatened to hang me then. I have been a Union man all my life. I have never been a sectional man. I commenced my political career in Tennessee in the memorable year of 1828, and I was one, thank God, of the corporal's guard who got up the electoral ticket for John Quincy Adams against Andrew Jackson. In the next contest I was for Clay. You and I and all of us cheer and applaud the mention of the name of Henry Clay. I purpose to move, when this rebellion is over, that we shall hold a National Convention, and I will put in nomination for the Presidency the last suit of clothes that Clay wore before his death. When the rebellion fairly opened, they saw the course my paper was taking, and they approached me, as they did every other editor of a Union paper in the country, with money. They knew I was poor, and they supposed it would have the same influence over me that it had over almost all the Union editors of the South, for they bought up the last devil of them all throughout the South. I told them as one did of old: Thy money perish with thee. I pursued the even tenor of my way until the stream rose higher and higher with secession fire, as red and hot as hell itself, and commenced pouring along that great artery of travel, that great railroad of Manassas, Yorktown, Richmond and Petersburg. Then it was, that, wanting in transportation, wanting in rolling stock, wanting in locomotives, they had to lie over by regiments in our town, and then they commenced to ride Union men upon rails. I have seen that done in the streets, and have seen them break into the stores and empty their contents; and coming before my house with ropes in their hands, they would groan out, "Let us give old Browlow a turn, the damned old scoundrel; come out, and we will hang you to the first limb." I would appear, sometimes, on the front portico of my house, and would address them in this way: "Men, what do you want with me?" for I was very select in my words. I took particular pains to never say "gentlemen." "Men, what do you want with me?" "We want a speech from you; we want you to come out for the Southern confederacy." To which I replied: "I have no speech to make to you. You know me as well as I know you; I am utterly and irreconcilably opposed to this infernal rebellion in which you are engaged, and I shall fight it to the bitter end. I hope that if you are going in to kill the Yankees in search of your rights, that you will get your rights before you get back." These threats towards me were repeated every day and every week, until finally they crushed out my paper, destroyed my office, appropriated the building to an old smith's shop to repair the locks and barrels of old muskets that Floyd had stolen from the Federal Government. They finally enacted a law in the Legislature of Tennessee authorizing an armed force to take all the arms, pistols, guns, dirks, swords, and everything of the sort, from all the Union men, and they paid a visit to every Union house in the State. They visited mine three times in succession upon that business, and they got there a couple of guns and one pistol. Being an editor and preacher myself, I was not largely supplied, and had the balance concealed under my bed-clothes.

Finally, after depriving us of all our arms throughout the State, and after taking all the fine horses of the Union men everywhere, without fee or reward, for cavalry horses, and seizing upon the fat hogs, corn, fodder, and sheep, going into houses and pulling the beds off the bedsteads in the day time, seizing upon all the blankets they could find for the army; after breaking open chests, bureaus, drawers, and everything of that sort—in which they were countenanced and tolerated by the authorities, civil and military—our people rose up in rebellion, unarmed as they were, and by accident, I know it was, from Chattanooga to the Virginia line—a distance of 300 miles—one Saturday night in November, at eleven o'clock, all the railroad bridges took fire at one time. It was purely accidental. I happened to be out from home at the time. I had really gone out on horseback—as they had suppressed my paper—to collect the fees which the clerks of the different counties were owing me, which they were ready and willing to pay me, knowing that I needed them to live upon; and as these bridges took fire while I was out of town, they swore that I was the bell-wether and ringleader of all the devilment that was going on, and hence that I must have had a hand in it. They wanted a pretext to seize upon me, and upon the 6th day of December they marched me off to jail—a miserable, uncomfortable, damp and desperate jail—where I found, when I was ushered into it, some 150 Union men; and, as God is my judge, I say here to-night, *there was not in the whole jail a chair, bench, stool, or table,* or any piece of furniture, except a dirty old wooden bucket and a pair of tin dippers to drink with. I found some of the first and best men of the whole country there. I knew them all, and they knew me, as I had been among them for thirty years. They rallied round me, some smiling and glad to see me, as I could give them the news that had been kept from them. Others took me by the hand and were utterly speechless, and, with bitter, burning tears running down their cheeks, they said that they never thought that they would come to that at last, looking through the bars of a grate. Speaking first to one and then another, I bade them to be of good cheer and take good courage. Addressing them, I said, "is it for stealing you are here? No. Is it for counterfeiting? No. Is it for manslaughter? No. You are here, boys, *because you adhere to the flag and the Constitution of our country.* I am here with you for no other offence but that; and, as God is my judge, boys, I look upon this 6th day of December as the proudest day of my life. And here I intend to stay until I die of old age or until they choose to hang me. I will never renounce my principles." Before I was confined in the jail, their officers were accustomed to visit the jail every day and offer them their liberty, if they would take the oath of allegiance to the Southern confederacy and volunteer to go into the service, and they would guarantee them safety and protection. They were accustomed to volunteer a dozen at a time, so great was their horror of imprisonment and the bad treatment they received in that miserable jail. After I got into the jail—and they had me in close confinement for three dreadful winter months—all this volunteering and taking the oath ceased, and the leaders swore I did it. One of the brigadiers who was in command of the military post paid me a special visit, two of his aids accompanying him. He came in, bowed and scraped, saying: "Why, Brownlow, you ought not to be in here." "But your generals," I replied, "have thought otherwise, and they have put me here." "I have come to inform you that if you will take the oath of allegiance to the Southern confederacy, we will guarantee the protection and safety of yourself and family." Rising up several feet in my boots at that time, and looking him full in the eye—"Why," said I, "I intend to lie here until I rot from disease, or die of old age, before I will take the oath of allegiance to your government. I deny your right to administer such an oath. I deny that you have any government other than a Southern mob. You have never been recognised by any civilized Power on the face of the earth, and you will never be. I will see the Southern confederacy, and you and I on top of it, in the infernal regions before I will do it." "Well," said he, "that's damned plain talk." "Yes," I replied, "that is the way to talk in revolutionary times."

But I must hasten on. I will detain you too long. But things went on. They tightened up; they grew tighter, and still more tight. Many of our company became sick. We had to lie upon that miserable, cold, naked floor, *with not room enough for us all to lie down at the same time*—and you think what it must have been in December and January—spelling each other, one lying down awhile on the floor and then another taking his place so made warm, and that was the way we managed until many became sick unto death. A number of the prisoners died of pneumonia and typhoid fever, and other diseases contracted by exposure there. I shall never forget, while my head is above ground, the scenes I passed through in that jail. I recollect there were *two venerable Baptist clergymen there*—Mr. Pope and Mr. Cate. Mr. Cate was very low indeed, prostrated from the fever and unable to eat the miserable food sent there by the corrupt jailor and deputy marshal—a man whom I had denounced in my paper as guilty of forgery time and time again—a suitable representative of the thieves and scoundrels that head this rebellion in the South.[4] The only favor they extended to me was to allow my family to send me three meals a day by my son, who brought the provisions in a basket. I requested my wife to send also enough for the two old clergymen. One of them was put in jail *for offering prayers for the President of the United States*, and the other was confined for throwing up his hat and cheering the Stars and Stripes as they passed his house, borne by a company of Union volunteers. When the basket of provisions came in, in the morning, they examined it at the door—would look between the pie and the bread to see if there was any billet or paper concealed there communicating treason from any outside Unionist to the old scoundrel they had in jail; and when the basket went out, again the same ceremony was repeated, to discover whether I had slipped any paper in, in any way. The old man Cate had three sons in jail. One of them, James Madison Cate, a most exemplary and worthy member of the Baptist church, who was there for having committed no other crime than that of *refusing to volunteer*, lay stretched at length upon the floor with one thickness of a piece of carpet under him and an old overcoat doubled up for a pillow, in the very agonies of death, unable to turn over, only from one side to the other. His wife came to visit him, bringing her youngest child with her, which was but a babe, but *they refused her admittance.* I put my head out of the jail window, and entreated them, for God's sake, to let the poor woman come in, as her husband was dying. They at last consented that she might see him for the limited time of fifteen minutes. As she came in and looked upon her husband's wan and emaciated face and saw how rapidly he was sinking, she gave evident sighs of fainting, and would have fallen to the floor with the babe in her arms, had I not rushed up to her and cried, "Let me have the babe," and then she sank down upon the breast of her dying husband, unable at first to speak a single word. I sat by and held the babe until the fifteen minutes had expired, when the officer came in, and in an insulting and peremptory manner notified her that the interview was to close. I hope I may never see such a scene again; and yet such cases were common all over East Tennessee. Such actions as these show the spirit of secession in the South.

It is the spirit of murder and assassination—it is the spirit of hell. And yet you have men at the North who sympathize with these infernal murderers. *If I owed the devil a debt to be discharged, and it was to be discharged by the rendering up to him of a dozen of the meanest, most revolting and God-forsaken wretches that ever could be culled from the ranks of depraved human society, and I wanted to pay*

4. William L. Pope and James M. Cate, east Tennessee unionist preachers.

that debt and get a premium upon the payment, I would make a tender to his Satanic Majesty of twelve Northern men who sympathized with this infernal rebellion. If I am severe and bitter in my remarks—if I am, you must consider that we in the South make a personal matter of this thing. We have no respect or confidence in any Northern man who sympathizes with this infernal rebellion—nor should any be tolerated in walking Broadway at any time. Such men ought to be ridden upon a rail and ridden out of the North. They should either be for or against the "mill dam;" and I would make them show their hands. Why, gentlemen, after the battle at Manassas and Bull Run the officers and privates of the Confederate army passed through our town on their way to Dixie, exulting over the victory they had achieved, and some of them had what they called Yankee heads, or the entire heads of Federal soldiers, some of them with long beards and goatees, by which they would take them up and say, "See! here is the head of a damned soldier captured at Bull Run." It is the spirit of murder of the vile untutored savage; it is the spirit of hell, and he who apologizes for them is no better than those who perpetrated the deed.

In Andy Johnson's town—and while Johnson's name is on my lips, I will make another remark or two here: if Mr. Lincoln had consulted the Union men of Tennessee as to whom they wanted for military Governor of the State, to a man they would have responded Andy Johnson. I have fought that man for twenty-five long and terrible years; I fought him systematically, perseveringly and untiringly; but it was upon the old issues of whiggery and democracy; and now we will fight for one another. We have merged in Tennessee all other parties and predilections in this great question of the Union. We are the Union men of Tennessee, unconditional Union men— and the miserable wretch who will attempt here or elsewhere to resurrect old exploded parties and party issues, and try to make capital out of this war, deserves the gallows, and deserves death. In Andy Johnson's town they had the jail full of prisoners, drove his family out of his house, and his wife being in the last stages of consumption, appropriated his house, carpet and bedding, for a hospital, and his wife had to take shelter with one of her daughters in an adjoining county; and Johnson has in him to-night a devil as big—and there is in the bosom of every Union man in Tennessee—as my hat; and whenever the federal army shall find its way there, we will shoot them down like dogs, and hang them on every limb we come to. They have had their time of hanging and shooting, and our time comes next, and I hope to God that it will not be long. I am watching in the papers the movements of the army, and whenever I hear that my country is captured I intend to return post-haste and point out the rebels. I have no other ambition on earth but to resurrect the Knoxville *Whig* and get it in full blast, with one hundred thousand subscribers. And then, as the negroes say down South, "I'll 'spress my opinion of some of them." But in the town of Greenville, where Andrew Johnson resides, they took out of the jail at one time two innocent Union men, who had committed no offence on the face of the earth but that of being Union men—Nash and Fry. Fry was a poor shoemaker, with a wife and half a dozen children. A fellow from way down East in Maine, by the name of Daniel Leadbeater, the bloodiest and the most ultra man, the vilest wretch, the most unmitigated scoundrel that ever made a track in East Tennessee—this is Colonel Daniel Leadbeater, late of the United States Army, but now a rebel in the secession army—he took these two men, tied them with his own hands upon one limb, *immediately over the railroad track in the town of Greenville,* and ordered them to hang four days and nights, and directed all the engineers and conductors to go by that hanging concern slow, in a kind of snail gallop, up and down the road, *to give the passengers an opportunity to kick the rigid bodies and strike them with a rattan.* And they did it. I pledge you my honor that on the front platform they made a business of kicking the dead bodies as they passed by; and the women— (I will not say the ladies, for down South we make a distinction between ladies and women)—the women, the wives and daughters of men in high position, waved their white handkerchiefs in triumph through the windows of the car at the sight of the two dead bodies hanging there. Leadbeater, for his murderous courage, was promoted by Jeff. Davis to the office of Brigadier General. He had an encounter, as their own papers at Richmond state, at Bridgeport, not long ago, with a part of General Mitchell's army, where Leadbeater got a glorious whipping. His own party turned round and chastised him for cowardice. He had courage to hang innocent unarmed men taken out of jail, but he had not courage to face the Yankees and the Northern men that were under Mitchell and Buell.[5] He took to his heels, like a coward and scavenger as he is. Our programme is this: that when we get back into East Tennessee we will instruct all our friends everywhere to secure and apprehend this fellow, Leadbeater; and our purpose is to take him to that tree and make the widow of Fry tie the rope around his infernal neck.

In the county of Knox, where I reside, and only seven miles west of the town of Knoxville, they caught up Union men, tied them upon logs, elevated the log upon blocks six or ten inches from the ground, put the men upon their breasts, tying their hands and feet under the log, stripped their backs entirely bare, and then, with switches, cut their backs literally to pieces, the blood running down at every stroke. They came into court

5. Union generals Ormsby M. Mitchell and Don Carlos Buell.

when it was in session, and when the case was stated, the Judge replied: "These are revolutionary times, and there is no remedy for anything of the kind." Hence, you see, our remedy is in our own hands; and, with the help of guns, and swords, and sabres, we intend, God willing, to slay them when we get back there, wherever we find them. In the jail where I lay they were accustomed to drive up with a cart, with an ugly, rough, flat topped coffin upon it, surrounded by fifteen to forty men, with bristling bayonets, as a guard to march in through the gate into the jail yard, with steady, military tread. We trembled in our boots, for they never notified us who was to be hanged, and you may imagine how your humble servant felt; for if any man in that jail, under their law, deserved the gallows, I claim to have been the man. I knew it, and they knew it. They came sometimes with two coffins, one on each cart, and they took two men at a time and marched them out. A poor old man of sixty-five, and his son of twenty-five, were marched out at one time and hanged on the same gallows. *They made that poor old man, who was a Methodist class leader, sit by and see his son hang till he was dead, and then they called him a damned Linconite Union shrieker, and said, "Come on; it is your turn next." He sank, but they propped him up and led him to the halter, and swung both off on the same gallows.* They came, after that, for another man, and they took J. C. Haum out of jail—a young man of fine sense, good address, and of excellent character—a tall, spare-made man, leaving a wife at home, with four or five helpless children. My wife passed the farm of Haum's the other day, when they drove her out of Tennessee and sent her on to New Jersey—I thank them for doing so—and saw *his wife ploughing, endeavoring to raise corn for her suffering and starving children. That is the spirit of secession, gentlemen. And yet you have a set of God-forsaken, unprincipled men at the North who are apologizing for them and sympathizing with them.* When they took Haum out and placed him on the scaffold they had a drunken chaplain. They were kind enough to notify him an hour before the hanging that he was to hang. Haum at once made an application for a Methodist preacher, a Union man, to come and pray for him. *They denied him the privilege, and said that God didn't hear any prayers in behalf of any damned Union shrieker,* and he had literally to die without the benefit of clergy. But they had near the gallows an unprincipled, drunken chaplain of their own army, who got up and undertook to apologize for Haum. He said: "This poor, unfortunate man, who is about to pay the debt of nature, regrets the course he took. He said he was misled by the Union paper." Haum rose up, and with a clear, stentorian voice, said: "Fellow-citizens, there is not a word of truth in that statement. I have authorized nobody to make such a statement. What I have said and done I have done and said with my eyes open, and, if it were to be done over, I would do it again. I am ready to hang, and you can execute your purposes." He died like a man; he died like a Union man, like an East Tennessean ought to die. As God is my judge, I would sooner be Haum in the grave today than any one of the scoundrels concerned in his murder. Time rolled on. One event after another occurred, and finally a man of excellent character, one of Andy Johnson's constituents from Greene county, by the name of Hessing Self, was condemned to be hung by this drumhead court-martial, and they were kind enough to let him know that he was to hang a few hours before the hour appointed. His daughter, who had come down to administer to his comfort and consolation—a most estimable girl, about twenty-one years of age—Elizabeth Self, a tall, spare-made girl, modest, handsomely attired, begged leave to enter the jail to see her father. They permitted her, contrary to their usual custom and their savage barbarity, to go in. They had him in a small iron cage, a terrible affair; they opened a little door, and the jailor admitted her. A number of us went to witness the scene. As she entered the cage where her father was—who was to die at four o'clock that afternoon—she clasped him around the neck, and he embraced her also, throwing his arms across her shoulders. They sobbed and cried; they shed their tears and made their moans. I stood by, and I never beheld such a sight since God Almighty made me, and I hope I may never see the like again. When they had parted, wringing each other by the hand, as she came out of the cage, stammering and trying to utter something intelligible, she lisped my name. She knew my face, and I could understand as much as that she desired me to write a dispatch to Jeff. Davis, and sign her name, begging him to pardon her father. I wrote it about thus:

> Hon. Jefferson Davis (I did not believe the first word I wrote was the truth, but I put it there for the sake of form:) My father, Hessing Self, is sentenced to be hanged at four o'clock today. I am living at home, and my mother is dead. My father is my earthly all; upon him my hopes are centred, and, friend, I pray you to pardon him. Respectfully,
>
> Elizabeth Self.

Jeff. Davis, who had a better heart than the rest of them, perhaps, immediately responded—for he could not withstand the appeals of a woman—to General Carroll, and told him not to hang that man Self, but to keep him in jail and let him atone for his crimes a certain time.[6] Self has served his time out and has gone home, and that girl is saved the wretchedness of being left alone without a father.

6. Confederate general William H. Carroll.

This is the spirit of secession all over the South; it is the spirit that actuates them everywhere; it is the spirit of murder; it is the spirit of the infernal regions; and, in God's name, can you any longer excuse or apologize for such murderous and bloodthirsty demons as live down in the Southern confederacy? Hanging is going on all over East Tennessee. *They shoot them down in the fields—they whip them; and, as strange as it may seem to you, in the counties of Campbell and Anderson they actually lacerate with switches the bodies of females, wives and daughters of Union men—clever, respectable women.* They show no quarter to male or female; they rob their houses and they throw them into prison. Our jails are all full now, and we have complained and thought hard that our Government has not come to our relief, for a more loyal, a more devoted people to the Stars and Stripes never lived on the face of God's earth than the Union people of Tennessee. With tears in their eyes they begged me, upon leaving East Tennessee, for God Almighty's sake to see the President, to see the army officers, so as to have relief sent to them and bring them out of jail. I hope, gentlemen, you will use your influence with the army and navy, and all concerned, to relieve these people. They are the most abused, down-trodden, persecuted and proscribed people that ever lived on the face of the earth. I am happy to announce to you that the rebellion will soon be played out. Thank God for his mercies, it will soon have been played out. Richmond will be obliged to fall very soon, for that noble fellow, McClellan, will capture the whole of them. I have confidence and faith in Fremont, and hope he may rush into East Tennessee. If Halleck, Buell & Co. will only capture the region round about Corinth and take Memphis, the play is out and the dog is dead. Then let us drive the leaders down into the Gulf of Mexico, like the devils drove the hogs into the sea of Galilee.

But a few weeks prior to the last Presidential election they announced in their papers that the great bull of the whole disunion flock was to speak in Knoxville—a man, the first two letters of his name are W. L. Yancey— a fellow that the Governor of South Carolina pardoned out of the State prison for murdering his uncle, Dr. Earl. He was announced to speak, and the crowd was two to one Union men.[7] I had never spoken to him in all my life. He called out in an insolent manner, "Is Parson Brownlow in this crowd?" The disunionists hallooed out, "Yes, he is here." "I hope," said he, "the Parson will have the nerve to come upon the stand and have me catechise him." "No," said the Breckinridge secessionists. Yes, we had four tickets in the field the last race—Lincoln and Hamlin, Bell and Everett—the Bell and Everett tickets was a kind of kangaroo ticket, with all the strength in

---

7. William Lowndes Yancey, Alabama radical secessionist.

the legs; and there was a Douglas and Johnson and a Breckinridge and Lane ticket. As God is my judge, that was the meanest and shabbiest ticket of the four that was in the field. Lincoln was elected fairly and squarely under the forms of law and the Constitution; and though I was not a Lincoln man, yet I gave in to the will of the majority, and it is the duty of every patriot and true man to bow to the will of the majority. But the crowd hallooed to Yancey, "Brownlow is here, but he has not nerve enough to mount the stand where you are." I rose and marched up the steps and said, I will show you whether I have the nerve or not. "Sir," said he—and he is a beautiful speaker and personally a fine looking man—"are you the celebrated Parson Brownlow?" "I am the only man on earth," I replied, "that fills the bill." "Don't you think," said Yancey, "you are badly employed as a preacher, a man of your cloth to be dabbling in politics and meddling with State affairs?" "No, sir," said I, "a distinguished member of the party you are acting with once took Jesus Christ up upon a mount and said to the Saviour, 'Look at the kingdoms of the world. All this will I give thee if thou will fall down and worship me.' Now, sir," I said, "his reply to the Devil is my reply to you, 'Get thee behind me, Satan.'" I rather expected to be knocked down my him; but I stood with my right side to him and a cocked Derringer in my breeches pocket. I intended, if I went off the scaffold, that he should go the other way. "Now, sir," I said, "if you are through, I would like to make a few remarks." "Certainly, proceed," said Yancey. "Well, sir, you should tread lightly upon the toes of preachers, and you should get these disunionists to post you up before you launch out in this way against preachers. Are you aware, sir, that this old gray-headed man sitting here, Isaac Lewis, the President of the meeting, who has welcomed you, is an old disunion Methodist preacher, and Buchanan's pension agent in this town, who has been meddling in politics all his lifetime? Sir," said I, "are you aware that this man, James D. Thomas, on my left, is a Breckinridge elector for this Congressional district? He was turned out of the Methodist ministry for whipping his wife and slandering his neighbors. Sir," said I, "are you aware that this young man sitting in front of us, Colonel Loudon [sic] C. Haynes, the elector of the Breckinridge ticket for the State of Tennessee at large, was expelled from the Methodist ministry for lying and cheating his neighbor in a measure of corn?[8] Now," said I, "for God's sake say nothing more about preachers until you know what sort of preachers are in your own ranks." And thus ended the colloquy between me and Yancey. I have never seen him since.

8. Landon C. Haynes, an important Tennessee politician and member of the Confederate States Senate.

JOHN W. WOOD

Union and Secession in Mississippi

(Memphis: Saunders, Parrish and Whitmore, 1863)

John W. Wood (ca. 1810–1870) said he was born in Virginia early in the
century into a slaveowning family. Little is known about his upbringing
or career save that he removed to Attala County, Mississippi, and took
up farming and politics. He represented his district in the state's secession
convention, spoke out against secession, and refused to vote for separation
from the Union. An ardent nationalist, he opposed the Confederate
government's activities in south-central Mississippi and suffered for his
actions. In 1860 Wood's personal wealth was slight, though he claimed to
own a few slaves. He disappeared from public view during the last year of
the war and does not appear in the 1870 census.

If not for this ardent unionist pamphlet addressed to "the few faithful
men of Mississippi," which he wrote in 1862 and had secreted to Memphis
and published there during the Federal occupation, this southern unionist
might be lost to history. In this pamphlet, Wood sought to stir his fellow
Mississippians to refuse aid and comfort to the Confederacy. In it he
described how radical antidemocratic secessionists had taken away the
liberties of peace-loving Mississippians and lied to them with promises
of Confederate victory. From his special place within the heart of the lower
Confederacy, Wood discussed how Confederate government authorities
impoverished the people and destroyed their personal property. He called
for Mississippi's prompt return to the Union.

For snippets of biographical information on Wood see Percy Lee Rain-
water, *Mississippi: Storm Center of Secession, 1856–1861* (Baton Rouge: Otto
Claitor, 1938); Thomas H. Woods, "A Sketch of the Mississippi Secession
Convention of 1861," *Publication of the Mississippi Historical Society* (1902);
and Lillian A. Pereyra, *James Lusk Alcorn* (Baton Rouge: Louisiana State
University Press, 1966).

* * *

PREFACE.

The great object of the writer in publishing the following pages is, to aid in effecting a re-union of the United States, for social and commercial advantages, as the only basis of a Union worth preserving. Having argued the questions before the people of Mississippi before secession, and a decision being rendered against me, I simply ask that I may again be heard upon a re-argument of the important issues involved. Whenever the minds of the honest masses of the people are convinced of their errors, they are always ready to correct them and move in the right direction, however obstinate or perverse may be their rules. Born in the old state of Virginia, in sight of Monticello, my ancestors being large slaveholders, and always a slaveholder myself, the tongue of calumny dare not impugn my motives. Whatever differences of opinion may exist as to the best method of restoring our country to its former prosperous and happy condition, the paramount consideration of every American citizen should be the integrity of the Government and the Union of the States.

CHAPTER I

Two years ago, our country presented the most pleasing prospect of general prosperity ever exhibited to the world by any nation upon the globe. Ever since the establishment of our Government, it seemed that He "whose kingdom is over all," has continued to pour forth his blessings upon us. Whithersoever we might look, evidences of peace, plenty and prosperity, were constantly before our eyes. If we glanced at our Western territories, we would there behold the thick-skirted forest tumbling beneath the woodman's axe. If we turned to our rich Southern valleys, we would there see them burthened by the very weight of luxuriance. The exhaustless mines of our newly acquired regions, were pouring out their willing treasures into the cup of awakened industry. The clang of the hammer and the hissing of the forge were borne to us on every breeze from the far distant North. The ships of the world, freighted with the rich productions of other countries, were clinging to our shores, all along our borders upon the East. The patriotic statesman of every State of the Union was accustomed to look upon the increasing grandeur and glory of the United States, with heartfelt emotions of pleasure and delight. He saw a great family composed of thirty-four States and nine territories, containing a population of upwards of thirty millions; of which, more than twenty-five millions were white. Casting his eye along our sea-coast, he saw that it embraced an extent of twelve thousand, six hundred and sixty miles. Following the course of our principal rivers, and estimating their length, he found ten of them extending twenty thousand miles. Looking upon the surface of our five great lakes upon our Northern border, he saw an area of ninety thousand square miles. Tracing upon the map the railroads in operation, he found twenty-five thousand miles, which cost upwards of one hundred millions of dollars; and among the longest railroad in the world, (the Illinois Central,) of seven hundred and eighty-four miles. He found five thousand miles of canals, dug out by hardy sons of Europe, who had come across the blue waters of the broad Atlantic, to seek the protection of our flag, and live in a land of freedom. He was astonished at the annual value of our agricultural productions, which summed up two hundred millions of dollars. He found that the most valuable production was Indian Corn, which yielded annually four hundred millions of bushels. He found the amount of registered and enrolled tonnage was four millions four hundred and seven thousand and ten. The amount of capital invested in manufactures was six hundred millions of dollars. The annual amount of our internal trade was six hundred millions of dollars. The annual amount of the products of labor (other than agricultural) was fifteen hundred millions of dollars. The value of farms and live stock was five hundred millions of dollars. The surface of our coal fields was one hundred and thirty-eight thousand and thirty-one square acres; and within our borders were eighty thousand schools, five thousand academies, two thousand and thirty-four colleges, and three thousand and eight hundred churches. Contemplate the grandeur, glory, magnificence and resources of such a country.

Let us contrast the present condition of our Southern country with its prospects two years ago. The sound of the woodman's axe is no longer heard in our forests. That weapon of industry has been dropped for the weapon of death. The plow has been left standing in the furrow of many a poor conscript's field, and his aged father, or poor little, barefooted sister, left to work out with the hoe the young corn just peeping from the ground. The clang of the hammer and the hissing of the forge have been hushed. The din of commerce no longer enlivens our cities, and the grass has literally grown in the streets of our blockaded ports. The necessaries of life have risen to almost fabulous prices; salt from fifty to sixty dollars per sack; cotton cards from twelve to fifteen dollars; boots and shoes, and many other necessary articles, to such enormous prices as to place them often beyond the reach of the poor. Coffee, a beverage of which our Southern people are peculiarly fond, is only found in the houses of the wealthiest, and the poorer classes have to substitute a decoction of toasted cornmeal, bran, potatoes, acorns, or such other substitutes as the ingenuity of the oldest dames can devise. Deserted villages are seen in every county. The few remaining merchants hang idly about their stores, with no customers to buy, and no merchandise to sell. The hotels are virtually closed. Many poor families, whom their richer neighbors had promised to provide for during the absence of their fathers or sons, have been suffered to want for the necessaries of life. The only men of business are the extortioners and tax-gatherers—the former with the quickness and voracity of a shark, are moving about from point to point, buying up the necessaries of life in proportion to their scarcity, and preying upon the wants and misfortunes of their countrymen; the latter, in obedience to the laws of the land, are gathering up the little remnants of gold and silver in the country, which has often to be purchased at a hundred per cent premium by the tax-payer with the proceeds of his poultry and dairy, to the great deprivation of his family. The rag money of the country is considered good enough for the people, but not good enough to pay the "Military War Tax." War—desolating war, has swept over the country with a storm of destruction—dragging along the unwilling conscripts to the field, and bathing with tears every mother in the South. Our school-houses are deserted, our churches languish, trade is prostrate, and all the best interests of the country have sickened and died. The planters, neglectful of their crops, linger about the villages, eager to hear the latest news from the war; even nature seems to sympathize with our misfortunes, and the sky has assumed a peculiar hue never before witnessed in this clime. Who are the authors of our calamities? It is time to pause and reflect. It is time for the sober second thought of the people calmly to consider the sources of the aggravated evils and intolerable oppressions which have been heaped upon us, and ask themselves the question, if they could not have been honorably avoided? To the doctrine of secession may be attributed the main-spring of all our woes. It is a doctrine never contemplated by the Constitution of the United States—false in theory, and destructive in its results.

CHAPTER II

The origin of the doctrine of secession may be traced step by step to the speech of Mr. Calhoun, on the Force Bill, in the United States Senate, in 1833, in which he uses this language: "Is this a Federal Union or Union of States, as distinct from that of individuals? Is the Sovereignty in the several

States or in the American people in the aggregate? The very language which we are compelled to use when speaking of our political institutions, affords proof conclusive as to its real character. The terms Union, Federal, United, all imply a combination of sovereignties, a confederation of States. They are never applied to an association of individuals. Who ever heard of the United States of New York, of Massachusetts, or of Virginia? Who ever heard the terms Federal or Union applied to the aggregation of individuals into one community? Nor is the other point less clear—that the Sovereignty is in the several States, and that our system is a Union of twenty-four Sovereign powers under a Constitutional compact, and not of a divided Sovereignty between the States severally and the United States. In spite of all that has been said, I maintain that Sovereignty is in its nature indivisible. It is the supreme power in a State, and we might just as well speak of half a square or half a triangle as of half a Sovereignty. It is a great error to confound the exercise of Sovereign powers with the surrender of them. A Sovereign may delegate his powers to be exercised by as many agents as he may think proper, under such conditions or with such limitations as he may impose, but to surrender any portion of his Sovereignty to another, is to annihilate the whole."

The fallacy of the fascinating doctrine contained in the foregoing extract consists in a total misconception of the true nature of the structure of our Government. The true doctrine, as fully explained by the great expounder of the Constitution at that time, is that the Government of the United States is a Government proper, established by the people of the States— not a compact between sovereign communities—that within its limits it is supreme, and that whether it is within its limits or not, in any given exertion of itself, is to be determined by the Supreme Court of the United States, the ultimate arbiter in the last resort—from which there is no appeal but to revolution. It is not my present purpose, however, to elaborate this question.

From the teachings of Mr. Calhoun, the Southern people very readily embraced the popular doctrine of State Rights, which, becoming blended with the name of Democracy, soon established the State Rights Democratic party. The doctrine of State Rights appealed to the pride and prejudices of the people, and required no investigation to commend it to the hearty approval of the masses. After the doctrines of the Democratic State Rights party had become so popular among the masses of the people, it required but one step further to induce them to embrace the doctrine of Secession. When the National Democratic party met at Charleston in 1860, they were divided upon a question of no practical utility whatever, at that time, viz: whether Slavery should be protected in the Territories, when really there was no territory whatever, since the settlement of the question in Kansas, where slavery was likely to go. But the leaders of the secession movement then saw what would be the result, and, doubtless, many of them designed to effect a division in the National Democratic party for no other purpose than to elect Abraham Lincoln, and thereby obtain a sufficient pretext for a dissolution of the Union.

Immediately after the result of the Presidential election, in 1860, was known, the leaders of the secession movement went to work calling county meetings, harangueing the people, forming companies of "minute men," and using all of those artful appliances so well understood by them, to get up a great political excitement. The Governors of the different States hastily called the Legislatures together. The Legislature of Mississippi assembled at Jackson on the 26th of November, and passed the following resolutions, introduced by the Hon. A. M. West, of Holmes:

"*Resolved by the Legislature of the State of Mississippi,* That in the opinion of those who now constitute the said Legislature, that Secession by each of the aggrieved States, for their grievances, is the remedy.

"*Resolved,* That the Governor be requested to appoint as many Commissioners as in his judgment may be necessary, to visit each of the slave-holding States, and designate the State or States to which each commissioner shall be commissioned, whose duty it shall be to inform them that this Legislature has passed an act calling a Convention of the people of this State, to consider the present threatening relations of the Northern and Southern sections of the Confederacy, aggravated by the recent election of a President upon principles of hostility to the States of the South, and to express the earnest hope of Mississippi that those States will co-operate with her in the adoption of efficient measures for their common defence and safety."

The Convention Bill provided that the election be held on the 20th of December, and that the Convention should assemble on the 7th of January, 1861.

Being called upon by the citizens of the central County of Mississippi, (Attala,) called by the Secessionists "the free State of Attala," to become a candidate for a seat in the Convention, I issued a list of appointments and mounted my horse for a canvass of the county, addressing the people nearly every day from two to three hours, and sometimes longer, till the day of the election. The result was, my election by a majority of only thirty-four votes. The Union candidate in 1850 was elected by only one vote. I made the issue upon the direct question of "Union" or "Disunion." Our tickets were printed "Union Ticket." The following extract from a circular in reply to a circular of the Secession candidates will give a glance at some of the views taken by me of the question at that time: "These gentlemen, then, are in favor of breaking up the present National Government, under which we have lived and prospered as no other people ever did, and trying to construct another one out of the State of Mississippi and such other seceding States as are willing to join in this undertaking. This they are in favor of doing without any effort being made to insure our rights in the Union; for no where in their circular do they propose anything else than *Secession* from the General Government. This proposition is infinitely the most momentous one ever submitted to the people of Mississippi; and, if adopted, will involve consequences which no eye can fully see, and no mind fully comprehend. It is REVOLUTION out and out. Whenever Mississippi secedes, she will become a foreign power to the remaining States of the Union. She will no longer have any interest in the General Government, or in the territories; in Congressional provisions for the establishment of Federal Courts, or in those for carrying the mails, or the establishment of Post Offices; but the remaining States, and the General Government, will be as foreign to her as is Great Britain or France.

"Are you in favor of taking this desperate step, and plunging into the dark abyss now opening at your feet? Have you carefully considered the consequences? Let us briefly glance at some of them. . . ."[1]

With arguments like these, I endeavored to convince the minds of the masses of the people of the danger of taking the awful step of secession. Although I succeeded in the central county of the State, a large majority of the people of Mississippi were deluded by false representations and false issues, made before them, some of which I will notice.

CHAPTER III

1. One of the greatest delusions which seemed to be all-pervading, notwithstanding the apparent preparations for war, was, that secession would be peaceable. The people could not realize the unwelcome fact that war was inevitable. The dangers of a dissolution of the Union had been so often

---

1. Wood here lists nine points: Loss of nationality meant no government to control the people. The burdens of an independent government will insure the new government will have to raise taxes. Equipment for national defense will be costly. There will be war. We will go bankrupt. All railroad building will stop. Mechanics will lose their jobs. The framework of society will be disorganized. Law will be suspended and disregarded, "and lawless violence and anarchy will take the place of law and order." No better government can be constructed than now exists.

sounded in their ears, that they had become somewhat accustomed to it. I always endeavored to impress upon them the sentiments of Daniel Webster, in his last speech in the Senate, on the 7th of March, 1850, in which he said: . . . [2]

Notwithstanding such lessons of wisdom as these, there were found secession leaders who professed to be willing to do all the fighting themselves, that would have to be done; but when the fighting came on, many of them proved to be reluctant to redeem their pugnacious promises.

Mr. Yancey had, long prior to the last presidential election, favored the plan of "precipitating the cotton States into a revolution," at the same time disclaiming that he was a disunionist! In his speech at Montgomery, a few days after the election, he said: "To-night I address a meeting of my fellow-citizens in Montgomery, in which has been witnessed the glorious spectacle of an actual fusion of all parties in our midst for one great purpose—the Union of the Southern men in order to a protection of the rights of the South, without the Union. Perhaps the boasted 'eighteen millions' may respect those rights when independent of their political power. . . ."[3]

I quote the above extract from the speech of the Ajax Telamon of the secession movement, as well for the purpose of showing that some of the leaders, at least, contemplated the probability of war, as to show the inconsistency of his position. For "separate State secession," and not a "disunionist!" Almost all of them, however, preached before the people the doctrine of "peaceable secession" and "bloodless revolution." The boldness of Mr. Yancey's position was entitled to more respect than those who taught many ignorant people to believe that "there would not be a gun fired!"

2. The next delusion of most importance which was disseminated among the people was, that in the event of war, England or France, or perhaps both, would certainly interpose in our behalf. That "Cotton was King," and that three or four millions of people in Europe were dependent upon our great staple for their daily bread. In this our greatest statesmen were in error, for they certainly knew, when plunging the Southern States into a contest so unequal, it would be impossible to succeed without foreign aid. They doubtless recollected that when Patrick Henry was inaugurating the American revolution in Virginia, and arousing our ancestors to battle, in a just and holy cause, he freely confessed to his intimate friends that he depended upon foreign assistance for their ultimate success. Our Senators

2. Wood quotes from Webster's assertion that secession would not be peaceful.
3. Wood had quoted at length from a speech of the Alabama fire-eater William L. Yancey.

in Congress, when leaving their seats, after the secession of their respective States, menacingly alluded to the assistance of the great powers of Europe. Much of the legislation of the Confederate Congress was based upon the assumed fact, that our Ports would be opened by foreign interference. Mr. Memminger's scheme for raising money by a "Produce Loan" was based upon that presumption.[4] Mr. Yancey had written home that our Ports would be opened prospectively, from time to time, about as often as some of the Northern Statesmen had designated the time of the termination of the "rebellion." The most strained efforts were made during the progress of the revolution to keep up this delusion. The telegraph was subsidized to gain its assistance. The "reliable Gentleman" had time and again heard a dispatch read at the head-quarters of such a General, that our independence was to be acknowledged at such a time, and our ports opened.

The position I assumed in the canvass before the people of Mississippi was: That we could not reasonably expect any assistance from foreign nations; that they were opposed to our peculiar institution which underlaid the revolution, and that their sympathies would be against us; that, however much they might rejoice at the dissentions existing here, and would encourage them to weaken us as a great rival, especially of England and France, they would not take part in the conflict. The Commissioners sent to Europe were so well aware of the prejudices of the English people against slavery that Messrs. Yancey, Mann, and Roost [sic], endeavored to place the revolution upon the grounds of the Tariff, and exhibited very great weakness in doing so.[5] Mr. Yancey, in his speech at the Fish-mongers Company dinner, said: "their pursuits, soil, climate and productions are totally different from those of the North. They think it their interest to buy cheapest and sell where they can sell dearest. In all this the North differs *toto coelo* from them, and now makes war upon us to enforce the supremacy of their mistaken ideas and selfish interests."

In a letter subsequently written by these gentlemen to Lord John Russell, the cause of the secession movement is attributed to the Tariff and not to Slavery. In this view of the subject those gentlemen were at least thirty years behind the times, and must have had their attention directed to the little nullification movement of South Carolina in 1832. Their great weakness, however, consisted in flattering themselves that Lord John Russell could be so easily deceived, when he understood, perhaps, a little better than those gentlemen, the true character of the American question.

4. Christopher G. Memminger, Confederate secretary of the treasury.
5. William L. Yancey, Ambrose Dudley Mann, and Pierce A. Rost.

CHAPTER IV

3. Long prior to the fall of Fort Sumpter [*sic*] on the 13th of April, 1861, the commencement of actual hostilities, a great effort had been made by the leaders of the secession movement to assimilate the revolution they were about to inaugurate, to the revolution of our ancestors, which established American independence. Our pretended grievances were summed up in imitation of the Declaration of Independence. Young Patrick Henrys sprung up in every county, and appeals to the patriotism of the people were made which far excelled all the powers of eloquence ever displayed by "the forest-born—Demosthenes." Many young orators, who had never before appeared upon the stump, made such strained efforts, that the hearer was irresistibly reminded of the young Shanghai rooster, so common in this country, that crows so hard, that he seems to be in imminent danger of crowing himself out of his knee joints!

Unfortunately these appeals to the people sent thousands of the brave young men of the South to the field, who never returned to their once happy homes. Instances might be enumerated of the many unfortunate poor widows, who thus lost all of their sons; and were thrown upon the cold charities of the rich, for a bare maintenance. Some young ladies were found simple-minded and silly enough to send aprons and dolls to those young men whose circumstances compelled them to remain at home, till forced off by that terrible engine of military despotism known as the "Conscript Law." An impression was made upon our young men that unless they took part in the revolution they would be regarded as the Tories of the Revolutionary War. This had a powerful effect upon the brave and impetuous youth of our country. The recollection of the success which had always attended our arms in all the wars in which we had been engaged—the revolutionary war—the war with England of 1812, and the Mexican war—inspired the belief that we could not engage in any war without success. The masses of the people did not stop to compare the resources of the different sections of the Union; nor pause to reflect upon the inequality of the conflict into which we were about to be plunged. Many of our young men are always ready for a fight, and when it is "a free fight" some care but little upon which side they are engaged, so that they are "in."

4. Another great delusion disseminated among our people was, the great superiority of our Southern soldiers to our Northern men. It was often said, that "one Southern man could whip half a dozen Yankees." This opinion has been formed from the appearance of the many delicate clerks and collectors who had been sent out by their houses, drumming and

collecting through the South, and who were more frequently met with the pistol and bowie-knife, than the ready money. It manifested a great ignorance of the history of the Northern Nations of Europe for bravery and endurance when compared with the more Southern tribes. This delusion has already been dispelled, especially in regard to the frontier men of the North-west. They seemed to be ignorant of the fact, that in the United States army would be met some of the best men of every civilized nation. It is undoubtedly true, that for impetuous bravery—the daring charge and dashing onset, the Southern soldier stands unsurpassed before the world; and in a war with any foreign nation, would do prodigies of valor, unequalled upon the pages of military warfare; but when fighting against the old flag, under which our fathers had fought and bled—endeared to them by all the associations of the past, and hopes of the future—under which Washington, Lafayette, Montgomery, Gates, Green, Jackson and Taylor had fought—that waved at King's Mountain, Gilford Courthouse, Camden, Eutaw, Cow-pens, Moultrie and Yorktown—against brethren of the same race, and often of the same family; whilst the hearts of many of them were never in the cause in which they were enlisted, it is wonderful that they displayed the heroism exhibited at Manassas, Leesburg, Belmont and Shiloh.

5. Direct Trade with Europe, was a favorite theme of indulgence by the secession leaders. Charleston, Savannah and New Orleans were to rival Boston, New York and Philadelphia. We were going to sell everything very high and buy everything very cheap. Our opponents told us, "we will have direct trade with Europe. Our commerce will flourish; industry will be amply rewarded. Our revenue from imports, instead of going into the treasury as now, to be expended in warring upon us, will be diverted into the Southern treasury to support our own friendly government. We will then be relieved of our vassalage in New York, and other Northern cities, which now subjects us to a monetary panic whenever there is a stringency in the New York money market, which began to be felt before the late Presidential election. In the present deranged state of the cotton market, we are experiencing the evil effects of this commercial dependence on New York. In our Southern Confederacy we will be free from all this. In withdrawing *we lose nothing and save all.*" This delusion led many into the snare. Loud expressions were heard of the great value that would attach to land and negroes in the event of secession, and some were heard to say that they would sell their lands and negroes at half price if Mississippi did not secede; but Mississippi did secede, and instead of land and negroes advancing, neither will bring half the price even in the rag money currency of

the State, and if put up for gold and silver, they would not bring one-fourth their usual price. The cities that were to rival the cities of the North have languished every day they have been out of the Union. Instead of selling everything very high and buying everything very cheap, we buy everything very high and sell everything very cheap; instead of direct trade with Europe, we have had no trade at all. We have no commerce; no revenue from our imports; no rewards for our industry—none of the golden promises of the secession leaders have been realized. Immediately after the secession of South Carolina, cotton dropped down to six cents, and we are told that it was owing to "a stringency in the New York money market!"

Financial men saw the dark storm that was approaching. That unfailing indication of the condition of the nation, the money market—the pulse of a nation—was disturbed; but its disturbance was produced by the secession of South Carolina. We were told that a sudden decline in cotton was produced by a stringency in the New York money market, but we were not told what produced that stringency. The first manifestation of any disturbance in England is exhibited by the money market—the decline in Consols. So in France, in the decline of the Rents—the pulse of the nation rises or falls, in proportion to the healthfulness of the nation; so it was with the money market of the United States, after the secession of South Carolina in December, 1860.

CHAPTER V

These delusions and many others—some of which were most preposterous, such as that unless secession succeeded the negroes would be emancipated and the poor would have to do the menial services of the slaves—were most artfully, ingeniously and sometimes powerfully impressed upon the people.

I always found a very strong attachment to the Union among the old men of the State. An incident of the canvass will forcibly illustrate this fact. At a precinct in the county of Attala, known as Crim's Box, where my opponent and myself were to address the "sovereigns" on the day of the Convention Election, I observed an unusual number of very old men, some of whom had fought in the revolutionary war. Seeing a fallen pine near the stand, I requested them all to take their seats together upon the log. In the course of my remarks I took occasion to paint the scenes of the revolution—the struggles of our forefathers—their hardships and sufferings—the character and conduct of Washington and his com-patriots—the principal battles and other reminiscences. When the polls were opened they all went up and voted together, and all voted the Union Ticket but one.

The Convention of Mississippi assembled at Jackson on Monday, January 7th, 1861. I had been requested by several members of the convention, before the hour of meeting, to call a conservative member to the Chair, in order that an organization as favorable as possible to the Union cause might be effected. This was anticipated however by an ultra Secessionist, who called the Convention to order more than thirty minutes before the usual time for such bodies to convene, and nominated the Hon. H. T. Ellett, an ultra member, as temporary Chairman. . . . [6]

The sound of the fife and drum was heard in every direction; the hotels were crowded to overflowing; the bars did an extremely flourishing business. Notwithstanding the unfavorable indications, and outside pressure, I determined to make a last effort for the old Flag, more as a protest than with any hope of defeating the passage of the ordinance, by a speech before the Convention, which I will submit to the reader as a part of the history of the times.[7]

CHAPTER VI

. . . "Mr. President: Your ears have been lulled by the cry of peaceable secession; but, Sir, there is no such thing as peaceable secession. It is revolution that you are inaugurating—a revolution that may not terminate before the heel of some military despot is placed upon the necks of the people. Peaceable secession! Sir, if ever the sun of this Union goes down, it will sink beneath the horizon bathed in the blood of thousands and tens of thousands of the best men in the country. This day, which has been ushered in with so much enthusiasm, by the assembled thousands here, I fear, will prove the darkest day that ever broke upon the State. Let us pause and reflect, before we plunge into the dark abyss now opening at our feet. Let us carefully consider the consequences that will surely follow the passage of the Ordinance of Secession. We go off to ourselves, without an army, without a navy, without a single vessel, and without any means of constructing a navy, even if one could be built in a day with the proper resources. We assume the responsibilities of a new government at a time when our State Treasury is bankrupt, and when the State herself cannot possibly borrow a dollar in the

6. Wood then prints the prayer that opened the convention. He also goes through the resolutions concerning the convention's committee structure, and he cites the debates and his side in the debate.

7. I print only the most important part of his long and rambling speech before the convention.

money markets of the world. When our State has neither money nor credit, how is she to carry on an independent government, either by herself or with the few States that are expected to go with her? Only by TAXATION. And, Sir, although the people may rest satisfied for a while, under the novelty of the new order of things, when you lay the iron hand of taxation upon them, and the millions of dollars in hard cash are wrung from the tax-payers, by the tax-collectors, a voice of indignation will rise in thunder tones from the masses of the people, which will shake the highest seats of the rulers of the contemplated Confederacy. Arms and munitions of war must be provided, and large bodies of men equipped for military service. The extensive military preparations now making, and the organizations of companies now going on, show, conclusively, that those who are urging this revolution onward, do not expect it to be peaceable. They smell the battle afar off, and are marshaling their forces. Complicated questions of boundaries; of the right to navigate the Mississippi river and its numerous tributaries; of duties on imports, exports, and many other equally difficult and perplexing questions, would soon rob secession of its peaceable character, and light up the flames of civil war. And what right have we to expect that the Government of the United States will peaceably permit its own dissolution? . . . [8]

"This, Sir, is not the only delusion resting upon this body. We have been taught to believe that 'Cotton is King,' and that England and France will be forced to intervene in our behalf. I fear, Sir, that this is a delusion. I have no confidence in foreign aid. The sympathies, not only of England and France, but of the civilized world will be against us. They are opposed to the institution which underlies this revolution. The great danger is, if our cotton is withheld to force them to our assistance, that when we again offer it to them, they will tell us they do not want it; that they have made other arrangements. It may cause them a temporary inconvenience, but their gratification at the dissentions in our republic, with the hope of an extinction of slavery, will rather induce them to forego that inconvenience, than to intervene in our favor. We cannot control the commerce of the world. It will seek its wants and necessities in other climes and countries.

"Mr. President: I do not intend to discuss this important subject further. You and I, and all the members present, have already fully discussed, before the people, all of the points involved. Let me only warn you and this Convention, that if Secession is carried out, there will be nothing but ruin and desolation follow in its course—war, war, inevitable war, the

8. Next Wood talks about the so-called right of secession and, like many other unionists, rejects it out of hand. He continues with comments on foreign commerce.

depreciation of every species of property, stop laws, and bankrupt laws, the neglect of agricultural pursuits, the collection of large bodies of troops, the diseases which will necessarily spread among them; and before the last act in the great drama is closed, not only war, but 'war, pestilence and famine' will spread over the land in a scene of devastation, desolation and destruction.

"The last words I have to say are, that posterity will hold you, Sir, and this Convention, responsible for the act which you this day commit."

CHAPTER VII

Seeing that the Convention had made up their minds to pass the Secession Ordinance I determined to take no further part in their proceedings, although I remained at the Capitol for ten days after the passage of the Ordinance. After my return home, I addressed a note to Mr. J. L. Power, the Reporter of the convention, requesting the publication of my speech, as a part of the proceedings, in order that my protest might go to the public, with the proceedings of the Convention, and received this reply . . . [9]

I was urged by many old friends, some of whom had held high positions in the United States Government, to sign the Ordinance, for the sake of unanimity. Indeed, I was told that it was "a second Declaration of Independence," and that my name should be upon it, to hand down to my children. My reply was, that I would not sign what my conscience and judgment did not approve; and that I would rather hand down to my children the remembrance of the fact that I was the member of the Mississippi State Convention who refused to sign the Ordinance of Secession. . . . [10]

CHAPTER VIII

. . . "Mr. Wood assailed many of the propositions enunciated by the gentleman from Harrison.[11] The greatest work, said he, that could be submitted to man is the building up of a good government. You are now trying a second experiment. No spot on the face of the earth now affords

9. Power promised that Wood's speech would be published, but it never was.

10. Wood then prints the ordinance of secession and the names of those who signed it.

11. Wood next prints part of the deliberations of the second session of the Mississippi secession convention beginning on March 29, 1861, and interjects his own views, especially on the issue concerning how the people of Mississippi were to ratify the convention's act of secession.

evidence of the perpetuity of the republican system; and he stated as his humble conviction that unless a course is adopted that will fasten the new government in the affections of the people, it would be of short duration. He thought that the delegates to Montgomery should be the first to desire their actions should be submitted to the people for ratification. There was no pressing necessity for the Constitution to be hastily ratified by this Convention. The very fact that this is a debatable question, proves that it should be submitted to the people. As a naked question, he believed that this Convention had the power, without the right—the power that the despot would exercise. . . ."[12]

I am thus particular in alluding to the proceedings of the Convention upon this subject, as it evidences the fact of the great distrust of the people, on the part of the Convention. Ever since the commencement of the Secession movement, a manifest disposition has been exhibited to hastily seize the reins of power, and never to let them loose again.

My ordinance was rejected, as I anticipated. The vote being 23 to 56— See Journal of March Session, page 34. The Constitution was then ratified by the Convention, only seven of us finally voting against it. A feeling of great indignation was manifested, in some parts of the State, in consequence of this flagrant outrage upon the rights of the people; but the tocsin of war had been sounded, and a military enthusiasm enkindled, which soon suppressed all exhibitions of feeling, save a loyalty to Jeff. Davis and the Southern Confederacy.

CHAPTER IX

I have heretofore made some allusions to the influence of Southern Democracy in causing the calamities which have befallen our country. The subject deserves a more particular notice. Thirty-four years ago S. S. Prentiss predicted what would be the result of the course pursued by that party. . . . [13]

Ever since the time when that purely patriotic citizen of Mississippi, whose bright genius has cast a halo of glory over the State, warned those

12. Wood then quotes from a speech of Gov. John J. Pettus of Mississippi and states that even Pettus knew it was dangerous to "alienate the affections of the people from this Government." He then presents his own ordinance, which called for popular ratification of secession.

13. Wood prints a speech of Sen. Sergeant S. Prentiss from Mississippi, which revealed the senator's fear that southern Democrats would lead the people to disunion.

"foolish men" of the awful consequences of their madness and folly, the political demagogue, under the guise of Democracy, who has been the loudest in his denunciation and vituperation of every person and thing north of Mason and Dixon's line, has been seen to receive the most rapturous applause of the people. Some of these reptiles have thus crawled up to the apices of the topmost pyramids in the State.

A very few individuals are often enabled to control the people of a State. The leaders about the Capitol keep the county leaders "posted," and they have been in the habit of haranguing the people upon Court days, at Barbecues, and upon such other occasions as the "dear people" can be conveniently assembled together. The County papers have been another very efficient means of diffusing the principles of the glorious Southern Democracy. A Democratic County paper has been considered as an "institution" as necessary to the prosperity of one of our towns as a hotel or retail grocery. Among the many misfortunes that have befallen our country, it is some little consolation to know that we have been deprived of the means of publishing these pests to the public welfare. When the pitiless storm of misfortune, which has burst with all its fury upon our devoted country, drenching our land with grief and sorrow, shall have passed over us, it is to be hoped that we shall live in a purer political atmosphere, free from the corrupting influence of political demagogues and partisan papers, whose chief aim, for years, seems to have been to undermine and destroy the best government upon earth.

CHAPTER X

The leaders of the Secession party, well knowing the strong attachment to the Union of their Fathers, among the people, and the horror with which they had viewed the monster Disunion, devised a scheme of breaking the subject more softly to their ears, by establishing a co-operation party. They professed to be violently opposed to separate State Secession, although their great leader, Mr. Yancey, had boldly announced the doctrine at Montgomery. They were for having a great Southern Confederacy of fifteen States; and many earnestly contended that Southern Illinois would join the list. New Mexico and Southern California would surely follow, and an empire was to be established, which our Statesmen delighted to compare, in extent, with combined empires in Europe. Old Virginia, the mother of States and Statesmen, the blue hills and sweet vallies of Kentucky, the mountainous regions of Tennessee and North Carolina (the Switzerland of America) the cotton and sugar regions of the Gulf States, the great State of Texas,

together with Arkansas and Missouri, were only parts of the great Southern
Confederacy. A question of serious difficulty arose in the minds of our
great Statesmen, upon which very able arguments were adduced, both
in the affirmative and negative, viz: Whether we should admit into our
Confederacy any of the free States of the North? Many contended that as
Southern Illinois was certain to go with us, it would be better not to divide
the State, but take in the whole, as it would be convenient to bring over
to the Northern part of the State, the large number of fugitive slaves who
had been for years collecting in those portions of her Majesty's dominions
known as Upper and Lower Canada. Others were still more comprehensive
and statesmen-like in their views, and contended that it would not be too
great a degree of condescension if we should admit, but not exactly upon an
equal footing, that extensive territory known as the Northwestern States,
although they were engaged in that homely occupation of raising meat
and bread, nothing doubting, that in process of time the whole region of
country, formerly known as the United States, would one by one gravitate
towards the Southern Confederacy, and become an integral part thereof,
excepting always that puritanical portion known as New England, which,
with imprecations deep and loud, they swore never should be admitted
into the Southern Confederacy. Such speculations as these were rife in the
minds of some who had held high positions in the country. It is deeply
to be regretted that the fond hopes and expectations of some, who had
been Union men in principle, such as the Vice-President of the Southern
Confederacy, (alas! for the frailty of human nature and the love of office,)
were to be so soon and so sadly disappointed.

The professed principles and speculations of the co-operationists presented, however, a magnificent theme for the stump orator to illustrate and
enlarge upon, before an excited audience; and many more were induced to
vote the Secession ticket, in that disguised form, who were utterly opposed
to separate State Secession; and were never more ready for a fight than when
called a disunionist.

Any one who has been a close observer of the Secession movement, could
not fail to see the artifices resorted to by the leaders to urge the people along
into the channel, by some means or other, in order to get the power out of
their hands. Having once seized the reins of power, they knew that they
would be enabled to drive them to the last extremity, rather than abandon
their nefarious purposes.

When the co-operationists met in the different State Conventions, they
proved to be the most ultra Secessionists. The reins were then in their own
hands, and they could do as they please; and they never intended to give
back to the people the power to control their actions, as was proven by

their refusal to permit them to vote upon the ratification or rejection of the Constitution. They knew that the effort that had been made in 1851, to stifle their love for the Union, had proven a failure, although led on by military chieftains fresh from the battle fields of Mexico, and now no means was spared to get at least the appearance of consent, upon the part of the people, to carry out their purposes. The true intention of the co-operationists proved to have been, not so much that of co-operating with other States and Territories, in forming the great Southern Confederacy, as to co-operate among themselves in getting the high offices in the new Government. By co-operation, this man who never could have attained to the high position of President of the United States, might get to be President of part of the United States, and that certainly would be better than never to be President at all; by co-operation that man who had never been enabled to obtain a seat in the Congress of the United States, might be enabled to obtain a seat in the Confederate Congress, and that would certainly be much better than never to have been honored with a seat in Congress at all; and by co-operation the other man who has been all his life fondly hoping for the happy period to arrive, when he would be honored with the high position of Envoy extraordinary and Minister plenipotentiary to the Court of St. James, or St. Cloud, but whose sterling merits and high qualifications have been so frequently and so unjustly overlooked, now sees his way clearly and speedily, into the honored presence of her Royal Majesty for Napoleon III. Take out from the leaders of the army of the Southern Confederacy all of appointed and disappointed office-holders and office-seekers, and there would scarcely be enough left, if fully supplied with artillery, to stop the course of the defenseless "Silver Wave" in any attempt she might have made to pass the city of Vicksburg. Seriously, this rapacious hunt after office has been one of the worst features in the Secession movement. Thousands upon thousands have prostituted their principles, and gone into the army for no other purpose than the gratification of avarice or ambition; while as many others have been compelled to go for a livelihood. For the latter, there is a ready apology, but for the former there is no extenuation. Upon a final reckoning, the righteous judgment of an outraged community will demand equal and distributive justice to all. The verdict of the country will be, "Let justice be done, though the Heavens fall."

CHAPTER XI

I assumed the position, that the election of no man, constitutionally chosen to the high office of President or Vice-President of the United States, was a sufficient cause for any State to separate from the Union. We ought to stand by and aid still, in maintaining the Constitution of the country. To make a point of resistance to the Government, to withdraw from it, because a man has been constitutionally elected, puts us in the wrong. We went into the election as one people, and took the chances of electing our candidate, and then to refuse to abide by the result, was unfair and dishonorable.

But it was said that Mr. Lincoln's policy and principles were against the Constitution, and that if he carried them out, it would be destructive of our rights. We should not have anticipated a threatened evil. If he had violated the Constitution, then it would have been time enough to hold him accountable. . . . [14]

With such manifestations of joy, as these, the most ultra Secessionists hailed the election of Lincoln and Hamlin, whom they had just previously denounced as the blackest Republicans and Abolitionists of the North. The cause of their joy is plain. They had long desired a dissolution of the Union, and now they were certain they had a pretext, which would be sufficient, with the people, to carry out their purposes. Some of the members of the South Carolina and Mississippi Conventions boasted that they had been Secessionists for thirty or forty years! It was, however, far beneath the dignity of those wise, far-seeing and venerable statesmen, to condescend to designate the particular cause or question, whether the protection of slavery, in the Territories or out of the Territories, or what other question, that at that early day, so justly entitled them to the merit of being the founders of the Secession party. The truth is, there was no cause then with them, or anybody else, for Secession, and the claim of those gentlemen was only antedated about a quarter of a century, to give age to their opinions, believing, no doubt, that their opinions, like their beverages, would improve with that commendable qualification.

It is true, that there had been, in the State of South Carolina, a deep-seated dissatisfaction with the general Government, since she had been humored with the compromise of 1832, of the nullification question, and she had been fretting and pouting like a spoiled child, upon every occasion she could find, likely to cause a disturbance in the family. Instead of the maternal tenderness exhibited towards that refractory child of the Union, upon that memorable occasion, if she had been given a smacking then, it would have proven far more conducive to the peace and quietude of the family, than anything else. But, having been so long humored in her

14. Wood next talks about and quotes headlines from secessionist newspapers that deplored Lincoln's election.

tantrums, she believed she could take almost any step, however shocking to decency or common sense, and Uncle Sam dare not say a word.

When the result of the Presidential election was known, if it had been intimated that the State which had been known as the Harry Percy of Chivalry—the game cock of the South,—should live in the Union under the administration of such a "*Monstrum horrendum*" as a big, Black Republican, a rope or a revolver would have been unanimously adjudged the proper desert of the unfortunate wretch who dared such an insinuation.

Before any of the other States had time to assemble their Conventions, the State of South Carolina was clean out of the Union. She passed the Ordinance of Secession, unanimously, on the 20th of December, 1860; one hundred and sixty nine members voting. The next State was Mississippi, on the 9th of January, 1861. . . . [15] The effect of the secession of South Carolina was very great in all of the Southern States, known as the Gulf States. Many of those States were settled by citizens of South Carolina, and a feeling of sympathy and State pride induced almost all of such persons readily to endorse the Secession movement. With but few exceptions, whenever a South Carolinian was met, he was sure to be found a Secessionist. It is a remarkable fact, however, that whenever a South Carolinian was found who was a Union man, he was the most thorough going and zealous Union man in the country; and the same may be justly said of those who have stood firmly in Mississippi, for the Union, throughout the whole Secession movement. For nearly two years they have endured a burthen of taunts, indignities, and opprobrious epithets, which have been heaped upon them by the dominant party—the sons of some of them have been arrested for treason, for expressing their feelings of indignation at the passage of the Conscript law—they have been continually reproached for "not going to war"—such a one "ought to be hung," has been constantly ringing in their ears—the term "abolitionist" has greeted them upon the corners of the streets—craven cowardice, the most degrading charge to a Southern man, has been imputed to them; even their families have not escaped the criminating reflections that have been so freely indulged by their Secession neighbors. It has often been exceedingly difficult for those in whom they had confidence, to restrain the indignation of the people at the countless oppressions under which they labored; and nothing but their defenceless condition, being deprived of arms or ammunition, and the means of obtaining them, has held the people in submission to the tyrannical military despotism of the so-called Southern Confederacy. The

15. There follows a listing by date of when each state of the lower South seceded.

fear alone of actual suffering among their families, for the necessaries of life, has kept back thousands, whose impulses would have led them to rush across the lines, and rally under the old Flag, under which their fathers fought and bled.

If the authors of our calamities, particularly in South Carolina, were the only sufferers from Secession, it would not be so much to be deplored, but the innocent, as well as the guilty, have had to suffer.

CHAPTER XII

One of the greatest difficulties to be encountered in eradicating the Secession sentiment, is with those who religiously believe that Secession is right. These men are honest in their belief, that Providence is on their side, and whether in victory or defeat, they have an ample fund of scriptural quotations at hand, with which either to rejoice or to cheer up the weak and faint-hearted. Within the last few years a set of political parsons have seized upon the subject of slavery as a Divine institution, and have rivaled the most fanatical enthusiasts of the North in their extreme views and zealous exertions. Should a Southern man dare to express the opinions of the framers of the Constitution of the United States, with whom slavery was considered an irremediable evil, he was a fit subject for the end of a rope, on the side of a black-jack. The evil produced by these political preachers illustrates the wisdom of our ancestors in drawing a line of separation between Church and State, for, whenever they have meddled with the affairs of our Government, either as Know-nothings or Secessionists, the result has been marked by the bloody foot-prints of their deluded followers.

If ever, in the Providence of God, it should devolve upon the President of the United States, in "the enforcement of the laws," to deal out even-handed justice to all, it would be "a consummation devoutly to be wished," that this peculiar class of individuals, whose holy calling presumes that they are always ready to be received "into Abraham's bosom," should be the first subjects of the law of treason.

Another misfortune, about as great as the horde of political parsons, with which the South has been cursed, which led more men astray, and turned the heads of more political aspirants and ambitious demagogues than any other event of the revolution, was the battle of Bull Run. If all the buffalo bulls of the Northwestern prairies could have been gathered into one herd, and all the panic-stricken Yankees in McDowell's army placed in their front, and chased throughout the extensive regions of the cotton Confederacy, it would have occasioned a degree of amusement and gratification, not exceeding that occasioned by the news of the victory which crowned their arms upon the banks of the aforesaid classical stream.[16] Although repeatedly told by the writer, and a few others, that it would have no effect upon the ultimate result, and only occasion a greater slaughter of our people, the masses were too intensely excited to listen to anything short of the extermination of the invaders—the capture of Washington—the reclamation of Maryland—the invasion of the North—the fall of Philadelphia, New York, and Boston, and the speedy "conquering a peace."

The calm, cool, calculating politician, who had cautiously looked on the contest, with nervous anxiety for an opportunity on either side, and it was no great matter on which, to distinguish himself, now thought he saw plainly the star that was to lead him on to fortune and to fame. The thunders of Bull Run had completely cleared away the mist that had enveloped his eyes. The grievous oppressions to which the young South had so meekly submitted for so many years of patient endurance, rose up afresh to his mind. His indignation was boiling hot to flesh his maiden sword in the cowardly carcass of some accursed Yankee. He longed for the time when he should

> "Fall like amazing thunder on the casque
> Of yon adverse pernicious enemy,"

His only serious difficulty was, whether as commander of a regiment, a brigade, or a division, Nature had designed him for the field; and to decide this perplexing mental controversy, "on to Richmond" was his rapid move. Soon clothed with a commission from His Excellency, the President of the Confederate States of North America, he returns in hot haste to the people to raise a company or regiment, with full assurance that he will soon be promoted to a brigadier. He calls meetings of the people and addresses them—his excited manner and nervous actions speak plainly that,

> "I am the rider of the wind,
> The stirrer of the storm,
> The hurricane I left behind
> Is yet with lightning warm."

He takes peculiar pleasure, in his speeches, in arraying the Secessionist against the Union man, and very wisely insinuating that certain individuals

16. Union general Irwin McDowell.

"ought to be hung as high as Haman." When his company is made up and ordered to rendezvous at some particular place, he almost always finds important business for the company to attend to in the region round about home. His health not infrequently gives way, under the arduous labors he has to endure for the glorious cause, and he becomes a prey to disease. When a great battle is "imminent," he is sure to be about home, but deeply laments his misfortune in not having the opportunity of correcting the gross errors committed by the commanders. Had he been there, things would have been otherwise. His criticisms are replete with learned historical illustrations. Caesar nor Hannibal, Napoleon nor Wellington, was ever so familiar with strategical movements. Had his advice been followed, Washington would have been taken long ago; the Potomac, as well as the Ohio, would have been crossed, and their army quartered upon the enemy's country, and they would have been made to feel the desolating effects of the war.

These vipers, in their mean endeavors to crawl up to some high places, have done more to poison the minds of the ignorant and credulous, than any other class of creatures that have cursed the Southern country. Really, regardless of the merits of the controversy, and generally too ignorant to understand the points of difference in the political questions involved, the only inquiry is, how can I make the most out of the troubles of the country? They seek alone to promote their own selfish purposes. Were they north of their lines, they would be equally clamorous for the Union, and for no better purpose.

There is but one other class of beings, engaged in the war, that sinks lower in the scale of human depravity than the one referred to, and that is the speculating extortioner. Whilst the political demagogue seeks to elevate himself, he does not even seek to raise himself above the low level of groveling gain. With wolfish relish, he laps the blood of the helpless innocent, and with tiger ferocity, he plunders the afflictions of age. The cries of the widow and orphan make no more impression upon his callous heart than the rattle of his dollars would upon the cold tombstone of the dead.

CHAPTER XIII

To any one who was a participator in the movements preceding secession, it is obvious, that if the people had believed that they did not possess the right of secession, but only the common right of revolution, they would never have given their authority to their leaders to inaugurate war. If the great speech of Daniel Webster, delivered in the Senate of the United States, on the 20th of January, 1830, in reply to Mr. Hayne, in which he so clearly refutes the South Carolina doctrine, had been generally read and understood by the people, they would never have voted for secession. It was attempted by the leaders to draw a distinction between the right to nullify and the right to secede, but the South Carolina doctrine of Mr. Calhoun and Mr. Hayne, was the foundation of the whole movement. . . . [17]

If the people of the United States only clearly understood the structure of our government, as it was intended to have been understood by its framers, there would never be any danger of its dissolution.

CHAPTER XIV

How any people could expect that Providence would favor a cause that had to be bolstered up by hypocrisy, dissimulation, duplicity, and even downright falsehood, is beyond the comprehension of any ordinary capacity to perceive, or even the brightness of genius to penetrate. The greatest leaders of the movement have used the utmost deception with the people, and in the most artful and fascinating manner. They seem to possess the

"Smooth dissimulation skilled to grace,
A devil's purpose with an angel's face."

Their daily conversation has been a tissue of the most disgusting fabrications. When in the presence of Union men, however, they frequently trim their conversation accordingly; and even men of Union sentiments, when in the presence of their Secession neighbors, have been compelled to resort to the same hypocritical course of duplicity, joining in with their tirade of extravagant falsehoods and mendacious exaggerations. Their only excuse is, perhaps, that it is better to follow the advice of Solomon, and "answer a fool according to his folly," for he tells us very truly, that "though thou shouldst bray a fool in a mortar among the wheat, with a pestle, yet will not his foolishness depart from him."

There is one subject in which there has been more falsehood and misrepresentation, perhaps, than upon any other, and that is the popular vote of the Seceding States. After many calls for the popular vote of Louisiana, it was finally published, and turned out to be a Secession majority of only about three thousand—not as many as there were voters in the

17. Wood then gives an abstract from Daniel Webster's famous speech.

State who did not vote at all, and who would have, no doubt, voted against Secession. In Mississippi, the papers represented that the majority was thirty thousand for Secession, when, in fact, if the votes of those who did not vote at all were counted with those who voted the Co-operation ticket, it will be found that the Separate State Secession ticket was in the minority; and it was only by a betrayal of the people that the Secession Ordinance was passed.

During the whole progress of the war, Mississippi has been represented, by the Secession papers, as a unit, when, in truth, in the central county of the State,—"the free State of Attala,"—during the whole contest, the strongest Union sentiment has prevailed; a sentiment that has been bold and out-spoken, despite the taunts and threats of the party in power.

The Southern ladies have been represented as unanimous for Secession. This is equally untrue. The following dialogue between an enroller of the conscripts and a lady, as related by himself, is a pretty fair sample of the sentiments of some, at least, in the country:

Enroller. Good morning, madam; where is your husband this morning?

Lady. He is over in Mr. Jones's field working out his corn. He promised to tend it for him while he has gone to the war.

Enroller. How old is your husband, madam?

Lady. He is somewhere between forty-two and forty-four. I don't know exactly, how old.

Enroller. You are certain he is over thirty-five?

Lady. Yes sir, he is; but what are you asking me such questions for?

Enroller. I am sent out by the authorities, madam, to enrol the conscripts between eighteen and thirty-five years of age.

Lady. I thought you were out on some such business as that. You are sent out by old Pettus, I reckon. If I had my way with him, I would souse his head in a whiskey barrel, and hold it there til he was drowned—an old villain, he is sending off all the men to the war, and leaving us poor women and children here to starve.

Enroller. If you did not souse it too deep, madam, I expect Governor Pettus would as soon have his head in a whiskey barrel as anywhere else.

Lady. I would souse it just deep enough to drown him: that's how deep I would souse it.

If the fate of the Secession leaders could be determined by a jury of the mothers of the young men, whose lives have been sacrificed in this most unnecessary, unnatural and unholy war, they would have about as much chance of an acquittal as the most obnoxious specimen of the canine race, upon proof positive of the slaughter of an innocent flock of sheep.

CHAPTER XV

The ardent desire of every American patriot should be to see a re-union in feeling among the people of the United States. Upon no other basis can our country ever be restored to its former prosperity and happiness. Now that the tocsin of war will soon be hushed, and the great family quarrel terminated, all eyes should be turned to peace and reconciliation. As we all have to live together in the same family, let us live together in peace and tranquility. Let us forgive and forget. Let us approach each other in the spirit of conciliation and friendship. Let all those who have been bound together by the mystic ties of brotherhood, renew their covenants, and meet as friends. Let those of extreme views agree to disagree, and bury their differences. Let each section say to the other, we will

> "Be to your faults a little blind
> And to your virtues very kind."

Let us rather contemplate the good, than the evil, that may result from this deplorable warfare. When re-united our government will stand upon a firmer basis than ever. The strength and power of the nation has been fully tested, and proven equal to any emergency. When re-united and harmonious, we will be the greatest military and maritime power on the globe. Uncle Sam will never be caught napping again.

Our navy has exhibited a power that has astonished all Europe, and now threatens to snatch the trident from old Neptune himself. What the boasted mistress of the seas, aided by the brave veterans of the Peninsula and Waterloo, failed to accomplish, the American sailor and soldier has promptly performed. Of our country it may now truly be said, that,

> "America needs no bulwarks,
> No towers along her steep;
> Her march is o'er the mountain-wave,
> Her home is on the deep."

The idea that the South is subjugated, seems to be a great obstacle with many of our people. This is not true. It is not the South that is subjugated, but secession that is subjugated; and no one should rejoice so much in its subjugation as the Union men of the South. They have suffered more, during the progress of the war, than any one else. Whilst the starving process has been going on, the secessionists have combined to starve out the Union men. The power which wealth always gives, has been brought to bear most heavily upon the poorer classes, producing a degree of suffering almost incredible in a country professing to be free. The Union men of the South, instead of being subjugated, have been liberated from the tyranny of contemptible, petty officials, and military despots. A love for the Union should be cherished, and renewed upon all suitable occasions. The fourth of July, and the twenty-second of February, should again be celebrated throughout the length and breadth of the country. With the same feeling that Napoleon embraced the eagles of France, the Old Flag should be hailed by every citizen of the United States. . . . [18]

18. Wood concludes with a poem on patriotism, quotes from Scripture, and a poem on peace.

The Wrongs to Missouri's Loyal People

(Jefferson City, Mo.: privately printed, 1863)

C harles D. Drake (1811–1892) was born in Cincinnati, Ohio, into the family of a famous Ohio and Kentucky physician. Drake served in the U.S. Navy before studying law; he passed the Cincinnati bar in 1833. In 1834 he moved to St. Louis, where he rose in legal circles and became an outspoken antislavery advocate. As a Democrat in the Missouri House in 1860 he fought the state's secession movement. He led the Missouri antislavery movement and in 1865 became vice president of the state constitutional convention that abolished slavery. In 1864 he published a volume of his speeches and pamphlets, *Union and Anti-Slavery Speeches*, which had a visible impact on the unionist cause in Missouri and other border states. He became a power in Republican state politics after the war, and the legislature elected him to the U.S. Senate in 1867.

An ardent pamphleteer and speechifier, Drake's contribution in this volume is his famous speech delivered in Jefferson City on September 1, 1863, in opposition to the continuation of slavery in Missouri. In it he supported the Lincoln emancipation proclamation and used the antislavery cause to force a division between loyal unionists and quasi supporters of the Confederacy. Thus he revealed much about the internal political tension in Missouri. Drake's comments on his border state's horrible guerrilla warfare certainly helped to unite the unionists with the abolition movement. No doubt he expected strong support from the national Republican party.

The only study of his life remains in dissertation form, but details of his political career can be found in works on Missouri wartime politics. See Daniel Drake, *Pioneer Life in Kentucky* (Cincinnati: R. Clarke, 1870); Charles D. Drake, *Union and Anti-Slavery Speeches* (Cincinnati: Applegate and Co., 1864); William E. Parrish, *A History of Missouri, 1860–1875* (Columbia:

University of Missouri Press, 1973); and David D. March, "The Life and Times of Charles Daniel Drake" (Ph.D. diss., University of Missouri, 1949).

* * *

I respond, without hesitation, to your invitation to address you; and as the period of our session must necessarily be brief, I will claim your attention no longer than may be necessary for a sufficient and truthful discussion of the circumstances which have led to our assembling.

Every member of this body will agree with me that those circumstances are extraordinary. From nearly thirty years' intimate acquaintance with Missouri, I am prepared to affirm that no Mass Convention of her people ever assembled under circumstances so extraordinary as those which surround us now. I congratulate you that you have the nerve and the patriotism to come from your distant homes, to show the world that you are able and willing to meet like men the exigency which is upon you.

We are loyal Union men, without any qualification or conditions; and we are, and are not afraid to declare that we are, RADICALS. That is, we are for going to the *root* of the infamous rebellion which has distracted our land for more than two years, and are for destroying that as well as the rebellion. That root is *the institution of* SLAVERY. From it the rebellion sprung, by it has been sustained, in it lives, and with it will die. And until that root is pulled up and destroyed, there is no hope of permanent peace in our country. Therefore I am for pulling it up, every fiber of it. And that is what I understand it is to be RADICAL. By that I stand or fall. The position is one which necessarily admits of no compromise. It is Country or Slavery; and he is a traitor who will compromise between them.

This, in a few words, is what I hold to be our character and position here to-day. I am not afraid to go before the world upon it. I should despise myself, if I took any other. It follows that I am for using every legitimate means to destroy the rebellion, and to crush down, wipe out, and utterly annihilate every development, form, and hue of disloyalty. I would pursue disloyalty through all its infinitive turnings and twistings, and hunt it down, ferret it out, and drive it forth, till throughout our State and our land no disloyal hand should be raised, nor disloyal tongue speak, against our glorious Union.

It follows, further, that I uphold the Proclamation of Emancipation issued by President Lincoln on the 1st of January, 1863. 1 believe that Proclamation to have been a Constitutional exercise of the war power of the

Commander-in-Chief of the Army and Navy of the United States, against public enemies. Were they foreign enemies, no American would question his right to strike at their main support: I affirm his right to strike at any and every support of our domestic enemies—the worse, by far, of the two. And it was a righteous exercise of his power. Slavery assailed the nation of which he was the head, and he was bound to assail Slavery in turn, even to its very death. And I hold that his Proclamation did, in law, free every slave in all the region it covered, on the very day it was issued. Not one of them has been lawfully held in Slavery since that day; nor can one of them, in my opinion, ever be lawfully enslaved again. The Proclamation is irrevocable—as irrevocable as death. No attempt at its revocation can ever make slaves again of those it made free. I accept and uphold it as the end of Slavery in the rebellious States, and I demand its enforcement there by the whole warlike power of the loyal people of the nation, as the only means of restoring abiding peace to our bleeding country.

And holding it right to use every lawful means to overwhelm rebellion, I rejoice that the President is enrolling among our country's armed hosts those whom his proclamation freed. I have no squeamishness about arming the negro. I am no half-breed Unionist, sensitive about seeing white men fight alongside of the "American citizen of African descent." No traitor is too good to be killed by a negro, nor has any traitor a right to insist on being killed by a white man. If for the sake of Slavery he turns traitor, let former slaves be his executioners; it is a just and fit retribution. Disaffection, if not disloyalty, lurks in him who opposes the arming of the negro, let him call himself what he may. For my part, I say to the President, *Go on in this good work, till the army of blacks shall be large enough to hold every rebel in subjection*; and then rebellion is at an end for ever and ever in this land.

I have been thus plain in the expression of these views, because I believe them to be the views heartily entertained by the entire body of the Radical Union men of Missouri. I do not believe there is one such man in our State who does not hold them, and who is not determined to stand by them. They spring from the deepest convictions of stern duty to our country and to the cause of Liberty. With him who opposes them we have nothing to do but to oppose him, and by all rightful means put him down. And that, my friends, is just the work which the Radicals of Missouri have before them.

To us are opposed a portion of the people of Missouri, who style themselves *Conservatives*. And who are they? Let the plain truth be spoken. *They embrace all the disloyal.* Every rebel in the State is with them. Every open or secret Secessionist is with them. Every guerrilla and bushwhacker is with them. Every Copperhead is with them.[1] Every man who opposes the radical policy of the Government against the rebellion is with them. Every man who is under bond for disloyal practices or sentiments, is with them. Every sympathizer with the rebellion is with them. Almost every pro-Slavery man is with them. And nine-tenths of the slaveholders, I believe, are with them. And along with this motley gang of open enemies to, or faint-hearted friends of, the Union cause, are associated just enough of real Union men to save the concern from going down instantly under the weight of its inherent and envenomed disloyalty. Nothing keeps that party alive this day but the presence of those Union men in its ranks, *and the concentration of official patronage and influence, State and National, in their hands*. They are the sugar-coat to the poison-pill which is sought to be administered to the people of Missouri. They alone give character to Conservatism in Missouri. They have suffered themselves to be identified with that class of our population, which would drag Missouri out of the Union in a moment, if they could; and they are supported and urged on by every man in the State whose hand or heart has been or is against his country. I profoundly regret that any of them should ever have been found in such company; but they are there, and must share the fate which surely awaits every disloyal man, whenever Missouri's loyal people can once have access to the ballot-box.

Such, my fellow-citizens, is what you and I know to be the position of parties in Missouri this day. It is not a matter of conjecture or supposition; we *know* it. We know that throughout this whole State there is not one single disloyal man in the Radical ranks. We know that every disloyal man in the State is a Conservative. We know, and desire the whole world to know, that the struggle now going on here, though ostensibly connected with the subject of Emancipation, is, in reality, *between Loyalty and Disloyalty*. The Union cause is at stake again, and the result will determine whether the destiny of this great commonwealth is to remain in the hands of its loyal people. For one, I will struggle, against all odds, in every lawful way, and to the last available moment, before I will yield the control of Missouri to her traitorous inhabitants. No such disgrace and disaster shall befall her, if in my power to prevent it.

As, from the moment of the outbreak of the rebellion, the spirit of shameless lying has characterized those engaged in it, and those who are with it in heart, so now the main weapon of the Conservatives of Missouri against the Radicals is atrocious and persistent falsehood. We are charged, as a body, with purposes which we have never expressed or entertained.

---

1. Border free state Democrats who favored reunion with slavery kept intact.

A strenuous effort has been made, upon the basis of false and wholly groundless imputations, to build up in opposition to us a so-called "Law and Order party;" and "Law and Order meetings" have been held in some counties, at which the Radical Union men have been denounced in the same category with rebels and bushwhackers. We have been stigmatized as "Jacobins;" as "revolutionary factionists;" as "engaged in schemes looking to revolution and violence;" as "in rebellion against the Union and the Constitution;" as "attempting to overthrow the State Government;" as "the party of commotion, and violence, and crime, and anarchy, and disregard of all law:" and "men of all parties, who are in favor of preserving the peace of the State, of enforcing the laws, and protecting citizens from violations of the laws," are invited to attend "Law and Order meetings;" where the "erring brother" returned from "Price's army," the bushwhacker, the Secessionist, the Copperhead and the "Southern sympathizer" skulk in, to help men claiming loyalty pass resolutions defaming and denouncing the Radical Union men of Missouri! It is the old game of the pursued thief crying "stop thief!" There is but one way to meet it, and I have so met it wherever I have spoken in this State. I say here, in the capitol of the State, as I have repeatedly said elsewhere, that whoever, directly or by implication, in speech, in writing, or in print, charges upon the Radical Union party of Missouri any intent of revolutionary violence or unlawful act, utters an atrocious *lie*. I like not to use that word in a public address: but the circumstances, in my opinion, demand it. The true Union men of Missouri have suffered enough of outrage and defamation at the hands of her disloyal people. We ought not quietly to submit any longer to be branded as unfaithful to our obligations as law-abiding and patriotic citizens. We are in heart and soul loyal to our country, to law, to duty, to honor, and to truth: and that is infinitely more than he who has been, in fact or in feeling, with this hell-born rebellion, can say, or in his conscience—if he has any—would dare to say he is.

My friends, that there is excitement among the loyal people of Missouri cannot be denied. The presence here to-day of this large Mass Convention, from every part of the State, affirms it. And there is cause for excitement. The loyal inhabitants of this ill-fated State have suffered more than those of any other State that has adhered to the Union. They have endured every form of aggravated and unmerited wrong. Loyalty to the Constitution and the Union has brought bitterness to them. Their property has been wrested from them by pillaging bands of traitors; their habitations have been given to the flames; they have been murdered in cold blood; and they have been disarmed by the authorities in whose support they were ready and willing to do all and risk all; thereby becoming an easier prey to the blood-thirsty fiends that infest wide districts of our State. Surrounded by treachery the most adroit and cruel; beset by devilish marauders, whose appearance they know not when or where to guard against; trembling by day and by night for their possessions and their families; worn and wasted by robbery, arson, and every outrage; and apparently given over utterly in many places to the grasp of the guerrilla and the bushwhacker; they are, in large portions of the State, harassed, impoverished, and overborne by accumulated calamity, beyond any conception of those who only read the meager reports which find their way into the public journals of the day. Is it a marvel that they are excited? Would it not be wonderful if they were not? What other people ever endured so much without excitement? Shall men sit quietly down and with indifference see themselves despoiled, beggared, and driven forth as fugitives from their homes? Have we got to that point when fathers can look with stoicism upon the slaying of their sons, and wives upon the murder of their husbands? If we have, then has the time come when popular excitement should be put down, as detrimental to the body politic. But that point is not yet reached. Our hearts are not yet callous to our own miseries, or to those of others. We are not able to see why such full, heaping measure of wrong, should be dealt out to loyal people, while the disloyal eat and drink and sleep and work and journey in peace and safety. We do not comprehend why protection should be so fully accorded, as we know it to be, to men of known disloyalty, while the loyal citizen is not only not protected, but has been required to forgo his Constitutional right to bear arms, and to surrender to the military power the weapons upon which alone he could depend for protecting himself, his family, and his property. We do not understand why military officers who pursued the miscreants of blood and plunder with an energy that threatened their extermination, should, without a word of explanation, be relieved of their commands, or mustered out of service, in the midst of their career, and succeeded by men under whose administration the work of spoliation and blood is plied with renewed vigor and success. We do not see why large numbers of men—or indeed any—who at the onset of the rebellion were outspoken and offensive Secessionists, should be appointed to high military positions under the State Government, while men always and unconditionally for the Union are refused such positions, or thrust from them. We do not perceive why men of thorough and consistent loyalty should be arrested and imprisoned by the military authorities, for no assigned cause, or for so small a cause as questioning the wisdom and purity of Governor Gamble's administration and policy; and we resent such arrests, and ought to resent them.[2] And

2. Reference is to Gov. Hamilton Rowan Gamble of Missouri. (Gamble's pamphlet is discussed in "Comments on Southern Unionist Pamphlets Not Selected for Inclusion.")

least of all do we comprehend why the earnest and beseeching appeals of Missouri's loyal and suffering people to the head of the nation for protection, should, apparently, be intercepted or neutralized, and he be made to believe that they proceed from a "pestilent faction," whose aim is to "torment" him. It is because of all these things that there is excitement among the loyal people of Missouri; and I say that they would deserve to suffer on, if they were not excited. But it is not an excitement which threatens or looks to any lawless or reckless proceeding. It asks only redress for incalculable evils, by lawful means; and this Convention is one of the means it takes to make itself heard and felt in quarters where, to hear and feel it, may remove or mitigate the sore trials under which our people have suffered. God grant that those in power may give heed to the voice of Missouri's loyal people, before that burden becomes intolerable!

But not in these matters alone, bitter and hard to be borne as they are, have the loyal Union people of Missouri been wronged. While Conservative policy has left them to be pillaged and murdered, it has gathered its strength and put forth its hand to wrest from them their rightful control in the affairs of Missouri, and to shape the fundamental law and the organic institutions of our State, *according to the behests of her disloyal people.* A coalition has been formed to overthrow the Radical Union party, and deliver the State over to the dominion of that Conservative party, which contains all the disloyalty of Missouri. At the head of that coalition is Governor Gamble; and he is sustained in it by almost every Federal office-holder of any note in the State; by a host of State officers appointed by himself to positions of high importance, civil and military; and by an army of politicians, who are seeking their own advancement, and know that from the Radical Union men of Missouri they have nothing to hope. No such combination has anywhere been made against the loyal people of any loyal State. It is the great feature of the day in Missouri. It is known to every observing man in the State, and it attracts the attention of the country. I wish to portray its course of wrong to Missouri's loyal people. I will do it plainly, fairly, and thoroughly; for I deem it of the greatest moment that, in this State and throughout the loyal States, the position of our affairs, and that of the men who have wronged that people, should be clearly understood. I will endeavor to present a historical summary of the leading facts, in such simple and connected form, that no man can fail to comprehend the whole matter.

The point at which I begin is the accession of Governor Gamble to the Provisional Chief Magistracy of Missouri, on the 31st of July, 1861; for from that time the course of public affairs in this State has connected itself directly with the circumstances of the present period. His first public declaration as Governor was significant of his own opinions and feelings, and of those of the people he was appointed to govern. On the 4th of August, 1861, he issued a proclamation to that people, in which, referring to his appointment, he said it *"would satisfy all that no countenance would be afforded to any scheme or any conduct calculated in any degree to interfere with the institution of Slavery existing in the State, and that to the utmost extent of Executive power that institution would be protected."* Concerning this remarkable declaration two things are apparent: *first,* that Governor Gamble was then, and desired it to be known that he was, a pro-Slavery man, and intended to be a pro-Slavery Governor; and *second,* that he believed the people of Missouri to be a pro-Slavery people; as, in my opinion, a large majority—perhaps seven-eighths—of them then were. This proclamation is the first point to be borne in mind; for it assumes importance in connection with subsequent events.

The sentiments of the people of Missouri in regard to the institution of Slavery underwent a radical change, not many months after that proclamation was issued. They came, by slow but sure degrees, to understand that this rebellion had but one origin and purpose—the aggrandizement of Slavery as a political power, the destruction of the noble Republic inherited from our fathers, and the substitution for it in the South of a great and strange Empire, based on Slavery, and intended for subjugation, piracy, and eventual dominion over this whole continent. When they saw it announced authoritatively by the parties engaged in the work of founding that empire, that they were only consummating what had been in conspiracy for forty years; when they saw that for Slavery the Southern aristocrats were striving to overturn the liberties of the American people, disrupt their Union, and destroy their Constitution; when they perceived that the success of this unexampled and incomparable scheme of outrage, fraud, perjury, and treason, would plunge this nation into perpetual war, and that as long as Missouri should be a slave State, she would be one of the chief victims of that war; when, I say, all these things became manifest to the loyal people of Missouri, a mighty revolution in their opinions concerning Slavery began, and from month to month moved on with tremendous rapidity and force. Never, I will venture to affirm, was there witnessed in this country so marked and swift a revolution of public sentiment in regard to so important a matter. And it was all the more glorious, because it sprung from a glowing and vital patriotism, which rejoiced in any sacrifice of opinion or interest in so holy a cause. While Southern traitors were demanding the emancipation of Slavery from contact with the free institutions of the North, the loyal people of Missouri demanded her emancipation from contact with that institution, which they recognized as aiming fatal blows at all they loved in the country, all they cherished in memory, and all they clung to in hope for themselves and their posterity.

The tendency of the public mind to the removal of Slavery from Missouri received a decided impulse in April, 1862, in consequence of the passage by Congress, upon the recommendation of the President, of a resolution, declaring "that the United States ought to co-operate with any State which may adopt gradual abolishment of Slavery, giving to such State pecuniary aid, to be used by such State in its discretion, to compensate for the inconveniences, public and private, produced by such change of system." The great obstacle to Emancipation in Missouri was the provision in her Constitution, prohibiting the Legislature from passing any law "for the emancipation of slaves, without the consent of their owners, or without paying them, before such emancipation, a full equivalent for such slaves so emancipated." As such compensation from our own resources was an impossibility, the resolution of Congress held out the hope of its coming from the National treasury, and feeling in favor of Emancipation received therefrom increased force and extension.

With the loyal sentiment of Missouri in this transition state from decided pro-Slaveryism to radical anti-Slaveryism, the State Convention assembled on the 2d of June, 1862, on the call of the Governor. On the 7th of that month, Judge Breckinridge introduced into that body an Ordinance proposing a plan of gradual Emancipation, to be submitted to the people for their ratification or rejection, on the first Monday of August, 1864, and supported it in a speech; at the close of which, on motion of Judge Hall, of Randolph, the Ordinance was laid on the table, by a vote of 52 to 19; and to use a well-known and significant expression exultingly applied, at the time, to the act, Emancipation was *killed at the first pop.* The Convention thereby pronounced itself opposed to Emancipation. It was a pro-Slavery body, and of course intolerant. It would hear no more on the subject than what Judge Breckinridge had a parliamentary right to urge, and having heard that, it was prepared to consign his proposition, and did consign it, to a tomb from which there should be no resurrection.[3]

Six days after this act of the Convention, on the 13th of June, Governor Gamble sent a message to that body, relating entirely to its action on Judge Breckinridge's Ordinance. He saw that that action "might be represented as rudely discourteous to the President and Congress," and "would, without doubt, be so misrepresented as to excite a hostile feeling to the State, among all those in authority who favor Emancipation, and thus *injuriously affect the*

3. William B. Hall and St. Louis conservative Samuel M. Breckinridge.

interests of the State." The object of that message, manifest upon its face, was to tell the members of the Convention how they might get out of the twofold scrape they had got into, with the National Government and with their own people. Not a word indicated the least sympathy with emancipation; not a word took off the keen edge of the pro-Slavery proclamation of August, 1861. The Governor was still Missouri's pro-Slavery Governor. Eighteen months of Slavery's war upon the Union had, apparently, implanted in his mind no sentiment against the peculiar institution, here or elsewhere; his sole anxiety was, that there should be "no appearance of a design to treat the offer of the President and Congress with neglect." He suggested, and most truly, that "it was not contemplated by the people, when electing the body, that it should *ever* act upon the subject of Slavery in the State, and therefore such action would be improper;" a reason as valid for all future time, as then. He suggested further, that "the public mind was so agitated already, that proposal of any scheme of Emancipation would produce dangerous excitement; a reason for non-action fully as forcible in June, 1863, as in June, 1862. These suggestions he accompanied with the following remarks: . . . [4]

As I said on a former occasion, so I reiterate now, that this language embodies and affirms the following five propositions:

1. That Emancipation is a social revolution.

2. That it is wholly unconnected with the relations between the State and the general Government.

3. That the people, in choosing the Convention, *never intended or imagined* that it would undertake to act on the subject of Emancipation.

4. That, therefore, the Convention was well warranted in declining to act upon it.

5. That whoever, understanding the principles of our Government, would object to the Convention's so declining to act, is willing *to disregard all principle* to accomplish a desired end.

No grounds could have been assumed more fatal to the propriety or expediency of any action by *that* Convention, at any time, upon the subject of Emancipation. We shall see, as we proceed, how the Governor maintained his own voluntarily-assumed position. . . . [5]

The resolution then copies, word for word, the paragraphs of the Governor's message above cited, except the first and last sentences. On the vote upon the adoption of that substitute, every member who voted for

---

4. Governor Gamble made a speech in which he declined to take up the issue of emancipation.

5. Drake cites a resolution from Hall similar to that of Governor Gamble.

it declared himself emphatically as sustaining the Governor's objections to *any* action by *that* Convention, at any time, on the subject of Emancipation. And yet, one year afterward, Lieut. Gov. Hall was one of the committee that reported an Ordinance of Emancipation for that body to pass; and fifteen of those who voted for his resolution in June, 1832, changed front in June, 1863, and voted for the ordinance then passed by that Convention!

Having seemingly given a death-blow to Emancipation in that body, the Convention adjourned to the 4th day of July, 1863, when, without re-assembling, it was to stand adjourned *sine die*. It declared its work done, and each man went his way, never expecting to return. But the door was left open for the re-assembling of the body, upon the call of the Governor. One man held the power to reinstate at any moment the rule of that Convention; and we shall see how he exercised it.

Five months after the Convention's action upon Judge Breckinridge's proposition, an election was held for members of the General Assembly. They were months of steady and rapid progress in the popular mind in favor of Emancipation. Every day the loyal people of Missouri grew more radical in sentiment against Slavery, their country's enemy. Missouri's Emancipation army was "marching on." The election resulted in the choice of a decided majority of Emancipationists in each House; but unfortunately, *mainly through the machinations of Federal office-holders, high in position in our State*, differences of opinion as to plans of Emancipation were created. The Legislature met on the 29th of December, 1862, and on the following day received the Governor's message. To the surprise of many who remembered his proclamation of August, 1861, and his message to the Convention in June, 1862, he declared himself in favor of Emancipation, and recommended action by the Legislature in relation to it. But he felt the embarrassment produced by the Constitutional limitation upon the power of the Legislature, before referred to. As it was impossible for the State, unaided, to pay any such equivalent for the slaves emancipated as that provision required, the Governor recommended that an act should be passed, providing that the children of slave women, born thereafter, should be born free, and should remain in the custody and under the control of the owner of their mothers until attaining a certain age; which plan, he considered, would require no compensation to be paid to the slaveholder but for "*the diminished value of the female slaves thus rendered incapable of bearing slaves.*" And such an act, so utterly impotent to remove Slavery from our soil,—for, standing by itself, it would never have secured freedom to one-tenth of the children born after its passage,—he intimated might be made to take effect, upon this provision being made by Congress for the small amount of compensation required!

This was gravely proposed by Governor Gamble as a plan of Emancipation; proposed as an "effectual mode of extinguishing the desire of the rebel leaders to have this State within the pretended Confederacy;" proposed as a means of "encouraging immigration from the free States!" It would have been about equal in its effects to dropping a homeopathic pill into the proboscis of a sick elephant. I refer to it, because it is a fact connected with the wrong done to the loyal people of Missouri, which is to be exposed.

The Legislature sat from the 29th of December, 1862, to the 23d of March, 1863, and then adjourned over to the 10th of November next, having done nothing to advance the cause of Emancipation. On the 18th of March, the Senate, by a vote of 17 to 15, passed a Concurrent Resolution, requesting the Governor to call the Convention together at an early period, for the purpose of taking into consideration the subject of Emancipation; every Conservative voting for it, and, aided by two Radicals, passing it. *No attempt was ever made to take up this resolution in the House,* nor could any such attempt have been successful. On the same day, the Senate passed a bill for the election of a new Convention, provided the old Convention did not, before the succeeding first of July, adopt a scheme of Emancipation. Two attempts were made to get this bill up in the House; but it required a two-thirds vote to suspend the rules; and each time the effort failed by a single vote. And with both resolution and bill thus pending in the House, and open for action when the Legislature should re-convene in November, the adjournment took place. But let it not be supposed that the effort in the House to get the bill up, indicated any desire among the Emancipationists there to pass it in the shape in which it came from the Senate. On the contrary, it was perfectly understood that if it had been got up, the provision referring to the old Convention would have been certainly struck out.

The facts which I have thus stated in detail are all necessary to a correct understanding of the case. Let us now examine their bearings upon the main point—the wrong done to the loyal people of Missouri.

I have placed before you Governor Gamble's message to the Convention in June, 1862, and his message to the Legislature in the following December; and how does the matter stand? Why, thus. In his judgment, at the former period, the Convention had no business to act upon Emancipation at all, because the people, in choosing it, never intended or imagined it would undertake to act upon that subject; and therefore the Convention was well warranted in killing Judge Breckinridge's Ordinance; and no one would find fault with it for so doing, unless he was *willing to disregard all principle.* So much for the Convention. Then, as to the Legislature, he finds that it is hampered by a Constitutional provision, which precluded any action on its part, except to declare after-born children of slave mothers to be born free; and that action was suggested to take effect only when Congress should provide the means for paying the owners of the mothers for the injury resulting to them from making the mothers incapable of breeding any more slaves. Here, then, was a Governor declaring himself in favor of Emancipation, and arguing in favor of it to a Legislature that was in favor of it, but almost powerless to do anything for it, which Legislature represented a people that were overwhelmingly in favor of it: what was the course he should have taken? Can any right-minded man hesitate in declaring that, if the Governor was earnestly an Emancipationist, he should and would have pointed the Legislature to some way by which the popular will might be carried into effect? As matters then stood he found the way blocked: why did he ignore the only way that lay wide open—*a direct appeal to* THE PEOPLE, *in the election of a new Convention?*

This is no idle question. Every man knows that he can often judge another as well by what he does not, as by what he does. If a man is drowning, and you do not throw a rope to him when you have one, because you have tried to save him with your hand and failed, would not all the world say, and say justly, that you were indifferent to his fate, or wanted him to drown? And so, when Governor Gamble recommended Emancipation to the Legislature which was powerless, and also held that the Convention ought not to act upon the subject, because it was not elected for any such purpose, and at the same time said not one word in favor of, or in allusion to, that other course which if pursued, would have secured Emancipation, and secured it as the people desired it, and so settled the matter forever: I demand, and have a right to demand, why he preserved that silence? Will it be said it was not his province? He is required by the Constitution of the State to "recommend to their consideration such measures as he may deem necessary and expedient." Will it be said it was not proper for him to suggest that particular mode of action? Why not? He could suggest to the Convention excuses and arguments to sustain their action on Judge Breckinridge's Ordinance; and he could suggest Emancipation to the General Assembly, and argue in favor of it; why not suggest and support the only means of obtaining Emancipation in such way as to satisfy the people? Will it be said that he could not have known that a recommendation from him on that point would have helped the measure? He had no right, for that reason, to withhold it, any more than to refuse to recommend any other measure, because he didn't know whether it would be adopted. But nothing is more certain, than that, *if he had advocated a new Convention, an act providing for it would have been passed.* But here came in a bugbear, that was paraded, during the whole session of the Legislature, to defeat the bill for a new Convention, viz: that if a new Convention should be called, there might arise a conflict between it and the old Convention. But that was impossible, unless Governor Gamble, after the new Convention was authorized should call the old one together again; for it never could meet again, except upon *his* call. And so it was perfectly in his power to have procured a new Convention, and also to have prevented the reassembling of the old one. Why did he not so do? I cannot say upon his authority, for he has never told me, or, so far as I know, told the world. I am forced to conclusions upon the facts as they are known to the public. If my conclusions are unjust to Governor Gamble, I am sorry for it; I do not *seek* them. I say, citizens of Missouri, that I can see no other reason for his utter silence in regard to a new Convention than that he did not intend that the people should have any further opportunity to say or do anything whatever, practically, on the subject of Emancipation. In other words, *he determined, if possible, to wrest the whole matter out of their hands, and force Emancipation upon them through the old Convention*, regardless of their wishes, and in defiance of their sacred right to shape their own fundamental law and their own domestic institutions. This is the only conclusion I can arrive at, and, before God, I believe it to be a right one.

That it was Governor Gamble's purpose so to use the old Convention, is manifest from subsequent events. The Legislature adjourned on the 23d of March, 1863, and on the 15th of April he issued his call for the Convention to meet on the 15th of June, to "consult and act upon the subject of Emancipation of slaves, and such other matters as may be connected with the peace and prosperity of the State." In his judgment, it was "of the highest importance to the interest of the State that some scheme of Emancipation should be adopted."

My friends, looking at this act of the Governor in the light of his previous declarations, and of the then condition of things in the State, I cannot but regard it as one of the most extraordinary exercises of Executive power that have ever fallen under my observation; and as indefensible as it was extraordinary. Why, look at it. Only ten months and two days before the date of that call, he had solemnly declared to the Convention, that the people, in choosing that body, never intended or—mark the word—*imagined* that it would undertake to act on the subject of Emancipation: and now he calls them to do that very thing! He had told the Convention, moreover, that it was justified in killing an Ordinance of Emancipation in the way it did; and yet he calls it together to pass such an Ordinance. He had, with a severity of expression unusual for him, declared, in effect, that no man of principle would have that Convention act on that subject; and yet he convenes it for that very purpose! What does this mean? Was it that the same man speaking in June, 1862, in condemnation of any action by that Convention upon that subject, who, in April, 1863, called them to act upon it? Yes, it was the same Governor Gamble in body, but unfortunately not in mind. A change, a wondrous change, had come over his opinions in that brief time. He no longer saw that it was wrong for that Convention to take Emancipation in hand and act upon it, but contrariwise saw it was right; *though the grounds upon which he had based his previous opinion remained precisely the same.* He no longer held that any man who wanted it so to act was an unprincipled man; for he wanted that very thing. He saw no more that Emancipation was a social revolution, wholly unconnected with the relations between the State and the general Government, which the people, in choosing that Convention, never dreamed it would undertake. And, above all, he forgot that for such a body, so elected, to assume to act upon such a subject, was a grievous wrong to a people who were at that very time represented by another set of men, in their General Assembly; who had been elected twenty-one months after the Convention, and actually had pending before them propositions looking to a settlement of the whole matter by a new Convention, to be elected for that express end.

It is due to Governor Gamble, and to the cause of truth and fair discussion, that I should take time and space to present whatever grounds I find anywhere taken by him in defense of his recall of that Convention, as it were, from the brink of its grave. He has twice expressed himself in relation to that matter; *first,* in his message to the Convention, at the opening of the late session; and *secondly,* in a speech he made in the Convention on the 27th of June. In his message he used the following language: . . . [6]

In these two extracts we have all that the Governor has said, so far as I know, in defense of his calling that Convention to act on the subject of Emancipation. The singular vapidness of the latter will attract attention. It gives no answer to the charge of inconsistency, takes back nothing, explains nothing. His justification, if any, is to be found in the passage quoted from his message to the Convention; and let us examine that.

He says he called the Convention together, because *first,* in his judgment, "very speedy action" was demanded; *second,* because the Senate had, by a majority of two votes, passed a resolution requesting him to do so; *third,* because the Senate had passed a bill for the election of a new Convention, provided the old one did not, before the first of July, 1863, adopt a scheme

6. Drake quotes Governor Gamble's message explaining why he now calls for emancipation. He also quotes the governor's speech at the convention to the same end.

of Emancipation; and *fourth*, because the friends of Emancipation in the House exhibited the greatest earnestness in endeavoring to have that bill acted upon by the House.

My friends, I confess to a feeling of sadness and humiliation at such an exhibition on the part of one so high in station, for whom, for more than a quarter of a century, I had entertained the highest respect. Never before, probably, did a high public officer in this country more expose himself to criticism and condemnation, than did Governor Gamble in that assignment of reasons for that act. The utter insufficiency, the absolute puerility of such a defense, must be apparent to the most limited comprehension. Nay, more and worse, does it not bear the plainest marks of insincerity? Why was "very speedy action" necessary? What circumstances forbade that Emancipation should be postponed until the people could act upon it through a new Convention? He states none, nor can any man designate any. But if they existed when he issued his call on the 15th of April, they must have existed before the adjournment of the Legislature on the 23d of March: why, if there was such urgency, did he not communicate it to that body, and let it provide for the exigency? The old Convention was elected twenty-eight days, and assembled thirty-eight days, after the passage of the act authorizing it; what was to prevent a like promptness in the election and assembling of a new Convention? Had the Legislature passed an act to call a new Convention, it might have met, passed an Ordinance of Emancipation, and adjourned, before the day he fixed for the old Convention to assemble; and so the "very speedy action" would have been had, sooner than it was had at the hands of the body which assembled in obedience to his sole will. As to the reasons based on the proceedings in the two branches of the General Assembly, they are not worthy of argument or notice. To the whole batch I simply oppose his own declaration, in 1862, *"that the people in choosing the Convention never intended or imagined that the body would undertake any social revolution wholly unconnected with the relations between the State and the general Government;"* and his still more emphatic announcement, in the same paragraph, that *"no person who understands the principles of our Government would object to such action [as that upon Judge Breckinridge's Ordinance], unless it be one who is willing* TO DISREGARD ALL PRINCIPLE *to accomplish a desired end."* Let Governor Gamble reconcile himself with himself, if he can. If he can escape his own denunciation, it is more than I could, were I in his position.

But not alone on the grounds so stated by Governor Gamble was it a wrong to the loyal people of Missouri to summon that Convention to the great work of Emancipation. Even if those grounds had not existed, there were others which made it offensive and injurious to the people for that body to handle that great subject. Elected in February, 1861, it was in no respect, except in the persons of the eleven members elected in May and June, 1863, to fill vacancies, an authentic exponent of the public sentiment of Missouri when it assembled to make its final record. *The constituency of 1863 was, in law and in fact, wholly different front the constituency of 1861.* The Convention itself, in June, 1862, had prescribed new conditions for the exercise of the elective franchise, requiring the taking of a solemn and searching oath of allegiance and expurgation from complicity in the rebellion after the 17th of December, 1861, as a pre-requisite to the right of voting. Every man who would not take that oath was banished from the polls, was disfranchised as a voter, was not one of the people whose will was to be considered. The control of the State had passed, by fundamental Constitutional enactments, into the hands of its loyal people, or those who would stand that test of their loyalty. That Convention, therefore, was no embodiment or representative of the will of the rightful constituency of 1863, but of a former and a different constituency; a large proportion of which was then in the armies of the rebellion, or pursuing the bloody work of the bushwhacker, or skulking at home in self-imposed abstinence from the right of suffrage, because he dared not appeal to God to witness its freedom from the stain of treason, or the sincerity of its allegiance to the noblest Government He ever vouchsafed to man. When, therefore, the Governor convened that body to perform the glorious work of Emancipation, he convened a body which, whatever its legal power, had no more moral right to do that work, without submitting its action to the present constituency, that is, the *loyal* people of Missouri, than the Legislature of Maine or Minnesota would have had.

Not only so, but more. It was a body which had shown itself, a year before, opposed to the consideration even of the subject of Emancipation, and it has never signified that its views had changed on that point. True, it ordained what it termed Emancipation; but not because it desired or favored that great measure; but because it was resolved to prevent its accomplishment by, and according to the desire of, the loyal people of the State. No man lives who dares affirm that a majority of that Convention were for Emancipation on principle, from conviction, or in feeling. It was essentially a pro-Slavery body. Of the fifty-one members who voted for the ordinance passed, forty were slaveholders; a few of whom should be honored for their advocacy of the cause of Freedom for its own sake: all the rest were but *playing a part.* And it was a body, the control of which was in the hands of men whose past acts there gave evident token of disloyalty. *Eighteen were there, who voted in July, 1861, against the deposition of Governor Jackson;* and sixteen of them—all who were present at the time, and more than enough to have changed the result in each case—voted, in 1863, against an election of a Governor and other State officers by the people, and for the exemption of slave property from taxation; and eight of them—more than enough to have changed the result—against submitting the ordinance of Emancipation to the people for ratification. Twenty-one were there, who voted, in 1861, against turning out the traitorous Legislature of that year. Sixteen were there, who voted against the abrogation by the Convention of the treasonable laws enacted by that Legislature. Twenty-two were there, who voted against the test-oath ordinance of June 10, 1862, intended to exclude traitors from the polls. Sixteen were there, who had voted against allowing our brave soldiers to vote in their camps beyond the limits of the State. The efficient control, in fact, was in the hands of those who had in such ways signalized their disloyalty; aided by seventeen, who were bound to the Gamble dynasty by offices of trust and profit received from it. And this was the body which, as Colonel Doniphan said at Liberty, after its adjournment, was convened by Governor Gamble, on the request of "certain *wealthy slaveholders* residing in different parts of the State." For what purpose? To ordain Emancipation according to the will of the State's loyal people? No; but that "*something should be done to save slave Property from utter waste and spoliation, and give to slaveholders a brief opportunity to make the best disposition in their power of their slaves!*"

From such a body, convened on such a principle, controlled by such influences, and working to such ends, what could be expected, other than has been realized? Called ostensibly to destroy Slavery, it labored disloyally for its preservation from the early doom which the loyalty of Missouri, if it could have spoken, would have awarded it, and postponed Emancipation, nominally, until the 4th of July, 1870, but in fact for a quarter of a century longer. While there were those who desired and labored for Emancipation for its own sake, and for the sake of Missouri and the Union, the potential influence was, at heart, against Emancipation on any grounds, and equally against every radical measure against Slavery anywhere. Few there yielded their pro-Slavery views in obedience to the anti-Slavery sentiments of their people; but there were numbers there who knew that they utterly misrepresented the popular will in the districts whence they came. Nothing concerning the body was more true or more apparent, than that, pretending to favor Emancipation, it was resolved to postpone it to the last possible moment, and to yield it on the least possible injurious terms to the slaveholder. And even that was done with the open avowal by some, that before the period fixed for the emancipation of the negro from slavery, and his transmission to a condition of servitude, *the people would elect three*

Legislatures; justifying the inference that, before that period should arrive, the work of the Convention might be repealed. Of Emancipation obtained at the hands of such a body, in the form it was pleased to grant,—pro-Slavery Emancipation, if such a solecism is allowable,—Governor Gamble was the chief engineer; showing himself still, to my mind, to be, as he was in 1861, Missouri's pro-Slavery Governor. True, the date he at one time proposed for Slavery to cease, nominally, in Missouri, was not that finally fixed; but even in the same breath that he expressed himself as desiring the 4th of July, 1867, he announced with remarkable accommodativeness, "I am willing to receive any action that, in *your* judgment, is best." But some action he was resolved should be had, then and there, and he staked his official position as Governor upon it. In his speech to the Convention, on the 27th of June, this paragraph occurs:

> "If, after having exercised my best judgment upon this subject, I have called this Convention together for the purpose of action, and it should separate with the expression of a contrary opinion, or without adopting any scheme of Emancipation, I would not feel myself at liberty to continue in the exercise of the Executive function. I would feel, as a Minister in England, when a proposition of his is voted down in the Commons, that it is a denial of the correctness of his judgment as to the proper policy of the State, and he resigns at once; so I would not feel at liberty to continue in the Executive office, if the Convention did not pass some scheme of Emancipation; because it would be a judgment adverse to what I think should be the policy of the State."

And the pro-Slavery Convention, the balance of power in which was held by men whose past acts there proclaim them disloyal at heart, bowed to the Governor's demand for *"some* scheme of Emancipation," because his continuance in office was necessary to them and their plans, and the price of it was *any* scheme of Emancipation *they* might choose to adopt! Easy terms! facile Governor! pliant Convention! and all that "something should be done to save slave property from utter waste and spoliation, and give to slaveholders a brief opportunity to make the best disposition in their power of their slaves."

Had Governor Gamble been half as solicitous for the people's approval of his administration, as he was for the Convention's—half as fearful of a popular denial of the correctness of his judgment as to the proper policy of the State," as he was of such a denial by the Convention, he would have been a wiser man and a better Governor. He would then have known that the loyal people of Missouri long ago abandoned all hope of him as a defender and supporter of true, uncompromising loyalty in our distressed and ravaged State; and that since what he deemed "the proper policy of the State" has been inaugurated by him, *there is not a disloyal man or woman in all Missouri that is not his backer.* Truly, "the laborer is worthy of his hire," and the Governor has received his. He enjoys position, power, influence, but at what a terrible price! But all his other mispolicies are of transient moment, compared with that upon which be put his hazard in that Convention. Almost the life-breath of Missouri hung upon action there. His influence shaped that action, not for the cause of Emancipation and the Union,—one and the same in Missouri—but for Slavery, the Union's enemy, and for slaveholders, almost all its enemies, too. He lent the weight of his age and office, his name and his personal character, to a scheme for the support of Slavery, and the overthrow of the great loyal party in Missouri, and in that Convention he won, but lost all with loyal Missourians. To a man hastening on to threescore and ten and the grave, what earthly gain can overbalance such a loss?

I have thus, my friends, endeavored to place before you the circumstances of the wrongs suffered by the loyal people of Missouri, through the policy of Governor Gamble, and the acts of the dead Convention, which he—the only man on earth that could do it—called to life again. In all American history there is no parallel to it, except in some of those Southern States, where secession and rebellion were forced upon the people by the aristocrats of Slavery. Thank God! however, there is virtue enough left in the loyal people of Missouri to raise their voice against the attempt to trample upon their most sacred rights. They raise it here to-day; not in revolutionary shouts, not in sedition, not in disregard of law, not in derogation of the duties of true citizenship, not in any unlawful or unauthorized way; but with the high and holy purpose that despotism shall be forced to recoil before the moral power of an aroused people. We are here to speak, to judge, and to do what becomes freemen, in a manner suited to freemen. The cry of the arch-traitor was, "*All we ask is to be let alone!*" and the pro-Slavery emancipationists of the defunct Convention shout the same cry. But they are not to be let alone. They are to be made to feel that they cannot commit treason against Popular Sovereignty, and be let alone. They are to learn that there is a People, to whom they are accountable, and upon whose necks they cannot put their feet with impunity. They are to be taught that they cannot snatch the work of Missouri's regeneration out of the hands of her loyal men, and then sing them to sleep. They are to understand that their work is rejected by the people, and they, too. They ask us to accept their ordinances as a finality: we do accept it as a finality—*of them!* But, conceived, as it was, in wrong to the people; planned, as it was, in the interest of Slavery; brought forth, as it was, by a body which was so conscious of its wrong, that it refused to let the people pass upon it, avowing through their leaders that the people would reject it; and upheld, as it is, by every rebel, Secessionist, bushwhacker, and Copperhead in the State; we, loyal men of Missouri, who love our country more than Slavery—who have borne patiently all that has befallen us, for the sake of the Union—who have consecrated our all to the maintenance of that Union against all enemies—and who are determined, come what may, to rebuke, denounce, and overthrow disloyalty, whatever form or guise it may assume—*we* REJECT *that Ordinance as a finality of* THE QUESTION. We, and our brethren in loyalty in Missouri, are able to manage the affairs of Missouri, and we will do it. We ask no interference or help from traitors or their friends, in office or out. We will bide our time, as loyal men should, looking for the day of deliverance. It will surely come. This is the day of the office-holders and the politicians, the rebels and their sympathizers, the pro-Slavery men and their courtiers; the day of the PEOPLE will come, and with it confusion, dismay, and defeat to all who have dared to take part in the attempt of that Convention to dominate Missouri in the interest of Slavery. Let it not be said, as Mr. Henderson is reported to have said, that the Ordinance is the best that could be procured *under the circumstances!*[7] Who made the circumstances? Who but he and those who acted with him? And shall they make the circumstances, and then plead them in their own extenuation? Let them stand aside, and the people will make other circumstances, from which something better will come forth, of measures and of men.

Let us not, my friends, lose sight of the great and vital truth, that not only is this a struggle for Popular Sovereignty, but for *loyal supremacy in Missouri.* In that view no man can compute its importance to us as a people. If we sleep now, all is lost. The loyal men of Missouri are her rightful sovereigns. If true to themselves and to the great cause which in the providence of God is committed to their keeping, all will be well. Missouri loyalty has become an honored name in the land. It imports all of dauntless bravery, stern resolution, and heroic fortitude, that could illustrate the character and glorify the history of any people. Let us be true to our record and our fame, through to the end. If we have no country, we are wanderers; if we have no Government, we are a prey to tyrants; if we have no Union, we have neither country nor Government. All lives or dies with the Union. Let our souls cling to it, our fortunes sustain it, our hands uphold it,

7. U.S. senator John B. Henderson.

and, if need be, our blood flow for it. For nearly three years we have had to defend it. Let us defend it thrice three more, if such will be the will of God; defend it against the traitor in arms and the traitor in heart; against the open and the secret foe; against the wily politician, the cunning plotter, the unscrupulous schemer, though he wrap himself in the bright folds of the Stars and Stripes; against perfidy, treachery, and disloyalty in every form, everywhere, always, to the glorious end that awaits us, if we are true. This our work is not in the South—it is here, in Missouri. We are beset on every side by the armed rebel, the prowling bushwhacker, the Southern sympathizer, the devotee of Slavery, all, openly or covertly, the Union's enemies. And they are ours, too. They are striving for the mastery in Missouri. The calling of that Convention to ordain Emancipation was a part of their game. The next move will be to secure a Legislature that will repeal the test-oath ordinance, which excludes them from the polls; and then will come the reign of disloyalty, the repeal of Emancipation, the triumph of Slavery, the hunting down and driving out of Union men—all, all will come. Meet the issue here and now. Proclaim that Loyalty *shall* govern Missouri. Demand of the General Assembly a law authorizing the election of a new Convention, wherein the people, not politicians and office-holders, shall speak. Demand that the people be permitted to elect their own rulers. Demand Emancipation, *immediate, unconditional, final.* Demand the perpetual disfranchisement of every man who has taken part, here or elsewhere, in this damnable rebellion. Enforce your demand by every lawful agency, device, and influence, with energy and fidelity, with firm confidence and steady perseverance; and there is no power on earth that can resist you. Justice and right are with you; every loyal heart in the land is with you; the great and precious principles of free government are with you; the mighty People are with you; and, in the not distant future, victory will be with you, and defeat and oblivion with all in Missouri who oppose the sacred cause of Popular Sovereignty and the Union.

The Institution of Slavery in the Southern States, Religiously and Morally Considered in Connection with Our Sectional Troubles

(Washington, D.C.: H. Polkinhorn, 1863)

B ryan Tyson (1830–1909) came from Randolph County, North Carolina, and belonged to a family of onetime wealthy Quakers. As a young man he taught school and sold farm equipment in Moore County. His real love was journalism, to which he devoted himself during the Civil War. Tyson was acknowledged as a North Carolina loyalist who sent unionist pamphlets and books North and throughout the state, and Confederate authorities eventually arrested him as a draft dodger. After his release, Tyson was rearrested on a train after he passed out copies of a reunion pamphlet. Thinking him demented, Gov. Zebulon B. Vance allowed Tyson to travel to Washington. Apparently, he was in and out of Virginia and North Carolina thereafter, as he managed to deliver his books and pamphlets even to Richmond, the seat of the Confederate government. Tyson supported the Democratic Party and became a willing propagandist for the Democratic National Committee in its bid to unseat President Lincoln in 1864. In Washington he came under the influence of former North Carolinian Benjamin Hedrick. It is said that the Republican government planned to arrest him, but Tyson fled Washington and went underground in nearby Bladensburg, Maryland. After the war, Tyson returned for a time to North Carolina, but he found no work and so went back to Washington, where he ran a mail contract business. In the 1890s he joined the Populist Party and ran for the U.S. Senate from North Carolina. In 1909 the authorities declared him insane.

In this pamphlet Tyson extolled the virtues of the northern Democrats and attacked the Republicans for a poor war policy. A southern proslavery unionist, he defended slavery to unionists back home and tried to influence northern attitudes on the subject. He weighed the pros and cons of slave society, attacked extremists North and South, and advocated a restored union with slavery left intact. But he also urged southerners to give up any support for the Confederacy. William T. Auman perhaps best captures Tyson's views when he says, "Tyson never forgave Lincoln for making emancipation a prerequisite for reunion because he believed that in doing so Lincoln had prolonged the war unnecessarily" (265).

No biography exists of Tyson, though his life has attracted some notice. See Richard L. Zuber, *Jonathan Worth* (Chapel Hill: University of North Carolina Press, 1965); William T. Auman, "Bryan Tyson: Southern Unionist and American Patriot," *North Carolina Historical Review* 62 (July 1985): 257–92; and Bryan Tyson, *A Ray of Light: or, Treatise on the Sectional Troubles, Religiously and Morally Considered* (Brower's Mills, N.C.: Published by the author, 1862). Tyson's papers are at Duke University and the Library of Congress.

* * *

But few subjects have been discussed with more interest, and, perhaps, none upon which greater diversity of opinion prevails, than the institution of slavery in the Southern States. Some argue that the institution is just and lawful, having been instituted under a Theocracy; others that it is unjust, inhumane, and ought to be abolished. One or the other of these positions is right and the contrary is wrong. God is on one side or the other of the question, and is opposed to the opposite.

It is now my purpose to inquire impartially into this matter in order, if possible, to determine which side of the question God and justice is on: and should we be so fortunate as to find a solution for the problem, it would then be an easy matter to determine which way the question should be decided.

It may, perhaps, be said that this is not a proper time to discuss the question, but I think never a better. I think a question that has caused so much trouble and distress as this should be discussed, and discussed freely, with an honest search after truth, rather than for the mastery, in order that it may be determined and settled in accordance with the word and justice of God, and settled forever. After our present troubles shall have been ended I hope our country will never again be agitated by this distressing question.

I will first take the affirmative side of the question, and show wherein it would be best for the servants to remain as they are. Then the negative, or arguments in favor of emancipation. And will then, in conclusion, compare the two together.

Whether or not slavery be right, certain it is that it has existed in all ages from the days of Noah, when a curse was laid upon Canaan, down to the present time. This, I presume, is a conceded fact, and I will, therefore, consume no time in proving this point, it being my object to prove the justness or unjustness of the institution, rather than to prove that it has existed for a long or short period of time.

According to my knowledge of the Old and New Testaments, being a earthly servant here does not appear to be a matter of so very great importance if so be that we are so fortunate as to gain eternal life in the world to come.

We find the word servant mentioned in the Scriptures some four hundred and thirty-five times. This word, however, has different meanings according to the sense in which it is used, but I will mention only a few of these texts, such as are calculated to elucidate the subject under consideration; by far the greater portion having no bearing upon the subject whatever.

We find the word servant mentioned in at least twelve places as pertaining to those that were held to involuntary service or labor. The first place that the word servant is mentioned in the Bible is, I believe, at Genesis, IX, 25, where Noah, awaking from his wine, lays a curse upon Canaan, saying: "cursed be Canaan; a servant of servants shall be unto his brethren." Soon after this we find by comparing Genesis 10, 2, with Ezekiel 27, 13, that Javan, Tubal and Meshech were trading among them upon the persons of men as merchandise. If this had been wrong it is reasonable to suppose that the practice would have been condemned by the good men of that day. But we do not find it thus condemned. The curse having been pronounced of Noah by inspiration, this was very probably a means devised for carrying it into effect. The sentence "a servant of servants he should be unto his brethren" was irrevocable and was bound to go into effect, let the private opinions of the people of that day have been what they might. It should therefore be the duty of the people in all ages to obey the commands of God, and perform the duties assigned them, rather than to cavil at his decrees, for it is evident that God who made the world can best govern it, and He may also, perhaps, have some object in view not known to us. Therefore we should submit to His commands and decrees. If we would always do this we would be apt to do well enough—better, perhaps, than many of us do. . . . [1]

Many things take place in this world that may not appear just and right unto us, but at the same time God may perhaps have some object in view not known to us. Thus, when Saul commanded to go and smite the Amelekites, he was commanded to smite every man, woman and child. Even the innocent suckling that had of itself known no guile, was doomed to death.

We are told in another place that God is a jealous God, visiting the iniquities of the fathers upon the children of the third and forth generations of them that hate Him. Thus it seems we belong to God, and He hath a right to do as seemeth well both with our lives and liberties also. This is exemplified in his works of the smaller creation.

If we turn our attention to the beasts of the forest we behold the more ferocious and formidable preying upon the weaker and lesser. If we turn our attention to the fowls of the air we there behold certain species armed with formidable talons, and supplied with carnivorous appetites, and every way fitted by nature for preying upon the weaker and lesser. And if we turn our attention to the fishes of the mighty deep we there behold the same thing. So in very nearly all of God's animate creation, except man, we behold the stronger species preying upon the weaker and lesser. These do not prey merely upon the liberties of the under species, but actually upon their lives, generally inflicting painful and excruciating deaths. So we find that the lives of one class are continually being offered up to support those of the stronger and more ferocious. Even so among men, so far as liberty is concerned, we find the superior, more intelligent and gifted by nature, preying upon the weaker and less intelligent, in reducing them to bondage, and compelling them to serve their superiors. This, no doubt, appears revolting to the feelings of any christian, humane man; but the institution of slavery has now got a foothold among us. The people of this generation are by no means responsible for the class of people being reduced to bondage. Therefore it becometh our duty as philanthropists, to study their case, and do by them what is best under existing circumstances, such as we would like to have done unto us under similar circumstances. I will treat of this more at length before I get through.

But says one, the servitude spoken of in the Scriptures is applicable only to the Hebrews, the command having been given especially to them, and

---

1. Tyson here cites a number of passages from the Bible to illustrate his argument. He prints 1 Peter 2, 18, 21 and 1 Timothy 6:1–10.

therefore we have no right to hold servants under that command unless we can establish that we are of Hebrew descent. I will acknowledge that there is some feasibility to this argument; and not wishing to lay any burden upon these people, not even so large as my little finger, I will not argue the question any farther in that light, nor will I take any advantage of the curse laid upon Canaan, but will proceed to argue it solely in a moral point of view, being not only willing but anxious that the question may be decided according to the best interests of the servants, be it which way it may. Because, admitting that the Scriptures would permit us to hold our own servants, there is no law nor obligation that I know of that would compel or bind us as our duty to hold them. And believing it to be unjust that one part of the human race should be deprived of their liberty and happiness in order to increase the happiness of another class, I think the interests of servants should be consulted exclusively in this matter, and let them be emancipated or remain as they are, according as their interests require. I will now proceed to argue this question in a moral point of view.

We will first look at this institution in a family where there are some thirty or forty servants. We find among them a good many women and children, and some old men and women who are not able to do regular field labor. So out of the whole we will probably not get more than four-ninths who are regular field hands. The children play about at their sports—the white and black almost invariably together, where there are children of each kind on a place—until they reach a proper age to put to work, which is light at first, but, as they grow older, gradually assumes a heavier form until they get so that they can do any work that is done on the farm. Their labor is now of some value, and a part of it goes towards supporting the women and children and the old men and women who are now too old to labor. They thus continue to labor, and in the course of time declining years set in and they too cease to be any longer regular field hands. They are now assigned some light work, such as boiling food and feeding stock, looking after and training the children, &c. The young negroes that they helped to raise, now, in turn, labor to support them in their declining years. So it appears to be one continuous copartnership, as it were, they having all things common, like as described in the fourth chapter of the Acts of the Apostles. The children, when they are too young to labor, likewise when they get to be too old, fare equally as well, as when they were at a proper age to labor. Thus, of the three stages—youth, middle age, and old age—through which servants pass, there is but one in which they are depended on as regular field hands. In old age they are taken good care of; and thus is the entire slave population rendered self-supporting. So, of the 3,953,760 that were in the United States in 1860, I don't suppose there was one of that number supported by public tax. Such an instance, I presume, is unknown among an equal number of industrial classes any where in the civilized world. If there has been any property accumulated from the labor of the servants during his younger days, that very same property stands pledged to take care of him in old age. I will ask where else on the face of the globe could you go to find, in a population of nearly four millions, no paupers?

The servants of the South, for the most part, receive good treatment, as is evident from the census returns of 1860. During that year there were 3,000 servants manumitted, and 803 escaped to the North as fugitives, making a total loss to the slave population of 3,803. Taking this as the annual loss for the past decade, there would thus have been a loss to the slave population of 38,030. But, with this odds against them, the slave population at the South increased during the decade ending in 1860, 23.39 per cent; which is faster than any nation in Europe increased during the same period of time. The free blacks during the same period, after having been augmented by about 38,030, increased only 12.33 per cent.

I will here give the statistics of some of the principal northern cities. In the city of Boston, during the five years ending in 1859, the city register observes: "The number of colored births was one less than the number of marriages, and the deaths exceeded the marriages nearly in the proportion of two to one. In Philadelphia, during the last six months of the census year, the new registration gives 148 births against 306 deaths among the free colored people. So we find that the slaves or servants of the South, notwithstanding that they were subject to two considerable drains as aforesaid, increased nearly as fast again as their free brethren. From this we would infer that the better treatment was in favor of the bond servant. This, I think, is the effect of their working in societies or copartnership as already explained. For thus situated, the women at times, when their health is delicate, are not required to labor, being taken about as good care of as a member of the white family under similar circumstances. I have known the owner, in cases where a large percentage of his servants were women and children, to have to labor himself very hard, and always have his nose down to the grindstone in order to raise these children, while they were running about, kicking up their heels, and seeing their pleasure. But they were willing to undergo this toil, with the hope that they would be able to pay for their raising some time.

The servants at the South are not only, generally speaking, well treated, but becoming respect is also shown them in old age. The white children are even taught to call the elderly servants uncle or aunt, as the case may be. I was thus brought up myself, and it still appears natural for me to do so.

Where servants are properly and well treated, I think they frequently fare better, and have more of the necessaries and comforts of life to go upon than many of the poorer classes of white people; and the reason of this is, that they attend more systematically to business; for while the voice of the former is heard loud and long at the tavern, or other places of amusement, these are attending to their daily avocations which furnish food and raiment for the body and employment for the mind; and being thus employed, they are kept out of mischief.

I think the unexampled increase among the servants is owing to the society or copartnership in which they live, together with the early age at which they generally marry. (I will speak of the mode presently.) In making matches, there are no questions of a worldly character to decide with them; for their women are all like Lycurgus would have those of Sparta, all equal as to property.

Among various laws that this learned sage introduced into Sparta was one that females should inherit no part of their father's estate, but that it should be equally divided among his sons. Being called upon to explain the object of this curious law he said, the young men in making matches would not then be picking and choosing after property, but would go for worth and merit. It also seems that some such a law would have an excellent effect in this day and time in encouraging early marriages and thus prevent the unnatural state of celibacy, with its many concurrent evils, for where people marry for wealth and character, they frequently keep picking and choosing after these until they pick through and get nobody. Therefore, under a discipline that would cause early and universal marriages, religion, morals, and school-houses would doubtless flourish.

The servants generally live up to this rule; for there being no questions of a worldly character to decide with them, they go in solely for "love and beauty." The consequence is, there are but few or no cases of celibacy among them; they have but few or no cares as to their rising families, and in old age they are taken care of. So, where they are properly and well treated, they are, in my opinion, about the happiest people the sun shines on.

In order that the reader may have some idea of the manner in which servants enjoy themselves, I will relate the following incident:

The past summer, a year ago, I was at a friend's house in Chatham county, North Carolina, who owned a good many servants. It was in time of wheat harvest. About dusk the hands came in from their laborious work. It would seem that all might have been tired enough without seeking farther exercise in diversions, but not so. After supper the banjo was brought forth, and preparations made for a social dance. They soon struck up in high glee.

I remarked to my friend that negroes saw a great deal of satisfaction and pleasure. Yes, said he, the most of any people in this world. He told me that wishing to finish a certain field of grain, they had labored very hard that day. But one would not have judged so from present appearances. When I went to bed they were in the midst of their glee, making the house fairly shake as their busy feet kept time to the music. So in what position in life could they be more happy? We should not form the belief because they have to labor that they are rendered unhappy; for the Bible, I think says: "The repose of the laboring man is sweet." They have to labor or their owners would soon be reduced to a condition such as to be unable to treat them well. Hence we may conclude if they be placed in a position where idleness would be encouraged, that their condition instead of being bettered, would thereby be worsted. For, as the saying is, "when idleness comes in at one door, want, with crime and its various attendants, come in at another." But servants, for the most part, live free from these evils, and are, therefore, a contented and happy people.

At all events, the felicity of the bond servant is such that I have actually known free persons of color to choose their masters and voluntarily enslave themselves. This may appear very singular to us, but unless they expected to better their condition, it is still more strange that they should thus voluntarily give away their liberty. It is to be presumed that they considered the matter well before entering into this engagement. But, inheriting by birth no wealth, and not being able to amass means sufficient, above the necessary expenses of life, to purchase lands, horses, &c., and thus put themselves in a comfortable situation for living, it seems that, rather than weary thus with the burdens of life, and hire themselves from house to house, and be dependent on uncertain means, they had rather pick out some good, kind, humane man for a master, who was well supplied with all the necessaries and comforts of life, and who they knew would treat them well, than to have their liberty and thus be taxed with the cares and concerns of life. After trying their new homes I never heard of any dissatisfaction on their part; so it is to be presumed that they were satisfied with the change.

To show the effect of emancipation on these people, I refer the reader to the history of Jamaica, Hayti and British Guiana, countries where emancipation has taken place. In these countries the negroes invariably ceased to work to much advantage after gaining freedom. To prove this I will mention a few facts.

In the year 1790 there was exported from the Island of Hayti 163,405,220 pounds sugar. After gaining their freedom the quantity began to diminish, and in forty-three years thereafter there was not a single pound exported from the Island, and the Queen Island of the seas was thus relinquished to barbarism, desolation, brutal licentiousness and crime, in every hideous form. I could multiply these instances, but, wishing to be brief, will let the above suffice.

It is said that bees when transported to the Island of Cuba soon cease to work and lay up honey, and divert themselves by flying about the sugar mills and stinging the hands whilst at work. The reason that they thus cease to labor is that they can always get a sufficiency of the necessary food without being at that trouble. Past experience has generally proved this to be the case with the negro where he has been emancipated—he soon ceases to work to much advantage.

It seems the negro should not be entirely idle, because he is well adapted for laboring on the cotton, rice and sugar plantations of the South, and can labor with impunity among various epidemic diseases where the white man would soon sicken and die. To prove this I refer to the following:

In the summer of 1855, during the awful scourge of yellow fever in Norfolk, Va., there died in that city about 3,000 persons. Of these were very few cases among the blacks. I was there for a considerable time among the fever myself, and I know I heard it remarked that it took but little or no effect on the black population. So they seem to be well adapted for working on the cotton, rice and sugar plantations of the South, in which the North, South and various European countries are interested. In warm countries, where serpents and alligators abound, there the negro flourishes to greatest perfection. But remove him from this to a Northern clime and he soon shows unmistakable signs of decay. It is therefore evident that his labor is particularly essential in rearing the tropical products, and experience has taught, that to raise these successfully, he requires the aid and superveilance of the white man.

I will now notice the negative side of the question and proceed to give the arguments that are generally brought against the institution of slavery.

Among the first and principal of these is the enhanced value of real estate in the Free States and the prevailing ignorance among the poorer classes South when compared with their Northern brethren. We will notice these arguments separately. In 1850 the average value of land in the Northern States was, I believe, $28 07 per acre. In the Southern, $5 34 per acre. But is this high price in the one case and low in the other attributable solely to the institution of slavery in the South? I think not. I think it is mainly owing to the very dense population of the Northern States and the more sparse or scattering of the Southern, together with the system of trade that has been carried on between the two sections. Thus, the people at the South have nearly forty-five acres of land per head, counting both black and white, great and small. The people at the North have less than twenty-one. So we should not wonder that lands are higher at the North, because scarcity always enhances the value of anything. It should also be recollected that city property, manufactories, &c., are counted in the above estimate; and the Northern States having larger cities and more manufactories than the Southern States, have greatly the advantage in this particular.

If we compare the Northwestern with the Southwestern States we shall find the average value of land in the Northwestern to be $11 39 per acre; in the Southwestern $6 26. So the lands of the Southwestern people are worth more per head than those of the Northwestern; for what they lack in price they more than make up in the number of acres.

But after all, is the enhanced or high price of land any advantage to the generality of people? I think not; no more than the selling of corn at five dollars per bushel would be to the buyer. Where lands are cheap the poor can buy them and every man owns his own tract of land; but placed at these enormously high prices, the rich alone can afford to be landholders.

As regards the superior intelligence of the masses of the people North compared with the masses South, I think that is mainly attributable to the system of trade that has been carried on between the Northern and Southern States, together with, perhaps, the better system with which schools have been conducted in the Free States. It is said that the South, poor as she is, has annually poured into the lap of the North about $230,000,000. This amount of money expended among the Northern people was calculated to make everything flourishing. Their manufactured articles all commanding ready sales, they could with the proceeds thereof, school their children and do almost anything else they desired, whilst at the South the people, banks, and everything else were languishing under this murderous system of trade. Had the necessary manufactories been built up at the South, and these $230,000,000 been expended annually among the poorer classes there, they too, I presume, would have been able to educate their children and business of every kind would soon have been in a thriving and prosperous condition. But after all, I am inclined to think that the superiority of the Northern people, in a literary point of view, compared with their Southern brethren, is not as great as has commonly been supposed. And as regards morals, I have it from reliable statistics that the religious persons South, according to population, exceed those North nearly in the proportion of two to one. So it seems what they lack in learning, if any, they make up in religion.

Let the institution of slavery have been what it might, it is evident that the Northern people got the sum and substance of it, while the Southern people got the shadow. The tide of trade had got turned to the North to such a degree that articles of Southern manufacture would scarcely sell; or at least the Northern was generally preferred as they were thought to be a little cheaper. Capitalists were, therefore afraid to invest their money in these enterprises, for it was evident without the benefit of the Southern trade they could not be sustained.

I will give an example of this. There were, in a certain small county in one of the Southern States, (Randolph, North Carolina,) five large and flourishing cotton manufactories, all being upon the same water course. These factories turned out large amounts of cloth and thread, but supplying none but the home market, they soon became overstocked with these goods, and in order to find sale for them, large quantities had to be sent to the Northern markets, principally New York, where they came in competition with the goods of Northern and various European manufacturers. Now, in order to find sale for these goods, they could not be offered at prices higher than the Northern and Europeans could be bought at. But, the profits of the Southern manufacturer being materially lessened by the expense of transportation, commissions, &c., what do you suppose was the consequence of this murderous system of trade? Why, several of these manufacturing companies soon failed to meet their demands, and some of their stockholders, who had not happened to have a surplus of means, had to sell their stock at a reduced price in order to meet their demands. So, with this prospect of things before the Southern people, it is not to be wondered at that they were afraid to risk their capital in manufacturing enterprises. The institution of slavery cannot, I presume, be brought as an argument against the want of success of these factories, because they were all operated exclusively by white hands. Nor can it be said that the Southern people were not able to sustain them, for they had means in abundance to do this, but these were, generally speaking, sent North. Their failure, then, was simply owing to lack of home patronage.

But soon after the Northern trade was broken up by our sectional troubles, these same goods advanced in value over 500 per cent. Many of the manufacturing companies throughout the South doubled the wages to their hands and still make enormous profits. If this state of things had taken place in time of peace, these enhanced prices would have caused other manufactories to spring up, and thus, in time, these goods, through competition, would have been brought down sufficiently low. Employment would then have been given to our poorer classes, and under these circumstances all would have journeyed on prosperously and happily together. I think we would then have been able to show our Northern brethren that the presence of a few niggers at the South could not keep us from manufacturing nor from doing anything else we wished to do. I desire to see the whole country prosper, both the North and the South, and for this purpose I think they should trade together as far as such trading would be of mutual advantage to each other. But I am not in favor of this trade being carried to such an extent as to enrich one section and impoverish the other, and then lay all the fault to the existence of a certain institution in one of the sections, while they themselves received a large amount of their profits from this same institution. I will endeavor to make this a little plainer by giving a fable that very probably the reader is familiar with: . . . [2]

If I had time and space I could trace this subject further and show that the panics that have been occurring in our money markets at the South, at intervals of a few years for a good many years back, were mainly attributable to the South overtrading with the North and the North overtrading with Europe; but I will leave this part of the subject with the reflecting reader.

I will here ask the emancipationists a question, and that is, if there be such an advantage in free labor over slave, why does not the people of England, Scotland, Ireland and other countries of Europe enjoy this to the same extent that the people of the Northern States have done? This question can be easily answered. In the first place the Free States are not so densely populated as those countries; and in the second place they have not had such a place to trade and draw their supplies from as the Northern States. But if the South would produce less of the raw material, and become to a certain extent a manufacturing people, mind you if the scale would not soon turn. Soon after the discovery of the cotton gin, cotton commanding very high prices, the Southern people became alive to producing the raw material. The climate of the North not being adapted to the growing of cotton, they erected the necessary manufactories and became a manufacturing people. Their goods too commanding high prices, soon increased their capital, which enabled them to build more manufactories. The Northern people having got their manufactories in successful operation, it would now be impossible for manufactories to be built up at the South, without affording them some protection in their infancy. And all the protection they would require would be for the Southern people to patronize them, let the price be

2. Tyson here recounts the fable of "The Ass, the Lion, and the Cock," and relates it to costs to the North if slavery were abolished.

high or low. In time, competition would bring all things right, as has already been stated.

The people of the Northern States boast of the rapidity with which their new States have grown up. This is owing to the emigration from Europe and other countries. But when these States shall have become as thickly settled as those European countries, in what particular will they possess an advantage over the people of those countries? I answer, in nothing, unless they have the benefit of the Southern trade.

Again, it is argued that servants are not properly and well treated; that they are kept in the dark and sometimes ill-treated also. This is even so, and I desire to see improvement in both cases.

As regards evil treatment I will admit that there are a few who do not treat their servants well, but the number is small in comparison with those who do treat them well. Would you then bring evil upon the whole race merely because there are a few persons who do not treat their servants well? The time never has been, and probably never will be, when, in a population of nearly four millions of people whether they be bond or free, that there will not be some acts of violence committed on the weakly and inoffensive.

But in order to remedy these defects, would you entail evil upon the whole race? I think not. I will illustrate this by the following:

Railroads are known to be great conveniences; but still accidents occasionally occur upon them which sometimes result in death. Now in order to remedy these evils, you would not do away with the entire railroad system, would you? No, I think not. I think you will readily admit that the good accomplished by them more than overbalances the evil.

But suppose a servant is harshly treated; that he has fallen into the hands of a hard taskmaster. In this case let him raise his petition to Christ, who is no respecter of persons, and justice will eventually be done. I have thought if there be an earthly temple fit for the Spirit of Christ to dwell in that it is a servant who is evily treated. God, in His infinite wisdom, did not intend that justice should be meted out in this world. If He had, there would be no need of a judgment in the next. Therefore, if the servant evily treated will raise his petition to Him who ruleth on high, it will, I think, in the end be of no disadvantage to him. The hard taskmaster will, in a coming day, stand at the bar of God, there to be judged according to the deeds done in the body, and there will be shown no respect of persons.

I wish to do these people justice throughout, and I, therefore, desire that they should be sent to school, and at least taught to read, so as to be able to read the Scriptures. It has been thought by some emancipationists that such a course would lead to enfranchisement. If it would, I am for it. The soul is evidently of more importance than the body, and should, therefore, be first cared for. I will remark, though, that the best servants I have ever known were such as could read, and were religious. It creates a moral worth in them. But still, should such a course lead to enfranchisement, I am for it as aforesaid. They would then be in a fit condition to take care of themselves. But turn them out in their present ignorant condition, and it is feared disastrous consequences would follow.

It is also argued that the servants at the South live in open adultery, never having been legally married.

In answer to this I will say, that a great many are married after book form; and they all, so far as my knowledge goes, have their choice in this matter, whether to be married after book form or cohabit under a vow. I will take occasion to state here that I believe the essential part of the marriage contract consists in a solemn vow between the parties, and a faithful observance thereof. There being so many different forms of marriage among the various nations of the earth, it is hard to tell which is right. But I am inclined to think that, where the parties cohabit under a solemn vow, and observe it faithfully, whether made privately or publicly, there is no adultery committed. So far as my knowledge goes, the servants that cohabit under a vow are fully as faithful to their companions as those who are married after book form, and in both cases they are generally true to their engagements. But still I am for granting the servants their discretion in this matter, and let all that wish to be married after book form do so. Or if it be found more in accordance with the Word and justice of God that they should be married after book form, I am, if you please, in favor of that, and even of compelling all to be thus wedded. Cohabiting under a vow seems to have been peculiar to ancient days: that of book form or public marriages to modern. So much for marriage among the servants.

Another argument that is frequently brought against the institution of slavery is the amalgamation of the white and black races. It is true this is an evil. But, it is thought, this could be effectually prevented by passing a simple law in reference thereto; and that is, that all such issues born of white parents on one side, should, as soon as capable of taking care of themselves, or, at farthest, at the age of twenty one years, go out free. In this case, as the owner of servants would not care to raise children who would be of little or no profit to him, it is to be presumed means would be adopted such as would prevent an increase of this kind among his servants. New cases being thus prevented, the mixed races now on hand would soon become extinct through the largely superior number of pure blacks. As is now the case, amalgamation is most prevalent in towns and cities; but it is thought the above would, in a few generations measurably wipe out the whole, and that the negroes would thenceforth be enabled to maintain their original purity.

Another argument that is brought against Slavery is, that it is the cause of the present war, and should therefore be abolished. I think in this case our duty as philanthropists, should be to study their case and place them in the position in which they would be most comfortable and happy, and then let the people of each section conform thereto.

Again: It is argued that servants should not be bought and sold, and thus parted from families and relatives. This does seem hard; and unless some one else were more in favor of it than I am there would be but few bought and sold, I assure you. But the principle at last tends to transfer them from a poorer section to one more fertile and congenial; and I doubt not many changes have thus been made by which the condition of servants were bettered, which was not apparent at the time. Thus, I am credibly informed, that in the Southern and Southwestern States a servant frequently makes for himself a bale of cotton in the time given him, which he appropriates to his own private purposes. In a less fertile section, probably in the one from whence he came, he could not do this. This age is one of emigration any way, and how often do we see members of a white family scattered into almost as many States as there are members!

As regards parting a man and wife, and small children from their parents, I am utterly opposed to that. I will remark, though, that in a sojourn at the South of over twenty years, I have known but very few cases where a man and wife were parted. There is a disposition among the people to keep them together as much as possible. But I would be glad to see laws passed at the South to prohibit a man and wife from being separated under any and all circumstances, and such is now the case in some of the States.

Another argument which is frequently brought against the institution of slavery—or rather against the rendition of fugitive slaves, which in substance is the same thing—is found at Deut. xxii, 15, 16: "Thou shalt not deliver unto his master his servant which has escaped from his master unto thee; he shall dwell with thee, even among you in that place which he shall choose in one of the gates where it liketh him best: thou shalt not oppress him."

The above text is capable of a two-fold interpretation: First, that the Hebrews were the only people permitted to own servants. This is verified by their being commanded not to deliver up fugitive servants, they being supposed to have escaped from some of the heathen nations round about. Second, that, as they were commanded not to deliver up these servants, and at the same time were not commanded to interpose so as to keep their masters from recovering them, the text merely means non-interference or neutrality.

I will illustrate this by the following: We will say your ox strays off and gets over on your neighbor's plantation. You miss him and go and search for him, and when you have found him, bring him home without, perhaps, your neighbor knowing that he had been there; he does not deliver him to you.

But if your ox go and get in your neighbor's corn, and he put him up in a stall and send you word, and when you come, he should then show and deliver him unto you, this might be called delivering. Even so in this case. You cannot deliver a servant unto his master unless you are instrumental in his recovery. It should seem that a servant escaping from his master and seeking refuge in a foreign land would be apt to have some just cause for so doing. In this case it would now be very cruel in you to hunt down this servant and be instrumental in any way in again placing him in bondage under his former taskmaster. But if you remain still, and do nothing, neither the one way nor the other, then is the case very different.

It is also argued that the servants should be emancipated, and if the whites need their services let them hire them and pay them wages therefor. The probability is, if they were emancipated their labor could not be commanded, not even for money, or at least not regularly enough for farm purposes; for experience has generally proven that when they have been emancipated they soon get to be like the bees when transported to the Island of Cuba—soon cease to work to much advantage, as already stated. It is, therefore, to be presumed that both themselves and cotton fields would soon languish under immediate and thorough emancipation. It should also be borne in mind that the relations existing between a master and his servant are quite different than those existing between the same person and a hired servant. In the one case he is considered and treated as a member of the family; in the other, but little regard is manifested for him after receiving his wages, and he is able to obtain but few favors—only such as he can purchase with his money—which in many instances are fewer than those the bond servants enjoy.

I will here ask the question how much does the richest man in New York get for taking care of his riches? I answer, only what he eats, drinks, and wears. "But they that will be rich fall into temptation and a snare, and into many foolish and hurtful lusts, which drown men in destruction and perdition." Therefore, if thou has food and raiment, therewith be content.

I will now treat of this subject in comparison:

In order to show the effect that religion, light, and the influence that the white man has had on these people, I will give a brief biographical sketch of [a Negro preacher].

A good many years ago there resided in the county of Moore, North Carolina, a negro whose name was Ralph. He professed religion early in life, and it was soon discovered that he had a gift for the ministry. By assiduous study he soon became learned and mighty in the Scriptures. The church to which he belonged, seeing that he was likely to be useful, contributed, bought, and gave him his freedom. Taking the name of his master, he was known thereafter as Ralph Freeman. He formed an acquaintance with a Baptist minister of the name of McGee. They soon became very intimate, and traveled and preached much together. At length they made an agreement that whoever died first the other should preach his funeral. Soon after this McGee removed to Alabama, where, after several years, he died, leaving his friend Ralph still surviving. In his will he left Ralph his horse, bridle and saddle, overcoat, Bible, and fifty dollars in money, and requested that he should be informed of his decease; which was accordingly done, and, by agreement, a time set for the preaching of the funeral. A few weeks before the appointed time Ralph, now grey-headed and well stricken in years, set out on his long journey to fulfil the pledge that he had made with his white brother many years before. He reached his place of destination in due time. It being a novel thing that a colored preacher should come from North Carolina to Alabama to preach a funeral, a vast concourse of people assembled on the occasion. To use Ralph's own words, "the whole land of Judea and region round about had come out to hear him." He said, the assemblage of people being so large, he feared he would not be able to realize their expectations. But he said he had not preached far before every bone in the old negro felt like preaching. His discourse was well received, and after services a collection was taken up, and $100 contributed for his benefit. Thus we see what effect light and religion has on these people.

Contrast the above with the following, or negro at home, by M. Jules Gerard, which you may find in the *Philadelphia Inquirer*, of September 7th, 1863: . . . [3]

I will now give the experience of some of the lately emancipated servants:

One of these, a negro man, told me in the streets of Newbern, that he was not as free now as he was before he came into the Federal lines. And also that he fared better particularly in sickness, for, said he, when I got sick I had some person to bring medicine out to me; but it is not so now.

---

3. Tyson here prints an abstract of an article by a prominent French journalist dealing with so-called primitive religion in Dahomey. He also recites black crime statistics in Massachusetts to predict that southern freed slaves would revert to crime.

I do not mention this in disparagement to the Federal authorities; for I, doubt not, they have taken as good care of these people as they could possibly do under existing circumstances. When we take into consideration the magnitude of our sectional troubles, and disturbed condition of the country, our great wonder is that they have been able to do as well by them as they have. . . . [4]

I will now give the experience of an old colored person with whom I conversed, at the market-house, in this city, but a few days ago. He said, a good many years ago, his master, living in South Carolina, emancipated himself and family, consisting of his wife and seven children—four sons and three daughters—and gave them money to bear their expenses to a free State. He said at first he hailed this change with much joy, as he expected to get aid from his children; but they had all scattered off; his wife was now dead, and he was dependent on his own labor for support, and now, being old, he was ill able to labor. I asked him which situation he would prefer, to be back with his master, or live the way he was now living? He said his master was a good and kind man, and if he was now back with him he would never consent to leave him again. Said he, I then had some time to rest, but I have none now.

If we contrast the present condition of the servants in the cases just mentioned with their former condition, and take their own word as evidence, how does the matter stand?

I will here remark that I have taken but little pains to inform myself on this subject, having conversed with probably not more than a half-dozen relative thereto, some of whom (I recollect definitely but one) said they were better satisfied since obtaining their freedom than before. These were mostly young, hearty laborers who were then working at good wages. Whether this state of things will continue after the war shall have subsided, and business become stagnant, and particularly after old age shall have set in, I am unable to say. We will, though, take it for granted that what has proven true in a few cases will in very nearly all similarly situated.

I will here ask the question, if these servants who have tried both modes of living say they were better off and lived more comfortably in their former than latter condition, how is it that the emancipationists, who know but comparatively little of the situation of slavery any way, should know so much better what suits them best than the servants do themselves?

Near where I resided, in North Carolina, there lived a family of free negroes, which consisted of a man and his wife and one or two children, the

---

4. Tyson makes another case, that of an ex-slave woman thrown out of work.

remaining children having been scattered off and left them. They had a very snug little tract of land, but in the course of time they became embarrassed and had to pawn their land for money. They are now old and well stricken in years and ill able to labor. So their creditor could, I presume, any time he saw proper to push his debt, have them turned out of doors. Here, then, would be two fit subjects for public charity, such as, I presume, you could not find among the whole population of servants at the South. (I call them servants because I hate the name slave. The word slave is a borrowed term and should not be used.) Contrast the condition of the members of this family with bond servants of a like age, where they are under the protection of a kind, humane man as master, and where they have servants to labor for them in their declining years, and tell me which you think is most happy.

The above family were the only free persons of color that lived immediately in my section, so I cannot be accused of being partial in selecting a case.

Again—it is argued by some that liberty is an inherent right; that we therefore have no right to deprive any people of their liberty, not even if their condition be bettered thereby. I will illustrate this by the following comparison, though simple, yet it will do to illustrate the point in question.

All will doubtless admit that the horse fares better in a domestic state than he would in his natural, or wild state where he could roam about at pleasure. Now, if these domestic animals were liberated and turned out to shift for themselves, they would soon become subject to great want and suffering, and as a consequence, would pine away and die. Now, no person, I presume would argue, that for the sake of giving these brutes their liberty, this should be done. Even so with the negro. Though he does not need the fostering care of the white man to the same extent that the horse does, yet it is evident that he does to a certain degree, from the fact that he thrives better with it than without it. . . . [5]

If men would reflect maturely on the subject, they would soon be convinced that liberty is a blessing to those, and only those, who are able to use it wisely. I will illustrate this by the following:

All waters are to a greater or less extent inhabited by fish. Even the waters of the mighty deep, although they are so salt that we can scarcely taste thereof, and much less support life therewith, are yet inhabited by immense

5. Repeating his argument of what will happen to freedpeople, Tyson continues with two further examples. One is the problem of ex-slaves doing town labor and being reduced to menials; the other is about slavery as the natural condition for black people.

multitudes of great and small fishes. Now, suppose we should conceive the idea, as fresh water is more agreeable to our taste, that the fish of the sea would also thrive better therein, and should transport some of them from thence to some fresh water course, what would be the consequence? Why they would soon pine away and die. The sea is their natural element, and before removing them from thence it would be well for us to work upon them and change their natures, so as to make them conform to the new element, and if we fail to do this it would then be best for us to let them remain where they are. You will doubtless admit this.

I will here compare the servants at the South to the fishes of the sea. Whether or not they occupy their natural position, certain it is that it is one in which they have prospered more than any other in which they have ever yet been placed. Therefore, before changing their social position, we should first change their nature so as to make them conform to the new element. We need not argue that they should first be placed in the new element as they are, and let them conform thereto, for this experiment has been tried over and over again—the results of which I presume are generally known; and if we now try the experiment again under similar circumstances, similar results will be apt to follow. Therefore, before placing them in this new element their nature should first be changed and made to conform thereto; and if after a fair trial we fail to do this, I think you will admit that they had best remain as they are, after correcting the evils of servitude as much as possible.

I know the word master sounds badly to a great many—even to myself. I am therefore for consulting the interest of servants exclusively in this matter, and am for continuing them in servitude or not, according as their interest require. If this is not doing as we would be done by, I should like to know what is.

A few words to emancipationists and I will soon conclude this already very lengthy article. As sensible men I beg you to pause and reflect, and consider well what you are doing. Listen to the words of one who has at heart the best interests of these people, ere perhaps a nation may be involved in irretrievable ruin. Have any of you proven that the negro would be better off emancipated than where he now is, under the protection of a good and kind man as a master. No, my friends, you have not done it; you cannot do it. And unless you can prove from the Scriptures, and from countries where emancipation has already taken place, that his condition would thereby be bettered, why do you wish to try the experiment on so large a scale? Before striking to free more of these people I would advise you to do something for those already freed and in your midst. It has already been shown that crime among the free negroes of Massachusetts, the State where they enjoyed freedom longer than those of any other State, is over thirteen times as great as among her white inhabitants. So if you desire to do something for these people, here is a field open to you. I will endeavor to make this plainer by the following illustration:

We will say that a master-workman gives an apprentice a job of work to do, and he instead of doing it bungles over it in some way, or perhaps does a part of it wrong. He then applies to his master for more work. Does he give it to him? No, he tells him to go and do well the work that he gave him before, and he would then give him more. Even so in this case. Before you desire more work, first do well what you have on hand and you shall then have more.

Again: It is the belief of certain of your sect (emancipationists) that a thorough abolition would tend to the extermination of the black race; that they would vanish under it as did the Indians from the presence of the white man. I have heard these words with my own ears; so I cannot be mistaken in making the assertion. Is this your belief also? If it is, I would advise you to desist. I don't believe God requires any such work at your hands. I don't believe He requires of you to sacrifice 1,000,000 human beings in order to place in the road for *extermination* 4,000,000 others. I positively do not envy the man his happiness that would advocate emancipation with such a belief as this.

The negro is as yet but a child in intellect. I therefore think it should be our duty as Christian people to treat them kindly, and place them in whatever position they thrive best. I think the white race at least owes them that much; for they were stolen from their homes in Africa and forced here against their will. Therefore, as we have plenty of room for them, and they can also occupy a useful position in society, why exterminate the poor creatures?

It is, though, to be presumed that the above is a mere exception to the general rule, and that by far the larger portion of emancipationists inculcate their doctrine of universal freedom purely through philanthropic motives. But they have read Uncle Tom's Cabin and played it in their theatres away up North, until, in my opinion, they have formed many erroneous ideas concerning this institution.

Again: If the owning of servants be such a monster of an evil, how is it that such few persons South, where they of all others have the best opportunities of seeing and judging for themselves, have been found to raise their voices against it? We have, I presume, some as great philanthropists South as can be found anywhere else, and if this has been such a crime as is frequently represented, it seems that some of these would have come out and spoke against it. It is true a few have done this, and prominent among them was Mr. Helper, of North Carolina.[6] But it is to be presumed that to better the condition of these people was not the object he had in view; as I have it from good authority that he hated negroes. The white man, then, seems to have been the object of his pseudo-philanthropy!

But suppose his object had been accomplished thoroughly—that all the servants had been emancipated—do you suppose the condition of the white man would have been bettered thereby? No; never a whit, as long as the South continued to overtrade to the North. He would then have found that he had been striking upon the wrong string altogether. For even if the servants had been emancipated, our merchants would still have continued to trade North as long as they could buy goods a few cents cheaper; and while this state of affairs continued how could manufactories have been built up at the South? For the Northern people having got their manufactories in successful operation, and having the channel of trade turned thither, and also selling such quantities, and running but little or no risk to effect sales for lack of custom, could, under these circumstances, sell cheaper than the Southern people. It was, therefore, to the advantage of the Southern merchant to trade North; but it would, in the end, have been to the advantage of the people and community at large to have had at least a portion of these goods manufactured and vended at the South, even if they had for the time being been some higher. For I hold if I buy your corn, cotton, flour, &c., that you could then afford to buy of me my manufactured articles. By reciprocal trade the prices on both sides would soon be properly regulated. Therefore, to have a universally happy and prosperous country, all sections must produce as many of the necessary articles of home consumption as possible. Having somewhat digressed from the subject I will now return to it again.

I expect to adduce a few arguments to prove that all men were not created or born equal, and that the negro is an inferior species of the human race. But, even taking it for granted that they were not created equal, and that the negro is an inferior race, I, by no means, consider this a justifiable excuse for reducing them to bondage to serve a superior race, provided their pleasures and enjoyments of life would thereby be curtailed. I think, in this case, they should be looked upon with commiseration, and that it would be our duty as philanthropists to do something to elevate and better their condition, rather than to pounce upon them and sink them still lower in the scale of

6. Hinton Rowan Helper, *Impending Crisis of the South*. Tyson must attack Helper if he wants to maintain credibility among North Carolina's proslave unionists.

human existence, merely because nature happened to do a little more for us than it did for them. My only plea, then, for retaining these people a day longer in servitude, is that, under existing circumstances, I don't think their condition would be bettered by changing their social position. I am for first applying to them the anointing oil of learning and christianity; and, whenever it shall have been clearly demonstrated that they are in a fit condition to take care of themselves, I am then for their going out free.

But if, after exhausting these means, it should be discovered that they had not made proper advances in the sciences and civilization, we might then fairly infer that God never intended that they should be placed on a level with the Caucasian or white race. I will now point out some of the principal features wherein the white and black races differ:

1st. They are born different anatomically considered. The white infant at birth has its brain enclosed by fifteen disunited bony plates. The negro infant is born with a hard, smooth, round head, like a gourd. The head of the negro infant is also smaller than that of the white.

2nd. The negro is a prognathos species of the human race, *i.e.* have receding foreheads. Prognathos is a technical term derived from *pro*, before, and *gnathos*, the jaws, indicating that the muzzle or mouth is anterior to the brain.

I could multiply these differences to a much greater extent, but think I have mentioned enough to prove conclusively that they do differ anatomically considered, and this difference too is of such a character as to indicate inferior intellectual endowments on the part of the black race. As a farther evidence of this, they thrive better in a state of servitude than in any other position in which they have ever yet been placed. Where the fetters of the white man have been broken they have, generally speaking, appreciated their liberties, and made advances in the arts, sciences, civilization and literature. But where the fetters of the black man have been broken they have, generally speaking, (I wish I could say otherwise,) made a retrograde movement, and started back for savagism, barbarism and mental decay.

Again. It appears singular that the words of Mr. Jefferson in the Declaration of Independence, "That all men were created equal," should be made to date back and apply as an interpretation of the Scriptures written by inspiration thousands and thousands of years before. No such doctrine is inculcated in the Scriptures, and it cannot be found within the lids of the Bible that all men were created equal, such an idea being wholly of human origin.

In conclusion I would say, as certain emancipationists and philanthropists will probably differ with me in the views herein set forth, that I have written what I have solely as a duty, I think, I owe to my God, my country and my countrymen. And, as regards the colored people, I presume there is no person, neither North nor South, who has their interest at heart more than I; I sincerely wish them well. Therefore, before condemning what I have written relative thereto, I hope you will give the subject your careful consideration, and, if we still differ, let us differ honestly, and appeal to a decision of the people at the *ballot box* to say who is in the right.

As the agitation of the slavery question, in connection with the territorial question, has had much to do in producing our present unhappy state of affairs, I deem it expedient to make a few remarks relative thereto.

The institution of slavery at the South was safe, and protected in the States where it existed; and already the Southern people had more than twice as much land per head as the Northern people, as I will show before I get through. And more than this, the Missouri compromise line would have given them far more than their just proportion of the Territories, for rightly apportioned there was only about one-fifth of the Territories coming to the Southern people. But, not satisfied with this, thinking that Cotton was King, their politicians thought they could sway things as they pleased. (I presume they will find by the time these sectional troubles are ended that Cotton is not King.) So, by their machinations and thirst after power and revolution, they managed to bring about a repeal of the Missouri Compromise, with the ostensible purpose of carrying slavery onto the Territories whithersoever they desired, thinking, it seems, that they had a right to do as they pleased in this matter, without consulting the non-slaveholders of the North and the South.

In order to make this plainer I have some calculations thereon, which are herewith submitted. . . . [7]

I think the territorial and slavery questions should be settled, and settled permanently. Have no more voting upon them. At these elections, when a State is to be admitted into the Union, with or without slavery, as the case may be, there is always too much excitement at them, too apt to be blood spilt; and the excitement thus got up extends throughout both sections, and it is not to be wondered at that much trouble should have grown out thereof. Therefore, let this danger be avoided in the future by settling these questions fairly, permanently, and forever. Had the Southern people struck for a compromise upon such terms as the foregoing, I have not a doubt but the business might have been settled fairly and permanently. But, instead of

---

7. Tyson's calculations are to establish that the southern states need no more Federal territory. He fears scattering slaves over a large amount of land.

doing this, they have come out under the protection of State laws, and have assailed the best government the world ever saw. Our Government, though good, had some defects in it; but it should have been our duty to remedy these defects, and not have disrupted the Union for trivial causes, and in place of the lesser evils have brought on others infinitely greater.

Let the interest of servants be which way it may, if the rebels of the South persist long enough in this wicked, unholy, and uncalled-for war, slavery will certainly be wiped out as a consequence of the war, if nothing else. So, let what will become of slavery, in the language of the patriotic Jackson, "The Union must and shall be preserved."

It has doubtless been looked upon with wonder and astonishment by the Northern people, as well as Unionists South, how the Southern people, under such great disadvantages, have been able to hold out so long. The population of the Northern States exceeds that of the Southern more than two to one if we except the servants of the latter. And besides this the States of Delaware, Maryland, Virginia, Kentucky, Missouri, Tennessee and Arkansas, have sent, I believe, 111 regiments of soldiers to the field to fight against the rebellion. In addition to this the North have a large and powerful fleet, and the Southern people as good as none. There is also an extensive Union sentiment in the States of North Carolina,[8] Georgia and Alabama, which has troubled the Confederate authorities much in the prosecution of the war. So, when we take all these things into consideration, it is much to be wondered at how the rebels have been enabled to hold out so long. This can only be accounted for in one way. The Federal army attacking and failing to carry their point at some of the rebel strong holds, instead of attacking them at the weaker and more vulnerable places, where important victories could easily have been gained and at, comparatively speaking, but little loss, together with the dissentions among the Northern people, have, in my opinion, tended more to prolong the war than any other two causes.

I will give an illustration of this. A few days before the seven day's fight before Richmond took place, I was in Wilmington, N.C., and heard the citizens of that place say, that for the Federals to take that city they had but to come after it. At that time the Southern people had such a perfect horror of a gunboat that I don't suppose there would have been a gun fired, or at least that was the talk of the citizens of the place. Therefore, if the Union forces had only made a feint upon Richmond and had gone round and have

---

8. Tyson in a long footnote looks at unionist sentiment in Randolph and Moore Counties, North Carolina. He is frustrated over the Federal government's poor efforts to liberate the state's unionists.

taken Wilmington and other vulnerable places, how much they would have been worth to the Union cause! If Wilmington had been taken at that time North Carolina would have been compelled to come back into the Union ere this, because she could not possibly have supplied her citizens with salt. Large quantities of this were manufactured in and around Wilmington, which sold at from forty to fifty cents per pound, and was scarcely to be had at that in sufficient quantities to supply the wants of the people. Therefore, if Wilmington had fallen, North Carolina would have soon have fallen also, and one star plucked from the Confederacy the remaining States would soon have followed. And the beauty of the thing is that all of this might have been accomplished with but little or no loss of life.

The failure of the Union forces to take Richmond at that time was probably owing as much to their having undertaken an impossibility under existing circumstances, as to anything else; for the whole Southern Confederacy was there, so to speak. Already there were a great many troops at Richmond, but for several days before the battle every train by Raleigh and Wilmington was loaded down to the full with soldiers "for Richmond." Therefore, if there had been a little strategy used at this time the rebellion would, in my opinion, have been played out long ago, and at great saving of life also.

It is also thought by some that the emancipation policy has had a bad, rather than a good, effect, and that, if its farther enforcement was withheld, say for ninety days, so as to give the rebs one more chance, and would then call for volunteers, that the road leading to restoration of the Union would be as plain as the road to market. I will remark that as far as I am concerned, I would be for the emancipation policy if I thought the Union would thereby be restored sooner, and at a saving of life and treasure. In fact, I am for any just and honorable means leading to this end, and am, therefore, for using the negroes in any way that they can aid in putting down the rebellion, by which their condition would not be permanently worsted. And that they can aid materially in this business, even without going into the army, there is no doubt. It is, therefore, evident, if the South have to be brought back by force of arms alone, that the emancipation policy would have been the thing, provided the North had hung together on this question. But, taking that into consideration, together with the extensive Union sentiment in many portions of the South, it is thought some milder means would probably have done as well.

It is also thought that a reunion, to be worth anything, must be based upon the will of the people governed, and that, therefore, to have a good and permanent Government the extremists North and South must yield, and let the question at issue be decided by a popular vote of the people.

I think it was in June, of the present year, that the Rev. Dr. Massie, of England, visited the United States. He brought with him a petition signed by some seven hundred and fifty Protestant Ministers of France, and some five thousand of those in England, for the purpose of furthering the emancipation policy, which he presented to the President and Cabinet. If these gentlemen could do anything calculated to restore peace and quietude to our bleeding country, most happy would we be for them to do so. But anything that is calculated to embitter the feelings, prolong the struggle, and thus make the breach between the two sections greater, we do not desire to see. We, therefore, think that when the services of these Reverend gentlemen are needed to interpose in our political affairs they should be notified thereof.

It is to be presumed that the Administration have resorted to no means for the prosecution of this unnatural and uncalled-for war on the part of the rebs, only such as was thought would be instrumental in restoring the Union and at a savings of life and treasure. Therefore, if any of these measures have turned out to be impolitic, we should take it into consideration that this could not be known until they had been tried.

The rebels have tried certain impolitic measures, and prominent among them was the law exempting the owner of, or person having in charge, twenty negroes. This was about to work a considerable disturbance in placing a distinction between the slave and non-slave holder. Their legislators seeing this, wisely for the cause of the rebellion, repealed the ordinance before any serious disturbance had grown out thereof.

But be the emancipation ordinance and certain military changes that have been made, politic or impolitic measures, I think we have now got to where we can see through the rebellion. Therefore, if we will pull together, pull steadily, and hold out faithful a little while longer, the stars and stripes will, as I believe, soon wave triumphantly throughout the entire length and breadth of the land.

But in order to attain this great desideratum it is expedient that we keep united at this most important period in our national existence, or we may yet, perhaps, through the dissensions and divisions of the people, lose the prime object for which the Union forces set out, after having borne the burden and heat of the day. Then all the fighting that has been done, and the much blood that has been spilt on the part of the Union forces, will all have been spilt in vain.—The stars and stripes, the flag of the nation, would go down with dishonor and disgrace, and another be built upon the ruins thereof. Shall we thus, through dissensions, be compelled to acknowledge that they were right in seceding when the causes were not justifiable? Acknowledge that they were right in firing upon and capturing Fort Sumpter [sic], when it might have been honorably avoided? Acknowledge that they were right in inaugurating this cruel civil war, in which seas of blood have been poured out and billions of treasure expended? Acknowledge that those who have had treasonable intents against the General Government for the last thirty or forty years, were right at length in putting them forth? Acknowledge all these things, and, above all, permit those secessionists to build up a government based upon usurped power and against the will of a majority of the people at the South? No! never, never! Never will I, for one, as long as breath animates my body and while there is even a remote chance for success, agree to this.

If we would not have all these evils, and even greater, to come upon us, we must keep united. Justice to liberty, our country and our God demand that we keep united. Justice to the gallant dead who have fallen in defence of the stars and stripes, and who now lay mouldering in the clay, demand that we keep united. Justice to the many loyal people South, who have held out amidst various trials and persecutions, and who still hold out with the hope, in the end, of seeing the stars and stripes wave triumphantly over them, demand that we keep united. We must keep united or all may yet be lost, irretrievably lost.

The Southern people are principally building their hopes of success upon the prospect of these dissensions and a consequent revolution among the Northern people. This I know. Therefore, if the people would now exhaust this source of aid and comfort by becoming united, the rebellion would, and, as I believe, with but very little more shedding of blood, vanish like a bank of snow before a summer's sun.

We will take it for granted that the *status* or standing of the General Government towards the seceded States has only been changed in such things as they were driven to by the acts of the secessionists. This is but fulfilling the Scriptures where it says "one evil word calleth for another." We will, therefore, take it for granted, as soon as the rebellion shall have been conquered, that the former *status* or standing of the General Government will be resumed, unless a majority of the people should say otherwise. Therefore, it would be better for us to yield our private opinions for the present, than to cleave thereto and thereby endanger the Union cause. For we should recollect, in proportion as we divide and relax our energies North, that in just this same proportion do we give aid and comfort to the rebellion South. We should, therefore, know no party at this most important crisis, "save the Union and it saved." This sentiment should rise paramount to every party consideration. We should, therefore, be willing to leave these questions of minor importance for the people to decide hereafter, as they would, doubtless, decide them *right*. Therefore, keep united, press forward, don't give up the ship, and when it gets hot for our Southern brethren let them come back into the Union where they ought to be, and from which, in my opinion, they ought never to have gone. And, having gone without a cause, they may at last blame themselves most for the many privations, hardships and sufferings they now endure. And should slavery eventually suffer, they may also blame themselves most for that; for they were warned and told in time that secession would in all probability lead to the emancipation of their servants.

The following is, in the main, intended for my Southern brethren, should it by chance fall into their hands:

My Dear Friends:—What have your politicians and the secessionists promised you? They promised you that it should be peaceable secession. Some in their speeches asserted that they would pay the cost of the war for ten cents; others that they would wipe up all the blood that would be spilt with a pocket handkerchief; and others still more generous, said they would agree to drink all the blood that would be spilt. To be short, they by making such speeches as the above, managed to deceive many of you, and to get you to volunteer, telling you that we must present a formidable front, and thus back out the North. Whether or not, these persons were conscientious in making these statements, I am unable to say, but if they were certain, it is, that it has turned out, that they were greatly mistaken. After getting a goodly number of you to volunteer, they soon got the war started, and after getting that started, they soon devised means for forcing the remainder of you into the army. They did this first by the draft, and then subsequently and more completely by the unjust conscription. Even those of you, who have been bitterly opposed to secession and its fruits from the start, and whom they had denied the just rights of freemen in not permitting you to vote directly upon this all-important subject, they now, by their unjust legislation, compelled to take up arms, and go forth and fight the battles of the war that they had themselves inaugurated, sometimes even hunting you down, casting you in prison, and sending you forth in irons to shed your blood upon some cruel battle field. Was it justice, that you as peaceable citizens should thus have been hunted down, torn from your innocent and dependent families, and compelled to go forth and enact scenes that were revolting to your feelings, revolting to christianity, and revolting to civilization? Was it justice that our politicians largely in the minority, should thus of their own arbitrary power legislate away, as it were, your lives, and thereby create desolation, ruin and mourning throughout the entire length and breadth of the land? It undoubtedly was not justice, and to sum up the whole in a few words, was in my opinion, a grand usurpation of power, and ought not to have been submitted to for a moment.

I think in all republican governments, a majority of the people should rule, and particularly upon these all-important questions like the present, which has involved us in so much trouble and distress. Therefore, as our politicians thought proper to bring on this war without consulting you, I now think it would be fair and just for you to end the war without consulting them by deserting and fleeing from them, and leaving those secessionists to fight their own battles if they want any fought. Yea, I think your outraged rights demand that you should speedily desert and flee from them like rats from a sinking ship, and let the structure founder, and go down with the secesh only on board should they choose to hold on, and the next time they wish to secede, let them consult the masses of the people.

I have by these sectional troubles been compelled to take one of three positions, which were: first, to take sides with my Southern brethren in the rebellion; second, espouse the Union cause; and third, remain neutral, which I could easily have done after getting rid of the conscription.

But I could not take sides with my Southern brethren in the rebellion, from the fact, that I did not think the causes justified secession. And when so many of my fellow men were fast passing from time to eternity, feeling that I had a duty to perform, I could not content myself to remain neutral. Therefore, believing that my Southern brethren acted with too much haste, first, in seceding, and then inaugurating this wicked war; and, also, believing that the only safe and permanent way of settling our difficulties, is by a restoration of the Union, I have considered it my imperative duty to espouse the Union cause, and vindicate its principles through weal and through woe.

But I have thus been placed in a very uncomfortable situation, for I have kindred, persons that are near and dear to me by the ties of nature in the Southern army, and oh! shall they go down, or shall I once more, in peace, be permitted to behold their happy faces? This is a subject that draws like chords around my heart, and nothing but a conscientious belief, that I was in the discharge of my duty would have prompted me to have taken the stand that I have. Yea, before I would have done anything in this matter that I conceived would be against the best interest of my Southern brethren, and country generally, I would have suffered the last drop of blood that is within my veins to run cold. But it being a matter of so very great importance, one in which the very life of our country, as well as the destinies of probably many future generations is involved, I considered it my imperative duty to espouse the Union cause, and stand by it, live or die, sink or swim. I have accordingly done this at much expense and great risk. At length for issuing and circulating certain publications, I was twice arrested and imprisoned, and being in danger of a third arrest for a similar offense, thinking it might not go so well with me, I had been told I would be tried for treason if arrested any more, I deemed it expedient to evade this by crossing the line, and did so. I am though glad to see free speech is once more becoming dominant in my native State. Old North Carolina will soon take her position once more under the stars and stripes, and one star plucked from the Confederacy, the remaining States would soon follow.

Before closing, I wish to give a plan by which I think the Union can be restored, and at comparatively little loss of life. I have endeavored to show that there is an extensive Union sentiment existing in various portions of the South. Measures that would now increase this sentiment would, in my opinion, be the plan. And, in my opinion, the best way for doing this would be to give them evidence that a strong conservative feeling exists North. And the best way to test this would be to submit the following resolution to the legal voters of all the free States, and let them vote thereon, for or against as they see proper; to wit:

"That this war is not waged on their part in any spirit of oppression, or for the purpose of overthrowing or interfering with the rights and established institutions of the States, but to defend and maintain the supremacy of the Constitution, and to preserve the Union with all the dignity, equality, and rights of the several States unimpaired, and that as soon as these objects are accomplished the war ought to cease."

If the above were submitted to the Northern people, and an extensive Union sentiment should thereby be shown forth, I believe it would have more effect in restoring peace and reunion than all the gunpowder in the United States. And if thus restored by conciliatory measures, the work would then be completed. We could then join together and journey on once more happily and prosperously together. But if restored solely by force of arms, conciliatory measures would at last have to be resorted to; for, as has already been said, "A reunion to be worth anything, must be based upon the will of the people governed." I therefore think the Union could be restored sooner, and at a greater saving of human life, by this plan, than by any other known to me. Or it might be so arranged as have a proposition submitted to the Southern people also; and that is, let the two Governments by mutual agreement come to the understanding that, if the proposition already mentioned were submitted to the people of the Northern States, should be carried favorably, that the Confederate authorities should then submit to the Southern people the question whether or not they would accept a reunion upon this basis. If we could thus get this question out of the hands of the politicians into those of the people, I think they would soon decide it, and decide it right.

It is also thought, as the Federal Government is vastly superior in strength and power, that the Administration could, without endangering the cause in the least, either submit or receive proposals leading to peace and conciliation.

I have so much confidence in the above plan that if it could be inaugurated I would be willing to risk my all, even my life, that it would result in a restoration of the Union.

But if force of arms alone be resorted to, the longer our sectional troubles remain unsettled the more new difficulties will spring up, and the harder it will be in the end to reconcile them. We need not expect to settle our difficulties, and particularly by force of arms, in such a way as to be satisfied immediately at the result; for, let us settle them as we may, it will take time, and a great deal of it at that, to effectually heal the awful breach that has been made. Many times, if we would do what is best, we must do things that we do not wish to do. So of this all-important subject, now before us. Let us consult our interest rather than our feelings, for it is a subject in which is involved the destinies of probably many future generations; and if such a subject as this will not justify our yielding in some of our mere personal feelings, I should like to know one that would. So before tearing up and consigning to utter desolation and ruin this once fair portion of the earth, let us make one mighty effort to restore peace and quietude to our now disaffected country by conciliatory measures. *But if in the end mild words and gentle means would not reclaim the wicked, they must then be dealt with in a more severe manner.*

I have endeavored to give my views impartially upon this all-important subject, and we now come to take our last view of the matter. But, before doing so, I would desire to urge upon you, my countrymen, the vast importance of the struggle in which we are now engaged. The destinies of unborn generations are depending upon the issue. We should therefore rise up in our might, and declare that the Union must and shall be preserved. Had our forefathers been here, do you suppose they would have disrupted the Union for the causes that existed at the commencement of our sectional troubles? No; never, never. A voice from our gallant dead, who had fallen in the achievement of our liberties, and who now lay mouldering in a common grave, would have come up before them, saying, "Down with your schisms and divisions. It was not for this that we fought, bled, and died. Keep united, and you will be a great, happy, and prosperous people."

Therefore, the difficulties between the North and the South should not be viewed as existing between foreign enemies, but between people that should be towards each other as brothers, both sides of which have erred and gone aside from the path of duty. If each side would now do away with these wrongs, and let the two sections be united upon just and honorable terms, will, I think, in the end, be for the best.

Shall the Monarchal Powers of Europe point to our country as an example and say, that man is incapable of self-government? I hope not. Let us then join together as erring brothers, and yet solve the problem "that man is capable of self-government." What do you think the Father of this country would say were he now back to take a view of his once beloved country? "United we stand: divided we fall," would probably be his words.

We were making onward and upward strides, and the United States, but for these sectional troubles were destined soon to have taken front rank among the nations of the globe. But oh! where are we now? I answer in the broad road that leads to ruin, speeding our way thither, as fast as the wheels of time impelled forward by the rage of an infuriated people, can bid us fly.

Oh! that those that were principally in fault, in bringing on our sectional troubles, may soon be brought to see their error, and that their course may be changed before it be everlasting too late; that the dark cloud which has lowered over us as a nation and people, may soon break away; and that peace, ah! blessed peace, may beam forth upon us; and that we may ere long be a united, contented, and happy people, is the sincere desire of one who has at heart the interest of both sections of the country.

EDWARD W. GANTT

Address in Favor of Reunion in 1863

(New York: Loyal Publication Society, 1865)

E dward W. Gantt (1829–1874) was born in Maury County, Tennessee, practiced law there, and served as a delegate to the Southern Rights Convention at Nashville in 1850. In 1854 Gantt moved to Washington, in Hempstead County, Arkansas, opened a law practice, and became active in local Democratic party politics. At that time he belonged to the ultra-secessionist Thomas C. Hindman faction of state politics. Gantt secured election to the U.S. Congress in 1861 but did not take his seat. Also elected to the First Confederate States House, he instead entered the army, raised the Twelfth Arkansas Confederate Infantry, and became its colonel. Commended for bravery at the Battle of Belmont in November 1861, he gained promotion to brigadier general, then was captured in Tennessee and exchanged in August 1862. He returned home to await further assignment, received none, and, disillusioned, turned unionist in the fall of 1863. He fled to the Union lines and then made a major address in Federal-occupied Little Rock on October 7, 1863, denouncing the Hindman forces and President Jefferson Davis, which was later printed as this pamphlet, circulated in Arkansas, Tennessee, Missouri, and the North. While in the North in 1864, Gantt met with the president over reconstruction in Arkansas, received a pardon, and spoke about the plight of Arkansas civilians. He supported the election of William Meade Fishback to the U.S. Senate and asked that he be seated. After the war he became a scalawag, served as a state prosecutor, supervised the Freedman's Bureau in southeast Arkansas, and in 1873 prepared a digest of state laws.

His October 7, 1863, pamphlet in this volume is unique as the only unionist pamphlet of a former Confederate States general officer. In it he showed how Arkansas Confederate leaders had failed to protect the people and described the horrors of Confederate treatment of Arkansas unionists. He also advocated that unionist senator William K. Sebastian return to his seat in the Federal Congress. Gantt thus used his pamphlet to seek support from the Federal government, to assist the growth of the unionist movement in the state, and to praise the unionists for resisting the Confederate guerrillas.

Gantt has not had a biographer, and historians of the war in Arkansas have suggested his rejection of the Confederacy resulted from his failure to get promoted. That seems unlikely, considering the risks he took to publish his views on the war. For some information on his life, see Bruce S. Allardine, ed., *More Generals in Gray* (Baton Rouge: Louisiana State University Press, 1995); Carl H. Moneyhon, *The Impact of the War and Reconstruction on Arkansas* (Baton Rouge: Louisiana State University Press, 1994); and Michael B. Dougan, *Confederate Arkansas* (Tuscaloosa: University of Alabama Press, 1976).

* * *

Fellow Citizens:—Since the third day of June I have been a prisoner in the Federal lines.

Having but recently been through the entire South—having studied its resources, and wept over its ruin, and having become fully acquainted with its condition, and the character of its rulers, I have chosen, after long hesitation, to remain here and address you, in preference to being sent home and exchanged. I am now out of the service, and can therefore speak with unreserved freedom.

My course in this struggle is known to this country. In the army and in prison, with a fire in front and in rear, I have been with you and of you so long as hope remained. And to-day I know no devotion so strong as that I bear to my Southern home, and to the masses of our people, whose terrible sufferings bind me closer to them now than ever.

I shall give you my views and counsel for what they are worth, frankly and fully in this address, and care not for the consequences to myself. It is the path of duty, and I shall follow it fearlessly.

I shall speak to you as an Arkansian—shall therefore confine myself more particularly to what has occurred in our midst since the commencement of hostilities, and may thus give a prominence, to events and persons, that they shall not otherwise deserve. As I fear no one, I shall spare no one.

In the commencement of this unfortunate struggle our State hesitated; but when the shock of arms came, she opened her treasury and poured out her best blood. Her troops were removed beyond the Mississippi River, upon the principle that there was the place to defend her soil. We acquiesced. The principle was doubtless correct. For a time all things went well enough with us. We were only annoyed by partisan feuds and broils—by that selfish faction which so long ruled our people and left their debasing influences upon society.

But the poisoned cup had been prepared for us in the very beginning. We were destined to drain its dregs to the bottom. Our people, plundered, whipped, and oppressed, were to bow their necks to the yoke of a political adventurer, clothed in lace and brass buttons, who owed all he was to their kindness and charity. Hindman and the Johnsons—names inseparably linked with the sorrow and ruin of our people—formed a coalition and drew into it the cast-off scum of all parties.[1] From that day may date the ruin of our people, if not of our whole cause. Not that I intend attributing to them great force or capacity, but that circumstances of long ago, linking Hindman to Davis, and intrigue on the part of Johnson, were to place Hindman on a larger wave than a craft of his size could ride securely. So bitter and rancorous had been the hatred of these men toward each other, that such a union, if made publicly, would have shocked and startled our people. But it was done by stealth. It leaked out by degrees.

The promotion of Captain J. B. Johnson, brother of Robert W. Johnson, in Hindman's legion, at Hindman's instance—the urging of Hindman's promotion by Mr. Johnson in the secret and corrupt ante-chambers of Richmond politics—the appointment of Mr. Johnson's near relative on Hindman's staff—the urging of Hindman's further promotion—and, stronger and stranger than all, the procuring, by a trick of Mr. Johnson's, of the transfer of General Hindman to this Department, are cumulative evidences of this corrupt bargain—a bargain in which the blood and treasure of our people were to go to enrich the Johnsons. Hindman was to be transferred to this Department, and by his aid a great party was to be built up in our midst, and the enemies of the Johnsons put down. Having for years used the public treasure to put down foes and build up parties, now the blood of the people is to be used for this same purpose.

Mr. Davis was eager to do any thing for Hindman—would scruple little about the means or the result to the people; yet, in this instance, he hesitated. Mr. Johnson assured him that our people wanted Hindman here. That he was the man for the occasion. But with all this, Mr. Davis would

1. Robert W. Johnson, Arkansas Confederate States senator; Confederate general Thomas C. Hindman from Arkansas.

not send him by "authority"; yet, would permit him to be smuggled across. Our people were amazed at his advent. More so when they found that Mr. Johnson had brought him, and that the press at Little Rock, heretofore his abusers, was subservient to him. It was voiceless so far as Hindman's usurpations and oppressions might be. No other reason has ever yet been given for its mysterious silence than the prompt appointment, by Hindman, to positions of influence, of near relatives of the editors of these papers. And so the plot thickens.

In all the instances of appointees referred to in this address, I do not intend accusing them of complicity with the leaders, and may as well say so here.

When Hindman came here we had no army on our soil—nor indeed any hostile army threatening us. [This needs modification. But the threat had passed before the army was organized.] The policy of the Confederate authorities had been announced. It was that no more regiments should be organized, but that all men liable to military duty should be enrolled in regiments then existing. This policy was in the way of Hindman's building up, for himself and the Johnsons, a great array of satellites, by the "appointing power." Therefore, in the teeth of this policy, and disregarding authority, he organized and officered some forty regiments. The poor soldier could not choose his own officer. He might not choose what would be regarded as Johnson-Hindman material. But the creation and continued existence of an officer, as such, depended upon Hindman's breath alone. It remained now to be seen what one, who had crawled in the dirt before the people, when he wanted place, would do when he held supreme power.

Among the first acts was to declare martial law all over the State, and to appoint patrols of ten, with a captain, in each township—a new military organization of his own creation. Among their duties was to assist in arresting and imprisoning, without charge or complaint, the suspected freemen of Arkansas. And many a poor creature, thus torn from home and family, died in a loathsome prison, or perished by the wayside. Would you believe it, my fellow-citizens, that two or three lines from Hindman or one of his subordinates has been all the commitment upon which respectable citizens, with their heads shorn, have lingered a year in the penitentiary, treated as ordinary convicts? The records are in the city of Little Rock.

But this is not all. He plundered our people most mercilessly. Anarchy and despotism vied in their reign. His Commissary Department was so miserably managed that, with an abundant country to draw and collect supplies from, it was so neglected, that, I am told, in many instances he took bread from the mouths of helpless women and children, whose only stay and support had perished by disease or the bayonet. He assumed to regulate prices. By this arbitrary and tyrannical means he caused great suffering, and afforded increased facilities for the growth of fraud and crime, while all honest men were well nigh impoverished. He ordered cotton to be burned in regions remote from navigation, and where an army will never tread, and where, if it should come, it could not more than transport supplies, much less haul cotton. And he sent brutal, rough men to execute these orders. If a citizen complained, he was snubbed, plundered, or imprisoned. Oftener all of these things. Of all these things Jeff. Davis was duly informed.

When long absences and tales of distress, coming from the plundered homes of toil-worn soldiers, impelled them, from impulses not to be despised, to force their way home, to stop the cries and suffering of babes and soothe the sorrows of heart-broken wives, with the intention of again returning to their command, he has not waited their return, but treated them as deserters, had them hunted with negro dogs, and when caught, executed with a fiendishness alike cruel and shocking to humanity.

He has, I am told, appointed military commissions which should keep no records, and from their midnight recesses spoken away the lives of citizen and soldier. In one instance this mysterious and worse than Jesuitical tribunal condemned, to six months' imprisonment, a citizen of our State. With a stroke of his pen he raised the penalty to capital punishment, and the victim was accordingly executed. What the supposed offender did, what he was accused of doing, there is no written record left. Voltaire says that in Africa, tyrants who execute with their own hands criminals condemned to death, are justly called barbarians. He would be puzzled for a name for the tyrant in this instance.

In other cases he is said to have caused men to be executed without trial, and even to have witnessed their execution. In others, again, he is said to have seized citizens and put them upon trial before military tribunals, and had them executed. In one instance, the offense being Unionism, it was ascertained, after trial and sentence, that the supposed offender was a good Southern man. A pardon from Hindman was started, but the bearer only reached there in time to see the lifeless form of the murdered man being borne from the desecrated spot of his execution. Of all these things Jefferson Davis was duly informed.

The story of the two young Texas soldiers I have often heard, and never heard it contradicted. They were twin brothers—young, handsome, and sprightly. Having just entered the service, and from a State noted for its peculiar ideas of personal freedom, they supposed that a few days' absence from camp without leave would subject them to nothing more than a slight camp punishment. And having relatives a few miles in the country, whom they had not seen for years, they concluded to visit them. Poor fellows! Hindman was fresh from Bragg![2] They were hunted down, summarily tried, convicted, and the sentence approved in one day. The young men, in person, urged their youth and inexperience as an excuse, and begged him to let them live, assuring him they would show him, if spared, what soldiers they could make. Their gray-haired sire, bearing about his person the marks of wounds received at the Alamo and upon battle-fields of Mexico, with breaking heart bowed before him and craved pardon for his thoughtless and innocent boys. And women, struck with their youth and innocence, with tears and intreaties implored mercy for the unfortunate youths. But in vain. The tyrant was inexorable. The noble youths fell, after a tender and touching farewell, victims to the ambition of one who was misled by the cruelty of Bragg, and who, in adopting the latter's style of discipline, took up the club of Hercules, and so, not being able to wield it, degenerated into a mere murderer.

He turned the Indians against us—thus leaving us defenseless, and threatened by a savage foe in the West, besides the loss of the whole territory. There was but one man on the continent who could control them. Nature, education, habits, and appearance, had peculiarly fitted him for the task. That man was Gen. Albert Pike.[3] He should have been permitted to remain there. Hindman and Johnson intrigued him out. Mr. Davis preferred risking the loss of that country, and our ruin, to the loss of his pet. He even permitted General Pike to be dragged through the country, like a common culprit, between a file of soldiers! What hope had a poor down-trodden citizen, when a general officer, and he one of the first men of the nation, could be thus treated with impunity at the instance of one of Davis' creatures? Of all these things Jefferson Davis was informed.

But our people, in the soreness of their agony, and from the depths of their oppression, petitioned Mr. Davis for relief. Month after month rolled by and no response. Still, month after month they groaned, and suffered, and supplicated. Their appeals for relief fell upon leaden ears. And while the people suffered, the Johnsons and Hindmans feasted and flourished, and were glad. But at last the current of agony and complaint was too great. The tardy response came. And what, oh, my suffering countrymen, do you suppose that answer is? It is that "Hindman is there without authority." What a terrible retribution we had a right to expect. The least we could

2. Gen. Braxton Bragg had a reputation for cruel treatment of his troops.
3. The scandal of the removal of Gen. Albert Pike from office rocked the Confederacy.

hope—had his acts been done by one here by authority—would be that he would meet removal and prompt punishment—and surely, that the one who, here, "without authority," had robbed, pillaged, and destroyed—oppressed and murdered, and crushed the very life out of our people, would be put upon trial as a culprit, and meet a felon's doom. We shall see.

In amazement, you would ask me if Mr. Davis knew of these things. All of them. Besides what private citizens all over the State had written him, General Pike, in written charges and in powerful published pamphlets, made most of it known to him and the world. But R. W. Johnson and his followers are supreme at Richmond. He owns the whole representation from this State, except Mr. Garland, who has all the sense and manliness of the concern. Verily, the "vessel of State must have been violently agitated, or such foul dregs could never have risen to the top!"

One Hanly did venture to whisper in his own room, with locked doors, to a few citizens, about these outrages; but he locked their mouths with a pledge of secresy before they left, lest "Bob Johnson" should think he had turned traitor to him. And poor old Mitchel would talk so much on both sides, that, as usual, he neutralized what he said, while Mr. Garland's utterances were stifled between affection on the part of Davis for Hindman, and subserviency to Mr. Johnson.[4] The latter gentleman will not desert Hindman yet. The harvest of place and power reaped by them is too great to lose. Better the people groan and suffer. So, after all his wickedness, Hindman is still to remain here. But to soothe the public, and blind it, a new man must be brought over—one they can use, of course. Mr. Johnson finds him—a weak, superannuated old creature, who has made "Lieutenant-General Holmes" for this express command—the interests of Arkansas being subordinated to that of the Johnsons, and to the hate of Mr. Davis—for our poor oppressed people demanded General Price—or rather, begged for him piteously, our days for "demanding" having passed.[5]

The acts of this poor, unfortunate, and pitiable old man are known to all. Our people breathed free for a moment after he came—for, the press here belonging to the coalition, he was eulogized excessively. But they soon saw the stroke of Hindman's odious orders, and the terrible scenes of oppression and plunder went on as before.

With all this our people were still willing to suffer and to bleed, if any military results favorable to us might flow from it. Our hopes were

4. Probably Augustus Hill Garland, a member of the Confederate House and Senate from Arkansas.
5. Generals Theophilus Holmes of Arkansas and Sterling Price of Missouri.

disappointed. Military affairs were neglected. Johnson and Hindman were intent on keeping up political prestige, and even induced poor old General Holmes to use the influence of his rank and gold lace upon weak members of the Legislature in the election for the Confederate Senator. Thus the time was passed in feasting and dancing, and political wire-working, while the poor soldier shivered under the bleak sky, and the poor citizen groaned under oppression and wrong, and trembled lest the last morsel should at any moment be taken from his helpless family.

General Holmes had no plan of campaign, no conception of his duties, and not manliness and honesty enough to give way to a better.

While this state of affairs existed I addressed a letter to Mr. Davis, as follows:

"Sir, if something is not done for Arkansas, we are ruined. Our people have been terribly oppressed. They are yet. They need relief. They want General Price. Send him, and he will winter in Missouri with sixty thousand men. If you don't, this Department is gone, and Arkansas must and will seek protection elsewhere.

"General Holmes has no plan of campaign. Hindman is in the Northwest, with some fifteen thousand men. But the centre, under Roane and a few other stupid political appointees of Hon. R. W. Johnson, is too far off to support him. The centre, in turn, can not be supported by the right under Hindman, or the left under Churchill, at Arkansas Post—while the latter place, if attacked, can not be supported, and must fall.[6] Besides, General C., although a good soldier, is, in my opinion, incompetent to the command. I speak of these things as against offensive movements upon the part of the enemy. As for the offensive movements upon our part, General Holmes has undertaken none. Nor does he even contemplate it. If our troops remain here, they ought to go into Missouri at once.

"But, as I said in my last letter, all the soldiers on this side of the river, except about five thousand mounted men, to keep out marauding bands, ought to be sent across the Mississippi River, for every man sent from this side the river forces the Federals to send one to meet him. Thus Arkansas would be relieved of a friendly and hostile army both. Then, holding Vicksburgh [sic] and its approaches, in the meantime, and our people being left free to sow and reap in peace, we can supply the whole army on the east side of the river. But, by all means, send Price here, and let him go into Missouri. He would be received with the wildest enthusiasm. If he is not sent, we are ruined.

6. Thomas James Churchill from Arkansas and John Selden Roane from Tennessee served under Hindman.

"I know that certain politicians from our State talk differently. They either don't know what they talk about, or are subserving some selfish ends at the cost of the people. I know that I have long been the victim of petty partisan intrigue there; but, as having been the chosen representative of half the people of Arkansas in the Federal Congress, and as that verdict has never been set aside by them, I have the right to speak, and do, in their name and behalf, most solemnly urge these views upon you. I beseech you not to listen alone to politicians, who, repudiated and kicked out of power in 1860, were so unmanly as to crawl back into like places when the country was in arms. I beseech you not to let their selfishness be our ruin. While I would scowl to ask this for myself, I can do so cheerfully for my people.

"This letter, for the present, I desire should be considered as private and confidential."

My appeals did not even elicit a response. Time wore on. My predictions proved true. Hindman was defeated at Prairie Grove. His shattered columns, over snow and ice, half clad and half fed, wound their toilsome way back to Little Rock. About five thousand went home by force. Churchill was attacked at Arkansas Post; but, being cut from the hope of succor, the place was surrendered after a feeble resistance. Mr. Davis had been warned time and again of these dangers. But Hindman was his pet and protégé. Sending Price would interfere with Hindman, and would likewise give opportunity for distinction to a man he hated. This noble and good old man, who is a statesman and a soldier, has been meanly and malignantly disparaged and oppressed by Mr. Davis since the commencement of the war.

Our people, after these reverses, were more disheartened than ever. They clamored for Hindman's removal and trial. General Pike preferred the charges, and went to Richmond in person to prosecute them. But Mr. Davis smuggled Hindman back on the other side of the river, and gave him the dignified and appropriate position of president of a court of inquiry, to investigate the conduct of one other pet of his, General Mansfield Lovell, who so ingloriously surrendered New Orleans—commencing in Louisiana what Hindman had completed in Arkansas. But, as if to add injury to insult, Mr. Davis at last "indorses" openly the acts of Hindman, and, to add to your shame and humiliation, gives him command of a division in Bragg's army. Humanity stands appalled, and reason aghast, at such acts of perfidy, baseness, and cruelty.

Oh, my countrymen, your suffering has been indescribable—inconceivable! We thought we were fighting for constitutional liberty, when a tyrant was most mercilessly treading that constitution under his feet by every act of outrage and oppression that a conquered people can feel. And, after nearly two years of strife, we awaken, from a fearful baptism of blood, to the terrible truth that the shadow of the despotism which we fled from, under Mr. Lincoln, dissolves into nothingness compared to the awful reign of tyranny that we have groaned under at the hands of Jefferson Davis and his minions. Will we profit by such awakening? It remains to be seen.

The army that Hindman raised and officered here, against authority, and "without authority," has, by disease, death, and destruction, dwindled to a mere handful of men. The same material, if it had never been thus organized, or if, after organization, it had been sent to Bragg as he entered Kentucky, would have enabled him to be on the Ohio line to-day. It certainly could have held Vicksburgh and its approaches, if assigned to that duty. Hence I said, in the early part of this address, that not only the ruin of our State, but of our cause, might be attributed to Hindman and the Johnsons. The forty thousand men sacrificed to their ambition could have turned the scale in any State—any Department.

But with all our sufferings and sorrows, we had hopes of success and better things while Vicksburgh held out. But Mr. Davis had a pet appointee here. His narrow stubbornness and great vanity would not permit him to remove Pemberton, because such removal would be an admission that Mr. Davis was wrong. Rather the people suffer than such admission. Pemberton was a bad appointment—clearly incompetent. Possessing the confidence of neither citizen nor soldier, and Mr. Davis cognizant of it, he was still retained in command. He lost Vicksburgh.[7] In his department were sixty thousand troops when General Grant undertook the bold and hazardous plan of running our batteries at Vicksburgh, and marching inland with less than fifty thousand men for duty.

Contrary to all military science and experience, Pemberton scatters instead of massing his forces. He leaves a weakened force, at Port Hudson, flanked on both sides—reduces the garrison at Vicksburgh, and leaves small forces at Raymond, Grand Gulf, Jackson, Yazoo City, and other points away up in Mississippi. General Grant was thus enabled, with his columns massed, to whip him in detail.

After the repulse at Grand Gulf—which forty thousand men on the defensive could have prevented, and which were in Pemberton's department—and the flight from Raymond, General Joe Johnston was sent to assume command. That noble officer, despised by Davis, and not even spoken to by that mercenary wretch, Benjamin—who controls, by indirection Davis and Cabinet—cheerfully repaired to Jackson. Arrived there, he is said to have shed tears over the hopelessness of affairs and the splendid opportunity lost.

7. John C. Pemberton surrendered his troops at Vicksburg.

You are familiar with the rest—our appalling loss at Edward's Depot, and the fall of Vicksburgh and Port Hudson with their brave defenders. Thus, with the loss of friends and relatives, came the blighting of your last hopes. And all to gratify the narrow obstinacy, mean selfishness, and personal hate and vindictiveness of Jefferson Davis and Judah P. Benjamin. Thus Arkansas was cut off from all chance of protection, if hope thereof she ever had. And thus stands the case to-day.

This gentleman has proven himself totally unsuited to the emergency. With the whole cotton crop and wealth of the South at his disposal, and the friendship of many European Powers, he has accomplished nothing abroad. His foreign policy has been a stupid failure. He has permitted himself to be over-reached and out-managed in every thing. His policy at home, while proving him to be strong in some respects, has shown him to be weak, mean, and malignant in others. He is cold, selfish, and supremely ambitious, and, under the cover of outward sanctity and patriotism, flows concealed the strongest vein of hypocrisy and demagogism.[8]

He has never been up to the magnitude of the undertaking. He refused troops for the war in May, A.D. 1861, because he did not "know that they would be needed." His idea at first seems to have been that hostilities would soon cease, and he bent his energies for a cheap war. His preparations and outfit were accordingly contracted and parsimonious. Awakened to a sense of his error, his next aim seems to have been to conquer his foes and put down every man that had crossed his pathway in life. The latter succeeded at all events. Instances of this are numerous; but that of Senator Brown—the peer of Mr. Davis in every thing, his superior in many, and his rival and successful competitor for the United States Senate—is pointed.[9] He joined a company in Davis's army, and was elected captain. He had capacity for any position. Yet Mr. Davis, not looking to the public interest, but to the gratification of his own private feelings, sees this opportunity to strike an old rival, and embraces it. He refused him all promotion, and left him the alternative of wearing himself out as captain of a company, or seeking position elsewhere. Mr. Brown's election to the Confederate Senate terminated the matter.

He drove General Gustavus W. Smith from the army. He was once ready to remove Stonewall Jackson, and only the success of the latter, backed by

8. Gantt obviously does not approve of Judah P. Benjamin, either as secretary of war or as secretary of state in the Davis cabinet.

9. Albert Gallatin Brown, fire-eating radical from Mississippi and two-term Confederate States senator.

a powerful and excited party, prevented it. He over-slaughed and oppressed Beauregard because he let the people know that he desired to move on Washington, at once, after the first Manassas fight, and was prevented by Davis. He drove General Walker, of Georgia, out of the service. He retained Hindman, in Arkansas, with a positive knowledge of his outrages. He removed him but to endorse his acts. He retains Holmes here, to gratify the Johnsons, at the ruin of our people. He has pursued and oppressed General Price, because, I suppose, the latter was made a brigadier in Mexico, and Davis was not. He retained Pemberton in command against the wishes of the army and the country, and, to add insult to it all, sends him to Mobile to take command, where he is execrated by every man, woman, and child. By a trick and a swindle he got General J. E. Johnston away from his command in Virginia, and gave him no other definite position until there was a pressing emergency, and a chance to damage him—thereby showing both his want of confidence in him and his malignity towards him. He drove General Pike out of the army to gratify Hindman and the Johnsons, and thereby lost to us the whole Indian country, and, if the war continues, will place the tomahawk and scalping knife at the throats of our women and children. He retains a weak and inefficient cabinet, and never calls them in council, that he may reign as sole despot over our people. He has had at his disposal physical force enough to carry out acts the most arbitrary and oppressive. He has used that force. He has shown his selfishness and disregard for the interest of the people by his appointment of Heath [sic], Van Dorn, Dick Taylor, Davis, and Mansfield Lovell—all relatives of his, and all alike incompetent.[10] He has alienated the people of Georgia—so much so, that were the Confederacy acknowledged to-day, Georgia would not remain two years under him. I heard a Confederate General of great prominence, who understands the feeling in that State, so declare. And, as significant of this, Governor Brown, of Georgia, gave to General G. W. Smith, meanly and spitefully driven out of the army by Davis, the presidency of the Etowah iron works, with a salary larger than that of his salary as Lieutenant-General. He falsified all the promises to Kentucky, and took General Humphrey Marshall's command away from him, turning it over to his old political rival, General Preston,[11] to gratify the partisan requirements of Kentucky citizens who had suddenly risen from the obscure position of pork packers to that of Senators and Representatives in the Confederate Congress, and

10. Confederate generals Henry Heth, Earl Van Dorn, Joseph Robert Davies, and Richard Taylor.

11. William Preston.

jugglers in that political Sodom. In a word, he has enriched and honored his friends, ruined and impoverished his enemies. Has given over the people, those of Arkansas especially, to plunder and oppression by his favorites, and in no instance punished the offender. I admit that in some things he looms above other men; but he has so many defects and weaknesses beneath others, that it reduces him to a very poor second-rate character. And you can never change him. His life has been warped by political intrigue. His prejudices have been narrowed and his hates embittered by years of partisan strife. And you had as well take the oak which has been bent while a twig and beat upon by the storms of centuries, when its boughs are falling off and its trunk decaying, and attempt to straighten it up toward Heaven, as to attempt the straightening of a character so warped and bent by years of political storm and intrigue.

What shall we do? This question naturally comes up after all that has preceded. If Mr. Davis, when he held the lives and fortunes of so many millions in his hands, so blundered as to lose his opportunity, what can we hope from him now that a scene of blackness, of anguish and desolation reigns where wealth, happiness, and plenty smiled? If he would not protect Arkansas when he could, but, instead, gave it over to oppression and plunder by his pets, what have we to hope now that he trembles in Richmond for his own safety, and wakes up at last to the terrible reality of his folly, weakness, and indiscretion? If we were not protected when we could have been, and if we can not now be protected, what must we do? Some say continue the struggle. Let the last man die, etc.

I think differently. We ought to end the struggle and submit. But you say, it is humiliating. No more than to surrender when whipped. We have done that often—always where we could do no better. I have tried the experiment twice, and found it by no means foolish. Submission is but surrender. We are fairly beaten in the whole result, and should at once surrender the point.

If we don't get the happiness we enjoyed in the old government, we can get no more misery than we have felt under Jefferson Davis. But I look for peace there. We had it many years. Even while we are arrayed against it, I find that hostile forces in our midst give more protection to citizens than they had when Holmes and Hindman were here. It is true the Johnsons tell you that General Steele[12] has imprisoned and oppressed people here. Not a word of truth in it. And they know it is all false. In a few months, when no

12. Union general Frederick Steele, leader of the Federal Arkansas expedition, and later commander of the Department of Arkansas.

more Confederate money can be invested, and nothing more made out of the people, they will sneak back and claim his protection.

But we are whipped—fairly beaten. Our armies are melting, and ruin approaches us. Will continuing this struggle help us? Every battle we might gain ought to wring tears from the hearts of Southern men! We are just that much weaker—that much nearer our final ruin. Anguish and sorrow and desolation meet us wherever we turn. The longer the struggle the more of it.

Don't let yourselves be deceived with the hope that the United States will abandon the struggle. They can never do it. They have toiled and spent too much to see the solution of the problem, and not foot up the figures. They scarcely feel the war at home. Their cities are more populous and thrifty to-day than ever. For every man who dies, or gets killed in battle, two emigrate to the country. Their villages and towns, their fields and country flourish as fresh as ever. They could sink their armies to-day, and raise new levies to crush us and not feel it.

How is it with us? The last man is in the field. Half our territory overrun. Our cities gone to wreck, peopled alone by the aged, the lame and halt, and women and children; while deserted towns, and smoking ruins, and plantations abandoned and laid waste, meet us on all sides, and anarchy and ruin, disappointment and discontent lower over all the land.

You rely upon foreign intervention. Alas, and alas! How many lives, hopes, and fortunes have been buried under this fatal delusion! It has held us on to a hopeless struggle while the belt of desolation has girdled us closer, and the sea of anguish and sorrow risen higher, flushed with the tears of ruined and bereaved ones. France will not interfere. Louis Napoleon has at heart the building of the transit route connecting the two oceans. If he can keep up this struggle until that is accomplished, the star of England's ascendency on the ocean goes out before him, and the whole commercial world becomes subsidiary to him. To keep up this struggle he will delude us continually with false hopes, recking nothing how much we bleed and suffer. I even suspect the pretended loans to us in France rest upon a policy of this sort, and that he is at the bottom of it.

But if Louis Napoleon does propose to interfere and take us under his "protection," what then? Another Maximilian for us—for Americans! "Forbid it my countrymen! Forbid it heaven!" Our fathers threw off colonial dependence upon a European crowned head! It would be ignominious in us to go back a half century and more to accept what they freed us from. Much less to risk a despot over us. So eager are some of our leaders for this interference that I am told it is proposed to give Napoleon Texas as a bonus for his good graces and his kindly aid! And the "Lone Star" may be handed over by Davis at any moment, so far as he can do it.[13] The thought ought to make the blood of every American citizen mount to his cheek. Whenever this is attempted I shall be one to meet the legions of France, under the old flag, to battle for the sacredness and safety of republican institutions. But suppose he offers recognition alone? It is a barren offering. Suppose he offers it coupled with assistance? It comes too late. *Timeo Danaos munera ferentes!* No more dangerous and destructive alliance, in our prostrate condition, could be formed, however eagerly he might, at first, have grasped it. For, even if we should succeed with his aid—and the struggle would be as doubtful as terrible (and he would abandon us at any moment), the French empire of Mexico, right at our doors, would swallow up Cuba and all the contiguous islands, and absorb that part of Mexico that we, as a nation, would hope to get. And the day we settle deliberately a monarchy on this side of the ocean, we prepare crowns for kings and fetters for the people on every foot of ground upon the American continent. But, as I said, there will be no interference.

Have no hopes from a divided North. It is on the surface—scarcely goes to the bottom of their politics, much less shaking the great masses of their determined people. Remember, too, that much of the South is with them. There is no division so far as fighting us is concerned. The mildest of them simply propose peace by reconstruction. That rejected, they are to press us with redoubled energy. Let us not, after all our misfortunes, construe the struggle between politicians for place into a sympathy for ourselves. But how could they propose peace? Who would bring the message? To whom would it be delivered? And should the proposition be made and rejected, we are that much worse off for it. We must propose peace, for we ought to know when we have got enough of the thing.

Do not rely upon splitting up our army, and adopting the Guerrilla mode of warfare. It will contribute nothing to the general result and only entail more suffering. If practiced behind the Federal lines, it subdues our own people. It converts many of our soldiers into robbers and plunderers, and brings down, oftentimes, terrible retribution upon the heads of our citizens. What does the shooting of a few friends and foes on a railroad train amount to? And your own friends, as prisoners, going or returning, are on nearly all of them. In order to shoot a citizen or soldier opposed to you, you risk taking the life of a relative, a friend, or perhaps a brother soldier, who,

13. French Emperor Louis-Napoléon had an army in Mexico. Some southern unionists believed President Davis intrigued with him.

having lingered long in prison, is returning with his sad heart full of home and loved ones.

And then to fire upon steamboats. It is dangerous to your friends—unmanly and unsoldierly in the extreme. Before a city is fired upon, it is the duty of the commanding officer to give his adversary reasonable notice to remove the women, children and non-combatants. Steamboats always have more or less of this class of people on board. A single shot may destroy a steamboat with all its passengers. How much stronger, then, the reason not to fire upon it until a like notice is served?

A few days since a Confederate officer was aboard a transport with his family. The boat was fired upon by guerrillas. He stepped forward and entreated the party not to fire, that their friends were on board. A ball entered his heart, and his widow and orphans are in the care of strangers. He was the only person touched.

On the boat that transported us were the wives, sisters, and mothers of Missouri soldiers, who had left home and country to join their husbands and relatives in the Southern army. How terrible was the thought which often occurred to me on our trip, that the ball of the guerrilla, in the foolish hope of killing a foe, might go to the heart of his homeless wife, then throbbing with anxiety to be once more pressed to his manly bosom. And this is a constant danger. Not a boat but contains more or less of these people.

But this mode of warfare, while contributing nothing toward the general result, breaks up the peace of communities. It has never whipped an army; never retarded its progress; never cut off its supplies, nor interfered materially with its operations. It recoils upon us invariably. For instance, we fall back before the enemy. Our family is left in his lines. The country around them has been devastated. The United States authorities permit the bringing of supplies. We fire upon their transports. No more supplies come, and our families are left on the verge of starvation. This thing has occurred both in Tennessee and Arkansas. I implore all of our citizens within the Federal lines to remain at home and keep quiet. Let West Tennessee be a warning to you. Long since, that country would have been quiet and the people recovering from their losses, had it not been infested with guerrillas, who, abandoning warfare, have plundered friend and foe, and kept life and property insecure. Indeed, a detailed account of their acts would be sickening and disgusting in the extreme. As the federal army advances through Arkansas let the sunlight of peace be behind it, however dark and threatening the cloud ahead. If we do not robbers and freebooters will take possession of our soil, and soon depopulate and convert it into a waste.

I am asked if Mr. Lincoln's Emancipation Proclamation will stand. If you continue to struggle, certainly. He has the physical force at his disposal to carry it out. If you cease now, you may save all in your hands, or compromise on gradual emancipation. But let, I beseech you, the negro no longer stand in the way of the happiness and safety of friends and kindred.

The changes of sentiment upon this question in the South have been curious. Not many years since it was by no means unusual for the press and public men, as well as for the people generally in the South, to concede that slavery was an evil, and regret that it had ever existed; expressing, however, no disposition or desire to be rid of it. Yet, a few years more—the demand for cotton having increased, the price of negroes having advanced, and the agitation of the slavery question having increased in virulence—finds us defending slavery as a divine institution. *DeBow's Review*, and other southern papers and periodicals, with Senator Hammond, of South Carolina, were prominent in this defence. Their object was to educate the Southern mind to this belief. Such a course had become vital to the existence of slavery; because, to concede that negro slavery was morally wrong, was virtually to concede the whole argument to the Abolitionists. As the controversy warmed we became sensitive, and so morbidly so, that the North might have threatened with impunity to deprive us of horses, or other property—yet the whole South would be ablaze if some fanatic took one negro. Such was the public sentiment South at the commencement of this most unfortunate and bloody struggle. But revolutions shake up men's thoughts and put them in different channels. I have recently talked with Southern slaveholders from every State. They are tired of negro slavery, and believe they could make more clear money, and live more peaceably without than with it. As for the non-slaveholder of the South, I honestly thought the struggle was for him more than for his wealthy neighbor. That to free the negro would reduce to comparative slavery the poor white man. I now regret, that instead of a war to sustain slavery, it had not been a struggle at the ballot box to colonise it. This will clearly be the next struggle.

I am of opinion that, whether it is a divine institution or not, negro slavery has accomplished its mission here. A great mission it had. A new and fertile country had been discovered and must be made useful. The necessities of mankind pressed for its speedy development. Negro slavery was the instrument to effect this. It alone could open up the fertile and miasmatic regions of the South, solving the problem of their utility, which no theorist could have reached. It was the magician which suddenly revolutionized the commerce of the world by the solution of this problem. It peopled and made opulent the barren hills of New England, and threw its powerful influence across the great North-west. Standing as a wall between the two sections, it caught and rolled northward the wealth and population of the Old World, and held in their places the restless adventurers of New England, or turned them along the great prairies and valleys of the West. Thus New England reached its climax, and the North-west was overgrown of its age, while the South, with its negro laborers, was sparsely settled and comparatively poor. Thus slavery had done its utmost for New England and the North-west, and was a weight upon the South. If, at this point, its disappearance could have clearly commenced, what untold suffering and sorrow might have been avoided.

Its existence had become incompatible with the existence of the Government. For, while it had stood as a wall, damming up the current and holding back the people and laborers of the North, it had, by thus precluding free intercourse between the sections, produced a marked change in their manners, customs, and sentiments, and the two sections were growing more divergent every day. This wall, or the Government—one must give way. The shock came which was to settle the question. I thought that the Government was divided, and negro slavery established forever. I erred. The Government was stronger than slavery. Re-union is certain, but not more certain than the downfall of slavery. As I have said, the mission of the latter is accomplished. And, as his happiness must always be subordinated to that of the white man, he must, ere long, depart on the foot-prints of the red man, whose mission being accomplished, is fast fading from our midst.

While I think the mission of the negro is accomplished here, I am clearly of the opinion that the time will come when civilization and learning shall light up the dark abodes of the four hundred million people in India, and when their wants and necessities will put the patient and hardy negro to toiling, and opening up the great valley of the fertile but miasmic America. But such speculations are out of place here.

Let us, fellow citizens, endeavor to be calm. Let us look these new ideas and our novel position squarely in the face. We fought for negro slavery. We have lost. We may have to do without it. The inconvenience will be great for a while—the loss heavy. This, however, is already well nigh accomplished. Yet behind this dark cloud is a silver lining, if not for us, at least for our children. In the place of these bondsmen, will come an immense influx of people from all parts of the world, bringing with them their wealth, arts, and improvements, and lending their talents and sinews to increase our aggregate wealth. Thrift, and trade, and a common destiny will bind us together. Machinery in the hills of Arkansas will reverberate to the music of machinery in New England, and the whir of Georgia spindles will meet responsive echoes upon the slopes of the far off Pacific. Protective tariffs, if needed, will stretch in their influence from the Lakes to the Gulf, and from ocean to ocean, bearing alike, at last, equally upon Arkansian and Vermonter, and upon Georgian and Californian. Differences of sections and sentiment will wear away and be forgotten, and the next generation be more homogeneous and united than any since the days of the Revolution. And the descendants of these bloody times will read, with as much pride and as little jealousy, of these battles of their fathers, as the English and Scotch descendants of the heroes of Flodden Field read of their ancestral achievements in the glowing lines of Scott, or, as the descendants of Highland and Lowland chiefs, allusions to their fathers' conflicts in the simple strains of the rustic Burns.[14]

Let us live in hope, my grief-stricken brothers, that the day is not far distant when Arkansas will rise from the ashes of her desolation, to start on a path of higher destiny, than, with negro slavery, she ever could have reached; while the reunited Government, freed from this cankering sore, will be more vigorous and powerful, and more thrifty, opulent and happy, than though the scourge of war had never desolated her fields, or made sorrowful her hearthstones!

The sooner we lay down our arms and quit this hopeless struggle, the sooner our days of prosperity will return.

I hesitated long, my fellow citizens, before I determined to issue this address. I dislike to be abused and slandered. But, more than all, dislike to live under a cloud with those friends who have not yet reached my stand-point—and, besides, all I possess is in the Confederate lines. Their leaders will deprive my family of slaves, home, property, debts due me—in a word, reduce them from competence and ease to penury. Aside from what I have inside the Confederate lines, I could not pay for the paper this address is written upon. But it may all go. Did I desire further promotion, and could bring my conscience to it, I would do like the Johnsons; safe from bullets and hardships themselves, they assist in holding you on to this hopeless and ruinous struggle, and at the end of the conflict will come back and say:—"I staid with you to the last!" "Honor me and mine." God deliver me from such traitors to humanity and to the interests of our bleeding people! To me the path of duty is plain. It is to lend my feeble aid to stop this useless effusion of blood. And though it beggars my family, and leaves me no ray of hope for the future, I shall follow it.

14. Sir Walter Scott, Scots novelist, and Robert Burns, Scots poet.

I have witnessed the desolation of the Southern States from one end to the other. This hopeless struggle but widens it. Each day makes new graves, new orphans, and new mourners. Each hour flings into this dreadful whirlpool more of wretched hopes, broken fortunes, and anguished hearts. The rich have mostly fallen. The poor have drunk deep in the cup of sorrow, while surely, and not slowly, the tide of ruin, in its resistless surge, sweeps toward the middle classes. A few more campaigns and they will form part of the general wreck. Each grave and each tear, each wasted fortune and broken heart, puts us that much further off from the object of the struggle, and that much further off from peace and happiness.

Viewing it thus, the terrible question was presented to me, as to whether I should continue my lot in an enterprise so fruitless and so full of woe, and help hold the masses of the people on to this terrible despotism of Davis, where only ruin awaits them; or whether I should be a quiet observer of it all; or, lastly, whether I should assist in saving the remnant of you from the wreck.

I have chosen the latter. I shall send this address to every hill and corner of the State, to the citizen and solider—at home or in prison, and shall send with it my prayers, to Almighty God, to arrest them in their pathway of blood and ruin. Why trust Davis longer. Had he twice our present resources, he would still fail. With success he would be a despot. But the whole thing is tumbling to pieces. Soldiers are leaving disgusted and disheartened, and whole States have gone back to their homes in the national galaxy; Maryland and Delaware will never again be shaken. Kentucky has intrenched herself in the Union behind a wall of bayonets in the hands of her sturdy sons. Missouri is as firmly set in the national galaxy as Massachusetts. Tennessee, tempest-tossed and bolt riven, under the guidance of her great pilot, steers for her old mooring, and will be safely anchored before the leaves fall; while the rays of light from the old North State, flashing out fitfully from her darkness across the troubled waves, show that she stirs, is not lost, but is struggling to rejoin her sisters. None of these States will ever join the South again. Then, with crippled armies, with devastated fields—with desolate cities, with disheartened soldiers, and, worse than all, with weak and corrupt leaders, what hope is left to the few remaining States, but especially to poor, oppressed, and down-trodden Arkansas? None! Better get our brothers home while they are left to us. Open the way for the return of husbands, fathers and sons, and bind up the broken links of the old Union. The people must act to do this. I tell you now, in grief and pain, that the leaders don't care for your blood. Your sufferings move them not. The tears and wails of your anguished and bereaved ones fall on hearts of flint.

While they can make a dollar, or wear an epaulet, they are content. Finally, with a grief-stricken and sorrowful heart, I implore mothers, sisters, wives, and daughters, to assist, by all their arts, in saving their loved ones from this terrible scourge, ere ruin overtakes you and them irretrievably. While God gives me strength, daunted by no peril, and swerved by no consideration of self, I shall give you my feeble aid.

To break the force of these utterances, honestly, patriotically, and sorrowfully made, the Johnsons and certain reptiles who crawl around Little Rock, under Federal protection, together with all other like men, who, from their own innate corruption, are not able to appreciate pure motives in others, will tell you that a desire to go to Congress has influenced my conduct. Do they suppose that I would lose the last dollar I have, and subject myself to their slander and abuse for the chance of running for an office when peace is made? Does not my refusing, upon principle, to take my seat in Congress in 1860, after a triumphant election, in which I carried twenty-two out of twenty-eight counties, show them what little value I set upon such a bauble? But I will stop their mouths by the solemn assurance that there are not people enough on the continent to induce me to go to Congress. I am sick, tired and disgusted with public life? Peace? peace and the safety of what is left of our noble and suffering people, is my only ambition! We must bear in mind, too, as we go along, that in conceding the chance of a "Congress," they acknowledge the failure of the Confederate cause.

The shortest way, in my opinion, to resume our relations with the Federal government, is to instruct Hon. W. K. Sebastian to take his seat in the United States Senate. It is by all means desirable that such instructions be so clear that the United States Government may be at no loss to see that our people are loyal, and that Mr. Sebastian may have but one course of conduct left. I feel sure that he will respond favorably to your wishes.[15]

Whenever it can be done, meetings should be held promptly, instructing him to resume his seat in the Senate. Where it can not be done, or where citizens can not attend meetings, let them get up petitions to that effect. The proceedings of such meetings, and the petitions, if sent to men, at this place, will receive prompt attention. We should do all this before the meeting of Congress in December. We will have trade open, and get all the other benefits of a government that much sooner.

15. William King Sebastian had been expelled from the Senate in 1861, but the Senate later rescinded the expulsion. Sebastian moved to Tennessee in 1864 and died there in 1865.

I must publicly acknowledge, here, my regret for the strong terms of disapprobation I used toward that distinguished gentleman, Hon. W. K. Sebastian, for his refusal to join us in this struggle.

To those who differed from me in the commencement of this rebellion—the extent and bloodiness of which no mortal could foresee—I must say, that developments show that you were right and I wrong. But let bygones be forgotten, and let us all unite to bring about peace, and to lure our Lost Pleiad from her wanderings, that she may again sparkle in our nation's coronet of stars.

What Is Unconditional Unionism?

(New Orleans: Printed at the Era Office, 1863)

G eorg Michael Decker Hahn (1830–1886) was born in Bavaria, brought to New Orleans in 1840, and later read law with Christian Roselius, a prominent Louisiana lawyer. Hahn at various times sold real estate, edited a newspaper, and practiced law, but mostly Democratic Party politics held his interest. As a unionist he opposed the John Slidell secessionist wing of the party, and Confederate States authorities forced him to flee the city when the war broke out. After the Federal army occupied New Orleans, he returned, gained election to the U.S. Congress, spoke openly against Confederate war policies, and advocated the return of his state to the Union. He edited the Republican *Daily True Delta*, became governor representing the Free State Party in 1864, resigned to serve in the U.S. Senate, but never pressed his claim for that seat. Wounded in the New Orleans riot of July 1866, Hahn was crippled for life. In later years he served in the state legislature and in the U.S. Congress as a Republican.

Hahn's pamphlet in this volume, delivered as a speech before the Union Association of New Orleans on November 14, 1863, reveals the high stakes of wartime reconstruction politics in Louisiana. In it he commented on the Lincoln government's plans for reconstruction and considered the divisions among the state's unionists. He explained why he favored a constitutional convention for Louisiana and called on his fellow unionists to support the end of slavery, but perhaps not the voting rights of ex-slaves, as a means to end the war and restore his beloved Union. Hahn, in addition, discussed the ethnic tensions that contributed to racial division within wartime New Orleans.

Although there has been much interest in his life, Hahn has not had a modern biographer. However, his wartime unionist activities have been well documented in Caryn Coose Bell, *Revolution, Romanticism, and the Afro-Creole Protest Tradition in Louisiana, 1718–1868* (Baton Rouge: Louisiana State University Press, 1997); Ted Tunnell, *Crucible of Reconstruction: War, Radicalism, and Race in Louisiana, 1862–1877* (Baton Rouge: Louisiana State University Press, 1984); William C. Harris, *With Charity for All: Lincoln and the Restoration of the Union* (Lexington: University Press of Kentucky, 1997); and Amos E. Simpson and Vaughan Baker, "Michael Hahn: Steady Patriot," *Louisiana History* 13 (summer 1972): 229–52.

* * *

I appear before you to-night in compliance with an invitation of the Union Association, and agreeably to the wishes of many citizens who value my political views, to address you a few remarks on questions of great concern to the people of Louisiana. I intend to avoid all effort at oratorical embellishment, and to speak to you in the calm and unvarnished style of reason and common sense. Instead of endeavors to arouse your passions, and to carry you along for the moment by tender appeals to your hearts, I will employ facts and reason, so that the impressions which I may make may be of lasting character. We have lately heard and read a great deal in this community about a free press and free speech. I intend to make the test to-night as to the truth of the boast that free speech exists among us; for I expect to utter sentiments and present views which differ in certain respects with those entertained by many persons in this Hall. And I will say now, that in consenting to address you on this occasion, I have not yielded in the slightest degree to the busy slanders of those who have unnecessarily and maliciously sought to injure me in this community, on the one hand by denouncing me as a "negro-worshiping abolitionist," and on the other hand by stigmatizing me as a "Copperhead." I have, I think, shown my indifference to such slanders. They do not affect me; I pass them by "as the idle wind which I regard not." Nor can I be prevented from speaking to you on such subjects as I deem proper, by the appeals of friends who think that I ought to abstain from expressing my opinions on certain points for fear of damage to my political prospects. Political prospects! Who ever knew me to conceal or disguise my political opinions with a view to personal advancement? Who ever knew me as an office-seeker? Those in high places who have the giving of offices, know whether I have sought or refused offices. I have no ambition except to remain a citizen of this great and prosperous Union. I shall, therefore, regardless of all outside influences, be they "wicked or charitable," speak to you from the honest convictions of my heart and mind, whether my remarks be received with applause or disapproval.

I can hardly say anything on the glorious theme of the Union which you have not already heard. On that subject I have frequently addressed you. The patriotic inscriptions which surround us on these walls, and the stars and stripes which hang over us, bear testimony to the patriotism of those who now meet in this Hall, and stand out in strong contrast with the appearance of this place when the Secession Convention of Louisiana plotted treason within this chamber. However pleasant might be the general theme of the Union, I feel that there are now other questions of an important and practical character which should engage our attention. I will, however, say that, if any man wishes to know how I stand politically, I will inform him that I stand fully and squarely on the platform of Abraham Lincoln. Call him "Abolitionist," or call him "Copperhead," with him I am ready to stand or to fall. Let him be true in the future as he has been in the past, and whatever he, in his honest discretion, shall deem good for the preservation of the Union, I will approve, and whatever he shall denounce as injurious to the Union, I will condemn. I bitterly regretted the defeat of my standard-bearer in the last Presidential election—the noble Douglas—yet I have had opportunities of studying the character, moral and intellectual, of our present beloved Chief Magistrate, and I can sincerely give it as my opinion, that a better man than Abraham Lincoln could not have been elected.

My friends, I regret to see the Union men of this State so much and so bitterly divided on a number of incidental questions, as to almost cause the question of the Union to occupy a subordinate position. I regret that before the rebel army has yet been entirely swept from our States, and while there is still so much necessity for harmony among the friends of the Union, you should allow your feelings and prejudices on minor questions to lead you so far astray as to resort to all manner of personal and political abuse, bickerings and divisions, calculated to seriously retard the progress of the Union cause, embarrass the officers of the Government, and delay the restoration of civil power in our midst. I can truly say that I have not aided in getting up any such divisions; and, so help me God, I shall not raise any of the questions which are the cause of so many bitter contentions among you, over and above the question of the Union. It needs no argument to show that the man who does not go for the Union unless slavery is abolished, or unless slavery is preserved, annexes conditions to his Unionism, and is, therefore, not an unconditional Union man. On this subject I agree with Owen Lovejoy, of Illinois.[1] In a debate which occurred in the House of Representatives of the United States, on the 29th of January last, Mr. Lovejoy, addressing Mr. Wickliffe, of Kentucky, used this language:

> "I will put the question to the gentleman now—if it is necessary to free all the slaves, and enlist them, in order to save the Union, whether he is willing that it shall be done?
>
> "Mr. Wickliffe.—I will play the Yankee on you, and ask you a question in return. If the Union is to be saved or the negroes freed, are you in favor of emancipating the slaves and of letting the Union slide?[2]
>
> "Mr. Lovejoy.—I am in favor of saving the Union first, last, and forever, by any means and all means, by abolishing slavery or by not abolishing it, as it can best be done. That is what I am in favor of. Now I want the gentleman to answer my question."

These are the noble words of a truly unconditional Union man. The man who does not approve this sentiment is no unconditional Union man. My own position is this: I am "for the Union *with* or *without* slavery, but prefer it *without*." I am emphatically an unconditional Union man. I will not make it a condition of my Unionism that slavery should be abolished, nor that it shall be maintained. I go for the Union in either case, but prefer it without slavery. We have the authority—if our common sense needed any—of the President for saying that these opinions, and various other shades of them, "may be sincerely entertained by honest and truthful men." Perhaps it would be well for us to read what he has said on the subject. In his reply to a committee, of which Mr. Charles D. Drake was chairman, representing a delegation of "radicals" from Missouri and Kansas, dated the 5th of October last, which was written while I was in Washington, and on the subject of which I heard the President's views orally expressed, the President uses this language:

> "We are in civil war. In such cases there always is a main question; but in this case that question is a perplexing compound—Union and Slavery. It thus becomes a question, not of two sides merely; but of at least four sides, even among those who are for the Union, saying nothing of those who are against it. Thus, those who are for the Union *with*, but not *without* slavery—those for it *without*, but not *with*—those for it *with* or *without*, but prefer it *with*, and those for it *with* or *without*, but prefer it *without*.

1. Abolitionist Republican congressman from Illinois.
2. Charles Wickliffe, longtime Whig congressman from Kentucky, gave up his seat in Congress to run unsuccessfully for governor as a Peace Democrat.

"Among these, again, is a subdivision of those who are for *gradual*, but not for *immediate*, and those who are for *immediate*, but not for *gradual*, extinction of slavery.

"It is easy to conceive that all these shades of opinion, and even more, may be sincerely entertained by honest and truthful men. Yet, all being for the Union, by reason of these sincere differences, each will prefer a different way of sustaining the Union. At once, sincerity is questioned, and motives are assailed. Actual war coming, blood grows hot, and blood is spilled. Thought is forced from old channels into confusion. Deception breeds and thrives. Confidence dies, and universal suspicion reigns. Each man feels an impulse to kill his neighbor, lest he be killed by him. Revenge and retaliation follow. And all this, as before said, may be among honest men only."

One of the questions which has lately been thrust among the Union men of this city, and which has acted like a fire brand in some quarters, is that with regard to the present *status* of this State. A few gentlemen, who make up in point of talent for much which they want in point of numbers and originality, have sought to maintain a doctrine—as erroneous as it is mischievous—that Louisiana is now a Territory, and not a State of this Union. The fallacy and injustice of this doctrine have been so ably shown by many of the best lawyers of the country, especially in the recent speech of Hon. Montgomery Blair, delivered at Rockville, Maryland, which has been so extensively published and commented on, that I will not stop to discuss that question this evening. Some gentlemen of this city have recently made a publication signed with their names, wherein they say:

"The Constitution of 1852, as amended by the Convention of 1861, was overthrown and destroyed by the rebellion of the people of Louisiana, and the subsequent conquest by the arms of the United States does not restore our political institutions."

The respectable source from which this bold and extraordinary declaration emanates entitles it to some notice. If our State Constitution, adopted in 1852, provided for a government Republican in its form, and contained no provisions conflicting with the Constitution of the United States, then it has not been overthrown, but still exists. The amendments referred to as having been adopted by the Convention of 1861, were no amendments at all, as they were in violation of the Constitution of the United States and enacted by a treasonable vote of a Secession Convention. The very object of the army of the United States in coming here was to do away with the secession acts of the Convention and to keep Louisiana and the neighboring

States in the union. The presence of the army among us at this time, and the necessity of the establishment of martial law, of course sets aside and suspends for a time the active operation of the Constitution and laws of this State, so far only as they conflict with the orders and proclamations of the military commander. In all matters not provided for by martial law, the laws of the State are not suspended. Do we not see the evidence of this every day? Go into our District Courts, named and regulated by our State laws, and you will there hear the members of the bar and the judges every day refer to the Constitution and laws of this State, which, we are told, have been "overthrown and destroyed by the rebellion of the people of Louisiana." The statement that this is a rebellion of the people of Louisiana is news to me. Indeed, I think it is news to the gentlemen who make it; for, if I am not greatly mistaken, they have frequently declared that Louisiana did not secede from the Union by a vote of her people. I should blush at the very mention of secession if I thought that a majority of the people of Louisiana had voted for a dissolution of this Union; and as a Union man, with my views of constitutional law, I cannot admit that a rebellion by all the people of a State has any legal effect, except such as may be produced by violence and brute force for the time being. As soon as this unlawful violence and insurrection is put down, the State resumes her position in the Union; and as soon as martial law is removed, her own loyal Constitution and laws, which have been temporarily suspended, regain their strength and go into operation. This proposition appears to me so plain, that I am really astonished to find a different opinion advanced by the able gentleman whose language I have quoted.

But, because I argue thus, it must not be understood that I am an admirer of the present Constitution, or that I am in favor of continuing it in force. I have discussed the matter as a lawyer, in its logical and legal views; but, as a citizen, I am in favor of a convention of the loyal people of Louisiana for the purpose of framing a new Constitution. I could see no wisdom, no propriety, no common sense, in the effort which was lately made by some of our Union friends to restore civil authority by holding an election for State officers, etc., in the curious manner which characterized their proceedings. If their course had not partaken so much of the Know Nothing proceedings of former days, they might have succeeded in their undertaking. If, at a proper time, say about two months, before the day designated in the Constitution for the election, these gentlemen had come out openly, publicly and manfully, and announced their intention to hold an election, their action might have been traceable to motives of disinterested patriotism. But, in doing as they did, enveloping their movements in mystery, meeting in secret, concealing their ticket and giving no intimation of their contemplated election until about three days before the election, they endeavored to fasten on the people of the State a government in opposition to their wishes, and without their knowledge. It is hardly necessary for me to tell you that I could not approve such proceedings. When I join in an election it must be one partaking of the character of real, genuine democracy. It must be one of the people, conducted in an open and honorable manner, and in a spirit of patriotism. It is somewhat singular that all the leaders of this movement, which so signally failed, are strong pro-slavery men; and the belief is almost irresistible that they were actuated more by a desire to preserve the "peculiar institution," than a real, sincere wish to restore civil authority.

The importance of establishing a civil government among us, and restoring Louisiana again to her proper position in the Union, cannot be overrated. Such an event would not only remove from us so many of the restrictions, burdens and inconveniences which now rest so heavily upon us, incident to the insurrection and the existence of martial law, and against which we hear so many complaints in the community; but it would also strengthen the Union cause elsewhere in our country, and have a salutary effect abroad. As soon as the Union lines are extended to embrace a few more parishes, which can be done at any time, we should reorganize our State Government, and place ourselves completely in line with the loyal States of the Union. There is no reason why we should not all unite in this great movement, and put an end to the stigma of disloyalty which still rests upon the fair fame of our noble State. The whole country looks to us for immediate action in this matter. The President feels a deep interest in it, and, with that tender regard for the rights of the people which distinguishes his administration, is anxious to give you the selection of your own civil officers. Indeed, even in December last, he told me that just as fast as we could name to him competent and loyal citizens of our own, he would fill the Federal offices of this State with them. He has already acted on this principle in the appointment of a Judge, District Attorney, Marshal, and other officers. Let us then, like good citizens, proud of our rights, come together in a spirit of harmony and patriotism, and place Louisiana where she belongs, and where she can be of service to the country.

But how are we to do this? Are we to resort to and continue to live under the present Constitution of Louisiana, or are we to call a Convention and make a new Constitution? Are we to recognize and protect the limited amount of slavery which still exists, or are we, by a new Constitution, to wipe slavery from our soil? These are important questions. They are deserving of our most serious attention and study. Many of us are quite rash, and many very timid, in coming to a decision; many are of one opinion, many of another; many are governed by calm reason and justice, others by interest and prejudice. I make neither plan a condition of my Unionism. I recognize good and true Union men on both sides, and I do not think that the cause which we all have so much at heart will be at all advanced by encouraging the bandying of such epithets as "Abolitionists" and Copperheads." But, as the time is fast arriving when every man must take sides on these questions, and as many of you have expressed a desire to have my views on them, I will briefly give them to you.

I think the easiest and most prudent and expeditious way of restoring this State to all her rights in the Union, and giving her a civil government, is to call a Convention and frame a new Constitution. But we are told by the mysterious gentlemen who meet in the Masonic Hall, that there is no authority vested with the power to call a Convention except the Legislature, and that the Constitution can only be changed in the manner pointed out by its own provisions. If this were true, we would have to wait a long time before we could obtain a new Constitution; for there is now scarcely a Legislature in existence, and even if there were, it is exceedingly doubtful whether it would be willing to call a Convention. The present Constitution itself was not framed and adopted in accordance with the directory provisions on that subject laid down in the former Constitution. But even the Legislature is not vested by the present Constitution with the power to call a Convention for such a purpose. Nor can the constitutional provisions which are relied on, prevent the people from exercising their sovereignty and power in calling a Convention, in their own name, instead of going through the machinery of a legislative body, whenever they choose to do so, especially in a time of war and treason on the part of their agents. No, the people of the State have a right to act thus, and if they wish again to enjoy peace, happiness and prosperity, the sooner they call this Convention and make a new Constitution, the better.

The present Constitution of the State is unjust to the city of New Orleans; discriminates unfairly between the slaveholder and the poor man, and is a barrier to the spirit of progress and humanity in our midst. It is, emphatically, the slaveholders' Constitution. The poor men of the State, recognizing it as the enactment of a majority, submit to it like good Democrats. But as the slaveholders themselves were the first to disregard and throw it aside, and to join in the rebellion, they cannot complain when we, who are in favor of the Union, are also desirous of setting it aside and making a new one to suit ourselves. Turn about is fair play.

I do not base my opposition to the present Constitution on its pro-slavery features exclusively. It has many other serious defects. I, and, I believe, every member of the bar in this city, object to the election of judges by the people. The respect and sanctity which should envelop the judicial robes forbid the ermine from mingling in the strifes of party contests. We want no judges on the bench elected by party spirit and carrying with them party prejudices. The appointment of judges by the Governor, and their confirmation by the Senate, will, of course, be somewhat influenced by party politics; but in such case the large number of litigants appearing before them will not be known as either friends or opponents of the judges, as they had no direct agency in their appointment, and can, therefore, reasonably expect impartial justice from the courts. From the experience we have had under an elective judiciary since the adoption of the present Constitution, I do not know of a single individual in this city, of any respectable standing, who is not in favor of a change in the mode of selecting our judiciary.

But the most serious objection to our present Constitution, and that which came nearer defeating it before the people in 1852, is that arising from the basis of representation which it prescribes. Article eighth commences thus: "Representation in the House of Representatives shall be equal and uniform, and shall be regulated and ascertained by the total population of each of the several parishes of the State." The iniquity of this provision can best be illustrated by supposing an example. Suppose the basis under this provision be fixed at one representative for every fifteen thousand inhabitants of all colors and conditions, and that the Parish of Jefferson has fifteen thousand inhabitants, all white and free, and the Parish of Assumption fifteen thousand inhabitants, of whom fourteen thousand nine hundred and eighty are slaves, and the other twenty are white men. Do you not see that in such a case the twenty white men in a slaveholding parish have the same vote and influence in the House as the fifteen thousand white persons in what might be termed the "freesoil" parish?

Is this fair and just to the small planters and farmers, the adventurous frontiersmen, the honest mechanics, hard laborers, the enterprizing manufacturers and merchants and the professional men of the States? No, certainly not. Why should a man, because he owns a plantation and slaves, have greater political rights than other men who have no such profitable investments? What gives such property a superiority over other property politically? When the Convention which framed the Constitution of 1845, had under consideration a similar proposition, Mr. Roselius, then a senatorial delegate from this parish, very properly said: . . . [3]

---

3. Hahn quotes Roselius, his mentor, speaking at the Louisiana constitutional convention of 1845 in opposition to including the slave population in allocating votes.

Such arguments defeated the proposition for the time. . . . [4]

. . . These quotations from the productions of two of our most talented and influential citizens, explain themselves and have a deep significance at this time, considering the opinions now entertained by those gentlemen. The same reasoning applies to the representation in the State Senate, which is not only based on the total population, but which limits New Orleans to a certain fixed number of Senators no matter what may be her population.

We have thus seen that the present Constitution is more calculated to protect and benefit the slaveholder than the other classes of our population. This is also the case with the laws of the State enacted by Legislatures elected on such a basis. Instead of developing the mechanical and manufacturing capacities and resources of the State—instead of paying some attention to the poorer and industrious classes of our citizens—instead of giving Louisiana a name for enterprise, arts and sciences, our Legislatures have confined themselves almost exclusively to legislating for the protection of the interests of slavery. Much has been said by the admirers of slavery— those who pretend to believe it a "divine institution;" about the spirit of humanity and Christianity of our laws. I must confess I have not been able to find much of this spirit. I certainly do not see it in the statutes preventing masters from liberating their slaves; providing for the mode of trial and punishment of slaves; making it criminal to teach slaves to read and write; and allowing slave families to be broken up, and the parents and children, husbands and wives, to be separated forever in this world. If the interests of slaveholders are sacrificed in this way, it is their own fault. Let us get over the difficulty as soon as possible, by emancipating the few slaves still in our State, and apply ourselves to the duty of devising some new plan for the prosecution of the agricultural interests.

Some slaveholders erroneously imagine that when the laborers on the plantation cease to be slaves the planters will be ruined, and no reasoning can convince them to the contrary. Let us go into figures for a moment, and see if they are correct. A good field hand was worth in times of peace about fifteen hundred dollars. A fair interest on this sum in most of the Southern States was 10 per cent per anum, making one hundred and fifty dollars, so that it may be said the planter pays, or deprives himself of, one hundred and fifty dollars a year for the services of his slave. He also runs the risk of the sickness or death of the slave, and escape from his involuntary servitude. When there is no slavery, and by adopting the "compensated labor system,"

4. Hahn next quotes Dr. Hugh Kennedy of New Orleans, who, in 1852, spoke out against the unequal voting rights given to the citizens of that city.

the planter can hire a negro for ten dollars a month, making one hundred and twenty dollars a year, and run none of the risks of the slave-owner, and receive a more willing and cheerful, and, therefore, more advantageous labor. Many other facts might be mentioned to show the advantage to the intelligent planter of the free labor system.

But many will say, "the negro when freed will not work." I humbly differ with them in this regard. Stringent and effective vagrant laws can be passed by the Legislature, which will secure their labor to the State, if they do not work otherwise. Some people say, "the negro, if free, will leave the plantation at the very time his services are most needed, when the cane is to be cut and ground, or when the cotton is to be picked." This can also be provided against. The contracts for hire can be so made as to allow the planter to retain in his hand several months' wages until the grinding or picking season is over, and in case the laborer should violate his contract a forfeiture of wages would be the consequence. Thus it will be seen the planter would not suffer at the least by the change. And if all this will not work well, then let the negroes be sent to colonies abroad, where they will cease to trouble us; and let the plantations be divided into small farms and cultivated by white labor. The cry that white labor cannot be profitably employed in this latitude could easily be shown to be erroneous, did my time permit me to enter on that field.

Many, and especially blacks, will object to any proposition to colonize the colored people. This suggestion of colonization comes from no ill-will towards the negro. Colonization has been advocated by some of the leading minds and philanthropists of our country. It is pretty well ascertained, I think, that Mr. Lincoln favors it, and that the Postmaster General has advocated it. John McDonough, whom you all remember as the philanthropic millionaire and the friend of the negro, gives expression, quaintly, to this impressive language in his instruction to his executors. . . .[5]

While I favor the emancipation of the slaves, and consider myself a friend of the colored people, I cannot but regret and condemn the course which some of them are now pursuing in this city. At a meeting lately held by them, the proceedings of which were reported in one of our newspapers, resolutions were passed demanding the right to vote with white men, and a petition was drawn to be handed to the Military Governor asking such right. These persons do not style themselves colored people in their resolutions and petition; they think the words "natives of Louisiana" more significant

5. Hahn cites McDonough on the advantages of colonization to save the ex-slaves from the brutality of their ex-masters.

and high-sounding, and appear to forget that the general term "natives," includes white persons as well as colored. The spirit of Know-Nothingism which pervades their document is more evident and more boldly expressed in the speeches of their orators.[6] One of their oracles was not satisfied with giving us his legal opinion that "Louisiana is a Territory, not a State"—for which opinion he had distinguished authority, as we have already seen— but thought proper to make an attack on our naturalized citizens, especially those from Ireland and Germany, which was as unnecessary and impertinent as it was unjust. "Go to the Registration office," said this colored Know-Nothing, "and see the crosses there of Irishmen and Germans who cannot write their names." This fling at the intelligent, honest and Union-loving citizens of German origin is as ill-timed and ungracious as it is untrue. The Germans as a general thing do not make their crosses, but sign their names, and in beautiful penmanship at that. They have excellent schools in abundance in the country of their birth. As to the Irish, the oppression of the British Government deprives many of them of a book-education; but their general vivacity, activity, wit and intelligence, is proverbial. No battle has yet been fought in the cause of the Union, in which Irish and German blood has not been freely and nobly shed for the good of the whole country. The deeds of those who went to battle and imperiled their lives in our country's cause, under the skillful Sigel and the dashing Meagher, will be imperishable in history.[7] The rash and imprudent statements of such speakers will do more damage than good to the cause of their race. The Union men of this State have a pretty heavy task before them already; they are sacrificing their dearest friendships in order to assist in saving the Union and giving freedom to the colored race. If the colored men are not satisfied with the efforts we are making towards general emancipation, but insist upon thrusting other issues and obstacles in our path, they may find all our efforts in vain. But let us see what principles they adopt where they have power. On the 26th day of July, 1847, the people of the Republic of Liberia adopted a Constitution, of which the 13th section of Article II reads thus:

> "The great object of forming these colonies being to provide a home for the dispersed and oppressed children of Africa, and to regenerate and enlighten this benighted continent, *none but persons of color shall be admitted to citizenship in this Republic.*"

6. The nativist and anti-Catholic party that so roiled Louisiana politics during the middle of the 1850s.

7. Union generals Franz Sigal and Thomas Francis Meagher, of German and Irish ancestry.

But, ladies and gentlemen, I feel that I have trespassed too much upon your patience. I think I have adhered to my promise made at the commencement of my remarks; I have studiously avoided any attempts at eloquence, and I have given you my views in an honest, plain and practical manner. I have been glad to have touched on other questions of importance, but it is time that I should close. In conclusion, let me appeal to you, as lovers of your country, to discard all personal controversies and irritating discussions calculated to divide Union men, and to sink all minor questions into the great one of unconditional loyalty to the Union. Let us imitate the noble example of our brethren in the great States of Ohio, Pennsylvania, and New York, whose unconditional devotion to the Union has crushed out all other questions; and who, in love of country, have cast aside all former party differences, have ceased for a time to be Republicans or Democrats, have divided on no minor issues, but have, in their recent elections, nominated Union men, and have worthily achieved a most glorious Union victory.

Address to the People of Texas

(New Orleans: Printed at the Era Office, 1864)

Andrew Jackson Hamilton (1815–1875) was born in Alabama and raised in a political family. Seeking a public career, this lawyer and farmer removed to Austin, Texas, in 1846, became a state attorney general in 1849, and gained election to the Federal congress in 1859, where he spoke openly against the southern secession movement. Forced by death threats to escape the state through Mexico, Hamilton for a time served as brigadier general in the U.S. volunteer army. President Lincoln appointed him military governor of Texas in exile in 1862, but Hamilton spent most of the war living in the North and New Orleans, where he spoke in favor of reunion and called for a Union army invasion of Texas. Hamilton launched his abortive reentry to Texas in 1864 from New Orleans, in hopes of alleviating the plight of the state's unionists and reopening the cotton trade with the North. In June 1865, President Andrew Johnson appointed him provisional governor of Texas, and he became a Conservative Republican during Reconstruction as he attempted to give legal rights to the freedmen, eventually supported black suffrage, and helped to draft the Texas constitution of 1869. He lost the race for governor in 1869 and retired from public life.

Hamilton's pamphlet of January 1, 1864, issued when he returned to Brownsville, Texas, with the Federal army, follows the pattern of many of his pamphlets directed at northern and southern unionist audiences. He even called on Texas moderates to join the Union cause. It reveals his support for reunion and his opposition to slavery. But most of all his pamphlet is a plea for Texas unionists to assist the many victims of the Confederate government. That is why he described their plight so vividly when he asserted that the Confederate government had treated Texans as slaves. Hamilton's pamphlet is thus a ringing condemnation of the failure of the Confederate government.

For another of his appeals to the North, see *On the Condition of the South under Rebel Rule* (New York: Printed by Order of the National War Committee, 1862). A recent biography is John L. Waller, *Colossal Hamilton of Texas* (El Paso: Texas Western Press, 1968); also see Carl H. Moneyhon, *Republicanism in Reconstruction Texas* (Austin: University of Texas Press, 1980); and James A. Marten, *Texas Divided: Loyalty and Dissent in the Lone Star State, 1856–1874* (Lexington: University Press of Kentucky, 1990). For an account of the brutal treatment of Texas unionists see Richard B. McCaslin, *Tainted Breeze: The Great Hanging at Gainesville, Texas, 1862* (Baton Rouge: Louisiana State University Press, 1994).

* * *

Through the instrumentality of ambitious and designing men, you have been, for more than two and a half years, engaged in rebellion against the government of the United States. Hunted as a felon and expelled the State because I would not join the conspiracy to overthrow free government I now, after an exile of eighteen months, return to it, charged with the duty of organizing such provisional State governments as may be best calculated to aid in restoring you to the blessings of civil liberty.

It is not improper, nor inopportune, briefly to review the past history of the rebellion, and from it to draw conclusions for the future. If, in doing this, I shall speak of myself, I do so because it is not only justified, but made necessary by our past and present relations.

When you were forced, by a minority, into rebellion, you were in the enjoyment of every blessing ever conferred by civil government upon men. Not a single wrong had you ever suffered from the Government. You had liberty, peace, prosperity, and were in the daily and undisturbed "pursuit of happiness." You will not fail to remember the promise of the rebel leaders, nor the predictions of loyal men. After an experience so sad in its results— so horrible in its details—I call upon you to answer, *who dealt truthfully with you?*

Let me recount some of the promises made to you.

You were told that secession was a rightful and peaceful remedy for anticipated evils; that the United States was inherently too weak to resist disruption, and that therefore the revolution would be bloodless. You were plied with a thousand arguments to induce you to believe that the South absolutely controlled the destinies, not only of your own country, but of the civilized world, because of her supposed monopoly of the production of a single article of commerce. *"Cotton is King"* was the arrogant and senseless declaration upon the lips of every man who was seeking the destruction of the Government. At the mere frown of this imperial despot, it was promised that France and England would bend in suppliant attitude and pray permission to serve you upon any terms. It was confidently asserted that the organization of the new government would break the chains that had so long bound the South to the commercial charriot-wheels of the North; and that it would at once inaugurate a new and unexampled prosperity among southern people, resulting in the attainment, for the Confederacy, of a national progress and power unknown in the previous history of the world. You were promised a government more potent to bless, and less liable to abuse than the one established by your fathers.

You were assured that in severing from the States of the North, you would promote national and individual happiness by the cultivation and practice of the wisest political economy, and the purest principles of morality and religion, uncontaminated by the terrible heresies of the North; that you would thus reach, at no distant day, a point of civilization from which you could gaze far down upon the benighted world outside of the Confederacy, and "thank God you were not as other men." All this was to come within the first decade of years—but it was not the limits assigned to the noble work destined to be accomplished by the all-conquering arm of the Confederacy.

Within the first quarter of a century of its existence this paragon of governments was charged with the duty of employing its moulding hand and humanizing influence in rescuing Mexico, Central America, and Cuba from decay and ruin by incorporating them as parts of its territory; and thus enlarged in capacity for the employment of slave labor and the unlimited production of cotton, present the blue waters of the Caribbean Sea and the Gulf of Mexico as the cradle and lap of the commerce of the world. No rebel ever doubted, when secession occurred, whether peace or war followed, that the Northern States would fall into a rapid decline, soon to end in the destruction of democratic government. They told you that the great commercial and manufacturing wealth of the North was just so much unjustly abstracted from the products of the South—and that the moment this source of supply was withdrawn her looms would be still—her people idle, starving and insubordinate—and the grass grow green and luxuriant in the streets of her great commercial cities. Famine—civil war—anarchy, was the doom of the North.

You were told by those who assumed to know, (and among them were northern men,) that if the *"imbecile and contemptible old government* should attempt to struggle for its existence, the effort would be a farce—that the

Yankees would not, *could* not fight Southern men." There was scarcely a Southern brave who did not pledge himself to despatch at least a dozen Yankees.

The terrible threat was made, that if war were waged by the Government to "coerce" the South—especially if the foot-print of a Yankee soldier should profane her sacred soil—she would muster her chivalrous and resistless hosts and seize the National Capital, and thence marching northward, lay in ruin successively Philadelphia, New York and Boston, and over their smouldering ruins dictate the terms of peace.

These are some of the things that you were promised. How many of them have you realized? If you dare not *speak*, let your *hearts* answer.

On the other hand, what did those who opposed disunion predict would be the consequences of that act of rebellion? I appeal to many of you who heard me, and others, to bear testimony to what we said, and labored to impress upon the minds of the people while the question of secession was still pending. We said the framers of our Government had not provided for the destruction of the fabric they were rearing—that no government was ever organized with a view to its own dissolution, and hence it was worse than a fallacy to talk of *legal* secession—that revolution against organized government was a *moral* right having its origin in the perversion of powers intended for good, and in the usurpation of others for the accomplishment of tyrannical purposes—that the Government of the United States had not abused its power nor tyrannized over any of its citizens—that no one had charged it with such a crime.

We said, also, that no great government was ever established or destroyed without a struggle involving war; and that the Government of the United Sates could not be permanently dismembered without its citizens wading through a sea of blood; that secession would involve war—a war in which the South would not only fail but forfeit the interest in behalf of which that war was waged; that revolution for the further security and perpetuity of slavery would sound its knell.

You were told that the institution of slavery owed to the Government of the United States all the toleration and consideration which it ever had in the civilized world—and that if left to combat the public sentiment of mankind alone upon its merits, it would go down—that whatever might be the intention of the leaders in rebellion, they would ultimately be forced to the alternative of making the new government a despotism—that the people would not long tolerate so disastrous a change in their interests and happiness, unless compelled by force. We said that "Cotton" was *not* "King"—that bread had ever been, and would ever be the chief necessary of individuals and of nations—that none of the governments of the old world could afford to jeopardize their moral status by openly aiding in the establishment of a government for the perpetuity of slavery—but that France and England would avail themselves of every opportunity to encourage civil war here, in the hope that the power and influence of Republican Government on this Continent might be broken and destroyed—that Mexico would be victimized by one or both of these governments whilst we were engaged in domestic strife.

We said the revolution would soon prove to the non-slave owner that it was not a war in the interest of his class—but in the interest of the *slave owner*, and destined to result in the disfranchisement of the poor, and thus compel them, in self-defence, to become the stern and uncompromising opponents of slavery. We warned you that the boasted wealth of the South was not, and could not be made, available in the contemplated struggle— that the institution of slavery, unlocked by the clash of arms, would deliver within the lines of the South, as the Grecian Horse did within the walls of Troy, a hostile force at its very citadel—that the government was strong and would exert its strength for the suppression of rebellion—that the issue would at last be between a Slave Aristocracy and a Democratic Republic.

Citizens of Texas, let truth be between us. Again, I call upon you to answer, whose promises have failed, and whose predictions have been verified? If a *single* promise made by the rebel leaders has been realized, I challenge you to name it!

Are you more free—more prosperous—more happy, than in former years? Are you more free to remain at home in the enjoyment of the society of your wives and children—more free to engage from day to day in such avocations as are most congenial to your tastes, and conducive to your interests? Are you more free to express your opinions, and to listen to those of your neighbors and friends—more free to come and go at will and devote your time to the interests of those you love?

Look around you and compare the present with the past. Ask the members of your households, your neighbors, and friends, what they have gained by the rebellion? Where is now the smile once seen in every face in our fair land, and the thrift that was fast converting our silent prairies into settlements of busy industry, and filling them with the homes of happy and contented citizens? Where all was peace, security, and contentment,—now all is strife, decay, and wretchedness.

Do you feel as secure of life, liberty, and property, as you once did? You know in your hearts that you are the victims of an odious despotism—*slaves* to the few who would crush the brightest hopes of humanity to perpetuate slavery. What has been your realization of liberty under the rebel rule?

Soon after the war commenced your ports were blockaded, excluding from your markets the comforts and necessities of life. Your substance was demanded in exchange for a worthless paper currency, which was forced upon you by the most insolent threats, in the form of Proclamations by Military Commanders, denouncing, as *enemies* to the new government, all who refused to take it as equivalent to gold and silver. In this form you have been daily robbed; while, at the same time, upon a thousand pretexts and by as many devices, you have either been denied the right to carry your cotton and other products to the only market open to you—the Mexican border—or you have, when there, been shamelessly plundered by government agents and military commanders, who have thus secured for themselves fortunes now safely deposited in foreign countries, and which they expect to enjoy while you suffer the evils which they have entailed upon you. Taxation in some form has been visited upon you day by day, until you are no longer able to meet the demands of your masters. And, at last, when every appliance to extort money from you had failed to satisfy them, because of the worthlessness of the currency they had compelled you to accept, agents were appointed to call upon you at your homes for one tenth of your crops—the proceeds of your honest toil.

Martial Law has been visited upon you; and in every town, and village, and neighborhood, some petty despot appointed, to whose edicts you were required to bow in meek submission. You have been denied the right to travel through the community near your homes on the most necessary business, without the written permission of one of those tools of tyranny. You dare not convey to market the products of your farms and your labor without permission. Your wagons and teams have been seized by government agents at home and on the roads to market, in order to compel you to sell to them your crops for a nominal price in worthless paper. No interest has been secure, and no right sacred. Law and order no longer exist among you. Public and social charity have disappeared; and in place of confidence, suspicion and distrust fill every mind. Intolerance, bigotry and barbarity, under the fostering hands of ignorance and tyranny, are every where dominant. Virtue is no longer a passport to public favor. The wise and good are not those whose influence is now felt either in public or private life. The vicious and depraved—the murderers and ruffians of the country—are banded together in secret societies, known as "Sons of the South," and are from day to day sitting in judgment upon the lives of the best citizens of the State.

Neither age, nor talents, nor public services, nor private virtues, may claim consideration at their hands. Murder is now the passport to the favor of the tyrants under whose rule you groan; and many have struggled to be foremost in acting the bloody role. Three thousand of your citizens have perished because they loved good government, and peace, and order in society—perished as felons. They have been hung, shot, and literally butchered—they have been tortured, in many instances, beyond anything known in savage warfare. On every prairie in Western Texas their bones are bleaching—their frames are still suspended from the forest trees, where they yielded up their lives in devotion to their love of liberty.

The thresholds of many homes are still red with the blood of husbands and fathers who were shot in the presence of their wives and children, because they loved the flag under which they were born and the government that had ever blessed them. Your State has been changed from the home of a peaceful, thriving and happy people, to an arena for assassination and robbery. Uncertainty, and gloom, and despair are resting upon you to-day like the frown of God. Are you in love with this, and do you desire it to continue?

I know that many of you are, and have long been praying secretly and devoutly for deliverance, while others, perhaps, are still unwilling to be "subjugated," in order to be relieved from the worst despotism that has ever outraged the rights of civilized man. If it be the *fact* of "subjugation" only, without reference to what follows, that is distasteful to you, then let your minds rest—you have long *been* "subjugated." The Government of the United States—your Government and mine—the only Government you have—*has* come to "subjugate" not peaceful citizens, but rebels and rebellion. Its flag now floats over Texas soil, as it does over the soil of every State represented by a star in its azure field. Its armies are here, and they will remain until peace and order are restored. Let those who brought this calamity upon you, and whose every promise and prediction has proved a delusion or a falsehood, again, if they will, essay to rouse you to desperation by shameless misrepresentations of the purposes of the Government, and the "atrocities of the Yankee soldiers." Let them tell you, as you were told by proclamation of your chief Executive officer less than two years since, that the "vile Hessians are coming with lust in their eyes, poverty in their pockets, and hell in their hearts," to violate your wives and daughters, despoil you of your homes, and property, and commit havoc and devastation throughout the land. And let them, as the proclamation referred to, advise you, upon their approach, to "apply the torch to your homes—commit your wives and children to the *Charnelhouse*—and retire to the woods with your *faithful slaves*, and share your last crust with them."

I hope the experience of two years has enabled you to appreciate such advice. You already comprehend that in the estimation of the rebel leaders the existence and sanctity of your homes, and the lives of those you most love, are not to be put in the balance against slavery. No! let every other interest perish, but preserve slavery! Tear down free government—destroy society—let Murder bare his arm and revel in the blood of our best citizens, until an agonizing wail goes up to heaven from every valley, and plain, and mountain-top—lay the torch with your own hands to your own homes— let your wives and children perish from cold and hunger, or, to prevent this, lay the knife to their throats, as you do the torch to their homes, and thus ridding yourselves of every encumbrance, devote yourselves to the higher and nobler duty of securing the faithful slaves of your wealthy neighbors.

The author of such advice to the people of Texas did not know that in one brief sentence he had presented a complete epitome of the rebel policy, and, as it were, exposed to the world the very soul and secret thoughts of its authors, who had determined to make the dearest and most sacred rights of the people subordinate to the accomplishment of their purpose; nor that he was, in so doing, securing for himself, beyond any accident or contingency of the future, *immortal infamy*. It is disingenuous in but one thing—while it would seem to be addressed to the owners of slaves, it was, in fact, rather intended for those who owned *none*. It was never intended that the slave owners should, as a class, imperil their precious lives in the war which was waged for their benefit. If so, how is it that the owner of twenty negroes is exempt from military duty under your laws of conscription? I am told that your leaders wax exceedingly wroth when they hear the rebellion characterized as "the rich man's war and the poor man's fight." It is not strange that they should regard with horror such expressions—they have cause of alarm—it is the utterance of a solemn truth that is awakening an echo in, and fast taking possession of, the minds and hearts of poor men throughout the South, and destined at no distant day to burst in a storm, that will sweep from its path those who so arrogantly denounce it.

Doubtless the cry will be raised that I am appealing to a class—to the prejudices of the poor against the rich. *I am appealing to a class—to the poor—not to their prejudices*, but to their manliness, to their love of liberty, and the memory of its full enjoyment under the Government of the United States—to their hopes for their children, their duty to God and posterity—to every noble instinct of the human heart. I appeal to them, not *because* they are poor, but because, *being* poor, they have been made the victims of another class, who have deliberately sought to use them in the establishment of a government in which they were to be disfranchised—reduced from the condition of free and equal citizens to become mere "hewers of wood and drawers of water." I appeal to them against the arrogance and selfishness of slave owners, who were not satisfied with political equality, but who aspired to the position of petty lords in a slave aristocracy. I do not mean to include in this class every slave owner. I know there are many noble exceptions—men who love free government more than they love slavery.

Do you doubt, men of Texas, you who labor for your daily bread, that you were, in the end, if the revolution succeeded, to be placed in a position of subordination to the wealthy? Unfortunately, for you, the whole truth has not been permitted to reach you since the rebellion commenced. But enough has emanated from your masters, from time to time, to clearly indicate the future character and policy of the new government. The leaders say that Democracy and Slavery cannot exist together. The Richmond and other leading papers of the rebel Government say, that the only true principle upon which to organize labor in any government, is, that it should be *owned*, whether *white or black*. They say that free suffrage is destructive of government—that political power should be in the hands of the property holders, who constitute the head of society, while the laboring class constitute its heels. How many owners of plantations and negroes have you heard, since the rebellion commenced, boldly asserting that Democracy is a failure, as evidenced by the weakness and inability of the United States Government to protect itself from dismemberment, and that a *stronger* government was necessary? If you yet doubt as to the real object and purpose of the rebel leaders, you would not believe "though one should rise from the dead."

You have been deceived and betrayed, until you are powerless to resist the tyranny of your masters. You have been plundered of your property—dragged from your homes and families, to fight a government that gave you freedom and happiness, without ever calling upon you for one farthing, or imposing upon you a single burthern. You have been compelled to exchange peace for strife—prosperity for decay and ruin—happiness at home for the hardships of a conscript camp in a rebel army. You are slaves to, and compelled to do the bidding of men from distant States, who have neither interest in, nor sympathy for you, and who use you only to pander to their own ambition. You have neither government nor society. You have not only been subjected to disgrace at home, but you have been humiliated abroad, by the disgraceful supplication of the thrones of France and England by your leaders, beseeching them to aid in the overthrow of free government on this Continent.

The men, women and children of Texas have been offered as so many cattle, together with the territory they inhabit, in the markets of foreign courts by Jefferson Davis and his agents abroad, as a consideration for the necessary aid in establishing his despotism in the other rebel States.

What answer do you make to your own hearts, when the question comes home to you, "for what am I fighting?" You are told that you are fighting for liberty—this you *know* is false; and you know, too, that it is no less false when you are told that you are to become the victims of the cupidity and barbarity of the Yankees, if you are conquered. Your own soldiers, who have been prisoners of war, can, if they will, satisfy you as to the treatment you may expect. The Government of the United States neither sanctions nor permits wrong, outrage or insult to any one. It is made the duty of its officers, military and civil, to give protection to every citizen not engaged in war against it. Your homes and families will be respected, and secure from insult and injury. Your own persons will be unmolested, if you will lay down your arms and renew your obligation of fidelity and loyalty to your government, and so *deserve* its protection.

I know with what assiduity those who have sinned beyond forgiveness seek to connect you, to the end, with their own desperate fortunes. They tell you that under the law you have already forfeited your homes and property, and that they will be taken away if you submit. But the government is able to, and *will* discriminate between the wilfully guilty and those who have been deluded or forced into rebellion; and when you are offered protection and security, you should, by your conduct, *merit*, if you would receive its favor. The Government will receive with joy to its embraces all whose sins are pardonable, if, like the Prodigal Son, they repent and ask to be forgiven.

The President of the United States, in a proclamation issued on the 8th of December, 1863, has offered a free pardon to all except the leaders—the real responsible agents of the rebellion.

He but requires you to give evidence of your desire to cease your warfare against the Government, by taking an oath that you will thenceforth be faithful to it; and that you will support and defend the laws of Congress upon the subject of slavery, and his Proclamation and Emancipation. Is this asking of you too much? He who will not joyfully accept these terms, is still in heart a rebel, and deserves no favor.

But what is still most relied upon by your rulers to inflame your minds and excite your passions, is, that you are to be brought down to a level with the negroes. This is an appeal to the meanest emotions of the human heart—envy and selfishness—predicated upon your supposed stupidity and ignorance. It is true that negroes in Texas are to-day *legally free*—but does this injure you? If you are yourselves free, the fact of all others being free also will not impair your rights nor abridge your privileges. The levelling process so much complained of is, indeed, very different from that intended by your masters; *they* intended to keep the negro in bondage, and *reduce* you to the same condition. The Government of the United States has determined that you *shall continue free*, and to that end has deemed it *necessary* to give freedom to the slaves.

Your position in government and society will remain unchanged—that of the negro will be improved. Let those who feel conscious that they cannot successfully compete with the negro for the prize of acknowledged merit and moral worth, chafe and complain. The man who is conscious of endowments, physical and mental, superior to the negro, and who intends to employ them for the good of his country and race, will feel no jealousy of the negro's freedom.

It is not out of consideration for your interests that these arguments are addressed to you by your leaders, but in the hope that you may still be induced, in obedience to an ignorant prejudice, to *bleed* and *die* to uphold an institution which aimed at once to destroy your Government and your freedom. The institution of slavery, by its crimes, has forfeited to the Government and the people its right to exist. Its doom has been pronounced—the sentence has gone forth, never to be recalled, "weighed in the balance and found wanting."

The President of the United States, in the exercise of his just power as commander-in-chief of its armies and navies, and in pursuance of the authority of the war making power—Congress—has proclaimed the freedom of the slaves, and upon the act when performed he invoked "the considerate judgment of mankind, and the gracious favor of Almighty God." The act *is* approved by the judgment of the lovers of liberty throughout the world, not one of whom doubts that it receives the approving smiles of a just God.

He has since said, in a noble letter, replete with argument, and the expression of determined purpose, that "the promise (to the slave) having been made, *must* be kept." To this declaration, the heart and voice of the nation enthusiastically responded. Again, in his recent Message to Congress, the President has reiterated the same determination. What have you, the poor and laboring men of Texas, to say to this? Do you deny its justice or its wisdom? What has slavery done for you, that you should become its champion and defend it to the death? It never benefitted you, materially, morally or politically. It has, in fact, been a clog upon your prosperity—the enemy of truth and virtue, and a sore upon the body politic for long years, producing constant irritation. It grew in arrogance as it increased in power, until, in the South, free government was practically overthrown long before open rebellion commenced.

The Constitution of the United States guarantees to all its citizens absolute "liberty of conscience and right of speech;" yet who among you, either in Texas or any other slave State, have dared, any time in the last ten years, to express even a *doubt* as to the divine origin of the institution, or its claim to the consideration and protection of government and society above every other interest? How many free citizens of the United States have been immolated upon the altar of this political and social demon?

In our own State, during the summer and fall of 1860, according to the published account of the murderers themselves, two hundred and fifty of our free citizens were hung as felons, and thousands driven from their homes and compelled to leave the State, because they were suspected of infidelity to slavery. And, finally, gathering temerity from its successful war upon the rights and lives of its citizens, it lifted its unholy hand to destroy the Government to whose protection it owed its power. In its efforts to accomplish this, you have only been considered as so much material to be used. Your lives, your homes, and families, your present good and future hopes for yourselves and children were not worth a moment's thought.

Still it is expected that you will yield to moral cowardness, and shrink from the name of "Abolitionist" as too odious to be borne, although you may believe in your hearts that slavery should perish.

Citizens of Texas—for the last seventeen years my fellow citizens—in a great struggle like this through which we are now passing, none should shrink from the responsibility of acting, when in a condition to do so, according to his highest convictions of duty. To fail in this is infidelity to posterity, and a crime against humanity. If, then, you believe, as I do, that the institution of slavery has merited and invited its own destruction, and that its doom, pronounced by the sovereign power of the nation, is an act of justice—more than human justice—attesting to the presence of an Omnipotent hand—then speak and act as men who deserve freedom for themselves and their posterity. The day is near at hand when the name "Abolitionist" will have ceased to be a reproach, even in the South; and when children, now daily the subjects of attempted insult on account of its application to their fathers, will thank God that they were so reviled.

When you shall have been—as you will soon be—delivered from your present bondage, say to those who would question you upon the subject, that you *are* an "Abolitionist," not only in respect to slavery, but abolitionists, as well, in respect to treason and traitors, in respect to every *power, interest, institution* or *thing* which opposes human progress, liberty and happiness. Tell them that slavery must die for the highest of all crimes known to human laws—an attempt to destroy the national life; that no government can tolerate that which seeks its death; that the issue is fairly made—made by the rebellion—and is now as fairly met—slavery against the Government. The struggle is for life. Slavery must perish if the Government survive—it must die that *Liberty may live*. Tell them that you can no longer give your sanction to an institution which crushes human sympathy, stifles human thought, and tyrannizes over the minds, and hearts and consciences of men; and which, in its efforts to destroy freedom, has sacrificed truth, justice, religion and humanity. And when those who were lately so defiant and denunciatory of the Government of the United States and its friends— who spurned the very thought of being again its citizens as the deepest degradation—and who have so often promised each to "die in the last ditch" rather than "submit to Lincoln," begin to tremble and turn pale as their fate approaches and cry aloud to you to aid them in restoring Texas to the Union *with slavery*—tell them first to repair the injuries they have inflicted upon the Government and its people.

Ask them to restore the lives that have been sacrificed by their agency, not of those who have fallen upon the battle-fields of this war against freedom, but of those also who have been victims of their hired assassins—to bind and heal up the wounds which they have inflicted upon so many hearts—to hush the groans and dry the tears of the widows and orphans, whose cries have gone up to God against the murderers of husbands and fathers— to banish hate and distrust, and restore confidence and fraternal feelings among our people, and rebuild their wasted fortunes—to blot from the pages of history, and from the memory of man, the crimes, cruelties and deep disgrace of the last three years—and then, perhaps, but not till then, will you consider their appeal.

The declaration has been constantly and persistently made, that this is a cruel war, forced upon you by the Government. But who of you is it who does not know the Government never made *preparation* for war, until you had, in Texas, made prisoners of her soldiers, sent here to protect your settlements on the Indian frontier, and seized her military stores, property and arms, to the amount of over three millions of dollars, by a rebel force organized for the purpose? A thousand acts of war had been committed by the South before the Government called for a soldier, or made any preparation for her own defense. The falsehood gains nothing by its repetition, although endorsed by those who pretend to minister in holy things.

You were assured, that you run no risk in fighting against the Government because you could not be conquered by its arms. What, now, is the prospect before you? Let your minds, for a moment, rest upon the actual condition of the parties to the struggle.

When the war commenced, the rebel government had undisputed possession of every slave State except Missouri, Kentucky and Maryland, and in the first two of these it claimed jurisdiction, and admitted their delegates to the rebel Congress. It had possession, with one or two exceptions, of the strongholds and cities on the Atlantic and Gulf coasts, from Virginia to Texas, inclusive. No dread was then felt of war upon the soil of the South— the only question was, what portions of the North should be conquered and kept. When the first gun was fired at Fort Sumter, no soldier of the United States was occupying Southern soil. To-day they are, to the number of hundreds of thousands, distributed throughout the South. And although your leaders and public presses have loudly and boastfully claimed a victory upon every battle field, still, one by one the Southern States have been penetrated by the Union armies, and entirely or partially redeemed from rebel rule. One by one the strongholds of the Southern armies, upon the sea coast and in the interior, have given way and are now held under the Stars and Stripes. Peace and quiet have been restored in Maryland; the rebel armies have been driven from Missouri and Kentucky, and the two former of these States, having tasted the bitter fruits of secession and rebellion, have determined to lay the axe to the root of the tree that bore them. In these States the fate of slavery has been practically sealed by the voluntary act of their people. A large portion of Virginia has been reclaimed and erected into a new State prohibiting slavery, and is now represented in the national Congress. Arkansas and Tennessee are nearly free from rebel soldiery and rebel tyranny. Louisiana, with the great commercial emporium of the South, is in the firm grasp of the Government. So, too, is the larger portion of Mississippi, including her capital. Alabama and Florida are partially occupied by her forces. Greek fire is raining upon Charleston, and in Georgia the fragments of the broken and routed army of Bragg are pursued by the victorious and invincible army of Grant.[1] North Carolina has openly manifested her detestation of the Richmond despotism, and will joyfully embrace the earliest opportunity to return to her allegiance to the Government.

1. Braxton Bragg. Hamilton was writing before Sherman mounted his Atlanta campaign.

The great Father of Waters is no longer a highway for the rebel Government, nor a line of defense for its armies. Every vessel borne upon its broad bosom floats under the National flag, thus isolating you from the States east of it. What can the Confederate Government now do for you? It is everywhere in extremity, and every day contracting in territory and wasting in strength. There are no longer men in the South to make armies. From boyhood to old age they have been conscripted and *hunted down* and forced to the field until none are left. Its currency has been depreciated until it is sheer mockery to call it money. In many sections of the South famine is inevitable—already women and children are crying for bread. Instead of that flood-tide of prosperity which was promised you, on every hand you see decay—your towns are deserted and rotting down—commerce is dead, and all industry suspended beyond that which is necessary to sustain life. No nation abroad has yet recognized the rebel Government, nor is any likely to do so hereafter.

What is the condition of the loyal States? I speak what I do know; what I have seen, when I say that their people were never before as prosperous as at this moment. Grass does not grow in the streets of their cities—on the contrary, they are filled to repletion with bustling throngs, and resound, day and night, with the rush and noise of busy commerce. Their people of all classes, and of every avocation of life, are thriving beyond anything known in former years. The hundreds of thousands sent to the war are not missed from the great hive of their population. The Government is full of *energy*, *resources* and determined to conquer the rebellion. It will be conquered—it is, in fact, conquered at this moment; its *power is broken—its fate is sealed.*

To those who feel conscious that their crimes have been such that they dare not remain among a people they have so outraged, and under a Government they have so deeply wronged—who have violated every principle of civilized warfare and every instinct of humanity, I have nothing to say. But to those who never loved rebellion, or who were either deluded or forced into its service, and who, after the bitter experience of more than two years, have seen and deplored the madness of its authors, *I now do appeal.*

Many of you have been taught to revile me and to stamp my name with infamy—and for what? For refusing to join in this great conspiracy against free democratic government—the greatest sin recorded or to be recorded in the annals of time—because I refused to aid in the accomplishment of your ruin.

I can and do assert, with the pride of conscious truth, that I have never deceived you. Neither the entreaties of friends, the threats of enemies, nor the hope of reward, nor the dread of danger, caused me to falter in my duty to my country and her citizens. Discerning the path of duty, I gave up home, and family, and friends, to tread it with an unfaltering step. I now challenge my enemies, with all their hate and malice, to point to an argument or prediction of mine not vindicated by the events of the war, or one promise of theirs which has been realized by the people to whom they were made. *In the sight of God and before the civilized world, I demand the verdict of your consciences upon the issues made between us.*

I appeal to you in behalf of your own interests, present and future, to cease a struggle so hopeless and disastrous. When you are told that having once engaged in rebellion you can expect no mercy from the Government, it is as false as when you were told in the beginning that you must take up arms to prevent the tyrant Lincoln from taking away your property and your homes. You will be exhorted now, as then, not to "submit to Lincoln." The President of the United States never desired nor asked you to "submit" to him. He has but required, and only requires now, that you, like himself, shall submit to the Constitution and laws of the United States, and respect its just authority. You have been told that he is a tyrant, and this will doubtless be repeated. Among the innumerable falsehoods and slanders originating in rebellion, none can exceed this. In the history of the world there cannot be found one example of a government dealing with a rebellion against its rightful authority, with the mercy and lenience which have characterized the United States in this war. Out of the multiplied thousands who have been taken in arms against the Government, *not one* has been made to suffer for his treason. How has it been in Texas, and throughout the South? Hecatombs of victims have been offered upon the altar of rebellion! The men who are responsible to society and to God for the blood of a thousand good citizens, are those who are prating about the tyranny of the President and the Government of the United States. I tell you that even at this late day—now, at the eleventh hour—you may rely with *confidence* upon the liberality and magnanimity of the Government, and the solemn promise of the President, if you will, by your acts, acknowledge the error into which you have fallen or been driven.

Come then, my fellow-citizens, and win for yourselves and your children the claim of having aided, at last, in the restoration of freedom, justice, and order, under a Government full of blessings for all its citizens, and full of hope for all humanity! If wrongs to me and mine have caused feelings of resentment to rankle in my heart, or a revengeful spirit at times to possess me, I can only say that I would have been either more or less than man if it had not been so. But whatever be the effect of such wrongs upon men and those who have perpetrated them, personally and socially, I am not here in an official capacity to gratify any personal or private feelings of myself or others.

It is my duty, as it will be my aim, to the utmost of my humble ability, to reorganize society in our distracted State, by the restoration of peace and order under a Provisional Government, and this can only be done by the administration of laws for the protection of innocent and peaceable citizens, and the punishment of the disorderly and guilty. And while I assure you that no unnecessary severity is desired by the Government, and that none will be attempted by me, I also assure you that the murderers, assassins, and robbers now infesting the country, must seek some other field in which to ply their trade, or be brought to answer for their misdeeds.

I sincerely trust that the necessity for the continuance of the office which I now hold may soon cease, and that Texas, again in the Union, under a new Constitution, recognizing the unconditional freedom of every human being within her limits, and prohibiting, forever, human slavery—with a population chastened by suffering and made wise by experience—may set forth upon a new career of prosperity, predicated upon truth, industry and intelligence, and that her citizens and their descendants, for ages to come, may contribute to and share the blessings of a Government devoted to the freedom, progress and happiness of the human race.[2]

2. Governor Hamilton was able to get this pamphlet delivered to Gulf Coast Texas unionists but was unable to remain in Texas himself.

ANDREW JOHNSON

Speech on the Restoration of State Government
(Nashville: Dispatch Printing Co., 1864)

Andrew Johnson (1808–1875), of whose career as president much is known, was born in Raleigh, North Carolina, to poor but supportive parents. Early in life he lost his father, and his mother apprenticed him to a Raleigh tailor. He removed to Greeneville in east Tennessee in 1826. This committed Democrat soon entered politics and used his magnificent speaking voice to advantage, serving in the state legislature, in the U.S. Congress, as governor, and in the U.S. Senate from 1857 to 1862. Most important for this study, he became military governor of occupied Tennessee, where he struggled with friends and foes alike to restore his state to the Union. Selected as Lincoln's running mate in 1864, Johnson became chief executive after the assassination of the president. A Republican House impeached him, but the Senate was unwilling to remove him from office. After his presidency he returned home, sought to restore his good name, and again entered the U.S. Senate.

While in the wartime Senate and as military governor, he wrote and published on the horrors of internal war, the evils of the aristocratic Confederate government, and the need for Tennesseans to accept the end of slavery, or at least he went on record favoring it by the end of 1863. His pamphlets received wide distribution and discussion in the North and the upper South and influenced the struggle for resistance to the Confederacy. Johnson's contribution to this volume, a pamphlet drawn from a speech of January 21, 1864, on the importance of electing union supporters to state offices, captures his anger, his self-mockery, and his enormous faith in a restored Union. In it he spoke against his aristocratic southern enemies and urged the citizens of middle Tennessee to understand that the state's return to the Union depended on its support for the abolition of slavery.

For Johnson, slavery had ended, and the beneficiaries would be the small, independent, republican farmers.

Although Johnson's Reconstruction career has been given critical scrutiny, his wartime accomplishments have been glossed over. The best work on his life is Hans L. Trefousse, *Andrew Johnson: A Biography* (New York: W. W. Norton, 1989). But also see the magnificent introductions in Leroy P. Graf and Ralph W. Haskins, eds., *The Papers of Andrew Johnson* (Knoxville: University of Tennessee Press, 1967–); Frank Moore, *Speeches of Andrew Johnson* (1865; rpt. New York: Burt Franklin, 1970); and Carmon Anthony Notaro, "History of the Biographic Treatment of Andrew Johnson in the Twentieth Century," *Tennessee Historical Quarterly* 24 (summer 1965): 143–55.

* * *

In responding to the call that has been made upon me, I do so not for the purpose of making a speech, but simply to enter into a conversation, as it were, upon the subjects brought to your consideration here to-night in the resolutions just adopted.

The time has come when we should begin to consider the true policy to be adopted. I know in making speeches it is easy to make a flourish of trumpets or a display of fireworks, and entertain an audience for a time, but at present we should be practical. Our business now is to commence the restoration of our State government, and if I understand the resolutions adopted to-night, I think they cover the whole ground.

Our object is to restore all the functions of State government. We have been involved, or, more properly, engaged, in a rebellion. Rebellions were anticipated by our forefathers, and their suppression provided for. And when a rebellion occurs it devolves upon the Government of the United States to suppress it. Admitting the functions of a State to be paralyzed for a time, it does not destroy the State, as has been very correctly remarked. In the progress of the rebellion, the governor of a State may fly to seek protection in foreign climes, the Legislature may disappear, the civil magistrates may cease to act, but that does not destroy the State. Its functions have only been paralyzed—its powers are only remaining inactive.

In the 4th section of the 4th Article of the Constitution we find that the United States shall guarantee to each State in this Union a republican form of government. Instead of petitioning the President or the Congress of the United States—instead of assuming the attitude of suppliants in reference to the restoration of the powers of State government, we stand in the attitude of demanding—claiming at the hands of the Federal Government the guarantee of a republican form of government. We are no suppliants— no petitioners. We stand upon the broad platform of the Constitution, demanding our rights—that the guarantees in the Constitution shall be secured to us—that is, to secure to us a republican form of government.

We find also in the Constitution of the United States that the President is required to take an oath of office. He is sworn to support the Constitution of the United States. He is bound to see that the laws are faithfully executed, and he, in the exercise of his constitutional obligations, may appear in the State of Tennessee in the person of an agent—I care not by what name, either military Governor, agent, or commissioner—but he can appear through his agent, and restore to the people of Tennessee, and to every other State in the Union, a republican form of government. He has been sending brave men and gallant officers to suppress this rebellion, and for a time the functions of government in this State have been suspended, we have no Governor, no Legislature, and but few Judges—and we have one of these here to-night, who has been discharging his duties in obedience to the principles I have been describing.[1]

But in beginning to restore the Government—in carrying out the obligations of the Constitution, preserving and guaranteeing to the people a republican form of government, we must have justices of the peace, constables, etc. There are many here, no doubt, to-night, who are not citizens of Tennessee. Those who are, are familiar with our regulations. For instance, our State is divided into counties, then civil districts, each one of which elects two magistrates and one constable. There are provisions and exceptions made for different towns to have additional justices of the peace and constables. We will say, by way of illustration, that the first Saturday in March has been the usual time for the election of all county officers— justices of the peace, constables, trustees, sheriffs, clerks of the county and circuit courts—and when we come to the constitutional basis, would it not be clearly constitutional—would it not be carrying out the behests of the Constitution, and would the Executive be doing anything more than discharging his duty, to say to the people of this State on the first Saturday in March next: Go to the ballot-box and elect your constables, sheriffs, justices, county trustees and clerks. And when elected, let them be commissioned as they ordinarily are. The agent of the Government supplies the vacuum. Is

---

1. Manson M. Brien, unionist judge and chairman of the state meeting Johnson addressed.

there anything outside of the principles of the Constitution in that? Is there any usurpation in it? There must be a beginning somewhere.

In the absence of government there must be steps taken, though they may be irregular, for the purpose of bringing back order? Then we take a step without precedent, but clearly justifiable, and proceed to elect our officers as we have done heretofore. In looking over the various judicial districts of the State, we find them without judicial officers. In turning to the laws and Constitution of the State we find that when vacancies occur by death, resignation, or otherwise, the Executive shall make temporary appointments, and these appointees shall hold their places until their successors are elected and qualified. Then we see how easy the process is. Begin at the foundation, elect the lower officers, and, step by step, put the government in motion. But it may be said this can't be done in all the counties throughout the State. But, if it is done in a half dozen counties, it is so much done, and that much done we can do more.

In this connection there comes up a very important question, and that is, who shall be allowed to vote? This is the touchstone. And let us talk about this in a plain, common sense way, and see if we can ascertain who ought, and who ought not to vote. I assume that an individual who has engaged in this rebellion, who has got his consent to give up the government of the United States, and with his person attach his fortunes to the Southern Confederacy, or to any other Government—I say he has been, by his own act, *expatriated*—at the very point of time at which he gets his consent to take up arms against the Government of the United States, he ceases to be a citizen of the United States. A man coming into the United States from Great Britain, Ireland, or elsewhere, does not become a citizen until he has filed his declaration and taken the oath of allegiance. We describe in our laws the process by which he may become a citizen. Renouncing his allegiance to all powers, kings and potentates, thus complying with our naturalization laws, he becomes a citizen of the United States. We know that a great many who went into this rebellion, went into it under a reign of terror; we know a great many were conscripted, a great many went from interest and speculation; and others—the intelligent portion—went into it for the purpose of changing the Government and establishing an Aristocracy or negro oligarchy. This we know; and now shall we act upon the doctrine that a man can't repent, or, upon the Christian principle, that a man can conscientiously acknowledge his error and once more become a citizen of the United States? This is the question. Shall we lay down a rule which prohibits all restoration, and by which all will be excluded from participating in the exercise of the elective franchise? Think: we are told that honest men sometimes do change their opinions. We are told upon pretty high authority that sinners sometimes repent, and honestly repent; and we are told that in this repentance there should be some evidence of it. That is the condition of the community. We want to restore the Government, and the restoring process is that you, the people, must go to the ballot-box and exercise the elective franchise in so doing. Now let us get at it practically. These three gentlemen sitting here to-night—who are reporting, I presume, are judges of an election. We want to elect our squires, our constables, our county officers and our judges. I am speaking of things to be done before we get to convention, about which I have much to say before I conclude. What rule will you adopt, by which you can tell disloyal from loyal men? Over there I can point to a man who has been standing out like Saul of old, head and shoulders above the rest for the Union, as everybody knows. Over there stands another who has been equally prominent on the other side. Of these two we can say at once that the one may vote and the other may not. But in this instance we have got two extremes—we have got a case which everybody or anybody can decide without difficulty. But is the whole community in this condition? You may discriminate for a while—these are union men, these are rebels—but after a while you approach a line where they have not been prominent, and then how many can tell which is which? Will you have no test? No rule? Will you confer the power upon these judges, to say that no person shall vote save those that be loyal? But they cannot tell; they may act correctly as far as their judgment goes. Then again, in addition, I tell you you are trusting a great deal, where you leave this matter to the discretion of judges. They may, in many instances, act right, and they may think they act right in all. Here sit the three judges; they look around the neighborhood and say: "Why, I do not like to discriminate in favor of one friend and against another—I hope he has done right, and if he has done wrong, I hope he has repented." Then what rule will you establish? We want some standard by which we can put he that has been a traitor to the test, though he has repented. Now what will it be? It is easy to talk that rebels shall not vote and Union men may, but it is difficult to practice this thing. What rule will you establish? I ask the question. I want information. I came up here to talk to you, and you to me.

I know it has been said by some Union men that we should not be placed in the attitude of culprits—of men asking for pardon. I do not feel that you, and you, should be required, for the sake of a vote, to ask for pardon. I am not a criminal—I have violated no law—I have not raised my arm against my government. Therefore, I do not want pardon. But in the election of officers who are to take charge of the government we want some test, at least, that the men who vote are loyal and will act with loyal men. In all the States of the Union there is a qualification attached to voters without regard to treason, traitors, or anything of the kind. And taking the State of Tennessee for an illustration, what is the qualification? We find that the person to vote must first be a citizen of the United States; next, he must be a free white man. I want you to understand that although I am going to talk about negroes presently, I am for a white man's government, and in favor of free white qualified voters controlling this country, without regard to negroes. Next, the voter must have been in the county six months immediately preceding the day of election. Then if we were to say in addition, before you can vote, you must take an oath something like the following:

I solemnly swear that I will henceforth support the Constitution of the United States, and defend it against the assaults of all its enemies; that I will hereafter be, and conduct myself as a true and faithful citizen of the United States, freely and voluntarily claiming to be subject to all the duties and obligations, and entitled to all the rights and privileges of such citizenship; that I ardently desire the suppression of the present insurrection and rebellion against the Government of the United States, the success of its armies and the defeat of all those who oppose them, and that the Constitution of the United States, and all laws and proclamations made in pursuance thereof, may be speedily and permanently established and enforced over all the people, States and Territories thereof; and further, that I will hereafter heartily aid and assist all loyal people in the accomplishment of these results. So help me God.

Is there any one, Union at heart, who can object to taking an oath like this? Is there a solitary Union man who cannot take this oath? Is there any Union man but what would take great pleasure in coming before the judges of election and take this oath to test him who has been warring against his country? You put him to the test, you don't come up asking pardon, but are only giving evidence of being a loyal and a qualified voter. These are simply the qualifications of a voter. On the other hand, if there is anybody in this large assembly of voters who needs and desires a pardon or amnesty, whether he seeks it in good faith or for the purpose of saving a little remnant of negro or any other property, I would say to him, "Go over there; there is an altar for you. There is President Lincoln's altar if you want pardon or amnesty—if petitioning to the President for executive clemency. If you want to escape the penalties you have incurred by violations of law and the constitution, go over there and get your pardon. We are not in need of it; we wish not to take that oath; that is the oath for him who has committed crime." Now, gentlemen, it seems to me this will be fair. We want a hard oath—a tight oath—as a qualification for everybody that votes. He that wants pardon must take the oath prescribed by the President of the United States; and I am free to say that I think the President has been exceedingly lenient in permitting them to do that. If this will not do, will you suggest something that will be better? What standard will you erect? Don't stand here and find fault with my suggestions and say they will not do; but suggest others that are better and more acceptable. I am for a rule that will test a loyal man as against a disloyal one; that is the rule I am for. I am free to say to you that I believe there are many even in the Confederate army, many who have deserted, and even some captured, who I believe are honest and loyal to-day and regret that they have ever been involved in this infamous, diabolical and damnable rebellion. I have had men come before me who evinced, by their emotions and the tone of their voice, that they were as much opposed to the rebellion as I am. If this be so, and they are now willing to support the constitution, and fight in vindication of it, as far as I am concerned, I am willing to admit them and give them a fair chance to return. We cannot put all in prison; we can't suspend all upon the gallows. No, this is not a war of extermination, but a war for the restoration of Government; and while restoring the Government, if we reclaim honest men we have only done our duty.

If we want to restore the government we must start at the foundation. Having elected our squires, constables, sheriffs and other county officers, as we can get men to serve, we have got the groundwork laid. Then what will you do next? Now mark: under the 4th clause and IVth article of the Constitution of the United States we have a pledge to secure to the States a republican form of government. To carry out the spirit and letter of the Constitution, as the people are the rightful source of political power, I should say the executive would have the right to invite the people to have a convention to restore government to the people. Then, even looking to the Constitution of the United States, we have a right to call a convention, and have the convention as a means of flowing from the constitution to guarantee the restoration of a republican form of government. We find in the constitution of this State that you can amend the constitution by the legislature, but it takes about six years to amend it in that way. But when we recur to the bill of rights, which is a paramount part of our State Constitution, we find that the sovereign people have the right to alter, amend or abolish their form of government whenever they think proper, and in their own way. This is perfectly consonant to the Constitution of the United States, and admits the great principle that all political power is inherent in the people.

I have unfortunately or fortunately, as the case may be, always been one of those who hold that all power is inherent in the people, and that the Government is made for the people instead of the people being made for the Government; as much so, at least, as the shoe is made for the foot, instead of the foot being made for the shoe. Government emanates from the people; and now, when your Government has been paralyzed or its functions suspended, is there any better way that can be adopted than to call a convention here? In other words: let us have the sovereign present in the shape of delegates; or, were it practicable, to appear in a large amphitheatre, and know what their opinions were in taking the steps to restore the workings of government, I would say let the people be convened in obedience to the Constitution of the United States and of the State, and in strict compliance with the fundamental principles of our Government, that power is inherent in the people. Who dare say the convention shall not assemble? Who dare say that the people shall not assemble in convention? I know there is a little croaking dissatisfaction among some that have been nominally Union men, and some that have been Rebels in this hell-born and hell-bound rebellion, who, now that they are subjugated, after having been instrumental in paralyzing to some extent the Government, and after having helped to produce the rebellion, hypocritically say: Oh! they don't want so much disturbance;—it will be too revolutionary to have a convention; it will not do to trust the people with the settlement of this great question. Let us think. Give me your attention, and I will show you that there is a cat in the meal. They turn to the Constitution as it now stands, and say, let us get the Legislature back here; let us patch up things and have no fuss. They think of that little clause in our Constitution which provides that the Legislature shall not emancipate slaves without the consent of their owners. Don't you see? Then if they get the Legislature back under the Constitution as it is, they think they can hold on to the little remnant of negroes that is left—the disturbing element that has produced all this war. I then say this: Bring the people forward in convention—the source of all power—they that made the Constitution, and let them act upon this important question and upon this momentous occasion. Let us have the people here, and when they assemble in convention—when the sovereign is present, he can do all that the Legislature can, and he can do a great deal more. Have a convention here, and it can put your State upon her legs in eight and forty hours. It could appoint these magistrates, these squires, these sheriffs, all the officers, and carry on the machinery of State to perfection in eight and forty hours. Let the people come forward and speak, and in speaking upon the negro question, my honest convictions are, that they will settle it, and settle it finally.

Now, my countrymen, it is not worth while to try to deceive each other, and thus play a hypocritical part as the soothsayers in olden times; while practicing their deceptions upon the people, when meeting, would always smile in each others faces. I know there is going to be division in Tennessee; and I tell them now, politically speaking, that my sword is unsheathed, and it never is to be returned until I fall, or until this great principle of free government has triumphed. Now is the time to settle it. This question of slavery has been the disturbing element in this Government, and the time has come now to settle it. The Rebels commenced the destruction of the Government for the preservation of slavery, and the Government is putting down the rebellion, and in the preservation of its own existence has put slavery down, justly and rightfully, and upon correct principles. It attempted to rise above the Government, and had it succeeded, negroes or their masters would have controlled the Government; but in making the attempt to control the Government, the mighty car of State has moved forward, and the institution has been crushed, and thank God for it.

But in this connection I have got a single word to say in reference to the brave and gallant men of Tennessee who have entered the service of their country. Is there any one who would like to deprive them of the elective franchise? Mr. Lincoln has done no such thing. He will not require these fifteen thousand heroic soldiers, who have been fighting the battles of their country, and of themselves constitute more than one-tenth of our voting population, to stand before him as petitioners for pardon and amnesty. I know his high appreciation of loyal men, of justice and right too well for this. I opposed his coming into power. I spoke and voted against him, and though I did this and in favor of another, I believe Abraham Lincoln is an honest man, and has done, and is doing, all in his power to preserve this Government and put down this infernal rebellion. Render unto Caesar the things that are Caesar's. I believe Mr. Lincoln is a patriot and a friend to his Government; I believe he is for free Government; and so believing, I shall stand by him. It is easy to find fault—to complain; but the next question comes up, who would have done better than he has done? He is the last man in the United States that would wish to circumscribe the privileges of the brave men of Tennessee in the matter of the elective franchise. Is there a Tennesseean here to-night, though he may have differed with me heretofore, who ever doubted me upon this question of free government? In an election for members of a convention or for county officers, how easy it will be for every Tennessee soldier, if he can hear who the candidates are in his district, to vote for the man of his choice wherever he may be stationed? Whether in Middle, or East, or West Tennessee, his voice can be heard and his weight goes into the ballot box in the settlement of this great question. That is the manner in which I want it settled. And when it comes to repelling and driving back the Rebel armies, then let him have on his whole armor—put on his shield and lock shield with his comrades, and never return till victory perches upon his standard. Who wants to deprive the army from Tennessee of the right to participate in the restoration of their Government? Will anybody make that allegation against me? Since this rebellion commenced, who has been hunted, persecuted, denounced, and calumniated by the Rebels? There is not one among the army of Tennesseeans but what knows that I would make any and every sacrifice by which their interest could be promoted. No, no; who ever dreamed or thought of their being deprived of participating at the ballot-box—they who have done so much for the restoration of the State?

Now upon this negro question, and I know the saying is sometimes bandied about that you are always prating and saying the negro is dead—if he is dead, why repeat it so often? Is there a man here that has observed this thing who does not know that the institution of slavery in Tennessee is dead? I have had some come to me and say, "Gov. Johnson, are you in favor of immediate emancipation?" I tell them yes. "Do you want to turn the negroes all loose upon the country? What will we do with them?" Why Sir, I reply, as far as emancipation is concerned, that has already taken place. Where are your negroes? They answer, "They are running about somewhere." I ask, what do you call that? They seem to be already turned loose. The institution of slavery is turned into a traveling institution, and goes just where it pleases. It is said the negroes are not qualified to be free; because they have been slaves so long they are unfitted to be freemen, and shall not be permitted to enjoy the privileges of freemen; but by way of making them competent, it is proposed to keep them in slavery nineteen or twenty years longer. In the first place it would not do to have them free, because they have been slaves, and in the next place they should be kept in slavery to qualify them for freemen.

We were proceeding to put up the State government—to elect clerks, justices, trustees, legislature, Governor and other things, that constituted the State heretofore. But the institution of slavery. There it lies; will you take it back? Leave out the disturbing element I say. It is now out; and to put the State in motion, start the machinery and leave negroes out of the question. Then the conclusion is, that in fact negroes are emancipated in Tennessee to day, and the only remaining question for us to settle, as prudent and wise men, is in assigning the negro his new relation. Now, what will that be? There are no more negroes to-day than there were yesterday—there being no more negroes free than there were slaves. The same space will contain them in one condition as in another, and the slaveholder need not be alarmed with the fear that negroes will be increased faster than they were before. Then the negro will be thrown upon society, governed by the same laws that govern communities, and be compelled to fall back upon his own resources, as all other human beings are. The God of Nature has endowed him with faculties that enable him to enjoy the result of his own labor. Political freedom means liberty to work, and at the same time enjoy the product of one's labor, be he white or black, blue or gray, red or green, and if he can rise by his own energies, in the name of God let him rise. In saying this, I do not argue that the negro race is equal to the Anglo-Saxon—not at all. There are degrees among white men; some are capable, others are not; some are industrious, others are not; but because we find inferiors among ourselves, shall every inferior man be assigned to slavery? If the negro is better fitted for the inferior condition of society, the laws of nature will assign him there. My own conviction is, that in less than five years after this question is settled upon the principle of hired labor, the negro's labor will be more productive than it ever was.

The argument used to be that "Cotton is King." But I think that idea is pretty well exploded. For a little experience has proven that cotton is a feeble King without the protection of the United States. I used to tell them that bread and meat were King, and if we look over in rebeldom now, we will find that a little bread and meat would be more acceptable than cotton.

I hope the negro will be transferred to Mexico, or some other country congenial to his nature, where there is not that difference in class or distinction, in reference to blood or color. If in the settlement of this question the providence of God should call a number of them there, I say let them go. And about that time I would not care much to see a large portion of our gallant sons go along to Mexico, too, and as they approach the city of Mexico or Jalapa, of which Louis Napoleon has taken possession, where he was going to send Prince Maximilian to govern, I would like our boys to be along there inquiring into that affair, and give him to understand that while we can fight for years and head a monstrous rebellion to boot, he cannot come upon this continent to establish a government anti-republican in its character.[2] We have not yet fulfilled our mission. We have got the negroes to dispose of. We will do that. And we have got other things to do. We should teach France and all other powers that we can crush down

2. Johnson, too, comments on the problem of the French emperor having troops on the U.S. border in Mexico.

a gigantic rebellion at home, and that the combined armies of the world cannot subdue the United States when united. I care not though all nations were arrayed against us in one solid phalanx. When the masses of the people of these United States stand united we can bid defiance to the combined powers of earth.

Let us go on in the performance of the great mission of restoring these States. And I fully concur in the doctrine I heard advanced here to-night, that a State cannot commit suicide—a State cannot destroy itself—a State has no right to go out of this Union, and the Federal Government has no right to put one out. None. The doctrine is as dangerous on one hand as on the other. If you accept either, your Government is destroyed and crumbles into pieces like a rope of sand, by its own weight. These States occupy a certain relation to the great whole, and the great whole to each part. The parts cannot destroy the whole, neither can the whole destroy the parts. It is undeniable: there is no way to destroy a State. We find in the Constitution that you can make States, create a Government, but there is no way to destroy it. I repudiate the doctrine *in toto*. It is contrary to the Government of our fathers—an emanation of Divinity—and we fail to discharge our duty, and commit as great a sin and error in permitting the destruction of this Government in that way, as though we had raised our sacrilegious hands to tear it down.

Though it was not my intention to speak on this occasion, in conclusion of what I have said, I am free to declare that I am for a Convention, after adopting some rule that will exclude disloyal and admit only loyal men. Under the Constitution, the people have a right to meet and appoint delegates. On the other hand, the President of the United States, through his agent, has the right by proclamation to say to the people: "On such a day elect so many delegates to take into consideration the restoration of the State." As I remarked before, sometimes we may do irregular things for the sake of returning to law and order. It might be irregular in starting, but when the Convention get together, they have a right to change, alter, or abolish, their government in their own way. I am disposed to think that the people, if they were together, would be inclined to remove the difficulties under which we labor. I am willing to trust them. I believe they are honest, and especially so in reference to governmental affairs. And even judging men by self-interest, I am willing to trust them, because it is their interest to have the best government they can get, and they will have it. I do not see why a Convention could not be trusted as well as a Legislature. Who is prepared here to-night to hesitate to admit the great principle that man is capable of governing himself? Have any of you reached that point? If you have, you had better go down and join Jeff. Davis; that is the locality for you. And now I am going to tell you a truth, and you know what I say is true: If there are any here who have lived in the county of Davidson, you know many men have been afraid and alarmed even to speak upon the negro question when the large slaveholders were about. Some of you have been deprived of your manhood so long upon this question, that when you begin to talk about it now, you look around to see if you are not overheard by some of your old masters.

In 1843, when I was a candidate for Governor, it was said, "That fellow Johnson is a demagogue—an abolitionist"—because I advocated a white basis for representation—apportioning members of Congress according to the number of qualified voters, instead of embracing negroes. I discussed the question alone, scarcely getting a paper to come to my support; and hundreds agreeing with me, sought me in private to give me comfort, but were afraid to strike openly. I know all about this negro question, and pardon me if I seem to be egotistical when I say that I am the only man that has dared at all times to discuss it in this State; and now some of you see what I have all along foreshadowed. I have known this question was coming, and that it was only a question of time. Standing alone, having but little means to command, and no press, but simply relying upon argument, with the great mass of the people I was sustained. Running against him who was called the "eagle orator," a lineal descendant from the forest-born Demosthenes, it was expected that I would be driven from the contest; but, thank God, I have always relied upon one thing: that there was a great principle of right lying at the foundation of all things; and that truth is mighty and will prevail.[3] Right goes forward; truth triumphs; justice is paramount; and slavery goes down. And now, I proclaim it, the time has come, God being my helper, I am willing to do my part, and am willing to wind up my political career in the final settlement of this question. The time has come when the tyrant's rod shall be broken, and the captive set free. Then, now is the time to strike; and he is a coward who desires to remain inactive and will not come forward to that altar and worship. Yet while right is triumphing, they talk about compromising this question. Compromise! Compromise with what? Compromise a great principle! Will you have truth to compromise with falsehood? Will you have right to compromise with wrong? Will you have virtue compromise with vice? I say, No. In the compromise of right with wrong, right is the loser; in the compromise of virtue with vice, virtue is always violated. Deity might as well have compromised with the devil,

3. Johnson ran against Gustavus A. Henry.

who was the first rebel, and made war in heaven. No compromise. None. No compromise with traitors while they have arms in their hands. I am no maniac or fanatic upon this question, but I feel devoted, attached and wedded to great principles. Sometimes I inquire in my own mind why this people have had no leader. Peter the Hermit led the Crusade, but was wild and visionary, yet he intended to redeem the Holy Land. The Crusaders had their leader; the Israelites had their leader; the Greeks had their leader; the Romans had their leader, and England had her leader. The Israelites had their Moses, and have this people got no Moses—no leader—or have they to rely for their deliverance upon the establishment of this great principle? The ways of Providence are incomprehensible to short-sighted, erring man. In the various periods of the world's history there have been manifestations of a power incomprehensible to us, and I believe that there is a direct and important connection between the moral and physical world, and the one is affected more or less by the other in bringing about great events. Going back to the history of the world, we find events and signs have preceded final results. This nation, many think, has been involved in a great sin. Nations as well as individuals must sooner or later be overtaken for their transgressions. Perhaps this rebellion will result in great good; the nation will become chastened and the sin removed. Who can tell? When we go back to ancient times and run over the pages of history, what do we find there? We find Pharaoh, after governing the Egyptians with an iron rod so many years, there was a rebellion there; the people were led by Moses to the shores of the Red Sea, when by the touch of his rod the waters parted and stood as a wall on either side, and Moses and his followers passed through dry-shod and reached the land of Canaan; whilst Pharaoh and his chariots and mighty hosts proceeded to follow on and were lost amid the waves, and were drowned in the sea. I do not say that this was a direct or special interposition of Providence; I will not undertake to argue that it was the result of a divine law. I refer to it as a great fact that Pharaoh and his hosts were lost in the Red Sea in pursuit of those trying to escape from bondage. If disposed, I might take you back to Babylon and there look at her people in their might, or to those mighty walls crowded with chariots. Those walls have crumbled; Babylon has gone down, and is no more. I will not say whether it was the result of a special providence, or of a general law, but I state it as a great fact. Some great wrong or some great sin had to be redressed. I might take you back to ancient Tyre, in the days of her freedom and splendor; but all her glories are no more, and her ruins are used only as a resort for straggling fishermen to dry their nets upon the rocks. I might take you back to Herod, in the days of all his pomp and splendor, when, on one occasion, he appeared before the people, and they stood amazed and exclaimed, "He speaks not as a man, but as God." But he was smitten by the Almighty, and eaten by worms. I will not say whether these were special interpositions of Providence or the results of a Divine law, but they are great facts. I might call attention to the journey of Saul of Tarsus to Damascus, when he was struck blind, as believed by some, on account of his persecutions of the Christians. But I will not say whether that was the result of a special interposition of Divine providence, or of a general law, but it is a great fact. I might take you to Jerusalem, and tell of the persecution by the Jews of Christ, and his crucifixion upon the cross, and now their dispersion to all parts of the globe. I will not assume that it was an interposition of Divine providence, or the result of a general law, but it is a great fact, and the Jews have been dispersed and rebuked. There are many ways in which the Almighty manifests his power. He sometimes unlocks the winds, and rends the forests, and strands whole navies upon the hidden rocks and desert shores. Sometimes He manifests His power in the forked lightning's glare, and sometimes His mutterings are heard in distant though threatening peals of thunder. Sometimes He lets the comet loose, which sweeps from one extreme of the universe to the other, shaking from its fiery tail pestilence and death. There are

> "Signs sent by God to mark the will of Heaven—
> Signs which bid nations weep and be forgiven."

Does not the mind irresistibly come to the conclusion that this great sin must be gotten clear of, or result in the overthrow and destruction of this nation? I say, then, remove the evil, obey the laws of Heaven, and always reach a right conclusion. As we have commenced the work of restoring the State, let us profit by past experience, and put the government in motion now upon correct and true principles. Let us go at it honestly. I know there are some that are finding fault and thinking about the places of State already. We should not be controlled by considerations of this kind. Let us forget that we have been divided into parties; let us commence the work of restoring and building the Government up, and then if we want to quarrel about local questions or questions of expediency, we will have a Government to quarrel in.

I will remark in this connection, that about the beginning of the rebellion, in conversation with Philip Clayton, Howell Cobb's Assistant Secretary of the Treasury, that gentleman said, after we had argued the question pro and con: "Mr. Johnson, it is unnecessary to argue this question further; a large portion of the South is unwilling to submit to the administration of the government by a man who has come up from the ranks as Abraham Lincoln has." And let me tell you, there is a good deal of this feeling and sentiment in the hearts of the leaders of this rebellion, because Abraham Lincoln rose from the masses. Abraham Lincoln is a democrat in principle; he is for the people, and for free government, and so I am for him, and will stand by him until this rebellion is put down. There are corruptions, of course, in such an immense expenditure. But what is a few millions or billions of dollars, when contrasted with the existence of this Government, and the suppression of this rebellion? What is it contrasted with the life and existence of a great nation which has not fulfilled its mission? It is easy to clamor and to find fault; but let us put the rebellion down, and then, if any body has done wrong, we will have plenty of time to punish offenders.

I did not come here to speak to-night. My intention was not to participate in the meeting, but I was anxious to see some steps taken which would indicate what you intended to do. If we have correct principles, it does not need previous consultation, and the result will be the triumph of those principles. Then take this great question; it is a question of state—of the existence of free government. Take it and think about it. Turn it over in your minds. Which is the best way? What is the best mode? How shall it be done? I stand where I have always stood, an advocate of free government. I am for the people having a fair, full, impartial trial of their capacity for self government, and I have confidence that they will triumph. And if these brave officers and gallant men, with what aid we can give them, will keep the rebel army from us, or drive them in the Gulf, (as I believe ere long they will,) before they reach the Gulf, Tennessee will "stand redeemed, regenerated and disenthralled by the genius of universal emancipation." Let those of us who are for restoring the government and leaving out this element called slavery, stand together, and in language often repeated, let us give a long pull, a strong pull and a pull altogether, and the union sentiment and free government will succeed. We have commenced the battle of freedom—it is freedom's battle,—and let me say it is not extended to the negro only, for this will free more white men than it will black men. I know what I say. There are men owning slaves themselves that will be emancipated by this operation. It is not my devotion to the black man alone, but a greater devotion to the white men and the amelioration of their condition. My humanity is broad enough for the white and the black man too. We have commenced the battle of freedom, and—

"Freedom's battle once begun,
Bequeathed from bleeding sire to son,
Though baffled oft, is ever won!"

Make high and strong resolves; let your principles go forth to the world, and, though slave-owners and negro-drivers, though hell stand yawning before you, go forward with the banner of Freedom and Free Government; pass the fiery cross around, and Freedom will ere long triumph, and the triumph, I hope, will last for all time.

Here in Tennessee, some say, "Oh, I am afraid of the slavery question!" They are so afraid of doing wrong that they are afraid to do right. Many yet are so afraid of their former masters, they still look around to see whether Mr. Bell, Mr. Overton, or the Ewings are standing about.[4] It is time, when talking about restoring slavery, to restore manhood. They know many of them have that taken from them which constitutes a man—their manhood has been emasculated. Get your consent that you have manhood enough to stand up here and take hold of the helm of State, and convince us that you are willing to do it. Let us commence the work this night. The shackles must fall from the limbs of all. You must have laws for the punishment and protection of all. Law is what we want. There is no freedom without law. As an ancient Greek has said, "The love of law is the soul of liberty." We must have law, and whether the black man is here or not, we must have government. There will be no difficulty about this question. I don't care if the negroes go to Africa or any other place more suitable to them—we can make more cotton after they are gone than has ever been made in the United States before. If you cut up these large cotton farms into small sized farms, each man with his little family getting hold of part of it, on good land will raise his own hogs, his own sheep, beef cattle, his own grain, and a few bales of cotton, better handled, and a much better article than we have ever had heretofore. With a greater number of individuals, each making a few bales, we will have more bales than ever were made before. And in addition to that, if the cotton-plant was lost, the world would not stop, for the vacuum would be filled by making a little more silk, wool, hemp and flax, and in a little while you would never know that cotton had been in the world. It is all an idea, that the world can't get along without cotton. And as is suggested by my friend behind me, whether we attain perfection in the raising of cotton

4. John Bell, Andrew Ewing, Edwin Ewing, John Overton, all political enemies of Johnson.

or not, I think we ought to stimulate the cultivation of hemp, for we ought to have more of it, and a far better material, a stronger fibre with which to make a stronger rope. For, not to be malicious or malignant, I am free to say, that many who were driven into this rebellion, I believe are repentant, but I say of the leaders, the instigators, the conscious intelligent traitors, they ought to be hung. Treason must be made odious, traitors must be punished and impoverished. Their social power must be destroyed, and the effects that give them power and influence must be taken away. I trust the time will come, when the Union men who have been oppressed, and the loyal heirs of those who have perished on the battle field, or starved in the mountains, will, to some extent, be remunerated out of the property of those who betrayed and tried to destroy their country. Common sense teaches that the transgressor should make restitution. What the common sense of every man suggests is but common justice.

This would not be considered a very politic electioneering speech, but I am no candidate for anything. I know some say that when traitors become numerous enough, then treason becomes respectable. I want that class hung to test their respectability. Fellow-citizens, I must say in conclusion, that I am very much gratified to find that there has been no dissension here to-night as far as I have observed. I am proud to say that I have not seen the slightest indication of prejudice or dissension. The resolutions as adopted, as I understand them, I think will cover the whole ground, and if we carry out these resolutions I think we can succeed in accomplishing the end sought for. I am also proud and gratified to see so many here participating in this meeting. Let it go to the country as an earnest of what is going to follow. Things must have a beginning, and you have put the ball in motion. I repeat, that I feel proud and more than gratified at this demonstration, and in conclusion, tender you my sincere thanks for your marked attention to this crude and desultory speech.

Letter to His Excellency the President and the Honorable Congress of the United States, on the Subject of Abuse of Military Power in the Command of General Butler in Virginia and North Carolina

(Washington, D.C.: McGill and Witherow, 1864)

F rancis Harrison Pierpont (1814–1899) was born near Morgantown, Virginia (now West Virginia), became a schoolteacher in Virginia and Mississippi, and by 1848 had a thriving law practice near Fairmont, Virginia. An antislavery Whig, he supported Lincoln for president in 1860 and organized the May 1860 Wheeling meeting, which elected him provisional governor of the Virginia government in exile. He campaigned for the creation of the separate state of West Virginia. The Lincoln government named him governor of the restored state of Virginia, and he moved the capital to Alexandria. As governor he sought help for refugees from Confederate Virginia, cooperated with congressmen from border Virginia and West Virginia, and planned for the restoration of the state to the Union. When the Confederacy fell he moved his government to Richmond, but he was ineffectual, and Federal authorities removed him in 1868.

Pierpont's April 18, 1864, pamphlet is an example of the troubles southern unionists had with some Federal generals in the occupied regions of their states. He tilted with Gen. Benjamin Butler and, in so doing, described much of the wartime hardships of Norfolk's unionist citizens. His work portrays Federal favoritism toward ex-Confederates, a Federal bureaucracy out of control, and the revenge of former Confederates against the outspoken coastal unionists.

There is one older study of this much neglected man's life; see Charles H. Ambler, *Francis H. Pierpont: Union War Governor of Virginia and Father of West Virginia* (Chapel Hill: University of North Carolina Press, 1937). See also

Anna Pierpont Sivitar, *Recollections of War and Peace, 1861–1868* (New York: G. P. Putnam's Sons, 1938).

* * *

It is a most painful necessity which has made it imperative on me to call your attention to the abuses of military power in Virginia. I have exhausted all the means known to me without success, to redress these wrongs. Your time is so much occupied that it is impossible for me to go to you individually and relate the contents of the following pages. Having so many other duties to perform, to economize time I have adopted this method as most convenient to myself, with a desire also to consult your convenience, hoping that you may find a leisure hour to look into the subject here presented.

In addition to what is herein stated in regard to General Butler's department in Virginia, I assigned to myself the task of stating some facts in regard to the military administration of General Slough in this city of Alexandria during the last eighteen months; but as General Slough's case has been referred to the Committee on the Conduct of the War, it may be considered premature for me to present the facts until that committee has had the opportunity to fully investigate the subject.[1] I have only presented a few of the cases at Norfolk, and could only do so of those in Alexandria, without swelling this pamphlet to too large proportions. In Alexandria arbitrary power has taken a less range than at Norfolk, but in some of its exercise it has been more damaging to the principles of our organic law. What I mean by arbitrary exercise of power, *is a capricious exercise of power outside of the rules of war* in a manner to justly render the military authority obnoxious to the friends of the Government and the Union cause.

With a most ardent desire for the welfare and safety of our common country, and the discharge of a most solemn duty I owe to those whom I represent, I submit this subject to your enlightened and patriotic consideration.

On the 13th day of April, 1861, the Virginia convention went into secret session. Hon. W. T. Willey, now United States Senator, wrote to his friends at Morgantown to prepare for war—the State would secede.[2] They must look for the worst. On the 22d of the same month a mass meeting was held at that place; that being court day, it was expected that speakers on

1. Union general John P. Slough, military governor of Alexandria, 1862–1865.
2. Waitman T. Willey, senator from West Virginia, whose pamphlet appears in this volume.

both sides would be present, to address the people. A delegation of four hundred Union men came from the east end of the county. Before they came into town they halted, and passed a resolution with General Jackson's oath, that no secessionist would speak in town that day. They kept their oath. At one o'clock, with drum and fife, and national flags carried by different delegations, flags displayed from almost every house, ladies and children welcoming, the procession was formed, which paraded the streets for an hour. A stand in the public square was erected, the masses gathered around, appropriate resolutions were adopted, two speeches were made denouncing secession and the conspirators. The crowd refused to disperse, and called one of the speakers back to the stand. Several old soldiers of 1812 were there. One of them in great earnestness, said: "You must tell us what to do." "Do!" said the speaker. "Don't in your wrath kill any of these secessionists, who, like spaniels, are slinking around town. They want to be martyrs in a small way, to make capital for their cause, and get an opportunity to punish you, or incarcerate you in a dungeon. We can't spare you in that way. Go home, call your children around you. If any are married, call them and your grand-children. Tell them that with your strong arms, you and they have cleared out your farms, built your houses, and filled them with the conveniences of life. Point them to your barns and stock; say to them that this is the product of the hard earnings of white men who never owned a slave; that now the slaveholders of the east, with the traitors in the west, are seeking to appropriate it all for the greater security, as they say, of their slaves. Say to your children, no; their object is to enslave the laboring white man, and to use your strong arms and all our substance to accomplish their wicked purpose. Then tell them to get their guns in order, and then in reunion let all, meekly kneeling around the family altar, promise before God to stand by the flag and Constitution of our fathers, and to defend it as long as life lasts. Then ask God, for the sake of his Son, to seal your covenant in heaven, and give you grace and courage to defend your section and country from the prey of the negro-ocracy of the south. That's what DO."

Upon this charge being received, the teeth of old men and young men chattered with rage, and they shouted, "we will DO IT."

In this spirit similar advice was given all over Northwestern Virginia. The people rallied, a great meeting was called by both parties at Fairmont, the center of secessionists, on the first Monday in May. Both parties were there in strength; both flags were flying; fist fights commenced before nine o'clock. By two, both parties had speakers on the stand; secesh in the court house, Union out of doors. Before four, the secesh attempted to break up the Union crowd, and the Union men whipped them in a fair fist fight of not less than eighty on a side. This broke the spirit of secession in West Virginia.

The first Wheeling convention was called under the auspices of the Hon. John S. Carlisle. The second was called, the State government reorganized and recognized by the Government of the United States as the government of Virginia, I think wisely and rightly.[3] The restored government put upward of eighteen thousand Union soldiers into the field during the first two years of the war. West Virginia has put in some three thousand since, in addition to which, a large number of the old troops have re-enlisted. These troops were as brave and as true as any who ever drew a trigger. The bones of many of them are now bleaching on almost every battle field, from the Peninsula to Vicksburg.

The State was divided by the consent of the Legislature and Congress. The officers and people endorsed the President's proclamation of emancipation, the policy of enlisting negroes in the Army, and the currency and the five-twenties. While West Virginia has put the troops above named into the field, her people have subscribed for a greater amount of the five-twenty loan than the State of Rhode Island, though one fourth of the territory is yet overrun by guerrillas; and Norfolk has established a national bank, with a capital of $100,000, and the amount all paid in.

After the division of the State, I consented to be elected Governor of the State, with the distinct understanding that I would govern it as a free State. The General Assembly was called together; it passed a bill providing for a constitutional convention; the members of the convention were elected by the people. The convention met on the 13th of February, 1864, in the city of Alexandria, and on the 10th day of March, with but one dissenting voice, adopted an amendment to the constitution abolishing slavery and involuntary servitude in the State forever.

The mode of organization of the State is complete, and as soon as the rebels are driven out, I expect to organize every county with loyal officers, under the old flag and a free constitution, without one cent of charge to the Federal Government.

I had the honor of acting as Governor of Virginia for two years, with the seat of government at the city of Wheeling. Troops were assembled there, mustered into the service of the United States, and sent to the field. Troops from other States passed through the city. The police regulations were, I think, about as good as they are in Norfolk and Alexandria. I had a small military force of two companies, with Major Darr for commander of the post and provost marshal. The military patroled the city, when disorderly

---

3. See Carlile's pamphlet in this volume.

soldiers were found, they were arrested and sent to the guard house. When disorderly citizens were found, they were arrested and handed over to the civil authority. When soldiers were passing through or stopping in the city, the places where liquor was sold were ordered to be closed. When the exigency passed the prohibition was removed. I had intercourse constantly with General McClellan, while he was there; with General Rosecrans, who succeeded him; then with General Fremont; then General Schenck and General Cox, General Scammon, and all the time with General Kelley.[4] This intercourse was of the kindest nature, always on their part showing every disposition to assist in building up the civil government, and establishing the authority of law. A question was started as to where the military authority stopped and the civil began. The first case that occurred was the shooting of one soldier by another, at Parkersburg. The case was referred to me. I answered, the military could try by court-martial, or the offender could be handed over to the civil court. The latter course was adopted. The jury did not hang him, but awarded him ten years in the penitentiary. He is now expiating his crime. All similar cases took the same direction. Harmony has always existed between the civil and military authorities in West Virginia. The result is a prosperous people, where they are safe, and the great majority truly loyal, feeling that the government is a blessing.

I make these prefatory remarks to you, gentlemen, merely to impress upon your mind the fact that I am not a late adventurer in this rebellion, and a stranger to civil and military rule working together; but to remind you that I have been right in the midst of the rebellion since the commencement, and know of what I am writing, thereby hoping to call your serious consideration to the condition of things on the Potomac, Chesapeake, and Albemarle Sound. I now promise you that the information I give you, I do not expect to be pleasant, but it is no less true and painful to me. I do it in the discharge of high official duty, believing that you do not understand the extent to which military power is abused.

In connection with the movement in West Virginia, I desire to make a single remark. In the border counties of Pennsylvania and Ohio, now represented by the Hon. Messrs. Dawson, Lazeer, White, and Morris, there was and still is a powerful secession element, ready to join the army of Jeff. Davis had they an opportunity.[5] In the fall of 1862, they gloried in wearing butternut breast-pins, and at their public meetings indulged in the

4. Union generals stationed in western Virginia and around Alexandria.
5. John R. Dawson and Jesse Lazeer, Pennsylvania Democrats, and Chilton A. White and James R. Morris, Ohio Democrats. None of them felt especially kindly toward the Pierpont administration.

refined exercise of lapping out their tongues in imitation of copper snakes. So bitter were they in their denunciation of the movement of the restored government of Virginia, both in Pennsylvania and Ohio, that I gave orders if certain leaders came into Virginia to arrest them and send them out of the State, as not safe to circulate there. If Western Virginia had gone into the rebellion with spirit, she would have involved the whole border of western Pennsylvania and southern Ohio, and God only knows what the result would have been. The masses of a great and time-honored party had been taught by their leaders that pro-slavery, secession, and democracy were all the same, and the highest duty they owed their country was to oppose Abraham Lincoln, abolition, and the Union. But fortunately for the country, many patriotic democrats came forward with a large number of the rank and file, and declared to the world that democracy, as they understood it, had a far different meaning, and have demonstrated the sincerity of their pretensions on many a hard fought battle-field, and are now shoulder to shoulder with the sincere Union men of all parties. Future generations will admire them for their courage in recognizing country before party.

By the act of the General Assembly, I was authorized to establish the seat of government in the bounds of the old State when West Virginia was organized. I fixed it at Alexandria. The county and municipal laws of Norfolk and Portsmouth and Norfolk county were put into operation about the 1st of June, 1863, by the election and qualification of proper officers, under the restored government of Virginia. Each officer, before entering on his duty, was sworn to support the Constitution of the United States as the supreme law of the land, and the laws of the restored government of Virginia—anything in the ordinance of convention which assembled at Richmond on the 13th of February, 1851, to the contrary, notwithstanding. Lawyers, doctors, merchants, and every person doing business under a license, and clerks in stores, were required to take the same oath. Accomac and Northampton, Alexandria and Fairfax had been organized before that time. General Dix, and General Viele, commanded at Norfolk. I saw but little of them. General Foster succeeded. I found him to be a soldier, every inch, and after we got acquainted, were strong friends, as far as I know. General Naglee I pass over. General Lockwood commanded in Accomac and Northampton. I found him as true as steel, working faithfully to restore law and order, ready on all occasions to do his duty in assisting the civil government to establish its ascendancy, for which I commend him. In November, General Butler was appointed to the command of the eastern district of Virginia and North Carolina. I sighed when I heard it—I remembered New Orleans. There was short rejoicing at Norfolk among the ultra Union men; but in a short time the wail of woe came up. I was satisfied he was going to abrogate civil government if he could; that Unionism availed nothing if it lay between him and his object. That he was the seventh vial poured out to try the faith of the saints.

I visited Norfolk about the last of December, and fully realized my apprehensions. Among the first orders General Butler issued, when he went to Norfolk in November last, was one threatening punishment to any person who used any disrespectful language to any officer or soldier in the Union army. Next was an order directing all permits granted by his predecessors to be returned to him. Then came an order charging one per cent on all goods shipped into his military district, to go to the support of the *provost marshal's fund*. All vessels clearing from his district pay from five to fifteen dollars according to size, to the same fund. Oyster men were taxed from fifty cents to one dollar per month for the privilege of taking oysters; if in one field, fifty cents, if in two, one dollar. The provost marshal's court was fully established, trying cases in controversy, from one dollar to writs of ejectment; judgments rendered in land cases, and writs of possession given in five and ten days from date of judgment. One man, unable to pay a large judgment rendered against him, was placed in a felon's cell in jail and a guard put over his house. Costs, on about the scale of a civil suit in court, with a percentage for collection were charged, bringing money into the *provost marshal's fund* in a stream. Rebels, whom he had forced to take the oath to support the Constitution of the United States, but who would not take the oath to support the restored government of Virginia, would go to their provost court to have judgments against their neighbors, and for the further reason that they paid no internal revenue if they went to the provost court. But if they went to the civil court before bringing their suit they had to take the oath to support the restored government of Virginia and pay for an internal revenue stamp, which went into the United States treasury. The provost court saved all this, which was distasteful to rebels. This same provost court was issuing prohibitions forbidding tax collectors to sell rebel property levied on for State and city taxes. While I was there the provost marshal turned two men out of jail who had been committed by a justice for a misdemeanor or a felony, and were awaiting their trial before a court of competent criminal jurisdiction.

I left Norfolk about the 30th of December, sick, mentally and physically, and came to this city; some time afterwards I wrote General Butler a letter, calling his attention particularly to the abuses alluded to, asking his co-operation in establishing the civil government, stating the opposition of the secessionists, and their desire to break up the civil rule. I also called his attention to military interferences with the city regulations of the markets, and reminded him that his provost court could make no sale of real or personal estate on its judgments and executions that would pass any title to the property sold. That a provost marshal's court was not the kind of court contemplated in the Constitution of the United States in which a party could be deprived of his property by due course of law.

The General replied to my letter, expressing a desire to sustain the civil government; and in regard to his provost court, said "that no debts shall be collected save against those who are in rebellion against the United States in favor of loyal citizens, and when the property might escape from *honest* creditor by reason of *confiscation*." In regard to the civil laws, he remarked: "The difficulty I find is that there are all the civil officers there known to the law, and none of the Government." He further said, "in regard to the stall in the market, I have only directed an interference to prevent a collection by the city government of a year's rent in advance, which would virtually close the market and stop supplies to my troops."

As I shall hereafter refer to this provost court and the markets, I shall not comment further on these extracts here. In regard to the officers of the civil government, without the government, it is easy to be seen that the best men in the world would be discouraged in the execution of the civil laws when there was a provost marshal in the city releasing criminals, forbidding sales, assuming concurrent jurisdiction in everything, and threatening to imprison the civil officers; and as to securing debts of honest creditors against debtors in rebellion, I informed the General that there was the Court of Hustings of the two cities, the Circuit Court, and the District Court of the United States, all open with full jurisdiction in all cases, and by the laws of the State any person in rebellion was a non-resident for purposes of attachment, and that the attachment was a lien on real estate from the date of issue, so there could have been no reason for his provost court.

The next thing I heard was that Tazwel[l] Taylor, of the city of Norfolk, was summoned to the council of the General to consult upon the civil affairs of Norfolk.[6] The Mayor was summoned also. When the Mayor went, who is a true and loyal man, he found, to his surprise, Tazwel in the room with the General. The General indecently catechized the Mayor for about an hour on the affairs of the civil government of the city in the presence of Tazwel Taylor, and through his promptings, much to the chagrin of the Mayor. Tazwel Taylor was the worst rebel in Norfolk, the agent for taking the confederate loan there; took $15,000 of it himself, and bullied others to take, until he raised about $75,000; was an aid on Magruder's staff while the rebels

6. Secessionist leader in Tidewater Virginia.

occupied Norfolk, and the most offensive rebel in the city to Union men, because he was the chief adviser of the rebels. Now, he becomes General Butler's adviser as to the restored government in the city. This may seem strange when you take General Butler's ultra views into consideration, but it is true. The General's letter was dated 10th of January, and his provost court is still in operation. The last civil case I heard of was the trial of a *habeas corpus* case, determining the custody of two children between husband and wife.

But to show the hollow pretense of taking Union men's rights: Harrington and Boyle, loyal merchants of Baltimore, brought suit and obtained judgment, in the Circuit Court of Norfolk city, against a rebel in arms against the United States. He had real estate in Norfolk city, and there was an order of sale, under an attachment duly issued. The order of sale, was directed to the city sergeant; and that those of you who are lawyers may see how easily a provost marshal issues a writ of prohibition, I will here insert the writ in full: . . . [7]

On the third of March he issued another in the same case, commanding him to respect the order of the 1st. Can there be a more flagrant usurpation of power than this? The man Barratt, who was living on the property, was a rebel; the owner was in rebellion, and this is the court that is to secure protection to loyal men of the North, lest the Government of the United States should cheat them out of their just debts. And this is only a sample of others. Immediately on the issuing of this order, Judge Sneed, of the Circuit Court, wrote a letter to General Butler protesting against this interference with the processes and orders of his court. On the 23d of this month Judge Sneed had no reply; so this is the act and order of General Butler. This provost court takes cognizance of all cases of drunkenness, or other violation of city ordinances, has the party arrested, brought to his court, fines inflicted and paid into the *provost marshal's fund.*

I was informed in December that the sale of liquor by importers into Norfolk was going to be made a monopoly, and only a few were going to be allowed to sell. I heard more, but it was so incredible and discreditable that I could not believe it. I propose now to give you a few cases, though incredible as they may appear, truth requires their publication.

DANIELS & ZANTZINGER'S CASE

This firm was one of the largest in Norfolk engaged in selling groceries and liquors and wood. About the first of January an officer called at their store

7. I have not printed the writ the provost marshal wrote.

and asked them how much liquor they had in the *store*. They replied about fifteen barrels. He examined the loft and cellar and found their statement correct. He then asked them how much they had in the shed. They told him he could go and see, and directed their clerk to go and show it to him. He went and found thirty-eight barrels there. He reported. They were immediately summoned before the provost court on a charge of fraudulently concealing from the officers of the United States the amount of whiskey on hand; and it was mentioned in the charge, by way of recital, that the whiskey was passed into the department, and being fraudulently retained, to the prejudice of good order and military discipline in the department. I here give the charge and evidence before the provost court. . . . [8]

The testimony closed here. One hour was required for consultation; verdict at the end of the hour: Fine one thousand dollars, whiskey confiscated. It was sold at auction on the public streets of Norfolk, about the 20th of January, for upwards of $14,000. Yes, I say, fourteen thousand dollars. Now, I ask the impartial judgment of any man living, on that testimony, after they had paid their city, State, and United States license, what is there in the case to inflict this punishment? What military order was pretended to be violated? But, you will mark, it was publicly known they had liquor in the shed: the officer knew it. He seems to be playing sharp; asks them "how much they had in the *store*?" They answered correctly. "How much in the shed?" "Go and see; clerk, go with them." Were they criminal in having it to the prejudice of good order and military discipline? Was it smuggled? Look to the record. With the verdict the following order was issued. . . . [9]

But the *animus* of General Butler can only be seen by connecting this case with

HODGINS'S CASE

In November, 1863, Hodgins bought a stock of hardware of a man by the name of Hartshorn, who was trustee for an old firm which failed during the rebellion. The hardware was in a storehouse belonging to William E. Taylor, who was in the rebel army. Mrs. Taylor, his wife, resided in Norfolk. Hartshorn had rented the house from her. Hodgins continued to occupy the house at fifty dollars per month, and paid her that sum for the month of

8. Pierpont lists the charges and gives elaborate details of the testimony.
9. Pierpont cites the order saying the firm could no longer purchase alcohol to resell.

December. Sometime in December Major Moss, the agent of the Treasury Department to collect and take care of abandoned property, called on Hodgins and told him he would probably have to pay the rent to the United States Government. Hodgins replied that he was willing to pay anybody that was entitled; that he had paid that month to Mrs. Taylor in advance, as she was needy. Major Moss took Hodgins's name and left. Between the 15th and 20th of January, Major Moss called on Hodgins and told him that he had received instructions from headquarters that the house he occupied was needed for military purposes, and he would have to leave. Hodgins used all the argument he could against leaving; that he had put repairs on the storehouse, that he was not able to move, and that it would cost a large amount to fit up another house. Major Moss called a second time, and the order was peremptory. The young man left; had to pay a Jew $300 for the key to another house; to fix shelving at a cost of $180, and remove ten thousand dollars' worth of small hardware. The house Hodgins was ordered to leave was the best and most eligible business house in the city, on Main, at the head of Market street. Hodgins got into his new house about the 9th of February. The day he left, the Taylor house commenced being fitted up for a liquor store, and in a few days it was occupied by a firm from Boston, with some $25,000 worth of liquors of all kinds, and groceries. About the same time another firm from Boston and another from Lowell, Massachusetts, came in with a large assortment of liquors, so that I am safe in saying that in thirty days from the time Zantzinger & Daniels's whiskey was sold, there were $75,000 worth of liquor in Norfolk, in the hands of Bostonians, when a native of Virginia, or any other State, could not get a permit for one gallon.

Put the charge against Zantzinger & Daniels with the orders to remove Hodgins out of the house together, and it only proves a fixed determination to close them up, break them up, put $15,000 into the provost marshal's fund, and make it a clear track for these Boston men to monopolize the whole business; and Major Moss says he talked with General Butler about requiring Hodgins to remove, and the General pressed his removal, but did not give an actual order. Hodgins went to the provost marshal and tried to get him to interfere. He asked Hodgins if he had a written contract with Major Moss for the house; he said, no. He then said he could do nothing.

Zantzinger is the brother-in-law of Commodore Farragut and a member of the loyal legislature of Virginia. Daniels is a loyal business man. Hodgins was in the confederate army, but left it at an early day, came home and took the oath, and has behaved himself and claims to be a loyal man.

G. W. SINGLETON'S CASE

G. W. Singleton was a resident of Nansemond county; was made postmaster on the 16th day of April, 1861, when no other man would take the place under Mr. Lincoln; had two stores, a farm, and seven slaves. When the Union army took Suffolk, he was the first man in the county who went forward immediately and took the oath; moved both stores together into Suffolk; had his dwellings, storehouse, and twelve other small houses on the bank of the river. When Longstreet attacked Suffolk last spring, the Union batteries were erected in Town Square, back of Singleton's houses. His storehouse was blown up and his dwelling and other houses were torn down lest they should take fire and prevent the working of the batteries. Singleton was sent to the mouth of the river, and piloted the magazine boat from the James river to Suffolk. He went back again and piloted up a gun boat. When the gun boat got opposite his farm they were attacked by the rebels, who occupied the farm. Singleton told the Union men to spare nothing; he had there 500 bushels of corn in the crib, 8000 pounds of bacon smoked in his smoke house, with all the other articles a thrifty farmer would have around him. It was all destroyed; not a dollar's worth of buildings, fences, corn, bacon, house, or anything else was left. After the rebels were repulsed he took his wife and children, and $3,500 in money, which was all he had left out of an estate of $40,000, and went to Norfolk. His money was running down, his eldest daughter ready to go to school, and something must be done. When he saw Daniels & Zantzinger's liquor was to be sold in Norfolk, it was natural to suppose the purchasers would be permitted to resell, so he purchased ten barrels, for which he paid $3,325, bought some groceries, and in the course of eight or ten days, opened a store, having paid State, city, and United States license. About seven days after he commenced selling, General Butler's famous order No. 19 came out, requiring all grocery and liquor dealers to obtain a permit therefor at his headquarters. Singleton immediately went to Fort Monroe with Governor Cowper. Cowper stated Singleton's case to Colonel Shafer, chief-of-staff. Colonel Shafer immediately gave an order to Captain Cassell, provost marshal, to grant Singleton a permit to sell groceries and liquors. Singleton returned to Norfolk, and in a few days, as his stock was running down, he made out a requisition for permission to bring from Baltimore liquors and groceries. General Wild signed it. He took it to Captain Cassell at Fort Monroe to get it approved; handed it to Cassell, who pitched it into a pigeon hole. Singleton requested him to sign it; Cassell refused, saying that Singleton had no permit. Singleton assured him that he had. Cassell asked to see it; Singleton handed it to him. He said it was a mistake; it was intended for a permit to keep an eating house. Singleton asked him to look at Colonel Shafer's order; Captain Cassell said he did not know anything about Shafer's order; he would have to wait until Colonel Shafer came home; he would be back perhaps next week, or the week after, or may be not at all. So Singleton went to General Butler and stated his case. General Butler said he would have to wait until Captain Cassell reported the case to him. But Singleton attempted to urge the matter, and General Butler replied, "you want to force me, do you. Now, the less you say the better." So poor Singleton had to leave, his permit taken from him, and there he is, with the residue of his whiskey on hand—no permit to sell. . . . [10]

NEWSPAPERS AND MAGAZINES

In February, General Butler issued an order asking for bids until the first of March, for the privilege of furnishing newspapers and periodicals in his district, by the month, promising to award the monopoly to the "*successful*" bidder, not to the highest. An old Jew by the name of Bohn was the successful bidder, at the price of $600 per month. All other dealers were closed up, among whom were Mahew & Brother, who had a news store in Norfolk, had paid a license to the city, State, and United States Governments, and were doing a fair business. They supposed the order did not refer to Norfolk, and as they had paid their internal revenue license, they continued their business. Soon, however, they were summoned to Old Point before Captain Cassell. When they got there, Cassell asked them if they took the papers. They replied, "We do." Said he, "Do you read them?" Reply, "We do." "Then," said he, "do you understand what you read?" Answer, "We do, or suppose we do." Said he, "Do you live in Norfolk?" "Yes." "Did you see the order awarding the privilege of supplying this district with papers and magazines to Mr. Bohn?" They answered, "We did." "Well," said he, "that order was issued by command of General Butler, and if you persist in bringing papers into this department, I will use all my influence to have you punished." Thus, American citizens from Pennsylvania, who have

10. Pierpont tells two more stories about loyalists who were denied the right to sell alcohol and groceries. Then he recounts the problems of the Norfolk Gas Works in dealing with General Butler, who placed a prohibitive tax on its owners. Pierpont also takes up the case of the widow Mrs. Tatem, who was kept from taking personal possessions from a bank. He discusses at length the plight of a Mr. Billsolly, who had silver taken from his house and nearly becomes Pierpont's symbol of the ill-treatment of a southern unionist.

resided in Norfolk near two years, are cut off from business. They paid the United States Government $1845 for internal revenue license alone, with a solemn undertaking on the part of the Government to protect them in their business. And this in addition to what they would pay on income; but the income has gone into the *provost marshal's fund.* . . . [11]

HOWARD ASSOCIATION

When the yellow fever raged in Norfolk and Portsmouth, in 1855, the good people of the neighboring cities sent in a large amount of money to some gentlemen who formed a society, under the name of the Howard Association. There was $60,000 left after the fever had abated. They were chartered by the Legislature of Virginia for the purpose of taking care of and supporting the orphans made by the yellow fever, and for other benevolent objects, when that was accomplished. The members of the Board have faithfully preserved the fund, using the interest for the purpose. There are some twelve or fifteen of the orphans which are still a charge upon them. Last year they had a small surplus of interest which they devoted to the poor. The money is all invested in loans, secured by mortgages on real estate and bonds with personal security. Some of the directors are disloyal, but the evidences of the debt are on record, and they are faithfully discharging their duty. On the 22d of March, General Butler issued an order, directing a committee of three, two of them officers on his staff, one a civilian of recent settlement in the city, to take possession of the assets of the association. On the 22d, Captain Edgar called on the secretary of the association, and demanded of him and obtained all the assets of the association; and on the 23d ordered all the board to meet him at the provost marshal's office.

General Butler, with the same propriety and more, might seize the assets of Girard College, or that of any professorship in Harvard University, for taking care of the poor in Norfolk and Princess Anne counties.

I will here make a remark in regard to the great clamor through the North about General Butler taking charge of the poor. He has a preacher going about trying to convince the people that General Butler is a very proper man; he is so liberal to the poor, thus using Heaven's liveried missionaries to make his conduct palatable. But General Butler can never get the co-operation of

11. The next case Pierpont discusses is Butler's charge to kill every fourth dog in Norfolk.

the Union people of Norfolk in any enterprise, however benevolent, while it is under the management of members of his staff and associates, simply because they have no confidence in them.

I desire to put to rest this clamor about Government taking care of the poor in Norfolk and Princess Anne counties, and the two cities. Ever since the Union troops occupied the cities of Norfolk and Portsmouth, the military have had possession of the ferry and boats between the two cities, using them for its own profit and benefit, collecting tolls from all civilians, and transporting Government troops and property. This ferry belongs to the two cities; they have not received one dollar from it. The military has got it all. The receipts of the ferry before the war, amounted to from $15,000 to $18,000 per annum. Since the military has had it I am satisfied that if the Government had paid for its use at the same rate that any similar service is paid for in the North, it would yield at least forty thousand dollars per annum, which is twice the sum appropriated for taking care of the poor. But this committee for taking care of the poor are holding meetings, are abusing the Union men for not rallying around them, and are trying to get up the idea that there are no Union men in Norfolk. The Union men won't rally under such leadership. The poor are from the oyster men, who are so taxed and fined that they can't make a living. The poor in the county are, many of them, made so by the destruction and plunder of the helpless, in military raids. A highly intelligent gentleman, and now a loyal member of the Virginia State Convention, told me that for three weeks after General Wild made his celebrated raid in Princess Anne, he could stand on the portico of his house and trace the track of the raid for ten miles by the turkey buzzards, feeding on the carrion made by destruction of animal life. Union men and widows shared the same fate; all they had was taken and destroyed, and thus many of the poor are made. I forbear facts and incidents. Many of the poor are the wives and children of rebels, either killed or now serving in the rebel army. The Union men have urged that the rich rebels left behind should take care of them. It was urged as a distinct proposition, that the rents of the property of rebels who were in rebellion, and at home, should go to their support. It was urged that Tazwell Taylor, the commissioner to procure a rebel loan in Norfolk, and who was a member of Magruder's staff while the rebels were there, and who took $15,000 of the rebel loan, should be taxed or compelled to contribute $15,000 to take care of the rebel poor. But strange to say, this same Tazwell remained a bitter rebel to the last, was General Naglee's closest companion, and was called in by General Butler to consult about the civil government of Norfolk.

Tazwell left the city and removed to Baltimore, without ever contributing one cent, as far as General Butler is concerned, for support of rebel poor; and now the support of the poor is made a scapegoat in the estimation of all General Butler's admirers, and a salvo for seizing and taxing everything; and because the Union men who have liberally drained their pockets to support the poor, will not come forward and follow the dictates of Captain Edgar, in whom they have no confidence, they are stigmatized as rebels, and forsooth, there is no loyalty in the city.

It is now too late to lay any contribution on rebel property holders in the city to support the poor. General Butler has required them all to take the oath of allegiance, with promise of protection, and the promise ought to be kept. The Union poor can be supported by the Union people, if the avenues of industry and enterprise are left open for them to work; but if part are taxed to fill the coffers of the *provost marshal's fund*, and others prohibited from following their avocations because they are in the way of Boston favorites, they will all soon be paupers and vagabonds. The rebel poor, whose friends and protectors are in the rebel army, must be cared for, either by cutting off their heads, sending them across the lines to their protectors, selling rich rebels' property who are in rebellion, and supporting them out of the proceeds, or the United States Government must support them. These are simple propositions.

The policy of supporting the poor out of rebel property was partially introduced. But when General Butler came it was all broken up. The houses were needed for his officers and Boston friends, who are occupying them free of rent.

THE WOOD BUSINESS

Shipping fire wood is an extensive and profitable business in Norfolk and that section. After General Butler went there the natives found it difficult to get permits—Bostonians got them. I will give a case. . . . [12]

SALE OF CORN

It is difficult to get a permit to send corn out of the department. I find no fault with the rule, but some do get permits. . . . [13]

12. Pierpont talks of loyalists being kept from selling wood in Norfolk because Gen. Edward A. Wild refused them a permit.

13. Another case is given where loyal citizens were not allowed to conduct business, this time to sell corn.

BUCK & CO.

This company is composed of Joseph A. Buck, Isaac M. Dennison, Peter H. Whitehurst, and Charles Whitehurst. This firm did a large business in dry goods and groceries, old iron, pewter, lead, brass, copper, old rope, sails, and grain. They were engaged in it before the rebellion. The vessel E. C. Knight, loaded with lumber, stranded on the beach of Princess Anne county, about the first of January last. The underwriters sold the cargo to the highest bidder. Quartermaster Godwin became the purchaser, and employed a Captain Caffee, a resident near the lumber, to haul it over the beach to a landing on Currituck Sound, where it could be loaded and brought to Norfolk. Great expedition was required, lest by rise of wind and tide the lumber should be lost. Caffee employed about one hundred hands, and got over one hundred and fifty-nine thousand feet of lumber, for which he was to get twelve dollars per thousand feet. He knew it would be some time before he could get his money, and they desired to have some groceries and salt to salt their pork. He called on Buck & Co., who had engaged to take two vessels and bring down the lumber, to furnish these articles to pay the hands for their labor, and wait with him until he got his money from the Government. Thereby he would be accommodated and they would make a profit. So Buck and Co. called on Quartermaster Godwin for permission, and he referred them to the provost marshal. . . . [14]

They went to Provost Marshal Whelden, presented their permit to his clerk, Tilden, who was sitting by the side of the provost marshal, showed him that they had taken the oath, and had paid their license. He endorsed it and handed it to the provost marshal, who signed it. Buck them asked him to whom they should take it next. The clerk, replied, "That is all right; every officer in the department would respect that." Buck, to be sure, repeated in substance the same remark, and received the same answer. They started on their journey and were arrested some fifteen or twenty miles from the city, and brought back by order of the provost marshal, who ordered them before the provost judge, to try them and confiscate their property for attempting to run the blockade. They waited ten days before a trial could be obtained, their vessels lying there. They had their trial, the facts turned out as above stated, and they were released, and went immediately to the vessels. Before they reached the store they were arrested again for having old brass and copper on hand belonging to the Government. They immediately appeared before the provost judge. He was on another case and they could get no trial for some seven days. They were finally tried and acquitted.

14. Pierpont here prints the Buck and Co. application.

They were thus detained about seventeen days with their vessels, at a cost of about twenty dollars per day, and had to give up their adventure. Since that time they have made five different applications for shipping the produce on hand, consisting of rags, cotton, old iron, copper, brass, lead, pewter, beeswax, old grease, bristles, old rope, sails, and wood, of which they have about ten thousand dollars worth on hand, all of which have been refused. Finally, Buck wrote a statement to General Butler of himself and his connection with Whitehurst, alleging his loyalty, the purity of his intentions, that General Wild had stated there was a cloud hanging over his character, and offering to prove as loyal and upright a character as any man in the department, civil or military, and asking that he might be placed on an equal footing with other men. General Butler referred the letter to General Wild, and General Wild made on the letter the following endorsement: . . . [15]

Now, gentlemen, without repetition, I refer you to the record. General Wild says shifting permits is inadmissible. Yet he advises it in the case of the wood permit, where a Boston friend profited four hundred per cent by it. Comment is unnecessary.

Peter H. Whitehurst is a native of Virginia, a man of high character, and as loyal a man as lives. The firm to which he belongs has paid more than three thousand dollars for the support of the poor and the Union cause, since our troops occupied Norfolk. Charles Whitehurst is a member of the loyal Virginia Senate, a Christian gentleman, and as pure a man, I think, as I ever met. Buck stands as high, I am informed, as an honorable merchant, as any in Baltimore; his loyalty undoubted. Denison, Buck's partner in Baltimore, was a secessionist in April, 1861. In June he joined one of the Union aid associations in Baltimore. In July, 1863, when Lee invaded Maryland, six months' volunteers were called for. Young Creamer was a clerk in some institution in which Denison was a director. After Creamer left, Denison moved that his company vote him fifty dollars bounty, and keep his place open for him until his return.

This is the class of men stricken down and all the avenues of trade shut up to them, charged with theft, after the General knew they had been acquitted, notified to sell their goods to some other person who would make the speculation by transportation, I suppose. Is this right; is it just, that these men, two of them living in Norfolk, with large families to support, and who have lost largely by the rebellion, should thus be blasted by the

15. Pierpont reproduces the endorsement and discusses the merits of the case to show the treachery of General Wild. Especially is he concerned that loyalists are depicted as guerrillas.

caprice of a commanding general? Peter Whitehurst had a slave named Charles, worth fifteen hundred dollars before the war. Charles remained with him until the order came to enlist colored men. Whitehurst went to Charles, although he was not free, and told him, "Charles, you now have a chance to fight for the freedom of your race. Go and join a colored regiment and show yourself a man." Charles said: "Master, I want to stay with you." "No," said Peter, "your country needs you more than I do, go." He went, and is now a soldier, and Peter has never made any demand for service or bounty. This is a Virginia Union man. . . . [16]

THE NEW REGIME

This is the title of a new daily newspaper, published in Norfolk under the auspices of General Butler. *New Regime* means new government, or order of things. Newspaper enterprises generally depend on private capital and enterprise. But the *New Regime* had two printing establishments, engines, presses, and type seized, belonging to men who had taken the oath. A restaurant keeper was turned out of the house he occupied because it was needed for military purposes—the quartermaster was required to detail hands from Government shops to repair engines and do carpenters' work to the amount of seven hundred and seventeen dollars and forty-five cents, which was charged to the United States Government, and Mr. Chase will have the money to provide to pay, to repair the engines and do carpenter work, to get ready for editing the *New Regime*. Then Captain Clark, one of General Butler's staff, was detailed with a civilian from Boston to edit the paper. Sixty printers—soldiers from the army—were detailed and sent to the office, thirty of them were chosen and now are acting as type setters, printers, and engaged in various ways in getting out the paper, and receiving their pay and rations from the United States Government; one of the editors paid as an officer. Suppose these printers to be all veterans, and if they are not veterans will have to take their place in the field. The Government, State and Federal, are paying now, seven hundred dollars bounty, besides clothing. . . . [17]

Captain Clark is on detached duty, and is entitled to commutation for rent, fuel, light, and rooms.

16. Here Pierpont tells a story called "Yellow Pine and Ship Knees," about military confiscation of loyalists' timber.

17. Pierpont lists the costs to the government in exile of printing the newspaper.

The editor's business notice is as follows: "The job printing department of this office is the most complete in Virginia, and as all our presses are run by steam power, we can afford to execute all kinds of work at the lowest possible price. Send orders to No. 33 Market street, corner of Commerce." Kept up as the *New Regime* is by the Federal Government, at the tune of $34,000 per annum, wearing out the engines, press, and type of men who had taken the oath under promise of protection, it would be supposed that they could do work cheaply. "But there is no need of these soldiers now." For that I cannot say. On the night of the 21st of March, the rebels came within eight miles of Norfolk and destroyed a considerable amount of Government property, and on the night of the 23d, they were within four miles of Norfolk. Rebels are running the lines almost daily. The printer soldier cannot attend to keeping guard or protecting property, were they to do so, this Boston gentleman could not do his work so cheaply.

The object of this newspaper is to create a sink to absorb as much as possible of the *provost marshal's fund* by way of advertisements. Nearly three fourths of it is filled with military orders as advertisements. Also, to prove that the civil government of Virginia should be abolished in General Butler's department and military rule substituted. I called the attention of the Secretary of War to some of the usurpations at Norfolk. Among other things, to the one per cent on merchandise that was shipped into the department. The *New Regime* takes up the gauntlet, and in his issue of the 7th March, he devotes nearly three columns to prove that the civil government ought to be abolished and military substituted in General Butler's department. Defending the one per cent charge, he denounces the opposition to it as the *"howl from a semi-loyal government."* It is exceedingly offensive to those who have imperiled all, and are still doing all in their power to advance the great cause of the country, to be denounced by a mere parasite as semi-loyal. No man's name appears as editor of the paper.

There are two daily newspapers in Norfolk and Portsmouth with a capacity to do all the printing required by the department.

THE MARKETS

They have undertaken to regulate the price of articles sold in market. I here give the military order containing the bill of prices: . . . [18]

All conversant with the prices paid in the Eastern markets for similar articles will at once observe that the prices here established are far below

18. He prints Special Order #30 from General Wild, which sets the price of groceries.

the price of any other market. Groceries ten per cent on Baltimore prices—they paid, when this bill was established, five per cent to United States Government, one per cent to General Butler, and at least two and one half per cent freight, cooperage, &c., making eight and one half per cent—one and one half per cent is left for profit. . . . [19]

This all proves one of two things, either the incapacity of the officers who undertake to regulate this subject, or a determination to have the articles produced in market for less than their value. It is immaterial to me to which cause it is attributable.

CASE OF CHAS. W. BUTTS

Mr. Butts is a lawyer in the city of Norfolk. Gen. Wild made an order confiscating the estate of a man in Portsmouth by the name of Williams. Williams was a rebel, but took the oath under the promise of protection. He heard before he took the oath that the military, with some Boston friends, coveted his dwelling house and handsome furniture. Shortly after taking the oath, an order was made confiscating his property. Williams then (being in delicate health) sent his certificate of having taken the oath prescribed by Gen. Butler, claiming his protection, to General Wild, who kept the certificate and endorsed the back of it "oath revoked," and ordered the officers in whose possession the books kept for the purposes of recording names, dates, and residences of persons taking the oath, and in which Williams's name was recorded, to erase from them all evidence of Williams's having taken the oath, which was done. Williams, with his wife and children, were turned out of their own house into the streets of Portsmouth, on the 22d of March last, during the prevalence of one of the most terrible snow storms I ever witnessed. . . . [20]

Judge Bates endorsed the letter and sent it to the Secretary of War. He endorsed it and sent it to General Butler. General Butler endorsed it and sent it to General Wild. Wild sent for Butts, asked him if he wrote the letter. Butts said he did; handed Butts a copy to read; and after reading asked him if it was a correct copy. Butts told him it was. Then Butts was shortly afterwards handed an order banishing him from the department. He went to General Butler and complained; asked Butler to rescind it. Among other things Butler told him he was in trouble with him, (General Butler,) and

19. Next he prints a letter from a John Newton opposing price-fixing.
20. Printed are Lawyer Butts's letter to Attorney General Edward Bates asking for assistance.

took from a pigeon hole a letter which Butts had written to the President, informing him of the dollar charge on persons going in and out of General Butler's department, which the President had referred to General Butler, and told Butts he was a dangerous man; he would not interfere with General Wild's order. So Butts had to leave, and at this writing is an exile from the home of his adoption and professional business, sitting in my office.

Who is Butts? He is a native of New Jersey, a republican in politics; the first political speech he ever made was advocating Mr. Lincoln's election. He was the second man volunteered in his county in the three month's service; was among the first who crossed from Washington to Alexandria when the lamented Ellsworth fell in that city. He served as a private; was in the New Jersey reserve corps, commanded by General Runyon at the time of the battle of Bull Run. When his term was out he returned home. He raised thirty men at once and joined Colonel Harlan's independent regiment, now the 11th Pennsylvania cavalry, and was commissioned 1st lieutenant, and served with distinction on the Peninsula, between James and York rivers. Butts has many certificates of which any young man ought to be proud, for acts of daring and gallantry on the field. I will quote the endorsement of Colonel Spear, the gallant commander of his regiment, on his request to resign: . . . [21]

GENERAL BUTLER'S MILITARY ADMINISTRATION IN THE FIELD

Since General Butler has been so vigilant in trying to impress the public mind that the civil government was inefficient at Norfolk, it may not be amiss to advert to *his* administration of military affairs in the field in that vicinity. The first movement was to send about one hundred men to Smithfield, on the James river, in the face of the enemy, with no mode of retreat, and only to be supported by gunboats going up a creek that is little more than a quagmire at low tide. The result was the loss of the whole command, and the destruction of a gunboat, which got aground.

The next was General Wild's notable raid into North Carolina and Princess Anne county. I never want to see the history of that raid until the war is over. The taking of Miss White a prisoner is only one of the occurrences.

The next was the projected raid on Richmond, for the liberation of the Union prisoners. The failure was much regretted. It was attributed to the desertion of a Union soldier, who carried the news to Richmond,

---

21. A letter follows, in praise of Butts's role in the war.

and gave them time to rally and defeat the project. And the public have been amused and satisfied with this story, and General Butler lauded to the heavens for the conception of the noble idea. He insulted the Navy by attributing to the officers unfaithfulness, and imprisoned a lady thirteen days, keeping her on bread and water, to force her to tell what naval officer had told her of the contemplated expedition to Richmond, when she knew nothing about it. Of all of this the public was duly notified through the press. But is it not strange how the soldier who deserted knew anything about the objects of the army, so as to give the information so long beforehand? It is said of General Harrison, when he commanded at Fort Meigs, in the winter of 1812, that there was a report of the approaching enemy, and some young man asked him what he was going to do, in case the enemy were at a certain point. The General replied that if he thought his shirt knew his thoughts, he would burn it.[22] I heard this when I was very young, and it impressed me. I was impressed when I heard the story of the deserter. I asked the first four or five men I met from Norfolk if it was known there publicly before the expedition started that it was going. Every one of them replied that they knew it from six to ten days before it started. The troops that were going, the object, route, and all about it. It was told by his own officers. General Butler knew to whom he had confided his plans. Why did he not strike there for the person who revealed the secret? I think it very likely that the news of the raid was communicated from Norfolk to Richmond, and it was suggested in the letter, "publish that you got this news from a Union soldier who deserted." But it was known at Williamsburg, and talked of among the soldiers for at least six days before the expedition started. Yet censure is heaped on everybody, to keep observation from General Butler and his confidential advisers.

The last military exploit I heard of, was a raid into North Carolina and the capture of two lighter loads of corn and meal, with some contrabands, and the selling of the corn at public auction, and the proceeds of the sale went into the *provost marshal's fund*.

With all the ridicule of General Butler, and the sneers of his *New Regime*, at the civil government of Norfolk and Portsmouth, it will stand out in bold relief as effective, when compared with General Butler's military operations in the field in that section.

The last I heard from the provost court, they were very desirous of trying a case of *habeas corpus* to determine the custody of two children, between a husband and wife who had separated.

22. Said to be a true statement from Gen. William Henry Harrison, later president of the United States.

WHAT BECOMES OF THE PROVOST MARSHAL'S FUND

I might answer this question by repeating the question, what does become of it? Perhaps this is about as satisfactory an answer as the country will ever get.

It does not go into the Treasury of the United States, nor do I suppose it relieves it of any of its burdens. It is estimated by those who have pretty good opportunity of knowing, that there has been collected since General Butler went to Old Point last fall, from two to three hundred thousand dollars into this fund. There has been a system of excessive fines introduced for one supposed offense and another, varying from fifty to five thousand dollars. In addition to this mode, property, captured and confiscated, all goes into the *provost marshal's fund*, with tax on goods shipped into and out of the district, tax on oysters and dogs, clearances of vessels, &c., &c.

Some repairs are being made on the streets. This is done by convicts, soldiers and citizens in penitentiary uniform, with Government teams to do the hauling, superintended by a contractor. He may be paid for all that is done. Advertisements in the *New Regime*, and it is said there are about forty detectives there, all under pay, perhaps, to keep down the fund. But as to its disposition, all is conjecture. One thing is certain, there is great interest taken in enlarging the fund. One man got a permit to bring in three thousand dollars' worth of goods, and paid thirty dollars. His wife was taken ill, and remained sick for some time. He could not leave home, and when she got well he had to decline his enterprise. He called to get his money back, but was refused. Buck & Whitehurst got a permit last fall to bring in thirty thousand dollars' worth of some kind of goods, but the permit was delayed so long that the season passed for the sale of the article; they only brought in ten thousand dollars' worth. They called for their two hundred dollars paid on the permit they did not use, and were also prohibited from shipping anything more; but they could not get back their two hundred dollars. The Government would refund under such circumstances.

In this succinct statement I have only given a few cases. I don't know that they are the worst cases. An elaborate history might be written of the acts there, all interesting in detail, and tending to illustrate more fully the existence of systematic abuse of military power. I am informed that the same system prevails perhaps to a greater extent in North Carolina than in Virginia, because there is less restraint there. Civil government seems to check it a little—hence the anxiety to break it up, in order that they may have a clear field.

It is strange to me that such a system should have grown up whereby military commanders collect tens and hundreds of thousands of dollars into this post or provost marshal's fund which is held by men who give no bonds. None of it goes into the United States Treasury, but little of it to relieve the Treasury of its burdens, and much of it expended for objects in no way connected with the suppression of the rebellion. This, to my mind, is a subject which needs attention.

THE EFFECT OF ALL THIS ON THE PUBLIC MIND

On going to Norfolk about the 20th of March last, I was humiliated. At Old Point and Norfolk, I met men, who, six months ago, stood erect and talked like freemen, who were proud of their country, and that they were American citizens. But now the hand of oppression is upon them, they look dejected and disheartened. When they spoke to me of their troubles, it was far from the presence of any one, and then in an undertone. When they came into my room to talk with me, they would look around the room to assure themselves that there was no spy concealed, and see that the doors were closely shut. The Union papers have been regretting that the Union cause for some time past has been on the decline in North Carolina. It is true. The wail of the oppressed there under General Butler's rule has gone out through the old North State and hushed the clamor of her liberty-loving people for the blessings of freedom they expected to enjoy under the old stars and stripes. And these oppressions now form the principal staple for the rebel Governor Vance in his canvass for re-election, to persuade the people to be reconciled to Jeff. Davis's despotism.

In October last I felt hopeful and buoyant at the prospect of returning loyalty, and the disposition of the people to sustain the restored government. General Foster was in command of the department. I found him a gentleman and a soldier, earnest in his profession and desire to do right. General Barnes was placed in command of the two cities.[23] He was from Massachusetts, an educated, earnest soldier, and all you would expect in a Massachusetts gentleman. Massachusetts, God bless her! I love her people. In Virginia's darkest day, in 1861, while the committee of safety was guiding, to a certain extent, the destiny of the loyal people of the State, the lightning of heaven brought us the happy dispatch from Governor Andrews that Massachusetts would let the loyal men of Virginia have two thousand

23. Gens. John Gray Foster and James Barnes.

muskets to be used in the defense of liberty in the State. A messenger was immediately dispatched for the arms. They came, and immediately on the reorganization of the State, I placed them in the hands of the men, where they did good service. The sending of the arms gave great moral strength to the Union cause and to Union hearts, and I say again, I love Massachusetts. It is an old adage, "that there are few mothers with many children but there are some black sheep among them." Massachusetts has hers, and I am after them. But I was speaking of General Barnes. He took great interest in the civil affairs of this section. General Lockwood was doing the same in Accomac and Northampton.[24] The civil officers began to feel assured that they were going to be sustained, were taking courage, and civil affairs began to move off smoothly. But General Lockwood and General Barnes did not suit General Butler, and they were removed from his department. Before General Butler went there, the Union men were buoyant with the hope of seeing their section settled and repopulated by people from the North. They welcomed Northern men among them. But now dejection, despondency and bitterness is seen where hope then existed, and deep sectional hostility is beginning to manifest itself. Oh! It is a deep, *bitter* contemplation, to see so glorious a cause as the Union cause thus stricken and wounded in the house of its friends. My heart is sick, *sick* at the contemplation. But there is consolation in knowing that the abuses only exist in this city and the district of Virginia and North Carolina, and that you, gentlemen, form a tribunal to whom we can appeal, which is too high and too pure to refuse adequate relief.

THE REMEDY

I am asked is it too late to remedy the evil and restore the cause? I answer, no. The remedy is indicated by the inspired prophet in his declaration that "righteousness exalteth the nation, and sin is a reproach to any people." Then the remedy is in doing right. This is the easiest matter in the world. Sin is a reproach, that is, doing wrong, and it always brings trouble. Rebels will never be fully punished in this world. Many universalists have abandoned their favorite dogma of a universal heaven since this war commenced. They see plainly that there can be no adequate punishment on earth for those who have brought the calamities of this terrible war on the country. If fifty men in Virginia had done six years ago what fifty thousand have done in the

24. Gen. Henry Hayes Lockwood.

last three years, they all would have been hung. But the Government thinks it is not wise to undertake to kill everybody who has turned traitor. I think that is right. When Korah, Dathan, and Abiram, with the two hundred and fifty princes rebelled against Moses, the earth opened and they were swallowed up; a consuming flame came out and killed the two hundred and fifty princes, and the people who were led away by them fled to the side of Moses and were not hurt. Perhaps we have an example in this, that it is right to extend amnesty to all but the leaders in rebellion. It is certainly the prerogative of the Government to fix the terms of amnesty to rebels. If the Government had declared that they all should be killed, and had killed as fast as we got to them, it would be difficult to prove that it was not a just act. Slavery was the root of the rebellion. Perhaps its abolishment, with confiscation, will be punishment enough. But the President, for wise purposes, determined that all who would return to allegiance, from the grade of colonel and under, and take the oath he prescribed, *should be pardoned and restored to all their rights of property*, unless it had been sold under the laws of punishing traitors. But if confiscations had commenced and not prosecuted to sale, the proceedings are to be dismissed upon the rebels taking the oath. The fullest and amplest protection is offered. General Butler has ordered all in his military district to take the oath with the solemn pledge of protection; the nation is bound to guarantee it. It is right to guarantee it after it is made. The Government, through the President, has prescribed the terms by which the rebel is to be protected. He conforms to the requisition, the terms must be kept on our part. A great Government like the United States cannot afford to do *wrong*. Now, it is *right* to redress all the wrongs General Butler has committed in his district as far as possible. It is *right* to return the gas works to the proper owners, with a fair charge for the repairs, and an account for the profits and especially to return the thirteen hundred dollars which were in the safe. It is *right* to return to Mrs. Tatum her silver cake baskets; to return to the property owners the silver taken from the house of Mr. Bilisolly, and also the wine and brandy taken from his house, and if it cannot be returned to punish those who have put it out of the power of the Government to do *right*. It is *right* to return to Daniels & Zantzinger the fifteen thousand dollars taken from them, and to reimburse Hodgins for violently turning him out of his house, and those who occupy the house should pay the money; and to require the speculators to reimburse the farmers whose land they have stripped of timber, if these farmers have taken the oath and have not violated it. Williams and all the other parties that have been turned out of their houses should have their property restored to them, where they have taken the oath and not violated it. This done, and there is no fair man living but will say it is *right* that it should be done; this would be that kind of righteousness which exalteth a nation. The news of it being ordered would thrill the hearts of the Union men in rebeldom. It would be grateful to every loyal heart in the nation, and would create a little jubilee in those desponding hearts in this section. Loyalty would prevail, and blessing would be poured out of grateful hearts upon the Government, where secret curses and imprecations are now being indulged in; and as General Grant goes forth this spring, hundreds of thousands will flock around his banner and kiss the old flag, conscious that no wrong will be suffered where it floats. It will disarm hundreds of thousands of their stubbornness and save the lives of thousands of Union soldiers. I am satisfied that these oppressions have done more to unite the rebels in the south and retard Union sentiment there, though confined to a narrow compass as they are, than any thing that has occurred since the rebellion has commenced, and if not corrected their warning voice will go into the south, and General Grant as he goes forward this summer, with his noble comrades, will have a hard road to travel.

The natural condition of men is under civil government. The military is an organized artificial force to aid the civil law to assert its power when resisted by force. It is *right* that the civil discharge all the duties assigned it by society; if resisted, the military removes the resistance; when that is done it has performed its function. Whenever it attempts to discharge civil duties it is *wrong*, and begets discord. It is *right* for the officers to attend to the duties assigned them by the rules of war; to drill and discipline the soldier; to prepare him for effective duty; to look after his health, and, as far as possible, to preserve his morals; to lead him in battle, and in all things to set him a good example. War is expensive, both in money and life, hence it should be short. I think there can be no controversy about these propositions being right in theory; and their practicable application is this. If the military will drive all the rebel army out of the State I will reorganize every county in the State in less than six months, with loyal officers to execute the civil laws. If they will remove all the soldiers from the limits of the city of Alexandria, Norfolk and Portsmouth, except what may be necessary to guard the public stores, and pick up straggling soldiers that come into the cities, I will ensure the good government of all three cities through the civil government, and save the Federal Government at least thirty thousand dollars per annum by way of pay to military brigadiers and their staffs, and superfluous bands of music, for which the civil government will not charge one cent. I submit, in all earnestness, that the city of Norfolk, for instance, with fifteen hundred women congregated there "who are no better than they ought to be," is not the place for soldiers or officers, who are expected to do efficient work in the field. In the city is not the place for an officer or soldier to defend the city. Philadelphia and Washington are defended and protected by the Army of the Potomac. Norfolk and Alexandria should be protected by the army outside of the cities, and there is no sort of military necessity for a military governor being in either city—a battalion with a field officer as commandant of the post is all that is necessary.

It will greatly relieve the complication of matters at Norfolk to open the port, and appoint an honest collector. He could attend to the business with half the cost to the Government and much more benefit to all concerned. This would greatly diminish the stock of goods kept on hand in those cities. This must be evident to any person who has observed the practical workings of the present system. A merchant now applies at Norfolk for a permit to ship goods into the city; he gets it signed there; he then sends it to Washington for approval; it is then sent to the custom house in Baltimore. This is done in a week; sometimes two or three weeks transpire; hence, a merchant to avoid trouble of permit, gets large supplies; and lest he should run out, replenishes soon; keeping on hand a large surplus; but open the ports, dispense with the permits, and he can send to Baltimore and get a return in 48 hours at furthest. Their cargoes with their invoices would be subject to inspection by custom house officers. The same regulations would still have to be kept up as to blockade runners. But I would dispense with much of that force by hanging or shooting all the blockade runners caught. These rascals have no claim upon their lives when they put the country to millions of expense to watch them, besides a large number of soldiers exposed to premature disease. In all such cases, when fairly detected, they should be hung. I think they are worse than spies. They combine the spy and the thief.

The loyal people of Norfolk and Portsmouth paid nearly $25,000 of internal revenue this year; I do not know how much this. Many of them, however, have paid large amounts of internal revenue for licenses that have not been permitted to use them; others commenced using and were closed up by the caprice of military commanders, and to make way for those who are in the same trade as monopolists. This is a reproach.

I submit these suggestions with great deference. But the subjects I have embraced are so deeply interesting to the people I represent, that did I not call them to your attention I should be grossly criminal.

I have been just as close to this war, ever since it commenced, as I could without much danger of being hurt, and have observed as closely as I could all the time. I think I understand the subject about which I am writing, and

I am satisfied that if the military rule had been practiced in West Virginia as it was in Alexandria for the least eighteen months, and in Norfolk for the last five months, that instead of the vast majority of loyal Union men that are there now sustaining the Government with men and money, and with happiness and prosperity around them, there would have been a vast majority of copperheads and secessionists, and civil government could not have been sustained. Regiments that now fill the Union army would have been in the secession army. I mean precisely what I say.

The question has been asked me, I am satisfied, a thousand times, "Do the President and Congress know of the oppression practiced on us?" The people say, "We have great confidence in the President's honesty and the purity of Congress, and they will redress our wrongs." I have an abiding confidence, gentlemen, in your justice.

I was born in Virginia. I desire to live in Virginia when this rebellion is subdued. I hope to see the old flag shortly unfurled in every county in the State, and the people acknowledging its majesty, and acknowledging with uplifted hands, the Constitution it represents to be the supreme law of the land. I never expect to have the *love* and *sympathy* of the rebels; but by the grace of God, by doing *right*, I intend to command their respect. My ardent desire and sincere prayer is, that this rebellion may be speedily crushed, that freedom may be enjoyed, not only in the State, but in all the broad limits of the nation, and that when the impartial historian comes to make up the record, he may be able truthfully to publish, that in accomplishing this great result the Government never sanctioned a *wrong* that was done to any man, however humble.

APPENDIX[25]

. . . I kindly proffered my aid and counsel to General Butler to assist in governing that "disarranged community;" but instead of taking counsel from me, he preferred calling in Tazwell Taylor to his counsel, the most noted secessionist in Norfolk, to counsel how he might overthrow civil government. Taylor had taken a prominent part in overthrowing the United States Government in a large part of Virginia. He was deemed fit counsel for General Butler, who desired to overthrow the restored government of the State. I prescribed to myself a rule in the outset of this rebellion not

---

25. Pierpont added a letter from General Butler filled with personal abuse of the governor.

to call into my confidence and counsel rebels against my Government, who were seeking its overthrow, nor to consult with generals who did; and when I found General Butler had called Tazwell Taylor to his counsel I resolved to not offer him mine, and I now inform him that he has done more to *disarrange* that community than any man living except Jeff. Davis and his followers.

"I have done what I believe to be right in this regard," says the General, "and neither the opinion of the assessor nor the abuse of the Governor will be very likely to move me from my position." I presume neither will be likely to move him from his position; but there is a very prevalent opinion that his blunders, if nothing else, in the command of his military department, will be very likely to "move" him from his "position."

Speech in the House of Representatives of the United States, May 17th, 1864, in Defence of His Claim to a Seat in That Body

(Baltimore: John Murphy and Co., 1864)

Joseph Eggleston Segar (1804–1880) was born in King William County, Virginia, where he practiced law and served in the state House. He was elected as a unionist to the Federal House in 1861, but the congress refused to seat him. Elected again by loyal eastern Virginians in 1862, he was seated and served ably to 1863. While in office he published a number of pamphlets that he circulated in the unionist regions of Virginia. When Segar presented his credentials to the Thirty-eighth Congress in 1864, he again was denied a seat. At the end of the war, Segar gained appointment to the U.S. Senate but was refused his seat. A loyal Virginia Republican, he finally received a plum post on the Spanish Claims Commission from 1877 to 1880.

Segar's pamphlet reveals his loyalty to his fellow unionists and again explains why some Virginians supported the nation. But mainly it is a fulsome request for a seat in Congress, a plea for representation for unionists, and an explanation of what failure to seat him would do for morale and loyalty in eastern and Tidewater Virginia. Segar also shows that he understands that Federal policy toward including his state in the restored Union might be changing. At the end of the pamphlet, he goes from an argument on the legal merits of his case to a wrenching and pitiable personal plea of his own loyalty to the Federal cause.

Information on Segar's life can be found in *The Biographical Directory of the United States Congress* (Washington, D.C.: Government Printing Office, 1973). Unfortunately, neither Segar nor other Tidewater Virginia unionists have received much study. For comment on Segar's ties to Governor

Pierpont see Anna Sivitar Pierpont, *Recollections of War and Peace, 1861–1868* (New York: G. P. Putnam's Sons, 1938).

* * *

In the fall of 1861 a small number of the loyal voters of the county of Elizabeth City, the county of my residence, appeared at the polls, in pursuance of a proclamation of Francis H. Peirpoint [*sic*], then the recognized loyal Governor of Virginia, and cast their vote for the humble individual before you, as their Representative in the Thirty-Seventh Congress. At the time I was far away from my home, treading, for the first time in my life, the soil of New England, and not even aware that an election was in contemplation. At first, I am frank to confess, I had no purpose of appropriating to myself the intended honor, having grave doubts of the legitimacy of the Wheeling government, under the auspices of which the election had taken place. But my doubts on that point having been removed by an able argument of the late Benjamin F. Hallet, of Boston, published in the Boston Post, and to which my attention was called by a distinguished member of the Boston bar, I determined finally to make claim to the proffered seat.[1] I accordingly appeared here to do so, but the House thought fit not to admit me.

The chief objections taken to my admission were, first, the one still raised, that *all* of the loyal voters of the district had not had an opportunity of indicating their choice at the polls, and, secondly, that the election having been one to supply a vacancy, it should have been held by writ of election, and not by executive proclamation.

Regarding the former of these objections as not soundly taken, and regardful of the rights of the State of which he was the acknowledged chief magistrate, Governor Peirpoint issued a writ for a new election. In this second election, I beg the House especially to note, only three counties voted—Accomac, Northampton, and Elizabeth City—and the vote cast was only 1,018, of which I received 559; and this number being a majority of the votes cast, I received a certificate of election, and a second time appeared in this Hall, seeking admission. You kept me out in the cold for some seven or eight weeks, but finally, either taking pity on me, or believing me entitled to the membership, you kindly rescued me from my shivering position outside, brought me within these doors, and conducted me to a seat in this House of Commons of this great nation. I took the seat; and

---

1. Benajmin F. Hallet was a Boston political leader and lawyer.

though it is not mine to boast a brilliant, I think I may not immodestly claim to have made at least an honorable record of my representative action. Elected as an unyielding Union man, I gave outspoken Union votes, having supported every vital measure of the Government for the suppression of the rebellion.

Well, supposing the point then as now raised against me to have been overruled by the solemn judgment of the House, and that the principle in my case had been definitely settled, I became a candidate for re-election, was elected by a large majority, and appeared here on the first day of the session to take my seat, never dreaming that the Clerk of the last House (Mr. Etheridge) would hesitate to place my name on his list of members elect—for I had presented a clear certificate of election, and had moreover been personally assured by him that my name was actually on his printed lists, my certificate of election being (as he said) all right—and still less conceiving it possible that the House, after the action of the last session, could for a moment hesitate over my admission.[2] And yet how stands the case? The Clerk, at a very late hour, thought fit to erase my name from the list on which he had put it, and this House, instead of standing by the decision of the last Congress, fairly and dispassionately made, has again kept me outside from early December till the summer solstice is almost upon us. In other words, though you admitted me the last session with a vote of only three counties of my district and a vote of 559, now, when I come here with the vote of four counties and a vote of 1,300—more than twice larger now than then—your committee tell me I have no right to a seat; and while you admitted the 559 loyal voters who sent me here the last Congress to representation on the floor, you now deny it to the 1,300 who sent me to the present Congress! And what is most remarkable and not a little mortifying, many of my old colleagues who voted to let me in in 1862 refuse to admit me in 1864!

Such are, briefly, the facts of the case; and I ask the House to bear them in mind while I proceed to demonstrate, as I am confident I can, my title to the seat I claim. Of my right to it on precedent, on principle, on law, on justice, and on public policy, I have no more doubt than I have of my right to my share of the sun light of heaven. And if my good friend from Massachusetts, the chairman of the Committee of Elections, will but give me a patient hearing, (as I am sure he will,) I am not without hope of

---

2. Emerson Etheridge was a Tennessee congressman who supported the Union cause. See Jon L. Wakelyn, ed., *Southern Pamphlets on Secession, November 1860–April 1861* (Chapel Hill: University of North Carolina Press, 1996), 395.

convincing him, not only that the conclusion of his report is erroneous, but that, on the very principles of his report, I am entitled to a seat in this body.

I rejoice, that this case comes up now disembarrassed of all complications. It is admitted to the committee's report that there is such a political organization as the State of Virginia—an admission for which I heartily thank them, for even that has been questioned in some high quarters; that there is such a district as the first congressional district of Virginia, duly laid off under an apportionment by the census of 1860; that the election was regularly held at the times and the places appointed by law; and that I have a proper certificate of election from the officer charged by law to grant it. So that there is but a single point in the case to be considered, so far as the committee's report is concerned, and that point is, that all the loyal voters of the district not having had an opportunity of reaching the polls, I cannot be said to be their choice, and therefore should not be admitted, for it is possible (they say) that some other person *might* have been preferred as Representative. I think I have fairly stated the point in the committee's report, and on that point I take issue with them. I maintain exactly the reverse of the committee's reasoning: that both principle and precedent are against the conclusion of the committee, and in favor of my admission.

I hold, first, that under a precedent long ago set, (as far back as the year 1826,) it is not competent for this House even to inquire whether or why any of the voters of my district, or any other district, were absent from the polls. I refer to the case of Biddle and Richard *vs.* Wing, (Contested Elections in Congress, p. 504,) in which it was charged by one of the claimants, Richard, that a sufficient number of his friends had been intimidated from voting to defeat his election; in other words, that but for actual intimidation practiced at the polls a sufficient number of his friends would have voted that did not vote to have given him a majority of the votes cast, and thus elected him. It was ruled that this inquiry could not be gone into at all. . . . [3]

Now, if ever a principle was set out with a pencil of light, here it is; and what is it? It is this: that so important is the elective privilege that an election should never be set aside except when there is an absolute impossibility of ascertaining where the majority of the votes actually given lies; that so vital is the right of representation in popular government, that it shall never be lost where it is possible to maintain it; that those who go to the polls shall not be deprived of the benefits of the inestimable privilege by those who do not go or could not go; that, no matter how many are absent from the polls, those who are not absent shall come in for freedom's great vital right

3. Segar gives an extended quote from that case of 1826.

of representation; and that however great the absence may be it shall not be taken into account, so as to interfere with the rights of non-absentees, unless there has been such a general fraud or corruption as would vitiate the whole election. This is the principle laid down by the committee of 1826, and it is a sound one; it is founded preëminently in reason and in wisdom; it institutes no superfluous inquiry; it is plain and incapable of perversion; it raises the simple and disembarrassing questions, who did vote, and who received the greatest number of votes given—an inquiry sufficient, where there is no absolute general fraud, for all the practical and useful ends of the elective franchise; it preserves to us unimpaired that essential principle of all free government, that taxation and representation should be "now and forever one and inseparable;" and it is deep-founded in the certainty and purity of the elective franchise, two qualities without which the privilege were as worthless dross. It discloses a rule which, from its simplicity and consequent incapability of fraudulent perversion, is suited for all times and all circumstances; for times of high party excitement and times of political quiet; for times of degeneracy and times of lustrous virtue; for "piping times of peace" and dark times of "grim-visaged war." And the best evidence of its soundness is that it is recognized in the election laws of every State in the Union, and has been from the very birth-hour of the Union, to this bleeding hour of civil strife.

Now, I ask my clear-headed friend from Massachusetts why he should not apply this philosophical reasoning of the Congress of 1826 to my constituents and their humble Representative? Is there not a peculiar and even touching applicability to their case? It looks to me as if the committee of the Nineteenth Congress has seen far down the vista of time, and, glancing with prophetic ken at the dark scenes of this unhappy rebellion, had fixed up (if I may speak) a set of maxims for our guidance in the very case before us.

Is not the "elective privilege as important" to my constituents as to any other people? Have they not, like those of other Delegates here, need for a Representative? Have they no rights to be shielded, no interests to be watched after?

When the people of my district went to the polls, were they not there "in the exercise of their constitutional rights?" and did they not "go through with the process of the election according to the prescribed rules?" The committee admit all this. Why, then, (to apply the just sentiment of the committee of the Nineteenth Congress,) "should they be deprived of the advantages accruing therefrom?"

And then, if you say that the votes of those loyal men who could go and did go to the polls shall go for nothing, do you not disfranchise all the loyal men of the district "of representation for a long period of time"—at least until "this cruel war is over?"

And is there any doubt who received the greatest number of votes, and was, therefore elected? The committee make no such pretension. I say, therefore, that an election having been made, and the result having been ascertained beyond cavil, this House, on the principle of *stare decisis*, has no such authority to do anything but ascertain "on whom the choice has fallen," and that, consequently, it has no right to open the question of who was absent from the polls, or of the reasons of the absence.

I might here rest my case, and demand my seat on the precedent set for our imitation by our predecessors of the golden era. But as it is insisted that a rule is to be now set for all time, I cannot forbear to look for a moment, by way of contrast, into the soundness of the one commended to us by the present committee, of inquiring into the number of absentees and the causes of absence, as a means of ascertaining the popular choice. Can any one fail to perceive that this modern rule—one of the offsprings of this hated rebellion—is utterly unreliable? You must either require the whole vote of a district to be out or within reach of the polls, or you must take the majority of the votes cast as an exponent of choice, or you may not hit the choice. I will illustrate by two of the very cases referred to in the report of the committee as illustrative of the soundness of its position. First, the case of Mr. Clements of Tennessee: Mr. Clements received in all the counties of his district 2,000 votes out of the usual vote of 6,000, one county, Warren, in rebel occupation, not voting.[4] Now, who knows but that if this county of Warren had voted there would have been a majority against Mr. Clements? And so in the case of Mr. Hahn, of Louisiana: he received in his district 2,799 votes, all others 2,319, a difference of less than five hundred.[5] But the parishes of St. Mary's and St. Martin's, being infested with rebel guerrilla bands, did not vote. Now *non constat* if these two parishes had voted, that Mr. Hahn would have been elected at all. The two parishes might have put the majority against him. And does not this show that the moment you begin to look into the matter of absent voters you may miss the object you aim at, to wit, the ascertainment of the popular choice, and that there is but one safe and certain rule, to wit, that which has been adopted by every State in the Union, of taking a majority or the greatest number of votes actually cast, without regard to absentees at all?

There is no other sound rule, and the proof of it is, that the moment you departed from the good old practice which has prevailed from the

4. Congressman Andrew J. Clements of Tennessee supported emancipation.
5. Michael Hahn, whose pamphlet is included in this book.

foundation of the Government until this rebellion began, of adopting the majority of the cast vote as the test of election, and relying on the official returns of the proper State officers as conclusive until fraud is alleged and proved, you involve yourselves in confusion, uncertainty, shifting decisions, and endless labor for your Committee of Elections, and the sooner you return to the old system, the sooner you will place the elective franchise on the most respectable and the securest basis, and the sooner you will take from the Committee of Elections the stone of Sisyphus, which it has been heaving up the mountain from the first moment this innovation on the elective principle and the old practice began.

My friend from Massachusetts, I know, will answer this argument and all others militating against his peculiar theory by saying that each House of Congress is the judge of the returns, qualifications, and elections of its members. True; and under that province this House may eject any member of the body, however legally elected, and there would be no redress except by another appeal to the people, and then another ejection might ensue, and so on, until a bare quorum would be left; so that this admitted function of Congress is to be exercised with a sound discretion, intelligently, rationally, honestly, not arbitrarily. Then, holding this power by the tenure of sound discretion and not arbitrary caprice, ought Congress so to exercise it as to subvert one of the noblest principles of American freedom, and more especially when under the Federal system there can be no extinction of a State except in the mode prescribed by the Constitution, and when, of course, the principle of representation must survive wherever there is a loyal population to vote? And until Congress shall intervene and take charge of this whole subject of elections, as it may rightfully do, ought not the State laws and State usages to prevail and control? Ought not, at least, this small respect be paid to State rights and State dignity? Ought you, in the absence of United States laws, to go behind the State laws and State returns? Resume, if you please, your rightful control over Federal elections, but so long as you leave this matter of elections to the States, respect them and the regulations which you yourselves invited them to adopt. And does not my friend from Massachusetts perceive that if we wish to establish the modern practice of opening the whole subject of elections in each case without regard to State laws and State returns, there is danger that, in times of high party excitement and demoralization, a broad margin may be left for political intrigue, and seats in Congress be given out and taken away by arbitrary party requirement? And does he not see the necessity, yea, the high policy, of not departing from the established precedents in this important matter of elections? In no interest of society is stability more necessary than in that of elections? Stability is indispensable there; and I will add that it is more necessary in reference to the elective franchise than it is to the institution of property itself, because the elective franchise is the source of the rights of property, and of every personal right, and not only the source, but the shield. I am looking ahead to the time when we may not have a Committee of Elections composed of as able and as honorable men as those of the present committee.

Now, I ask my friend from Massachusetts, in all respect, if this precedent of the days of yore—those pure and happy days of the Republic, the days of the second Adams, whose administration was a bright era in our land, and was as faultless and pure as that of Washington himself—is not one that comes to my relief on the present occasion, entitling me to a seat with him in this Hall? In the face of this precedent, can he do anything more than inquire whether I had, or had not, the majority of the legal votes cast?

But, leaving this precedent out of view, are there no other precedents to entitle me to membership in this body? I marvel much that the Committee of Elections, while they were looking up the precedents and declaring that all precedent was against me, did not think of one of very recent origin, and perfectly in point, the case in the last Congress, of the unlucky individual whom you have so long kept out in the cold, my humble self. I can only account for the omission by the fact that I was so silent and obscure a member that gentlemen have actually forgotten that I was a member at all. And so I crave leave to refresh the recollection of the House and to remind it (as the Journal will show) that I was a veritable member of the Thirty-Seventh Congress, and that I obtained my seat in the very teeth and in defiance of the very principle on which the committee now seek to exclude me, and on the very state of facts now existing. My friend from Massachusetts will say, I suppose, that his committee, being unable to agree, did not make report of the specific objection now taken, and so asked to be discharged from the further consideration of the subject, leaving the House to decide the matter for itself. True, but the committee reported the facts of the case, as in the present instance, leaving the House to decide the principle, and to apply it, without regard to any opinion of the committee, and the House did decide and apply it. . . . [6]

The only material difference is that in the first election seventeen counties composed the district, and only three voted; while in the late election twenty counties, under the new appointment, formed the district, and only four

6. Segar shows that his majority in 1863 far exceeded his majority in 1861.

voted. So that there is no substantial difference, in principle, in the two cases.

True, the addition of three counties to the district increases its population, but that addition is more than offsetted by the increase of the aggregate vote cast and the increase of my own vote in the last election over the first.

The able chairman of the committee will argue, I can foresee, that this case of mine is not a precedent. He will tell you that when it was up in the last Congress he declared that the House might, without interfering with any position of the committee, either admit or reject me. But I hold it to be indisputable that the House in admitting me did so either as matter of personal compliment or on principle.

But it could not well have been on personal compliment; for I suppose it is my hard lot to be one of the least popular members that ever sat in this body. That, however, is more my misfortune than my fault; for an excessive infirmity of vision, besides giving me the appearance of almost clownish awkwardness and a seeming stiffness, much disqualifies me for recognizing faces and associating faces and names; and so I am debarred the pleasure of an extensive acquaintance with the members of the House, which I deeply regret, for I know I am socially and personally much a loser by the exclusion inflicted by this defect.

So the House must have voted on principle, and not on mere compliment. Well, all I have to say is, that if you voted on principle, stand by it, for principle is a thing to be stood by; and if you voted for me for compliment's sake, please pay me the compliment once more, for I am as worthy now as then. The objection, then, that is taken to my admission now is the identical one that was in the mind of the House when I was admitted in 1862, and which, by my admission then, was expressly overruled by a conclusive vote. Nay, more. My case is far stronger now than it was then. Then, but 1,018 votes were cast in my district; now, there are near 1,700. Then, I received only 559 votes; at the late election, 1,300. So that while you gave my district a Representative with a vote of just 1,000, you propose to deny it one with a vote of 1,700; and while you awarded me my seat when I had only 559 votes, you talk of ejecting me when I received 1,300!

Now I do not mean to say whether consistency is a jewel or not, or whether it is a rare jewel, or one worth keeping bright; but this I do aver, that my case was decided, and I think rightly decided, when, on the 6th of May, 1862, I was admitted a member of the Thirty-Seventh Congress, because then there could not have been a single conceivable objection to my admission but the one now urged—that the whole vote of the district was not in reach of the polls. And I maintain, further, that the faith of this

House is most solemnly plighted to yield me and my constituents the seat we claim. You cannot reject me without breaking your faith. Declare me elected to one Congress and rule me out of another, when the principle is identical, and the facts even stronger in the last case than in the first! Is that the way you keep sparkling the jewel of faith? Is that the way this honorable body, the representative of the morals of the nation, cherishes its consistency and honor? Is this the example the law-makers of a great and proud nation are to set to the citizen masses? Invite me, on the faith of your past action, into a most laborious and expensive canvass, and then turn me adrift, to be the sport of the envious and malicious, and an especial object of confederate taunt! I trust this House will bring upon itself no such reproach. Let it be just to itself and just to me, by re-inscribing my name on the list from which the late Clerk so improperly struck it off.

But is there no other precedent of the same purport? Why, my friend from Kentucky, Mr. Casey, was allowed to take his seat in the Thirty-Seventh Congress with about seven hundred votes, just about half of my vote; and when, we are assured by an honorable gentleman now a member from that State, (Mr. Smith,) that a considerable portion of Mr. Casey's district was held by rebels, and could not reach the polls.[7] How is it that you "make fish of one and flesh of another?"

I could bring up many other instances of gentlemen reaching the honors of this floor—some of them here now—who received a very inconsiderable proportion of the votes of their districts, but I have cited examples enough to show that when the committee said that the precedents are all against me they were decidedly wrong. I insist that precedent, both old and new, time-honored and recent, lights the way to a seat in this body, as plain as the road to the parish church. Indeed, after the vote of the last Congress in my favor, the question of my admission is not now an open one. On the principle of *stare decisis* it cannot be reopened. To all intents and purposes it is *res adjudicata*.

But a large portion of my district being in rebel possession, and not voting, the committee argue that I cannot be said to be the choice of the loyal voters of it, for (may be) if the loyal men in the counties in possession of the rebels *had* voted I might not have had the majority. How did the committee ascertain that there are *any* loyal men in that portion of the district which is in the rebel lines? How do they know that there is one single loyal man there? The *presumption* is that there are *no* loyal men there.

7. Congressmen Samuel S. Casey and Green C. Smith from Kentucky supported emancipation.

When a portion of a State rests under rebel rule, civil and military, the presumption of common reason is that *all* its people, or certainly most of them, are rebels; for if they prefer the Government of the Union to the rebel government why have they not left the one and sought the other? There is not a county in my district that is not in easy reach of the stars and stripes; and there is not a loyal man in any one of those counties that could not in a few days put himself within the Federal lines and the protection of the United States. Why have they not left the rebeldom and sought protection under the old flag? I, for one, fled from the one and sought the other. I had made up my mind, immovably, that I would under no circumstances live under treason's government; and so I fled from the very heart of rebeldom, and fled, and fled on, until I caught sight of that glorious flag which is power and strength and protection wherever its proud folds are flung to the breeze. If there are any loyal men in the rebel-held portion of my district, why did they not as others did, "come out from among the wicked?"

The argument, then, of the Committee of Elections, that I am not entitled to my seat because there was a greater portion of the loyal men in the rebel part of the district than in the loyal part of it, is based altogether *on a naked assumption*. They do not state an ascertained fact, but put forth only an airy speculation. They *assume* what they ought to *prove*. They forget that the *onus probandi* is on them. I come here with a proper certificate of the proper returning officers of my State, which raises at once the presumption that I had all the votes necessary, both in quantity and quality, to elect me; and I come here also with the presumption in my favor that all those in rebel lands are rebels; and yet these presumptions, these most rational presumptions, to the benefit of which I am entitled as against any other contestant, and indeed against all the world, until legitimately repelled, are to be rebutted and set aside, How? By facts and proofs? No, by another and an inferior, less rational presumption—by a naked speculation!

Now, I am not much of a lawyer, but I did learn this principle in the elementary law-books, that where a presumption arises in favor of a party, that party is entitled to the benefit of it until it is rebutted and the contrary made to appear. Now, I ask, in all candor, have the committee fairly and squarely rebutted the presumptions with which I come here in my favor? I am here, as I just said, with the presumption, first, arising from a proper certificate of election, that I had all the votes necessary to elect me; and I am here with that other most rational presumption, that in a rebel land there are but few loyal men to break the monotony of treason's song; and how, I ask again, do the committee rebut these presumptions and take from me the benefit of them? Why, by the bold and bald assumption that as there were 1,700 loyal votes in the counties that did vote, there must be a proportional number of loyal men in those that did not vote! And having settled the basis of proportion, they work it out, by the principles of Cocker and Pike, that as there were 1,700 loyal votes in the voting counties, there must be at least 5,100 in the counties in rebel possession and not voting! There are (to put the argument in semi-syllogistic form) 1,700 loyal votes in the four counties within the Federal lines that voted: *ergo*, there are 5,100 in the sixteen counties in the rebel lines that did not vote!

On what principle is it that the committee make the loyalty of the four counties that voted the basis for calculating the loyalty of the sixteen counties that did not vote! The circumstances of the two are totally different. The counties of Accomac, Northampton, Elizabeth City, and York, early came back within the blessed scope of the Union. The proud emblem of our national sovereignty and power as it streams from the liberty-poles at Fortress Monroe, and Fort Wool, and Camp Hamilton, and Yorktown, and Williamsburg, can be seen by the naked eye of the people of the counties of Elizabeth City and York, as each fold flutters in the breeze. The two large counties of Accomac and Northampton, in six months from the date of Virginia's secession, came, by the expedition of General Dix, within the protection of the Union, and at once acknowledged its supremacy. Not so with the rest of the district. The Federal arms had made no lodgment there. Practical protection had not been guaranteed or offered. The stars and bars, not the stars and stripes, floated there, and there rebellion and treason still their vigils keep. Now, in such entire dissimilarity of circumstances, how can you reason from the loyalty of the people in the protected, loyal portion of my district, to the loyalty of those in the unprotected, rebellion-bound portion of it?

Five thousand one hundred loyal voters in the portion of my district in occupancy of the rebels? I wish in all my heart it were so. It would be *imperium in imperio*. It would be a power in that section more potent than the power of the rebellion itself—a power that might "beard the lion in his den." It would put the Union party there long way ahead of the secession traitors. In the whole of this portion of my district, the entire vote in the presidential election of 1860 was 7,840. The loyal vote in it now, say the committee, is 5,100. So that according to the committee's reasoning it has 2,745 more loyal than disloyal voters—a thing which cannot be predicted of any congressional district in Virginia. The same reasoning, as I have ascertained by actual calculation, would make the number of loyal voters in the whole State 54,400, and of the disloyal 44,019, thus making the loyal voter greater by 10,381 than the disloyal; a result which will, I am sure, expose to the chairman of the Committee of Elections the entire fallacy of the calculations on which he proposes to oust his friend from Virginia from a seat beside him. Five thousand one hundred loyal voters in this most "copperhead" region of the whole State! I tell you, in all candor, that the counties outside the four that sent me here, are the very last locality in my State to find loyal people in. It was in the soil of those counties that Mr. Calhoun sowed broad-cast those seeds of nullification and sectionalism which have ripened into a fruitful harvest of rebellion and treason. I have often heard it remarked, and the remark was but too true, that there were more disciples of the Calhoun faith in the first congressional district of Virginia than in all the State beside. I know it to be so. I was often the Whig elector in that district, was the representative of a portion of it in the State Legislature for more than twenty years, and I speak from personal knowledge when I say that there has been from the time of Mr. Calhoun's celebrated Fort Hill manifesto in 1831, less attachment to the Union of these States in this than in any other portion of the Old Dominion. It has been a soil more fruitful of a dividing and alienating sectionalism and of disunion doctrine than any in this whole land, except peculiarly traitorous South Carolina. Look at the antecedents! When I first knew the district, it was represented in Congress by old Burwell Bassett, a politician of the extremist State-rights faith. Soon after came Richard Coke, an ardent nullifier, whose Magnus Apollo was John C. Calhoun. Next came Henry A. Wise, who ran against Mr. Coke on the avowed ground of secession against nullification—the secessionist against the nullifier. True, Mr. Wise redeemed himself not a little in the dark times when executive prerogative in the hands of Andrew Jackson was laying foul hand on the most sacred principles of the Constitution. He gallantly stood up for the "union of the Whigs for the sake of the Union." He even said that "office could not add a cubit to the stature" of Henry Clay—a tribute as righteous as beautiful, and that will be echoed back by the wise and good of the world, "to the last syllable of recorded time."

But alas! *Quam mutatus ab illo!* Mr. Wise relapsed and beat badly Hill Carter, a gentleman of the olden standard, and an uncompromising old-line Whig of the Henry Clay and Daniel Webster school. I shall be no further his historian, but bring to your notice his successor, Thomas H. Bayly, a man of noble parts of both heart and head, but of extreme State rights and southern proclivities, and one of the most enthusiastic admirers of Mr. Calhoun. He was succeeded by a gentleman well known to many members of this body—Muscoe R. H. Garnett, whose political notions were at war since his boyhood with all national statesmanship, who regarded a labor to subvert our blessed Union a labor of patriotism and of duty, and who, since his pernicious doctrines eventuated in fragmenting that noblest fabric of human workmanship, held a seat in the rebel congress. From such antecedents, you can scarcely expect to find in a certain part of my district, the army of Union men which the Committee of Elections have so kindly assigned to its custody.[8] Why, even the old-line Whigs of the western shore portion of my district have forgotten their instincts. The Critchers and the Lewises and the Saunderses and the Smiths and the Roanes and the Lacys and the Carters and the Wilcoxes and the Shields and the Howards and the Greshams and the Cloptons and the Fleets, and hundreds of the like quondam politics, who shouted for "Tippecanoe and Tyler too," who sprung every nerve to make President noble, magnificent, immortal Henry Clay, who admired Daniel Webster as an intellect that any country might be proud of, who looked upon Millard Fillmore as one of the most unselfish, most patriotic, and most sagacious statesmen the North has ever given to our common country, and who "did yeoman's service" in the cause of Bell and Everett at the last presidential election as being *par excellence* the Union ticket: all these and thousands of others, the very élite of Whig chivalry in district No. 1, have gone off on "the pride of former days." They "kept step to the music of the Union," and sang anthems to the Union while Virginia and the Union were together, but now the harp of Tara sleeps on Tara's walls. Roused by the bugle-blast of their native land, they have flung away the clarion with which they were wont to ring out joyous notes to the Union of their Washington. There never was a class possessing in reference to their State—their *natale solum*—more of the Cavalier spirit than do my old comrades, the old-line Whigs of Northumberland and Lancaster and Richmond and Westmoreland and King George and Essex and King and Queen and Glouchester and Matthews and King William and Middlesex and Caroline and James City and Williamsburg and New Kent and Charles City. They loved the Union while their State and the Union could go on harmoniously together; but when the conflict came, they became clannish, and, taking a position for their loved Old Dominion, they soliloquized, each to himself, in the language of Roderick Dhu's resolve:

> "This rock shall fly
> From its firm base as soon as I."[9]

8. Biographical information on the above-mentioned radical Virginia congressmen may be found in the *Biographical Directory of Congress*.

9. Roderick Dhu, Highland Scottish chief, killed by King James V, and described in Sir Walter Scott, *The Lady of the Lake*.

And hence it was that, without reference to old party, they united almost to a man in ratifying the secession ordinance of their State.

Why, all the blockade-running and carrying of supplies to the rebels from across the Potomac takes place through the very heart of the non-voting portion of my district. Could this contraband passing and traffic be well carried on if there were scattered over it 5,100 loyal voters? The two recent raids upon that land of submissive loyalty, the eastern shore of Virginia, emanated from the county of Matthews, one of the non-voting counties, and in which I do not believe there is one loyal man or woman. And throughout the western shore of my district a merciless conscription has sent nearly the whole arms-bearing population to the camp and the battle-field. . . . [10]

And a prominent citizen of Lancaster county, William N. Harris, Esq., who left that county because it was no place for a Union man to live in, assures me that scarcely a Union man is to be found in the whole northern neck of Virginia.

Now, I ask my friend from Massachusetts how he expects to find among such people, at this hour of peculiar estrangement, 5,100 loyal voters? "You may call spirits from the vasty deep, but will they come?" The 5,100 loyal men are not there. They exist only in the fabulous comparison of the election committee. Instead of that large number, I am satisfied there are not 250 loyal men in that portion of my district that failed to vote at the late election. I do not mean to say that there will be no returning loyalty there, I am persuaded that when our armies shall have possessed this region so that those who shall return to their homes may have assurance of security, thousands of the small farmers and mechanics and working men will, as it was in the counties of Elizabeth City and York, joyfully wend their way back to the hearth-stones they love. But at the time of the late election, I know I do not err when I say that not 250 loyal men were there to vote. But say there were 500, or 800, and still it will be manifest that I received a majority of the loyal votes of the whole district; and a majority *of the loyal vote*, as I understand, is all the committee require.

Now, I appeal to my friend from Massachusetts if I have not made good my position, that, on the principles of my own report, I am entitled to a seat in this body. Let it be borne in mind that the Committee of Elections do not require me to have received a majority of the entire vote of the district.

10. There follow letters from Judge E. P. Pitts of the Eastern Shore Circuit and Thomas R. Bowden, a Tidewater Virginia lawyer, to affirm Segar's assertion of disloyal counties.

They do not estimate for the disloyal voters at all, for disloyal men are not expected or allowed to vote. The military power has been even used to exclude them from the polls. All that is required of me, I repeat, is to show that I received a majority of the loyal votes of the district; and I submit it to the House if I have not so made it appear.

But concede that there are the 5,100 loyal votes assumed by the committee, and I contend that on all principle, and in all reason, I am to be credited with that entire vote, just as much as if it had been written down on the poll-books for me.

In many cases in practical life, as in law, finite beings must act upon rational presumptions, because they cannot always have the solutions of fact. Now I hold that one of the most rational presumptions the mind of man can conceive, is, that those loyal men in my district who could not reach the polls would ratify the choice of their more fortunate brethren in loyalty who did reach them. Is there anything more consonant with reason, or, if you please, the instincts of the human constitution? Why, what do people ordinarily want a Representative for? Is it not to have their rights and interests looked after and protected? Suppose that in your absence some considerate person undertakes to attend to some important matter of interest for you—saves, for example, the sacrifice of your property—is it not the most rational supposition in the world that you would ratify the action of that considerate person, and give him your thanks besides? And is not this the very case between myself and the loyal voters who could not reach the polls, and more especially when what little capacity I may possess to serve them is as well known to every man in the district as the road to mill? Will not this be their reasoning: "Well, we couldn't get to the polls ourselves, but we are glad our loyal brethren elsewhere did get there to elect a good, loyal man to look out for us and help bring this unhappy war to a close?" If they would not so reason they would falsify all the instincts of our nature.

This presumption that those loyal voters of my district who could not reach the polls would approve, ratify, and even rejoice at the choice made by their more fortunate brethren who did, is so strong, so rational, so instinctive, that it ought to prevail, and I ought to have the benefit of it until by some popular loyal demonstration to the contrary the presumption is overturned. I appeal to the House if this is not legitimate logic.

Why call for positive proof that I am the choice of the loyal absentees, when, on every just principle, I cannot but be that choice? I am as well satisfied of it as I am that death awaits all mortal flesh, that, if the truth could be ascertained, there is not one loyal voter in the whole of that portion of my district outside the Federal lines that would not accept me unhesitatingly as his Representative in Congress. And why deal in mere technicalities and non-essentials at this trying hour when the life of the nation is at stake? And why are we not taught by the enemy? They have in their congress senators and representatives from Tennessee, Kentucky, and Missouri States that are not in the rebellion, willing, I suppose, to have aid from any and every quarter. Why will you deny us loyal men of Virginia the privilege of aiding you as far as we can in bringing this war of ruin and death to a close, and re-lifting the star-lit banner of the Union over an undismembered land? We do not claim to be master-workmen, but we shall be content to do the best we can in our humble way. Maybe we can carry to all the master-craftsmen the cement to reunite the disjointed fragments of a once magnificent fabric of liberty and Union.

It is not necessary (say the Committee) that all the loyal men of a district should be at the polls to constitute an election. If they have an opportunity it suffices, because if, having the opportunity, they stay away, the doctrine of acquiescence holds. On this point I have to say that by an ordinance of the Wheeling convention passed in August, 1861, providing that the voters of any county may vote in any other county and at any precinct, a large number of the voters within the rebel lines in my district might have voted if they had had the will and the nerve.

But they were intimidated, or kept from voting by the fear of consequences, it is alleged. Be it so; but according to the ruling in the case of Biddle and Richard *vs.* King, if intimidation prevailed, and voters were kept back by intimidation, the votes thus lost are not to be taken into the account, and the result is to stand on the votes actually given in.

But concede that the whole loyal vote of the rebel portion of the district was kept off by intimidation or duress or coercion: does it follow that we of the loyal portion of the district who were not intimidated or coerced are to be disfranchised of our representation in Congress? A portion of the people of my district were intimidated from voting, or were under duress: *ergo*, those who were not intimidated, or not under duress, are to be stripped of their representative rights! I confess to no such doctrine, because there is no justice in it; because it is the punishing of one set of loyal men for the helpless misfortunes of another set of loyal men; because it is the blending of the innocent and the guilty; and because, above all, it is ignored by one of the fundamental and most sacred maxims of Anglo-Saxon liberty, which ought to be dear to every American heart, because at America's Runnymede, Boston harbor, it lit the fires of the Revolution which blazed out into the broad, lustrous radiance of American independence and American freedom; and that precious, liberty-born, liberty-preserving, century-honored principle is, that there should be no taxation without representation. . . . [11]

There, you have it in figures! Near twenty thousand dollars tax per annum under your internal revenue laws, all of which has been actually paid in, and cheerfully paid; and yet I am told that the people who pay this uncomfortable taxation are not to have a Representative on this floor! I trust the House will not subject my good constituents to so unjust and humiliating a discrimination. I invoke for them the intervention of my friend from Massachusetts—a Representative of that noble State that gave birth to the dauntless patriots who threw the tea overboard in Boston harbor. Why cannot my friend be as generous to the loyal people of my district as he was last year to the loyal people of Louisiana, when they sent Mr. Flanders and Mr. Hahn here, and when the chairman of the Election Committee so zealously pleaded for their admission?[12] I quote from the committee's report on that occasion. After urging, most strenuously, that the military governor had the power to order an election, the report says:

> "The constitutionally-elected Governor of Louisiana had turned traitor,
> and refused to discharge his constitutional obligations. What were the
> loyal voters to do? Were they to turn traitors also, or to be disfranchised?"

I ask, in all deference, and in the committee's own language, "what are my poor constituents to do?" Are they to "turn traitors also, or to be disfranchised?" . . . [13]

Now, all I ask is that this constitutional and generous logic be applied to the loyal voters of my district as it was to the loyal voters of the first and second districts of Louisiana. The armies of the Union have, in a portion of my district, "driven out the rebel usurpation" and restored the civil authority there. But let me remind you, in the language of your committee, that your "work is not ended until there is representation here."

The committee further say:

> "Are this people to wait for representation here until their rebel governor
> returns to his loyalty and appoints a day, or is the Government to guaranty
> that representation as best it may?"

11. Segar talks of the heroics of the American Revolutionaries who resisted taxation without representation. He then cites the taxes his constituents paid to the Federal government.

12. Congressman Benjamin Flanders of Louisiana.

13. Segar further cites the Election Committee's report on the Louisiana election.

I beg to submit the same question as to the people of my district. Are we to go without representation until "Honest John Letcher" or "Extra Billy Smith" returns to his loyalty and helps to re-hoist over his State the old flag, or until Jefferson Davis and his wicked accomplices lay down the arms of treason and rebellion? Or, rather, ought not the "Government to guaranty to us representation as best it may?" That is the idea. Representation in some form or other—in the best form you can! Do for us the best you are able—"guaranty it to us as best you may," and we shall be satisfied.

Forbear this invidious discrimination against my constituents. Give us representation, or tax us not. And I call upon my friend from Massachusetts, the moment I am ejected from a seat here, to rise in his place and vindicate a great principle, and his own consistency and the consistency of the House, by offering a bill to relieve the people who sent me here of all Federal taxation.

I am now to consider the last, and, I suppose the most formidable objection to my admission, though I am happy to say, it has not been raised by the Committee of Elections, and I presume, accordingly, has not its sanction. It is urged in some quarters that we have no State. It was argued in the debate in the Arkansas case that a "State should exist with a government." And I know well that some gentleman on this floor entertain that most extraordinary idea that there is no such political organization as the State of Virginia. Well, if that be so, most certainly I can have no right to come here as a Representative from Virginia. But is it so? I think not. There certainly was once a State of Virginia. What has become of her? Has she gone up to the clouds? Has rebellion swallowed her down and abrogated her political existence? I hold that as a State she is, under our system of government, indestructible; once a State always a State, until let out by the three-fourths vote, or until successful revolution and general international recognition shall have animated into being a new nationality.

But so long as we profess to be governed by the Federal Constitution, we cannot extinguish a State. You may by arms subdue the people of a State to obedience to the Federal laws, and to their primary allegiance to the Federal Union; but you cannot, without violating the Constitution, and giving up the whole theory of our system and the whole theory of rebellion, extinguish the State organization, because a State, in our system, occupies relation to, and is indeed part and parcel of, the Federal Government, and is subject to and to be governed by the Constitution of the United States as the supreme law. And on this principle Virginia is yet an existing State, and I think I can make it apparent to the House in a very few words.

The Constitution expressly provides, and it is one of the wisest provisions in it, because, without it, the Government of the Union would not last a lustrum, would have been a rope of sand, a helpless organization without the energy of self-preservation; I say the Constitution provides that it shall be in no respect changed without the concurrent assent of three-fourths of the States that formed it, or subsequently became parties to it. So that Virginia is still a member of the Union, owing primary allegiance to it, until she shall have been let out by the regular action of three-fourths of her sister States. Now, would not the making of the number of States one less in number be a change, and a radical change, in the Constitution? Would it not be a destruction, *pro tanto*, of the Constitution, the knocking away of one of its pillars? And if you can, without the joint action of three-fourths of the States, knock away one pillar, may you not knock away another and another, until the whole fabric shall have fallen into ruins? I say, therefore, if you cannot "dot an *i* or cross a *t*" in the Constitution without having the consent of the constitutional majority of three-fourths of the States *à fortiori* you cannot perform the momentous act of ending, at your will, the life of a State.

Virginia, then, is somehow or somewhere a State, and to us, her loyal citizens, whose interest it is to keep posted about her, it is no difficult task to find her whereabouts, and to explain how she came where she is. You will find her sitting in her qualified sovereignty and in her loyalty about eight miles off, down in Alexandria. There she has a Governor and Lieutenant Governor residing, and her auditor, treasurer, secretary of State, and attorney general. There she had recently, in actual session, a convention to revise her constitution, and adapt it to the extraordinary posture of affairs induced by the rebellion. Very recently her Legislature was in regular session, and will shortly be again in extraordinary session. The people of the loyal counties that acknowledge this Government pay their taxes with punctuality and alacrity; and I am happy to inform the House and our rebel friends in Dixie that the treasury of this State, much as some people turn up their noses at her, is in a very prosperous condition—plenty of money, and not a very expensive government to maintain. It would be most fortunate for the rebel government if it could exhibit so flattering a balance-sheet, and I rather think that Uncle Sam himself might well be congratulated if his fisc [finances] were in so enviable a condition. She had some short time since two Senators in Congress; one, most lamentably, sleeps in a premature grave; the other still sits and votes in the other wing of the Capitol. She has her civil authorities, judges, magistrates, sheriffs, coroners, clerks, constables, and all the officers of a regular government, in full exercise of their respective functions. She has, then, all the external and apparent characteristics of a State; and the only other question that can arise in relation to her is, is she *legitimately* a State? Just as much so, in my judgment, as a man is a human being or a mule a brute.

Let history speak. Shortly after the old State, in evil hour, seceded from the Union, the people of the northwest who desired to live yet under the Union of their fathers, held a convention at Wheeling and put into operation what is usually known as the Wheeling government of Virginia, and more recently as the restored government of Virginia. This government originated in the irresistible necessities of the loyal men, who could not follow their State into the treason and ruin of secession, and it was founded on the idea that the loyal people of the State constitute the State, or the political power of the State. From time to time other counties than those of the northwest attached themselves to this new organization, and among them the four that did me the honor to depute me their representative here. In course of time West Virginia became a separate State, but the counties in eastern and Piedmont Virginia that did not belong, geographically, to that division, and that did not of course desire to become a part of the new State, adhered to the restored government, and such is their present position. If the Wheeling government was a legal one, so is the present government in Alexandria, because the latter is an emanation from, and a continuation of, the Wheeling government.

Then, was the Wheeling government a legal organization? Undoubtedly it was; and the argument is brief. Its legality rests on the high ground of a decision of the highest judicial tribunal in the land, the Supreme Court of the United States.

In the case of Luther *vs.* Borden, the celebrated Dorr rebellion case, the Supreme Court ruled that where there are within the limits of an already existing State two conflicting political organizations, that is the legal, rightful one, which is recognized by the Federal Executive. And the court decided (Chief Justice Taney delivering the opinion of the court) that when the recognition is officially made by an official act of the Federal Executive, there is no going behind it. President Tyler, by the act of proffering Federal troops to the Governor under the old charter government of Rhode Island, recognized the latter government (the Supreme Court say) as legitimate, and so it ruled that the Dorr government was a usurpation and a nullity.

Now, after the Wheeling government of Virginia was organized, the President of the United States recognized it in various ways. Through his heads of Departments he held official correspondence and business relations with Francis H. Peirpoint, Governor of the State under the Wheeling organization. As Governor, the latter was called on for troops, and furnished the quota of his State.

The recognition by the Federal Executive was all that could be properly required, but both Houses of Congress acknowledged the new government as legitimate. The Senate admitted two Senators for it, though it embraced not more than one fourth the population and territory of the original State; and this House recognized it by admitting to this floor three representatives, my friends Messrs. Brown, Blair, and Whaley.[14]

So the Wheeling government, having been acknowledged by the Federal Executive, was a legal, constitutional government, and the present restored government, being a continuation of the Wheeling government, and resting on the same principle, is equally rightful and lawful; and here I might dismiss the question. But I am unwilling to place the restored government on any mere inferential basis. I say that it has been specifically recognized by the President of the United States subsequently to the formation of the new State of West Virginia, and since the present restored government went into operation. To say nothing of other acts of recognition, Mr. Lincoln, in his amnesty proclamation of the 8th of December last, expressly recognizes all "loyal State governments that have all the while been maintained." Such a government is that of the restored government of Virginia. By him it is acknowledged a "loyal State government all the while maintained," and therefore he excepted it from his general plan of reconstruction. Perhaps I had better quote his words, and here they are:

> "To avoid misunderstanding, it may be proper to say that this proclamation, so far as it relates to State governments, has no reference to States wherein loyal governments have been all the while maintained."

Most evidently the President had in his mind this very restored government of Virginia.

The case has been supposed in this House of a recognition by the Executive and non-recognition by one or both Houses of Congress, and then it has been asked, where will a State government be found? The answer is obvious. I hold that no recognition by either House of Congress is necessary. It is the Executive acknowledgement that stamps legality upon a State whose organizations conflict. Congress has no part nor lot in establishing the legitimacy. The Executive, and the Executive alone, can

14. Congressmen Jacob B. Blair, William G. Brown, and Kelian V. Whaley from Virginia's Wheeling government. (All three were elected to the Thirty-eighth Congress from West Virginia.)

exercise the legalizing function. And when it does exercise the function, Congress itself cannot look behind the act done. It binds not only Congress, but every citizen of the United States.

This restored government of Virginia is as legitimate as the old charter government of Rhode Island as against the Dorr government, and as legitimate as that of Massachusetts and New York. And I put it to my friend from Massachusetts, how is it that a State can have two Senators in Congress and no Representatives. If Virginia is not a State, how can she have Senators in Congress, and if, as a State, she is entitled to Senators in Congress, is she not sufficiently a State to be entitled to Representatives also, and to her electoral vote likewise?

In the name of the Union, do not ignore our young and may be feeble government, by denying us representation in this body. We are not strong, but we are none the less a State. Why, the little State of Delaware, scarcely equal in territorial extent to a single county in Virginia, is, nevertheless, just as much a State as her empire sister, New York; just (to use the language of Vattel) as a "dwarf is as much a man as a giant, and the smallest republic as much a State as the greatest empire."

Ought not our weakness to be even our protection? Suppose you see the brawny giant strike down to the earth the helpless dwarf: what emotion rises in your bosoms but of execration of the cowardly act? And so, if the strong arms of the mighty Government shall fell to the earth this youthful State in her weakness, sweeping away her whole civil establishment, and substituting for it the chafing harshness of a pure military government, and thus depriving her of what the Constitution guaranties to every State, a republican form of government, what will be thought of us and said of us by the Christian nations of the earth? What will be our portion but an enlightened scorn? How will the thing read in history? Let the historian write it down: "Here was a State (it will be noted) that could not brook rebellion, and that set up for itself, to avoid the crime and penalties of rebellion, a nascent nationality struggling against treason, yet loving the old flag and clinging with fond devotion to the blessed Government which is the 'brightest particular' conception of human statesmanship, and which made us the freest, the happiest, and the greatest people on the globe, promising to be the nucleus for a grand gathering of future loyalty, until the whole length and breadth of the Ancient Dominion shall be brought under the gentle sway of peace, and back to allegiance to the best Government on earth; and yet a State like this, with promises and prospects like these, was, in her helplessness, struck down by the crushing arm of the all powerful Government of the United States!" Shall we write any such chapter in the history of our country? Let us, as the President of the United States has done, recognize her as a "loyal organization all the while maintained;" and let us take her in and keep her in, until her weakness becomes strength, and the song of redemption shall ring through all her ancient domain.

And I will venture to say, that if it be really desired to bring back the "mother of States and statesmen," in all her ancient consequences, within the scope of re-construction, you can in no way so surely accomplish the great desideratum as by preserving unharmed her restored government. It will be a sure nucleus for loyal formations. As the federal armies advance and rear the standard of the Union, men who were forced into this cruel war against their will, and those that tire of it—having tasted its bitter fruits—and those who at heart sigh for the old flag and for peace, will hasten within the lines where they will find a double protection, the civil protection of their own accustomed municipal authorities, and the military protection of the United States. And I venture to express the opinion—and I do it very confidently—that the best possible system of re-construction is that of restored State organization and gradual accretion. It will be far more effectual than the territorializing policy or the establishment of military governments. There is not in it the harshness, the alienation, the embitterment, the rending, the crush, the crash that will follow any system that waits for general subjugation before it is applied. Its operation will be gentle and soothing, because gradual and restorative; and under it the people will find themselves almost imperceptibly back at their homes, and almost unconsciously remitted to their local governments and associations, and to the blessings of the Union of their fathers. Just as the amputation of a limb under the sedative influence of chloroform: the surgeon's knife does its gashing work, and his saw its hackling, and the limb is off, and when the patient wakes up he feels no pain, and is unconscious that a limb is gone!

We need no intervention of Congress to provide for us "a republican form of government." Spare us, we beseech you, all such graciousness. *Non tali auxilio, nec defensoribus istis!* Whatever call there may be for the guarantying of republican forms of government in other States, there is no necessity that the United States perform that office for us. We call not on Hercules for help. Our own shoulders are at the wheel. We have already a republican form of government—one far more republican than any that Congress is likely to assign us; for give us one when you will, it will be more or less a military government, and no military government can be republican. Gentlemen of this people's branch of Congress, spare this government to us! It is our own handiwork—the emanation of our own free will and choice—the creation of our own native people and not of strangers—a government grappled to us by the strong hooks of a thousand dear associations of nativity and home, and twice a thousand sweet memories, yet lingering around the broken vase, that will bid us look wishfully back to the stars and stripes, and "bring the light of other days around us." I invoke you again, wrest not this our own cherished government from us! "Woodman! Spare that tree."

Let us remember, unceasingly, one thing, that which should be written "in letters of living light" over the lintel of every American door and deep engraven on every American heart, that in this country Governments spring from the people, not the people from Governments.

And is it clear that Congress has any rightful authority to interfere aught with this Government of ours? Can it interpose by virtue of its obligation to guaranty to each State a republican form of government? Mr. Madison, in the forty-third number of the Federalist, expressly declares that his obligation extends only to a guarantee against "aristocratic or monarchical innovations." Has there been in our State government any aristocratic or monarchical innovation? Have we any privileged classes, any titled nobility, any sceptered king? None. Then Congress cannot intermeddle. There is nothing to guaranty. As to us, it is *functus officio*. In this regard its "occupation is gone;" or, rather, it never had any.

And according to the same illustrious authority, having maintained continuously republican institutions, we have a right even to "claim the Federal guarantee." And this is just what we do. We demand your assurance of this our republican form of government. We claim protection, not extinction, at your hands. If you do not give us the protection you fail of your constitutional duty, and thrust us into revolution.

One more point and I have done. I am not unaware that whispers have been going around of my disloyalty. I am not unaware that calumny, guided by sordid meanness and black corruption, has escaped to "filch from me my good name" in this regard. I know it well. Villainy generally aims to cover up its foot-marks, but sometimes, as if Providence were looking on to punish it, it does not put soil enough over to disguise them. In this matter I have trailed its tortuous track, and traced out all its dark doings. By letters clandestinely used in 1861 in this Hall—so clandestinely that I never got sight of them, though I did learn casually the base purport of them—it made its stealthy effort to prevent me from taking my seat in this body that it might be filled on a new election by one of the arch-conspirators, who is unworthy to unloose the lachet of any Union man's shoes; and from that hour to this this puppy villainy has been barking at my heels, never once halting at hypocrisy, falsehood or fraud. But this I will say, no man of honor and truth, and no one himself truly and disinterestedly loyal, ever impeached my loyalty. And I must say that if I am disloyal I have a strange way of showing it. I do not deny that I made an effort to go with my State. Following the instincts that bind us all to the land under whose sod the bones of our ancestors rest, and where loved kindred live, I did endeavor to find arguments to reconcile me to secession. It was the struggle of a not uneventful life. I saw the bark of my State as she was about to set out on her perilous voyage. There she was, "all in the Downs." I watched her as she left her moorings and neared the pier to take in her freight of human life, and I gazed on the eager throng as it pressed down to the pier.

Among the first to tread her decks was my own and only son—a noble boy, around whom had gathered the honors of the university of his State, but who, alas! yielded to that fatal infatuation that a citizen must go with his State, right or wrong. Another look, and two unbearded youths, fresh from the college hall, my orphaned nephews, loved and cared for as my own children, followed that son. I looked again, and there stepped aboard as magnificent a specimen of mortality as ever eye rested on. And beside him stood one of queenly mien, his beautiful wife, my own dear child. And clinging to the mother was her cherub boy. There they all were; the son and the nephews were there, Aeneas was there, and Creusa, and the boy Ascanius. But old father Anchises was not there. He stood upon the shore eyeing the flapping canvas, a struggle going on in his bosom which loosened the very heart strings, a struggle which I pray God may never wring my soul again—an agonizing struggle between instinct on the one hand and conscience on the other—a struggle whether I should follow the most loved on earth or stand by my country. But, blessed be God! conscience triumphed over instinct. I loved the stars and stripes better than my own flesh and blood!

I disloyal! I who have loved this Union from my boyhood; who have worshiped at its altars with as pure and deep a devotion as ever bowed down votary there; who (as I have said on other occasions) have all my life regarded the Constitution of the United States as "the best system of civil liberty that ever emanated from human hearts and human heads, and the accumulated political wisdom of the world from the time of Magna Charta to 1789!" Disloyal to that Union which (I have often said) is connected in my mind with a thousand, and twice a thousand, glorious associations; with the wisdom that conceived and the blood that cemented it; with our prosperity and strength at home and our power and glory abroad; with that gallant flag that flings out the stars and stripes of our great country on every ocean, lake, and gulf, and sea; with that renown which exhibits her unconquered on a thousand battle fields; with all the bright glories of the past and brighter hopes of the future—disloyal to a Union like this! No, no!

Letter

(Philadelphia: J. B. Lippincott and Co., 1864)

J eremiah Clemens (1814–1865) was born near Huntsville, Alabama, attended the University of Alabama, and graduated in law from Transylvania College in Kentucky. He served in the Alabama legislature from 1839 to 1844, commanded a regiment during the Mexican War, and entered the U.S. Senate in 1849. Before the Civil War, Clemens also wrote a number of novels in which he argued against southern radicalism. In 1859 he lived in Memphis, Tennessee, and edited a unionist newspaper. As a member of the Alabama secession convention, he vigorously opposed secession but did not vote against it. Early in the war Clemens led an Alabama regiment, but he soon entered the Union lines, escaped to Philadelphia for medical treatment, and wrote a number of pamphlets under the auspices of the Union League that he addressed to Alabama's unionists. He also wrote the novel *Tobias Wilson* (1865), in which he depicted the harsh, physical violence perpetrated on Alabama's unionists.

The pamphlet included herein, written in October 1864, was directed to a friend in Alabama. In it Clemens discussed why some Alabamians stuck with the Union, castigated the war effort of the Confederate government as evil and destructive, and urged his friends to support reconstruction of the state. Rumors, vivid stories, and quotations from aggrieved victims of the Confederacy abound in this fictionalist's most effective pamphlet. Clemens even suggests an evil foreign power is in league with the Davis government to invade the United States.

Despite his important political and writing careers, Clemens has had no major biographer. For information on his life see William Garrett, *Reminiscences of Public Men in Alabama* (Atlanta: Plantation Publication Co., 1872); Virginia Clay-Clopton, *Belle of the 1850s* (New York: Doubleday, Page and Co., 1904); and Edward McPherson, *The Political History of the United*

States during the Great Rebellion, 1860–1865 (Washington, D.C.: Phelps and Solomon, 1865).

* * *

I have heretofore called your attention to the delusions under which the Southern people have so long labored, and the arts by which they have been led on from the surrender of one right to another—from one calamity to a still greater—from independence, prosperity, and happiness, to misery, humiliation, and slavery. Secession, in any aspect, was a wrong and an outrage. It never presented itself in any form which was not repugnant and repelling. It was based upon the destruction of a great government, whose people were the happiest the sun of heaven had ever warmed, and it launched a whole nation upon an unknown sea, whose shoals and quicksands no plummet had ever sounded, and whose winds and currents no mariner had ever tested. Wild and dangerous as the experiment was, many good, and wise, and virtuous men, who had battled against it to the last, when the mischief was once done, from feelings of State pride, or local affections, gave it their earnest support. Others, again, united in it under the delusive belief that they could in that way best avert some of the calamities they dreaded in the future. At first we had none but fair and glorious promises. The rights of the States were to be scrupulously regarded; individual liberty to be protected; and freedom of the press and speech guaranteed to every citizen. We were to have the best currency in the world; our commerce was to be world-wide, and the prosperity and wealth flowing from it illimitable. In short, there was no governmental good for which a citizen could ask which was not to be secured to us. These were the promises. What has been the fulfillment? The rights of the States have been trampled under foot so often, and so ruthlessly, that they have ceased to regard themselves as anything more than mere corporations. They are altogether ignored as sovereignties. When Jeff. Davis wants soldiers, he does not make a requisition upon the Governors of States, but sends his own minions to run down and catch hapless citizens wherever they can find them. When he wants provisions, he sends out a press-gang to rob at will. In January last, he read the Governor of North Carolina a lecture upon the subject of "traitors" in his own State, whose treason consisted in a respectful petition for the appointment of Commissioners to treat for peace, and which petition had been called to his attention by an equally respectful letter from the Governor himself. He very cavalierly informs the Governor that he does not know anything about his own people, and that although the Governor may believe them "to be sound at heart," their "loyalty is more than suspected elsewhere." He further warns the Governor to "spare your State the scenes of civil war, which will devastate its homes, if the designs of these traitors be allowed to make headway." It was perfectly right and proper for North Carolina to leave the old Union, under which she had grown great, powerful, rich, and happy. It was then a sacred and inalienable right to violate a compact by which the State had agreed to be bound forever. Then there was not an unfledged chicken, in the whole Secession brood, who could tolerate the bare idea of "coercing a sovereign State;" and, for attempting to preserve unimpaired the Union our fathers made, Mr. Lincoln was, and still is, denounced as a tyrant, the Federal Congress as a band of ferocious miscreants, Gen. Grant as a butcher, Gen. Sherman as a merciless ruffian, Gen. Butler as a beast, and, lastly, the people of the North were proclaimed incapable of self-government—miserable tools of the "basest and most degraded despotism," who had "profoundly disgraced themselves" by an "ignoble love of gold and brutifying fanaticism." These, and many other *mild and gentlemanly* epithets, were applied to all who dared to doubt the right of a single State to destroy the liberty and happiness of the whole. But all that is changed when the principle of Secession comes to be applied in Jeff. Davis's dominions. The people of North Carolina are now told that they shall not even *consider* the question of restoring the Union; and their Governor is warned that if he does not repress the expression of every wish for a return to more peaceful times, his State will be desolated with fire and sword.[1] Good God! how blind must that infatuation be which bows the necks of an unquestionably brave and gallant people beneath a yoke so galling—a despotism so pitiless as this!

The *Mobile Tribune*, in an article, unblushingly acknowledges that the whole land is "only a great camp," in which, of course, neither States nor individuals have rights, save at the will of the Dictator who controls it.

I could add a great deal more, but this is enough to show how faithfully promise No. 1 has been kept.

The next was the protection of individual liberty, and freedom of speech and the press.

Need I go further than to ask you what liberty you enjoy? You have indeed a Constitution which assures you that your property shall not be taken for public use without due compensation. Let me suppose that you are sitting

---

1. Clemens is referring to Gov. Zebulon B. Vance and the North Carolina peace initiative of 1864.

in your back piazza upon a summer's day, refreshing your memory by a reperusal of that charter of your liberties; upon raising your eyes from the page, you see five or six men, with bowie-knives and revolvers belted around them, making an examination of your stable yard. You walk out, book in hand, to inquire their business. "We want horses for the Confederate army," is the response.

Q. What authority have you to take mine?

A. The order of our Captain.

Q. What authority has he to issue such an order?

A. We don't know, and don't care. We want horses, and he told us to take them wherever we found them.

You go on to remonstrate: "But, gentlemen, I have but one good horse; the others have already been taken by the Confederacy; and this Constitution says you shall not take my property without due compensation."

You are answered, "D—n the Constitution, and you too! We must have the horse, and, as for pay, we will give you a receipt, and if you will come up to the camp the quartermaster will give you a voucher." A voucher, be it remembered, to be paid in Confederate notes, at some uncertain time, worth somewhere from three to five cents on the dollar! You are helpless, and you turn away. But if you imagine you have got rid of them, you are mistaken. You have hardly reached your own door before you are followed with a demand for something to eat. You have nothing cooked. "Well, give us your smoke-house key." And while some are helping themselves in the smoke-house, some are killing your poultry in the yard, and another has found his way to your weaving room, and is deliberately cutting a piece of cloth from your wife's loom.

About this time your son comes up. The marauders have loaded themselves with plunder, and they now turn their attention to the boy. "How old are you, my lad?" "Seventeen." "Just the right age for a soldier. There is a conscript officer at camp who will be glad to see you. So come along." You argue, you remonstrate in vain. You tell them the Constitution gives the President no power to call out any but the militia, and that what constitutes the militia is determined, by law, to be only those persons between the ages of eighteen and forty-five. The answer you probably receive is, that "you are a d—n-d old Union traitor," and that you had better hush up or it will be the worse for you. And thus you are compelled to submit, in powerless agony, to personal insult, the robbery of your property, and the kidnapping of your child. As a last resource, you resolve to appeal to the commanding officer. On the way you discover that forty or fifty more horses are feeding on your growing crop, and that your fences have been torn away to make cooking fires for the soldiery. You approach the commander; you state your case; but the soldiers have been before you,—you are informed, in no delicate language, that you are suspected of being a Union traitor, and are forthwith hurried off, *on suspicion*, to some higher military authority.

I do not say that all these things have happened to any one man, but they are all liable to happen, and all of them have happened, some to one, and some to another citizen. You and I can both point to many instances. We know of one citizen who was arrested and carried far beyond the limits of his State to the camp of Gen. Forrest, who manifested his chivalry by striking his manacled prisoner in the mouth.[2] We know of another, who was barbarously cut down with a sabre for daring to remonstrate against the impressment of his horse. But it would be too tedious to enumerate all the cases of wrong, outrage, and robbery within our own knowledge. There is already enough to show what amount of *personal* liberty you enjoy.

How stands the case as to freedom of speech and of the press? There is not a paper in all the land whose proprietor dares to publish one syllable which indicates a feeling of love and reverence for the old Union, or the slightest desire to return to it. And when friends of the Union meet, they speak in whispers, or retire to back rooms beyond the hearing of any listening ear. This is the sort of freedom of speech and of the press which you know, as well as I do, that you are now enjoying.

The next promise was, that you should be supplied with the best currency in the world. If this were only a failure—if it only appeared that those who deceived you were themselves deceived, there might be an excuse for pity as well as cause for censure. But such is not the case; the Confederate government deliberately violated a published contract. It issued notes bearing interest at the rate of eight per cent per annum, and when these notes had been widely diffused among the people, Congress repudiated the interest, thus diminishing the value of the notes, and robbing its own citizens in a far greater ratio,—the actual repudiation not being their only or greatest loss; because the destruction of all confidence in the honesty and integrity of the government which resulted from it caused a greater depreciation, and was as much a robbery as if the sum had been directly taken from the pockets of the people. The next step was to *tax its own notes* twenty-five per cent, and now they are to be taxed one hundred per cent, (just all,) unless they are returned to the Treasury by the first day of January next: a species of knavery too open and undisguised to be termed chicanery.

2. Confederate cavalry general and sometimes guerrilla Nathan Bedford Forrest.

Thus, by the acts of the Government itself, its currency has been rendered so worthless that it has no market value at all, even in the city of Richmond. I will not say that there would not have been great depreciation in any event, but, as long as the people believed the Government honest, it could not have fallen so low.

Of like character were the commercial promises with which you were deluded. Instead of an illimitable commerce, you have none at all. Families accustomed to every luxury are now compelled to put up with the plainest clothing and the humblest fare. Eight months ago a lady's parasol, of no extraordinary fineness, was estimated to be worth four hundred dollars in Augusta, Georgia. Sugar and coffee are now in many places unattainable, and soon they will be unattainable everywhere. Even your cotton is comparatively valueless. In the beginning of the war you were told that *Cotton was King.* If so, three years of blockade have sapped the foundations of his throne and the monarch has tumbled into dust. You cannot transport it beyond the Confederate lines; if you sell it at home, you get nothing but Confederate scrip; if you keep it, the first petty officer in Confederate uniform who has a fancy to look upon a bonfire will burn it before your eyes. You have no commerce, absolutely none; but you have the consolation of knowing that you have nothing to sell which your Government will let you sell, and no money to buy anything with.

This picture of your free, and happy, and glorious Confederacy, I know you will feel in your heart is rather under than overdrawn. But I do not expect you to say so, or even to *think* it, *within sight* of one of Jefferson Davis's officials or toadies.

How long will this be borne I cannot tell. I have been absent for months from the happy land of Dixie, and in revolutionary times great changes are often effected in a much shorter period; but it is evident that the Powers at Richmond think you are prepared for still further debasement. But recently I read an article in a Southern paper which made all the blood tingle in my veins. Here it is. Read it, and remember that it comes from a South Carolina journal—a journal not only of high, but the highest respectability and widest circulation in the State:—

From the *Charleston Courier, Sept. 23.*

"It can do now no added injury to reprint in the *Courier* the report below, given from the Richmond correspondence of the *Constitutionalist:—*

" 'I wrote you, a short time ago, in regard to a contemplated arrangement between the Confederate Government and a commissioner representing a certain European population. I am now in condition to state, that the desired *entente cordiale* has been fully established.

" 'The envoys, consisting, as stated in a previous letter, of two army officers and a clergyman of the Catholic church, were admitted to an audience with the President, and an arrangement was effected that cannot be otherwise than conducive to our interests. This agreement, as I have heard, gives us the service, most probably, at an early day, of some thirty thousand soldiers of approved valor, and of a race famous for military endurance. The President promised to use his influence with the respective State Governments in the matter of securing for those whom the Commissioners represented, as much land as would suit them for colonizing purposes. Of course the President could not guarantee the colonists the allotment of lands in the States, and, as the scant Confederate territorial possessions are, for the most part, in but a dubious occupancy of our arms, it would have been useless to enter into any compact by which the immigrating population would have been compelled to rely upon a comparatively unprotected section for a home.

" 'It is, however, understood that all of those who enlist in our armies, and probably nine-tenths of the able-bodied men among the colonists will do so, are to receive the soldier's land bounty, thus meeting in a measure the requirements put forth by the Commissioners, who are now on their way to Europe to carry out the arrangements of the treaty. I understand that there will be no difficulty in the departure of these immigrants from their own country, and as they are expected to arrive during the winter months, we may confidently hope (should nothing occur to mar the plan) to witness at the beginning of the spring campaign a grand army of foreign allies, of a race that, centuries ago, smote the Saracen's power in Europe, and drove back the tide of Turkish aggression upon Constantinople.' "

What has become of the boasted chivalry of the South? Where are the braggarts who could kill two Yankees, and run away two more every morning for breakfast? And what strange change has come over the hero President, who promised you, at the Huntsville Depot, that the war would be waged on Northern, not on Southern soil? Is this negotiator with foreign adventurers; this trafficker for the swords of a mercenary band, alike ignorant of our laws and our language, the same haughty chief who proudly proclaimed to his army that the next time the hated Yankees crossed the Potomac he would be among them, not to say "go on," but "come on?" Has the head of a great nation descended so low as to barter with individuals for the bayonets of ruffians, and to promise them in payment for their blood lands which are not his, and can only become his by the plunder of Southern citizens? Are these the hopes which were held out to you when, every evening, lovely forms gathered about the depot, and lovely hands scattered bouquets of flowers upon every passing soldier; while still more lovely eyes grew brilliant with added lustre as words of thanks for their sweet encouragement were mingled with earnest promises to achieve a glorious independence, or an honored grave? Alas! those roses have withered, and the proud leader of a once great, and still courageous people, is bargaining away their lands for the support of the runaway slaves of a despot.

One of the inducements to secession was, that we should have a homogeneous population, speaking the same language, having the same interests, the same laws, and institutions. Mr. Davis proposes to fulfill this stipulation by importing from the heart of Europe a body of colonists who have never heard, much less spoken, a word of English—who never saw a negro, and who have about as correct notions of well-regulated liberty as those of a Poland bear. It is not to be presumed that in his dealings with these men he proposes to practice a fraud upon them, and if he does not, how is he to fulfill his agreement to settle them upon the rich and inviting lands of the South? The Confederacy does not own an acre of land, and the only means it has of obtaining it is to take away the land of citizens.[3]

That he has long cherished some such idea I do not doubt. I do not think my title, or yours, or that of any other original Union man, would be worth much, except in the case of some few individuals, who have wiped out the sin of voting against Secession, by becoming the blind and pliant tools of the Autocrat of Richmond. The success of the rebellion would be certainly followed by an instant robbery, and merciless proscription of the old Union men. If you have not *felt* this already, I have, and you have *seen* too many indications of this remorseless purpose to entertain any doubt upon the subject. It will be of no avail to you that your sons and nephews have thrown away their lives in this most wicked and inhuman war. It will not profit you that you have surrendered, one by one, all the rights and privileges of a freeman, without resistance or remonstrance; the sin of having voted for the Union remains, and for that there is no atonement but abject submission to the will of Jefferson Davis, and unscrupulous obedience to his orders. Even that will be insufficient unless your aid happens to be also necessary in carrying out his future plans.

If the old Union men will not see that to this "complexion *they* must come at last;" if they do not feel that they are a proscribed class; if they cannot now understand with what eagerness every pretext will be seized to confiscate their estates for the benefit of any body of hired ruffians who will undertake to prop Jeff. Davis's throne with their bayonets, they are already half lost.

---

3. I have not been able to verify this charge. However, it smacks of the nativism to which Clemens at one time subscribed.

To them it will be useless to recall the examples of history. It will be idle to remind them that when Rome employed foreign mercenaries to fight her battles, instead of the mistress, she became the scorn of the world. Or, to take an instance from their own ancestral records, how, when England called in the Saxons to defend her against the Danes, in a little while Englishmen became the slaves of the Saxon. Pregnant with instruction as are the lessons of the past, they would be thrown away upon men who refuse to exercise their own senses, and walk on blindly to the grave of liberty, as well as to their own poverty and degradation. I hope better things from those among whom I was born and whom I have cause to love with all a brother's love. I hope they are not prepared for this last act of suicidal infamy. I know that none but the aged and infirm are left among them. I know that the young and the strong have been dragged away by an unsparing conscription, and that their bones are whitening every battlefield from the Potomac to New Orleans: but there is a mode of escape from the soulless tyranny under which they are groaning, and the still greater tyranny with which they are threatened, and whenever they indicate a wish to resort to it, weak and feeble as I am, I shall be among them to point it out, and aid in its successful accomplishment.

Do not for a moment understand that I have the least apprehension that Mr. Davis's negotiations can result in anything of importance. Before he can land this addition to his "homogeneous population" on the Continent of North America, they must cross an ocean three thousand miles in extent, over almost every wave of which the glorious flag of our fathers is floating, and it will be but little short of a miracle if his land-hunting ruffians do not find their possessions at the bottom of the Atlantic. I only refer to it to show what he would do if he could, and as an illustration of what he will do if the Union armies are ever withdrawn, and a peace is patched up which will enable him to pursue his plans for your enslavement without restraint.

I trust you will not take these for the opinions of a man whose feelings are too bitter to allow him to think calmly or reason justly upon the subject. True, I never had any love for the Southern Confederacy, and no faith in its success. I opposed it earnestly to the last; but when the fiat went forth, too many of my friends and relatives became involved in its meshes to admit of continued opposition on my part. Many of those friends, and the nearest and dearest of these relatives, are now in the grave. The experiment of Secession has had a long and bloody trial. Its inevitable results are now apparent to the meanest comprehension. If you succeed you are slaves, and failure—immediate failure—is the best wish the best friend of the South can frame. I think I can look at it calmly and reason upon it dispassionately.

I have no longer any personal interest in the struggle, but I would gladly do something to save your families from the desolation which has visited mine. To insure this there is but one course to pursue, and that is to return to the allegiance which was so recklessly thrown off. I tell you now, as I told you in 1860, that the people of the North will gladly meet you half way. There is none of that bitterness of feeling toward *the people* of the South which your leaders tell you exists. They understand far better than you imagine how you were dragged into rebellion, and have no disposition to lay the sin at any door but where it justly belongs. Dismiss from your minds the delusions by which they have been clouded. You cannot get foreign aid, and it would not be worth the price you must pay for it if you could. Put no faith in divisions among the people of the North. There are party divisions it is true; there are differences of opinion as to the mode of conducting the war, and the best means of bringing about an honorable peace; but upon the one great question, that of restoring the Union, there is unanimity.

The election of McClellan, if that were possible, would only prolong the war, and make the desolation of your land more complete.[4] He might suspend military operations for a time, and negotiate for a peace, but the only terms Jefferson Davis will ever offer him will be such as he dare not accept. Mr. Davis has no idea of abdicating his sovereignty; and if McClellan were so mad as to accede to his demands, his own residence would soon be a less comfortable one than the White House at Washington. From this source, therefore, you have nothing to expect but still greater eventual destitution and prolonged misery—evils, it is true, which will be shared in some degree by the North; but that is a poor consolation. The plain and direct road to peace is before you. You need not consult Mr. Davis, or Mr. Lincoln, or Mr. McClellan on the subject. You went out by separate State action; you can come back in the same way. In the Southern Confederacy, at least, there ought to be no denial of your right to do so. It was the doctrine the leaders inculcated when they wished you to please them by going out of the Union, and they cannot object to it when you wish to please yourselves by going in. This is your remedy—a remedy independent of the will or wishes of those who are compromised too deeply to expect ready forgiveness, and who wish to make you the sharers of their own destiny, provided always that destiny is calamitous.

If the love of law, order, and tranquillity still holds a place in your bosoms—if you are wearied with carnage, and worn out by exactions—if

4. The reference is to the presidential election of 1864 and the Democratic candidacy of former general George B. McClellan.

the sanctity of your homes is yet dear to you, and if the freedom and welfare of your children and your children's children, for generations to come, claim a serious thought, you ought to abandon at once the attitude of armed resistance to a Government which never wronged you, and a people whose hearts now bleed in sympathy with yours over the miseries which the mad ambition of your leaders has produced. Return, as you may now do without dishonor, to the protection of that banner which has been for nearly a century the symbol of freedom and the harbinger of happiness. You have exhibited on the battle-field a heroism which, in a better cause, would have won for you immortal honor. Prove to the world that you are capable of the still higher heroism of *daring to do right* in defiance of the scoffs or sneers, or threatened coercion of the guilty criminals who led you astray.

Letter to the Hon. Henry Winter Davis

(New Orleans: H. P. Lathrop, 1864)

Thomas Jefferson Durant (1817–ca. 1874) was born in Pennsylvania, came to New Orleans as a youth of fourteen, worked on newspapers, and became a Democrat. When the Civil War began he served as a private in the Louisiana militia. After the Union army captured New Orleans, Durant joined the Louisiana free state party and soon became a leader of its radical antislavery faction. He went into opposition against Gov. Michael Hahn and Anthony P. Dostie when he accused them of trying to slow down the movement to end slavery in the state. An ardent reconstructionist, Durant opposed the state constitutional convention of 1864 and became a close ally of northern congressional abolitionists. His role in the breakup of the state's unionist faction certainly hurt the reconstruction loyalist cause. Although he did not come under direct attack, Durant left Louisiana shortly after the New Orleans riot of 1866. There is little information on his later life, save that he probably lived for a time in Washington, D.C., and perhaps New York City.

This pamphlet, printed from a letter of October 27, 1864, to Congressman Henry Winter Davis of Maryland, reveals much about the role the Federal Congress and the occupying Federal army played in Louisiana unionist politics. In it Durant asked for congressional support in behalf of the New Orleans freedman. He also tried to undermine the voting power of the established unionist leadership in the city. He insists that the Federal army controls too little of the state to execute a valid election. There are some hints in the pamphlet that these battles among wartime unionists may have begun even before the war.

A most supportive study of Durant's wartime activities is Joseph G. Tregle, "Thomas J. Durant, Utopian Socialism, and the Failure of Presidential Reconstruction in Louisiana," *Journal of Southern History* 45 (November

1979): 485–512. For a corrective to Tregle, see Ted Tunnell, *Crucible of Reconstruction: War, Radicalism, and Race in Louisiana, 1862–1877* (Baton Rouge: Louisiana State University Press, 1984), and William C. Harris, *With Charity for All: Lincoln and the Restoration of the Union* (Lexington: University Press of Kentucky, 1997). There are Durant papers in the New-York Historical Society.

* * *

The letter addressed to Hon. J. H. Lane, U.S. Senator from Kansas, which appeared in the New Orleans papers of the 24th September last, signed by Major General N. P. Banks, has, no doubt, received a full share of your attention.[1]

The reputation which Gen. Banks brought with him to Louisiana for statesmanship and administrative ability, gives to all he says on civil matters, here, a claim to respectful consideration; while his character as a gentleman, repels the idea that he has in any instance, or in any degree, in the course of his communication, been led into wilful misrepresentation. He has, however, in my opinion, fallen into some essential errors of fact and law, which, in the most respectful manner, as a citizen of Louisiana, it becomes my duty to point out.

The letter to Senator Lane treats of "the Reconstruction bill" which passed both houses of Congress at the last session: seeks to show "its agreement with the new Louisiana Constitution," and enters into a defense of the Louisiana elections held under his orders.

The act of Congress for guaranteeing republican government to the States declared to be in insurrection against the United States, was inferior in importance to no measure that has ever been considered in the national councils. Its immediate relation to the rebellion, its effectual scheme for permanently removing the curse of slavery, together with the exalted patriotism and ability of its authors, had made a deep and general impression upon the mind of the nation.

The bill was reported to the House of Representatives early in April last, was fully debated there, and passed on the 4th of May. It was reported to the Senate on the 27th of May, debated there, and finally passed as it came from the House, on the 2d of July.

---

1. Gen. Nathaniel P. Banks was the military commander in New Orleans.

On the eighth day of July, the President published his well known proclamation with regard to this bill, annexing thereto a copy of the act in full. This proclamation was received in New Orleans by the 19th of July, when the Constitutional Convention elected under General Orders No. 35, from the Head Quarters of the Department of the Gulf, was in session, and we are told "that the proclamation of the President, and the protest of the Hon. Messrs. Wade and Davis, relating to this measure, attracted general attention here"; which indeed could scarcely have been otherwise, as the bill was an authoritative condemnation by the only branch of the Government invested with power over the subject, by the Constitution, of all that the Major General commanding the Department was then engaged in, so far as the reorganization of civil government was concerned, though until recently, before the 24th of the following September, he had "not had an opportunity to examine the bill passed at the late session of Congress, providing for the reconstruction of Government in rebel States," a period at which examination became supererogatory, as the work of the Louisiana Convention had been submitted to the vote of what is called "the people of Louisiana," and proclaimed adopted.[2] We are further told that in the mean time "no attention was given to the provisions of the bill for reconstruction of government in seceding States, and but little interest was manifested in legislation on that subject."

This inattention to a question that was worthy, in itself, of the deepest reflection, arose from the fundamental difference of opinion which exists between the Congress and the President in relation to their respective powers over the subject of reorganization of civil government in the insurrectionary States. The President pretends to the right, in his military character, as commander-in-chief, to organize State Governments designed to survive the war, and, in the mean time possessing the right to participate in the government of the country by sending Senators and Representatives to Congress, and to cast votes, as States, in the presidential election. This power, the Constitution and Courts of the country, have declared does not exist in the executive department, but belongs exclusively to Congress. Gen. Banks adopts in its fullest extent the presidential idea, saying, "no declaration of war can be made without consent of Congress, but once waged by its order, it cannot restrict the power of the President as commander in chief." Giving this language its full meaning, would place the President above all law, and render the deliberations and acts of Congress useless

---

2. The reference is to the Wade-Davis reconstruction bill of Sen. Benjamin Wade of Pennsylvania and Rep. Henry Winter Davis of Maryland.

in time of war; but limiting the application of the language to the subject matter of debate, it plainly means, that when the President chooses to order a Maj-General to organize a State Government in a State in insurrection, his power to do so is supreme, though exercised against the will of Congress. Such a doctrine is of the most dangerous character, and it is to be hoped will not be adopted by the Representatives of the Nation. It is not to be supposed that a reconstruction bill in Congress would attract much of the attention of the military department, when such views of the power of the Commander-in-Chief were entertained.

The whole course of proceedings, then, in regard to the reorganization of civil government in Louisiana, must be judged under the knowledge, that their managers conscientiously believed that the President, in his military capacity, was the sole master of the situation, and that his will alone was the law of the case.

The will of the President, however, is not exclusively relied on, and General Banks endeavors to show that his action in "Louisiana corresponds completely to the requisition of Congress."

To this portion of his letter it is necessary to devote some attention. An account of what was actually done in Louisiana, so far as it can be examined from an outside point of view, will convince you that neither the provisions of the act of Congress, nor the Constitution and laws of the State of Louisiana, supposing them to be in force, were complied with.

The act of Congress contemplates a civil organization: what was done here is purely military. The first section of the act of Congress directs the appointment by the President of a provisional Governor by and with the advice and consent of the Senate. The provisional Governor of the State of Louisiana, Mr. Hahn, was appointed by the President alone and in his military capacity, and as far as the letter of appointment shows, without the concurrence of any member of his cabinet.[3]

The second section of the act provides that the reorganization of the state government shall commence only when "the military resistance to the United States shall have been suppressed in the State." So far from that happy condition having been achieved, the rebels had undisputed control of far more than half the territory of the State, during the whole time of these proceedings. The same section of this act also provides that the Marshal of the United States, (a civil officer) shall make an enrolment of citizens, preparatory to a proclamation of the provisional Governor, calling upon the

3. Michael Hahn of New Orleans, whose pamphlet in this volume represents many who opposed Durant.

loyal people of the State to elect delegates to a Convention, to declare the will of the people, as to the re-establishment of a State Government.

The third section of the act provides that the convention shall consist of as many members as both Houses of the last Constitutional State Legislature, to be apportioned by the provisional Governor among the counties, parishes or districts of the State, in proportion to the white population returned as electors by the Marshal, &c.

On this point General Banks says: "delegates to the Convention were apportioned to the white population, not of enrolled electors merely, but of the whole State, and the number fixed as prescribed by the Constitution and laws of the State applicable to Legislative Assemblies."

You may ask why, in the above paragraph, is the expression, "enrolled electors," put in apposition to the words "the whole State"? It is because, in only a part of the State were electors enrolled; for in the greater number of parishes, no enrollment was made, nor was any possible, as they were under the control of the rebel government; notwithstanding which, an election was gravely ordered to be held in every parish of the State, though impossible to be effected; and a convention assembled under this order which purported to represent all the parishes. . . . [4]

Two capital errors must be considered in this declaration. In the first place the military power of the United States is only competent for military purposes, and cannot constitute a civil government of a State; and in the second place no such officers elected in such a way could be a civil government under the Constitution and laws of Louisiana; because those enactments pointed out an entirely different mode for the election of officers. The result of the action prompted by General Banks' proclamation, was in accordance with these views; the form of election which was gone through with was considered by the President merely as the indication of a fit and proper person for the office of military Governor, and the Commander in Chief of the Army and Navy conferred an informal appointment of that character upon Mr. Hahn, who had been returned as having received a majority of the votes cast at that election. The commencement and the end therefore were purely military, and partook in no degree of a civil character.

On the 11th of March, 1864, General Banks issued, from his Head Quarters, Department of the Gulf, "General Orders No. 35." They said: "An election will be held on Monday, the 28th day of March, at 9 o'clock, A.M.,

4. Durant here prints General Banks's January 11, 1864, proclamation on holding an election.

in each of the Election Precincts established by law in this State, for a choice of Delegates to a Convention to be held for the revision and amendment of the Constitution of Louisiana."

One might suppose from this, that there was no opposition to the authority of the United States in Louisiana; and that to hold an election in each of the precincts established by law in the State, was a matter that no Union man would hesitate to undertake. Yet, the fact was, that in more than one-half of the Parishes of the State no avowed adherent of the National cause could be found. It will be observed that this Order is for a revision of the Constitution existing, which harmonizes with the prior Proclamation of the General, declaring the Constitution and Laws of the State (except such as related to slavery) to be in force. The second section of the General Orders No. 35 declares that "the several Parishes shall be entitled to elect the number of Delegates herein assigned to each, upon the basis of white population exhibited by the Census of 1860, to be chosen in each Parish, on one ticket, by the qualified voters of the Parish, except in the Parish of Orleans, in which Parish the election shall be held in the several representative districts established by law, for the number of Delegates herein assigned to each District, as follows, to-wit:" then going on to name each one of the forty-eight Parishes of the State, stating the white population of each from the Census of 1860, and assigning to each its number of Delegates in the Convention; making an aggregate of one hundred and fifty members, of which sixty-three were assigned to the parish and city of New Orleans.

This was done under a distinct declaration that the Constitution and Laws of Louisiana—except in regard to slavery—were in force; and is followed by the statement, in the letter to Senator Lane, that "the number of delegates was fixed as prescribed by the Constitution and Laws of the State, applicable to Legislative Assemblies." . . . [5]

The General Orders No. 35, established a representative number of two thousand two hundred and fifty-one, and the basis of the white population. The Constitution and laws of Louisiana established a representative number of six thousand nine hundred and twenty and the basis of the total population.

The General Orders No. 35, assigned to New Orleans city and parish sixty-three Delegates; the constitution and laws of Louisiana gave them twenty-six.

5. Durant quotes the Louisiana Constitution of 1852 on the number of delegates.

By General Orders No. 35, the Convention was to be composed of one hundred and fifty Delegates. By the constitution and laws of Louisiana, it should have consisted of one hundred and thirty members only.

Thus General Banks's order for an election of Delegates to the Constitutional Convention was an absolute departure from the Constitution and laws of the State, and in plain contradiction of the Act of Congress.

He apportioned the representation on the white population only, instead of the whole.

He ordered one hundred and fifty members to be elected to the Convention instead of one hundred and thirty.

He obliterated the Senatorial Districts and the legal provision for their representation.

He gave New Orleans sixty-three Delegates instead of twenty-six.

He essentially changed the representation of the other parishes.

Nor was this done without deliberation. Before issuing General Orders No. 35, he appointed a committee consisting of Rufus K. Howell, Alfred Shaw and James Ready, three citizens of New Orleans, "to consider the questions connected with the calling a State Convention and the election of Delegates." In their report to the General, made on the 3d March, 1864, the Committee say, their attention was directed *by him* to the following questions: . . . [6]

Now, inasmuch as all these questions were definitely settled by the Constitution and laws of Louisiana, proclaimed to be in force, the fact that the Major General Commanding referred their solution to a committee, showed that he did not intend to be bound either by law or Constitution. The report of the committee solved most of the questions in a sense contrary to the Constitution and the laws, and their report was, in its leading features, adopted by the Major General and embodied in his General Orders No. 35; and therefore, he cannot but be in error in saying that the Constitution and laws were followed.

Although the General Orders No. 35 directed, as has been seen, an election of Delegates in each of the forty-eight parishes of the State, yet it was well known that in a majority of parishes no elections could be held. Accordingly the third paragraph of said Orders states that "Any parish *not now* within the lines of the army shall be entitled to send Delegates as herein specified, at any time before the dissolution of the Convention, should such parish be brought within the lines of the army."

6. Durant lists the questions, including one on the basis of representation.

which is an acknowledgement that the programme announced could not be carried out, though silence is preserved as to the real extent of this impracticality. . . . [7]

The vote in the Convention on the adoption of the Constitution as a whole, was in the aggregate eighty-two, of which sixty-six were in the affirmative, and sixteen in the negative—see journal p. 165; and as the whole number of Delegates ordered to be elected by "General Orders No. 35" was one hundred and fifty, and as a quorum to do business consisted of not less than seventy-six, it appears the Constitution was finally adopted by a vote less by ten than a quorum, and only equal to the number of Delegates from New Orleans, with three Delegates from the country; so that New Orleans and Jefferson, which are as closely allied as New York and Brooklyn, were enough to constitute this "regenerated" State.

On the report of the Committee on Enrolment, the number of members who signed the Constitution was only sixty, being sixteen less than a quorum. See Journal, p. 170.

The Convention has not been dissolved, a resolution having been adopted, sixty-two to fourteen—a bare quorum—to re-assemble again in certain contingencies—same page.

One curious feature may be noticed here, although not strictly within the scope of the present branch of the inquiry. On the last day of the sitting of the Convention, Mr. Fish offered a series of patriotic and loyal resolutions, referring in a preamble to the Secession Convention and its treasonable Ordinance of separation; and declaring, 1st, that the people denounce the doctrine of State Rights and sovereignty, interpreted as a justification of secession: 2d, declaring a primary allegiance to the United States, and that the ordinance of secession was a nullity; 3d, declaring the desire of the Convention that Slavery should be abolished through the whole country by an amendment to the Constitution of the United States. These concurrent resolutions were, indeed, adopted, but by only sixty-eight in the affirmative and eight in the negative; thus showing that not even a number equal to a bare quorum of the Convention could be found to endorse the principles laid down.

On recurring to the report of the Secretary of State, and to that of the Committee on Credentials above referred to, it will be found that S. A. Lobdell is returned as elected from the Parish of West Baton Rouge, but he never, as I am informed, appeared in the Convention. It

---

7. Durant cites the members elected from the various parishes to the convention in order to show that New Orleans received too many delegates.

is difficult to understand how an election could have been held in that parish, or in Avoyelles, Rapides or Madison, nor have the public ever had any official information on that subject. Certain it is, however, that when the Constitution was submitted to the popular vote for ratification, no votes were cast, according to the Proclamation of Governor Hahn of 19th September, 1864, in the parishes of West Baton Rouge, Avoyelles or Rapides, either for or against the Constitution; so that no election could be held at that time in these parishes which it was maintained had sent seven members to the Convention. On the other hand, by the same Proclamation of the 19th September, it is declared that the question of ratification was voted upon in the parishes of Pointe Coupee, St. Martin, St. Charles, Iberville and St. Landry, though these parishes were not returned as having elected any members to the Convention, and no members sat in it from those parishes. . . . [8]

It is clear, that such a Board as this could make no pretension to be organized according to law, and therefore no commissioners appointed by it would be "legal," in the true civil meaning of the word; they would derive all their powers from the military authority of the United States.

The Board thus constituted, proceeded to perform the acts required by the laws of the State. . . . [9]

Such are the official proceedings of the Board. They speak for themselves. Their official publication had been perverted and falsified, none of those present appeared to know by whom. When such things can be done with success, what assurance or guarantee have the people of fairness in the election? or how can it properly be said that such an election was conducted according to the laws of the State?

By the official returns of the election published in the True Delta of September 7th, it appears that the following votes were polled at the four extra legal polls interpolated upon the advertisement of the Board of Commissioners, on the question of adoption of the Constitution. . . . [10]

These votes were not cast according to the Constitution and laws of Louisiana.

The General, in his letter to Senator Lane, further says, "the Delegates were chosen by white male citizens of the United States, 21 years of age, who had the qualifications required by law."

---

8. Durant lists the commissioners of election and discusses how they were selected.

9. Durant says the board met and added additional precincts, which it was not supposed to do. He also cites a letter opposing the board's actions.

10. Durant publishes the vote from the illegal polling places.

"Soldiers who had enlisted in the Army from the State were permitted to vote at the polls opened at their respective commands by regularly appointed Commissioners of Elections, not by Officers where it was impossible for them to vote in established legal Precincts."

The General pays a just tribute to the merits of the soldiers who have enlisted from this State, when, in another part of his letter he says—

"Nearly ten thousand white troops, and fifteen thousand colored soldiers have been enlisted here in the armies of the Union. They are among the best men in the service. Every battle field from the Rio Grande to Port Hudson and Florida has been honored by their valor and hallowed by their blood."

Every patriot will say with the General, all honor to the brave soldiers of Louisiana. These twenty-five thousand men were as well entitled to participate in the reorganization of civil government as any other equal body of men to be found; fifteen thousand of them were, most likely, all native citizens of the United States. But by the laws of Louisiana, which alone are in question here, not one of the twenty-five thousand was a qualified elector. The 12th Article of the Constitution says: "No soldier, seaman or marine, in the Army or Navy of the United States, shall be entitled to vote at any election in this State."

How many soldiers voted, no means are at hand to ascertain; their votes are not distinguished from others in any official report. . . . [11]

It is publicly stated, and by many believed, in New Orleans, that persons were registered as voters, who had resided only six months in the State, and one month in the Parish, and this too without the proof of citizenship. I have seen a statement to this effect sworn to before a Justice of the Peace who was a clerk in the Registers' office, but have no means of ascertaining what number of voters were so registered; however, if the statement be true, of which I have no doubt, the registration was illegal, and the whole subject ought to be subjected to a satisfactory investigation.

Enough has been shown, in what goes before, to demonstrate that the laws of Louisiana with regard to elections have not been complied with, but that there have been departures from them of the most essential character.

The Act of Congress of the last session, which the President did not sign, provided that at elections "no person who has held or exercised any office, Civil or Military, State or Confederate, under the rebel usurpation, or who have voluntarily borne arms against the United States, shall vote or be eligible to be elected as Delegate at such election." And in reference to this feature General Banks' letter says: "so far as is known no person who

11. Here he cites the laws of who is eligible to vote.

has held office under the Confederate Government, or who has borne arms against the United States, has participated in these elections."

This does not appear to meet the difficulty. Congress desired these persons to be excluded from voting, and serving in the Convention. The rules adopted on the subject of the call of the Convention in Louisiana made no provision for excluding them either as Voters or Delegates. As the vote was by ballot, no means are now at hand of knowing whether any such voted at the elections. But it is known that several who would have been excluded by the Act of Congress, held seats as Delegates in the Convention.

Nor is any such exclusion as the above extract from the Act of Congress provides for, embodied in the new Constitution of Louisiana. The reason of this omission is explained by General Banks' letter. He says—"The only provision of the bill not embodied in the Constitution is that which denies the elective franchise to men who have borne arms against the United States. The Convention would have readily adopted this provision, but, although the State, under the Constitution, establishes the condition of suffrage even for Members of Congress, it was impracticable for Louisiana, to overthrow the policy of the General Government in this respect. The principal officer in the Treasury in New Orleans, held a commission in the Rebel army, and the Quarter Master and the Chiefs of other Departments have been ordered to employ in public services deserters from the enemy."

There appears to be an error in this statement; the policy of the General Government cannot be held to be such as is declared, for the Act of Congress, the only means we have of ascertaining its policy, is entirely different. The policy of the Executive, may be correctly stated by General Banks, but the Executive is not the General Government; and the reason assigned for the omission of the Convention, is therefore insufficient. This difference between the Act of Congress and the new Louisiana Constitution is of an important character. Under the Act of Congress it is designed to put the State government in the hands of the real friends of the Union, whereas, if the government of the new Constitution could be spread over the whole State, there is danger that the result would be of quite another kind.

The entire want of compliance with the forms required by the Constitution and laws of Louisiana, in the various orders and elections which have preceded the formation of this Constitution have been insisted on, not merely on account of their own importance, but because the attempt is made to recommend the instrument to favor by alleging that these forms have been complied with.

The far weightier objections are, that all these movements were impelled by mere Military authority; that the resulting Constitution is no more than a Military rescript; that the whole proceedings has been in opposition to the will of Congress, which alone, possesses the constitutional power to act on the subject; that not one-half of the Parishes or Territories of the State had any thing to do, even nominally, with the Elections of the Convention; and that of that portion of the State, which did not participate, there is nothing to guide us but uncertain conjecture as to the amount of population; that the Parishes nominally represented in these elections and the Convention are only partially controlled by the National arms; and that no satisfactory census of their population, whereon to base representation in a Convention, has been taken.

General Banks, devotes a portion of his letter to an estimate of the population of the State. On this subject, it must be premised that if the rebellion of the State has produced no change in its relations to the General Government, if its Constitution survived, and, without any enabling Act of Congress, the citizens, or a fraction of their number can send Senators and Representatives to Congress, and cast an electoral vote for President, then the question of population becomes of no importance, for no matter how much it may have been reduced, the rights of the State to representation under the census remain unimpaired, unless the causes effecting that reduction have also changed the relations of the State.

But if such be not the condition of the political relations of the inhabitants of Louisiana, if the State has forfeited its rights by rebellion, as we believe, then there must be an enabling act, and an enumeration of the people, not conjectural but actual.

General Banks says: "the statement that Louisiana does not control half the population or half the territory of the State is very far from being true."

Let us examine the question: The Constitution framed by the Convention assembled under General Orders No. 35, was submitted to the vote of the people of "this State," on the first Monday of September, 1864.

On the nineteenth of the same month Mr. Hahn, Military Governor of Louisiana, issued a Proclamation, declaring the official vote "cast in the State, as far as received for and against the Constitution according to returns received at the office of the Secretary of State," to be as follows: . . . [12]

In looking at this table, it is found, that the vote in favor of the Constitution in Orleans, is greater than the aggregate of all other votes, both for and against the Constitution, so that the State is made by the city alone, and would have been so made had every vote outside of it, been unanimously cast against the Constitution. Now it is precisely in

12. Durant lists the vote by parish. The vote was 6,836 for, and 1,566 against.

New Orleans, there is the strongest reason for believing that influence and patronage carried the election, and where a Congressional investigation would most probably show that the majority consisted of electors who were not duly qualified, and that the influences at work overpowered dissent.

When you look for the above named parishes on the map, you will find them all except St. Martin, St. Mary, Assumption, Lafourche, Terrebonne and St. Landry (six in all), lying on both sides of the Mississippi river; and inquiry will assure you that in most of them above Jefferson, but little more is possessed by us, than the immediate bank of the river; while in regard to St. Martin, St. Mary and St. Landry you will not find that we control one half of either. . . . [13]

Showing that the area of all the parishes which voted on the Constitution does not, in the aggregate, much exceed one third of the entire area of the State, and of this portion we have not actual control of more than a half, even if so much.

It is impossible for any one to say, with accuracy, what the population of Louisiana is, at the present time. It might be taken as a fair presumption that it has decreased in about equal proportions in all parts of the State, and in that case, by far the greater part of the population is under the dominion of the rebel Governor Allen.[14]

The letter of General Banks controverts this theory of equal diminution of the population and insists that the decrease has been greater outside of the Union lines than inside: a conjecture which may be right or wrong, but nothing else than an enumeration can determine which it is.

According to the United States Census of 1860 and the Report of the State Auditor of Public Accounts made to the Legislature of Louisiana in January 1862, the population of those parishes, which according to Governor Hahn's Proclamation recently voted on the Constitution, was as follows: . . . [15]

The above will show the inaccuracy of what purports to be official censuses, taken within a few months of one another. . . . [16]

This, at the first glance, admitting the population to have remained unchanged, would seem to show a large majority within the parishes which voted on the Constitution. But this appearance will vanish when it is

13. There follows a list of the square milage of the parishes concerned and of the state.

14. Henry W. Allen, Confederate States governor of Louisiana.

15. The total from the 1860 census is 423,811, and that from the U.S. census of 1861 is 286,360.

16. Durant subtracts the total for the parishes he is studying from the U.S. census total for the entire state.

considered that in a number of those parishes, though real or pretended elections may have been held in some points of them, yet that the control of our forces does not extend over a third of their territory; . . . [17]

Of these Parishes, we do not hold, on the average, one-third of the area; but assuming that proportion, then the population being unchanged, we would have a right to count one third of it, i.e., 47,884 as within our lines, leaving 95,770 outside, which, deducted from the aggregate of the twenty Parishes above, leaves 328,157, less than one half of the population of 1860.

I, of course, am well aware that the population has not remained unchanged; and I am equally well convinced that the proportions are not such as are stated, but that in point of fact, there is a much smaller proportion within the Union lines than allowed above: all which serves to show that, as a preliminary to organization, a trustworthy census should be taken.

I now give the votes cast in these twenty Parishes in the Presidential election of 1860, and the vote for the ratification of the Constitution in 1864. . . . [18]

Now, admitting all the votes proclaimed as having been cast on the 5th September last to be genuine, which many are very far from believing, compare the vote of 1864 with that of 1860, and we find the former is not one third of the latter: and if we should suppose that the vote in the whole State—the Convention election was ordered to take place in every Parish—has fallen off in the same ratio as in the above named Parishes, then the vote in Parishes where no election was held on 5th September last, would be found to be 7,530, making an aggregate of (by supposition) 15,932 votes in the entire State at this time. This result, however, is entirely inconsistent with what I believe to be the facts of the case, and also with the estimates contained in Gen. Banks's letter.

That letter tells us that from forty-two to forty-five thousand men have enlisted from Louisiana in the rebel armies. His sources of information are probably correct; and if all these were voters, there would be left only eight thousand in the State, as the total vote polled on the Presidential election of 1860 was 50,510, whereas there must be, according to the estimate made above, nearly sixteen thousand. So that it is impossible to arrive at any satisfactory conclusion either as to the number of voters or the population by any estimate or conjecture. This becomes more apparent when we learn

17. A table of the parishes' population.

18. Durant takes his figures from New Orleans newspapers and comes up with 26,694 votes cast in 1860, and 8,402 votes cast on the Constitution of 1864.

further from the General's letter, that ten thousand white men have enlisted in the National Army, making a total enlistment (by supposition) in the two Armies of fifty-two to fifty-five thousand men, far more than the whole number of voters in 1860; and yet when these are disposed of, for the forty-two to forty-five thousand rebel soldiers or voters are all out of the State, we still have some sixteen thousand left; such results demonstrate the fatal errors of the estimate and must serve to convince all, that no means have been adopted to ascertain with reasonable accuracy the number of electors in the State and, not even of that portion of them within the Union lines, or which can, in any degree be deemed satisfactory by one who seeks correct or safe results.

General Banks avows the belief that from forty-two to forty-five thousand men, most of whom he says were politicians—meaning I presume voters—left the State as soldiers in the rebel Army. That one-fourth of the slaves have perished; and as the whole number by the census of 1850 was 331,726; the number who have disappeared is 87,931. That a number of negroes, equal to the rebel enlistments, accompanied their masters, or fled with their own powers to surrounding States. And that the diminution of the white population is nearly equal to the loss among the blacks. If I rightly understand the General, then, he estimates a total decrease of population in the State of 265,862: but this is not his complete meaning, for he says immediately afterwards, that the entire population of the State at the present time is 451,000, of which number he thinks that two thirds are within the Union lines. Two thirds of the number stated are 300,700, about; and leaves only 150,300, in the remainder of the State; such estimates are not supported by any sound conjectures, and even if they were are not a proper basis to place reconstruction upon. If there are really such large number of persons now within our lines how is it that the Constitution received so meagre a vote as 8,402, when it is pretended we have a population of 300,700?

But while these estimates are claimed by General Banks to be correct, we find a Convention assembled under his General Orders No. 35, assuming the powers of a Legislature, dividing the whole State into five Congressional Districts, as if they controlled it all, and actually causing to be elected five members of Congress, the number to which only the total Census population of 708,002 was entitled; when the electors in all of them did not reach, at the election of 5th September, 1864, eight thousand three hundred.

On the whole an impartial examination of the statements of General Banks in regard to the population of Louisiana, will fail to bring conviction to the mind of their accuracy. They are, indeed, mere conjectures. They may possibly be right, but they are probably wrong, as many here believe. The nation cannot and ought not to permit the Executive, by military orders, to substitute conjecture for facts; or to cut the knot with the sword.

Louisiana is not a State in the constitutional sense of that word. Her relations with the Government of the United States have been broken by rebellion. She is a State in insurrection; so decreed by Act of Congress, which the Executive cannot do away with. By the same power of Congress she must be reconstructed and readmitted, on such terms and conditions as may be found consistent with justice and safety.

The foregoing remarks are devoted to a consideration of objects unconnected with the intrinsic merits of the Constitution itself; these, however, General Banks, has been pleased to speak of in terms of high laudation.

Some of these claims to exalted praise are worthy to be examined. General Banks' letter says, speaking of the Convention: "And what was the result of their labors?"

"In a State which held 331,726 slaves, one half of its population in 1860, more than three quarters of whom had been specially excepted from the operation of the Proclamation of Emancipation, and were still held *de jure* in bondage, the Convention declared by a majority of all the votes to which the State would have been entitled, if every Delegate had been present from every District in the State:

"Instantaneous, universal, uncompensated, unconditional emancipation of slaves."

The slave population above stated is less than half of the total population in 1860.

The slaves in the parishes excepted from the operation of the President's Emancipation Proclamation of January 1, 1863, are stated in the Census to be . . . [19]

Such was the number excepted by the President from emancipation: while the whole number in the State was 331,726: so that far from there having been two thirds of the whole number, excepted from emancipation, there was but little more than one fourth of the whole number left in slavery.

On page 74 of the official Journal of the proceedings of the Convention is found the vote on the adoption of the report of the Committee on Emancipation. It there appears that there were in the affirmative seventy-two votes and in the negative, thirteen. The next day two more votes were added to the affirmative, making seventy-four. The whole number of

19. Durant cites twelve union parishes holding 93,162 slaves.

members of which the Convention was ordered to consist was one hundred and fifty, of which seventy-six was a bare majority, and also a *quorum*. Now, neither seventy-two votes, nor seventy-four were "a majority of all the votes to which the State would have been entitled, if every Delegate had been present from every District in the State." And more than that, there were Delegates present, as representing parishes in which, as has already been shown, no vote could be taken, when the Constitution was submitted to the people, and who therefore represented, legally speaking, no constituencies.

The seventy-two or seventy-four Delegates, who voted for emancipation, were, no doubt, in favor of the measure, but at the same time it must be remembered that the Convention had no choice in the matter.

The Convention, Journal page 3, commences in these words—"Wednesday, April 6, 1864, The Convention met in Liberty Hall, New Orleans, at 12 M., in pursuance of paragraph XI, of General Orders No. 35, of Major General N. P. Banks, the Commanding General of the Department."

Those general orders, with the proclamation of January 11, were the parent of the Convention. They were purely military in their authority.

Martial Law had been proclaimed in the Department of the Gulf, on May 1, 1864, and exists up to the present day. The Proclamation of Major General Banks of January 11, 1864, paragraph VI, said that, "The fundamental law of the State is Martial Law."

The first paragraph of the same proclamation said that "the constitution and laws of Louisiana, which recognize, regulate or relate to slavery, must be suspended, and they are therefore, and hereby declared to be inoperative and void."

This was the abolition of slavery by Martial Law, to which the Convention itself was subject. What could that Body do, then, but abolish slavery, if they touched it at all? And what difference would it have made had they not gone through the form of abolishing it? None whatever, as all laws in relation to it had already been declared void by a power superior to that of the Convention. They only registered a decree, and can claim no merit for the ministerial act. The benefit was conferred by the Commander of the Department. . . . [20]

On page 71 of the Journal of the Convention, it appears, that the Report of the Committee on Emancipation being under consideration, Mr. Abell offered the following proviso to section 3d.

---

20. Durant cites information to the effect that "the whole political power of the State is vested exclusively in the white citizens."

"Provided always, that the Legislature shall never pass any Act authorizing free negroes to vote, or to immigrate into this State under any pretence whatsoever."

The question was divided by the words "to vote," when the first clause was carried by sixty-eight for, to fifteen against.

The next day, the debate was cut off with the amendments by the previous question, but the sense of the Convention, at that time, as to the extension of the suffrage to persons of African descent had been expressed by an emphatic majority against it. This was on the 10th day of May, 1864.

It appears a change was produced in the sentiments of the Members of the Convention, by what influence is not publicly known. On the 23d of June, Mr. Gorlinski, offered the following as an additional article to the general provisions, as follows:

"The Legislature shall have power to pass laws, extending the right of suffrage to such persons, citizens of the United States, as by Military service, by taxation to support the Government, or by intellectual fitness, may be deemed entitled thereto." This was adopted by forty-eight in the affirmative, to thirty-two in the negative. See Journal p. 130. It is understood to have reference to persons of African descent, but is ambiguous, under the decision of the Dred Scott case.

This is the only approach towards equality—another word for justice, which is made in the Constitution. If the authors of that instrument were really in favor of the principle, why did they not establish it? Can it be supposed, that a more opportune occasion will ever arrive, or one where there will be more generosity or less prejudice?

Let us suppose, that the Major General Commanding the Department of the Gulf, had called a Convention consisting exclusively of Members of the other race—that he had permitted only *black* citizens of the United States to vote—that he had allowed only his black soldiers to participate in the election—and that the Constitution had allowed only blacks to vote and hold any office, executive, legislative, or judicial? And that, he had proclaimed this as establishing equality before the law? What answer would the white citizens have given to such an assertion? It is easy to see, and equally easy to know, that a clause permitting a future Legislature, to extend suffrage to whites, would hardly have been deemed very satisfactory by the latter.

The Constitution does not make all men equal before the law; and no such claim can be consistently set up for it.

Seventy five years ago the great Apostle of American democracy said: "With what execration should the statesman be loaded, who permitting one half the citizens thus to trample on the rights of the other, transforms those into despots, and these into enemies, destroys the moral of the one and the amor patriæ of the other."

There are other objections to the Constitution which are rather of a moral than a political character, but equally worthy of consideration. . . . [21]

It is not difficult to make a good Constitution, we have so many to copy from; but it is difficult to make a State by a military order. Such a consummation deliberately abandons its functions, under Executive dictation.

21. Durant facetiously cites other actions of the constitutional convention, including a lottery, to show its illegal activities.

The Political Position of Thomas J. Durant

(New Orleans: Printed at the Office of the True Delta, 1865)

Anthony Paul Dostie (1821–1866) was born in Saratoga County, New York, where he trained as a barber and a dentist. He moved to Chicago, then to Michigan, and finally settled in New Orleans in 1852 to practice dentistry. A courageous union man, Dostie refused to take the oath of allegiance to the Confederacy, was imprisoned in Nashville, and then escaped to Chicago, where he spoke in support of the Union cause and advocated a Federal invasion of the Gulf Coast. He returned to New Orleans in August 1862 and wrote and lectured in favor of reconstruction; his January 1864 address at City Hall calling for an end to slavery is well known. He also served as state auditor under the free state governor, Michael Hahn. Dostie broke with his ally Thomas Durant when the latter attacked the free state government. Dostie's candidacy for congress in 1864 failed to gain reformist support, but he continued as a unionist leader and led in the constitutional convention, where he advocated the emancipation of slaves and the arming of ex-slaves from Louisiana to fight to restore the Union. He lost the state auditorship when the war ended because he favored suffrage for ex-slaves. He was mortally wounded in the 1866 New Orleans riots as he courageously spoke out for the rights of the freedmen.

The pamphlet included herein, which originated as a December 29, 1864, letter to Henry L. Dawes, chairman of the House of Representatives Committee on Elections, announced Dostie's call for a new convention that would support black voting and require the Federal congress to accept Louisiana back into the Union. Dostie's pamphlet, a systematic and forceful denunciation of Thomas Durant, reveals the bitter divisions of wartime Louisiana unionists over reconstructionist policies.

Although obviously biased, the best study of Dostie's life is that of his daughter, Emily Hazen Reed, *Life of Anthony Paul Dostie: Or the Conflict in New Orleans* (New York: W. P. Tomlinson, 1868). Also see William C. Harris, *With Charity for All* (Lexington: University Press of Kentucky, 1997).

* * *

I see by the newspapers that the Congressional delegation from Louisiana has been met by a protest from thirty-one citizens of Louisiana under the leadership of Thomas J. Durant.[1]

Although this protest was drawn up and signed in this city, the free State men of this State knew not its contents until the document had quietly been sent to Washington, and after being printed by order of Congress, found its way back again to this city, and was published in one of our newspapers this morning. The friendly spirit which you manifested towards the Union men of Louisiana in your successful efforts for the admission of her Representatives to Congress in February, 1863, and the important official position you occupy with reference to questions of this kind, lead me to address you hurriedly some remarks with the view of enlightening you on the political antecedents and antics of Durant, so that his statements may not be received for more than they are worth.

The machinations and insidious efforts of this man to thwart and defeat the restoration of Louisiana to the Union, make it highly proper, if not necessary, that some notice should be taken of his movements. He appears to have the reputation abroad of being associated with the Free State movement here and to have caused many citizens of other States, including members of Congress, to believe him to be the Magnus Apollo of our cause. He is not in any wise a reliable exponent of the Free State men of Louisiana, as I shall conclusively demonstrate. Was Louisiana the tribunal before which the questions involved are to be decided, I should not find it necessary to notice or expose Durant. He is well known here. His movements and his inconsistencies are thoroughly understood, and need no ventilation. His party has been reduced to thirty-one. His organization has dissolved; his partisans of yore have found that there was neither virtue nor prophecy in his oracles. They are now reduced to thirty-one; and a considerable portion of these thirty-one are, or have been, applicants for office under the present State Government; showing, though they have yielded to his request for their signatures, they have no faith in the results of his efforts. So much for Durant as he is, and appears to us at home.

1. See Durant's pamphlet in this volume.

But during the past summer he performed a pilgrimage to the North, and while the friends of the Free State cause were battling for their principles before the people at the polls, he was traveling about misrepresenting their efforts and the conditions of affairs, and electioneering against President Lincoln. That he has deceived many good and honest men, is evident. It therefore seems necessary that the true character and past history of this man should be known abroad as well as at home.

Thomas J. Durant has been known in Louisiana for the past twenty or twenty-five years as a prominent office-seeking politician. He was United States District Attorney under Polk; and when more recently, in the co-operation campaign, he was accused of having opposed the annexation of Texas, on grounds of hostility to the extension of slavery, he vigorously and publicly denied any such motives. But his more recent political tergiversations, it is more to the purpose to examine.

During the reign of the Confederacy in this city he was one of its most obedient adherents. Although above the age to be required to do militia service, he with much alacrity entered as a private into the ranks of the citizen soldiery, and his stately and measured tread and perfection and accuracy of drill were emulated by the admiring youth of the city who were wont to look to him as an example.

He conformed to the requirements for members of the bar and entered as one of the earliest and most active practitioners in the "Confederate States District Court." In doing this he showed much more readiness than after the arrival of the Union fleet when he refused to practice his profession for some six months on account of having to take the oath. . . . [2]

His house was a manufactory of Confederate soldiers' clothing, where rebel ladies used to assemble, and with their tongues and their needles give proof of their devotion to the cause of rebellion. These asseverations he cannot deny.

When at last the hearts of the Union people of New Orleans were gladdened by the arrival of the Union forces, who among the citizens went out with rejoicing and welcome upon his lips? Was it Thomas J. Durant? No; he stalked sulkily and sullenly about with his hands in his pockets, finding fault with everything. He was invited to attend the first Union meeting at No. 44 St. Louis street, in Polar Star Hall. He did so, but what did he do? When the formation of a Union *Association* was proposed, he resisted it; said it was no time; that our sons and brothers were upon the battle-fields; many had gone forth "under our own Beauregard"—(these words have been

2. Dostie prints a letter to prove Durant practiced law with Confederates.

publicly attributed to Durant, I hope erroneously, but without denial); that the result at Corinth was not as yet known; that it behooved the people of New Orleans to await results; that Butler was enticing the negroes to the Custom house and shielding them from the authority of their masters; and that it was best to know first whether our rights to "our property" were to be respected or violated. When the meeting, notwithstanding his speech, proceeded to organize the first Union Association of New Orleans, he withdrew.

Major Bell, the Judge of the Provost Court, after most of the leading members of the bar had commenced practicing in his Court, sent Col. Thorpe to invite Durant to do so also, but was refused on the ground of his objection to taking the oath to support the Constitution of the United States.

When the heart of every true Union man thrilled with joy to see the welcome blue coats frequenting our streets, Durant coldly and heartlessly said: "I hate the very sight of a soldier; to me it is emblematic of tyranny and despotism."

Desiring to take a trip to the North for the *benefit* of *his* health, and unable to procure a pass through the usual channels without taking the oath, he succeeded in obtaining one from Gen. Butler.[3] When the latter learned too late, that through his means he had gone North without taking the oath, he gave way to the strongest and most indignant vexation.

He wrote letters to the President of the United States, calling, or, as with the voice of John Hook, hoarsely bawling for protection to negro property as a *sine qua non* to submission or loyalty. Perhaps the President still has Durant's appeals for aid to the cause of slavery; if not, at all events, Mr. Lincoln's patriotic reply is no doubt on file at the Executive Mansion.

This man sets himself up as a sort of model upon the slavery question; in fact, his "I-am-holier-than-thou" sort of professions upon everything concerning the colored people—his refusal to give credit to the Free State movement for what it has done for their cause, make it necessary that I should analyze his antecedents strictly upon this question. I should not do so but for his unfairness and unjustness. Far be it from me to question any man's past who is patriotically working for our country's future. I freely and frankly admit that though I was never a pro-slavery man, and never bought and sold human flesh, I was in favor of letting the "peculiar institution" alone and against the unceasing agitation of the slavery question throughout the nation, and therefore against the abolition plan of carrying on the war; but

3. Union general Benjamin Butler, former military commander in New Orleans.

when the implacability of the rebellion manifested itself and the experience of the war showed slavery to be its strong pillar, when the necessity of its destruction was shown in order to secure the safety of the Union, I publicly declared myself for immediate abolition. I threw off all the previous conservatism of my policies when I saw my country in danger, and made the first public anti-slavery speech in New Orleans in 1862. Throughout the Union the most staid and conservative were changing their ground for their country's sake, which they had previously held, as they thought also, for their country's sake, and in the same spirit. Our glorious President by his proclamation of September 23, 1862, foreshadowed an entire change of policy in conducting the war so far as it affected slavery. I would not blame Durant for his multitude of inconsistent positions on the subject of the Union, slavery, reconstruction, State and Territorial Government, had they changed with an enlightened progression in favor of the cause of the Union, freedom and restoration. I shall simply narrate his political antics, and if they are explainable on any grounds other than those of selfishness, political disappointment, acridity of temper and jealousy that anything could be accomplished as well or better by other hands, I will leave the task to his vindicators.

His first appearance as a Union man to my recollection, was upon my invitation to address the Union Association of New Orleans in 1863. He had, however, as I am informed made a Union speech in Jefferson City, one of our suburban towns.

The first notable proposition he made was to restore Louisiana to the Union by a convention. He made several speeches in favor of immediate restoration by that method, and after most earnest and persevering efforts he succeeded in carrying one of the Union Associations in his favor. Those who opposed him believed in his views but deemed them premature. This was in February, 1863. He continued agitating on the question in the district or local clubs. He became Attorney General under the military authority of Gov. Shepley, and commenced a registry system for the voters of the city and country parishes.[4] He had registers appointed in all the parishes within the lines. He got up a plan for a convention upon the white basis, to consist of one hundred and fifty members, apportioned among the parishes almost identically as was adopted in the calling of the Convention of 1864. It was understood that Durant was the active promoter of the scheme of a convention, but that Gov. Shepley always found cause for delay. Excepting

4. George Foster Shepley, governor of Louisiana, 1862–1864, and a Union army major general.

his *penchant* for delay, he left everything in Durant's hands; and with this Durant was well pleased. But a *certain letter* was received from President Lincoln, who, not pleased with Shepley's delays, placed everything in the hands of Maj. Gen. Banks.

Here was the beginning of Durant's hostility to the plan which had been substantially followed in the restoration of Louisiana. Before that time there was, according to *his own speeches, territory enough* and *population enough fully* to warrant such a proceeding. Taking the thing out of Shepley's hands was taking it out of Durant's hands. Although all the propositions and plans of Durant have been substantially, nay almost identically followed, his opinions have undergone a radical change. What caused that change to come "o'er the spirit of his dreams?" Disappointment and ambition. He could not rule as "master," therefore he has striven to *ruin.* On November 22, 1863, at Lyceum Hall, Mr. Durant said: "In this contest there could be no neutrality; if one was not with his country wholly and enthusiastically, he was co-operating with the enemies." Also: "He who fails to uphold the Administration in all its measures helps the rebellion to tear the country to pieces." In this speech he expressed his belief that he was addressing an audience that was willing to lay their all upon the altar of their country, to preserve the Union and establish freedom to all mankind.

> "But we are not a territory in the *common* acceptation of that term—such, for instance, as Nebraska and Nevada—we are merely in a state of insurrection, under military rule and without a State Government, and when the time comes, if the people themselves will step forward and frame a Constitution, recognizing the principles of freedom as laid down in the Emancipation Proclamation, and without slavery, the return of the State to her allegiance will be hailed with one universal shout of joy from all her free sisters; but until they do this, they must be content to live under the laws made by our military rulers, or as a territory of the United States."

That is the closing paragraph of one of his most elaborate speeches made but a little more than one year ago. The State's integrity is not assailed; State lines and State rights under the Federal Constitution are forcibly and eloquently defended. He says, in his letter to the Hon. Henry Winter Davis, that the friends of freedom were thwarted in their efforts by the executive at Washington. He says he has watched the progress of the Davis bill with anxiety because he perceived it would give "us" relief from the incapacity and infidelity of the executive administration. He, in his letter, is suddenly apprised of the great efficacy of the Davis plan of reconstruction. From the moment I had the honor to invite him to identify himself with the cause of

Unionism and liberty he urged, in his powerful arguments, that Louisiana had not seceded, that she was still a constituent member of the Union, that she could not disconnect herself from the hallowed bonds otherwise than by the provisions of the Constitution that formed it and made for us the great and glorious Republic; and now he speaks of the Davis' bill as being the only *constitutional* power known to the Government for the restoration of which in his ablest arguments he claimed had not been lost, and he dares to abuse the great and wise President in seeking to perpetuate in Louisiana "*all* that incapacity and selfishness can render odious to the citizens."

That Durant has been no stranger to the system of slavery, the following document, which may be seen at the Conveyance Office of this city, will show; he did not scruple to traffic in, and buy women and children. He said recently in a letter to the New York Tribune, that the people of New Orleans knew what he had done with his slaves. Yes, they do know. He kept them til the close of 1863, when, having got all the work he could out of them, and Gen. Butler's administration against his remonstrances having rendered them of no further pecuniary value to him, he ostentatiously emancipated them in open court, not quietly like hundreds of other citizens, telling them that they were free, and contracting for their services as free laborers without a forced and unreasonable display of pretended generosity. What magnificent philanthropy! . . . [5]

I now give an extract of his remarks at a united Southern action mass meeting at the Orleans Theatre, as published in the Daily True Delta, January 4th, 1861: . . . [6]

He says "no free State Constitution had, on the 8th day of July, been adopted or installed in the fragment of Louisiana held by the military forces of the United States." On the 11th May the Convention, representing fully two-thirds of the entire population of the State, passed the Ordinance of Emancipation. Eighty-five members of the Convention were present and voted upon the great question. Of this number seventy-two voted in favor of the Ordinance, declaring slavery forever *abolished* and prohibited throughout the State, and inhibiting in their fiat the Legislature from making laws recognizing the right of property in man, and proclaiming that all children, from the ages of six and eighteen years, shall be educated by maintenance of free public schools; also, that all able-bodied men in the State shall be armed and disciplined for its defence, and that the black man may receive

5. Dostie prints a notice of Durant's slave sale from May 1851.
6. Dostie prints a letter in which Durant says he would be happy out of the Union.

the full rights of citizenship. Are these not jewels of liberty? With these invaluable jewels the Constitution was adopted in the hearts of the people. The form of ceremony of ratification had not been gone through 'tis true; but Mr. Durant, from his knowledge of the loyalty of his fellow-citizens, could scarcely help knowing it would be ratified by an immense majority, and if he was imbued with that patriotism and love of liberty his eloquent speeches in his saner and more generous moments portray, he would feel to thank those who stood by the helm of the ship when he was in the hold endeavoring to scuttle and sink her.

Durant participated in the election for State officers in February, 1864; he was chairman of a committee which conducted the campaign for one set of candidates; he made numerous publications and speeches, and his partner, Chas. W. Horner, who now "certifies" the protest, went before the people on Durant's ticket as a candidate for Attorney General! The Durant ticket obtained only about one sixth of the entire vote cast. Finding the weakness of his party, and abandoning all hope of being returned to the Constitutional Convention, he suddenly came to the conclusion that he would not be a candidate, "because the whole movement was irregular!" His partner was, however, again a candidate, and again unsuccessful. If Durant or his partner had been elected, it is fair to assume that we would have had none of their pigmy efforts to retard the great Free State movement in Louisiana. And if the President had, in compliance with his wishes, directed Gen. Butler to respect slave property, Durant would not have sought (as he did in his published letter to H. Winter Davis) to ridicule our glorious President, by quoting the lines:

> "Full well they laugh, with counterfeited glee,
> At all his jokes, for many a joke has he."

But I fear the length of this letter may tire you. I have written hurriedly and therefore incoherently. Let the patriotism and earnestness of my heart compensate for my delicacy of style. I have written more in a spirit of sorrow than in anger. My aim has been nothing to extenuate nor aught to set down in malice; but I have considered it my duty as a good citizen to unmask the conduct of one who has immodestly and unjustly sought to thrust himself before the country as the only consistent Union and Free State man of Louisiana, and thus sought to injure the glorious cause of loyalty and restoration, under our new Constitution. How far he will succeed in his mischievous and disloyal practices or in his effort to control the politics of this State, remains to be seen. With regard to the amount of his success at a distance, where he is not known, I can not prophecy. But for the people of Louisiana I can safely say that they have no confidence in his political integrity or wisdom.

P.S.—While closing the above letter a number of additional documents have come into my possession, throwing further light upon Durant's record, which I shall, if necessary, make the subject of another letter.

THOMAS C. FLETCHER

Speech on the Occasion of the Reception by the Legislature of the News of the Passage of the Convention Ordinance Abolishing Slavery in Missouri

(Jefferson City: W. A. Curry, 1865)

Thomas Clement Fletcher (1827–1899) was born in Jefferson County, Missouri, clerked at the county courthouse, studied law at night, and became a lawyer in 1856. A supporter of the Thomas Hart Benton wing of the Democratic Party, he opposed secession. During the Civil War he served as a colonel in the Missouri Union Infantry. He was wounded at the battle of Chickasaw Bayou, captured, and imprisoned until 1863. Finally exchanged, he fought at Lookout Mountain and commanded a brigade in the Atlanta campaign. Elected governor in early 1865 as a Republican, Fletcher took the lead in the abolition of slavery in Missouri. He served as governor until 1869 and presided over various accommodations that allowed Confederate sympathizers to participate in reconstruction political affairs. Afterward he practiced law in St. Louis and Washington, D.C.

His ringing speech delivered on January 11, 1865, at the Emancipation Jubilee at the state capitol, which fittingly ends this volume, was published as a pamphlet, and ten thousand copies were circulated throughout Missouri and Tennessee. In it he proclaimed ecstatically the end of slavery in his native state. For Fletcher, the white people of Missouri had been removed from a terrible burden. He urged all true unionists to rally round abolition and continue to fight to end the war, and he attacked Missouri's pro-Confederates as guerrillas bent on destroying the loyalists. Fletcher also hoped that all loyalists would repopulate their own counties and restore effective local government.

For an account of Fletcher's role among Missouri's unionists, see William E. Parrish, *Missouri under Radical Rule, 1865–1870* (Columbia: University of Missouri Press, 1965).

* * *

I thank you for the invitation you have given me to mingle my voice with yours on this occasion of our general rejoicing. In the lightning's chirography by the fact is written ere this over the whole land—Missouri is free! I do not feel like talking now. At the end of a long war, after the last blow is struck and the crowning victory won, words fail to give an impression of the real feelings of the victory.

Forever be this day celebrated by our people. Let us teach our children, on the annual recurrence of the eleventh day of January, to meet around the altar of Liberty and renew their thankfulness for our deliverance; and, in the historic contemplation of our redemption, renew the songs of our jubilee. Through all coming time this day should be celebrated in the manner indicated by John Adams for celebrating the fourth day of July—by bonfires, ringing of bells, firing of cannon, and waving of flags. There is something in the feelings of an old "Black Republican," an old Abolitionist, who has endured the proscriptive and intolerant rule of the arrogant slave power in Missouri for the last fifteen years, that language is entirely inadequate to express. In this free atmosphere he feels himself a head taller.

To-day we remember the acts of that party which, when in the incipient stages of rebellion, declared "that Missouri should share the fate of her sister slave States." For once they told the truth. Missouri has obtained the lead, and "her sister slave States" will share her fate. . . . [1]

The white men of Missouri are to-day emancipated from a system which has so long lain with crushing weight upon their energies. We are now rid of every weight, and ready for the race. And the black man, too, is free. The gates of a bright future are open to him as well as to us.

Let us now set to work as becomes men, to rid ourselves of all the effects the damnable system of slavery has left behind it. Not the least among these are the bushwhackers, redhanded marauders and robbers, fit allies of the institution which enslaved the souls and bodies of men.

I anticipate that the action of this Legislature, in coöperation with the policy of Major General Dodge, will enable us to hold in security, what we have so fairly possessed ourselves of.[2] MISSOURI BELONGS TO THE LOYAL MEN OF MISSOURI, AND TO THEM ALONE. They have bought it with the price of blood, and their title is such as is respected by all civilized nations. If there is but one single loyal man in any one county of this State, he shall

1. Fletcher prints a short, bad poem on liberty.
2. Union general Grenville M. Dodge.

stand up at the county seat of his county and defy Jeff Davis and the whole rebel Confederacy.

We will so organize our forces as to give perfect security to every man in his life and property. Let our loyal men be of good cheer. Let them go back and repopulate the deserted counties of the border. They shall possess their homes again, and no man shall dare molest or make them afraid.

Major General Dodge, commanding the Department of the Missouri, is not a talking general: he is a thinking and an acting one. He don't value any species of disloyalty. It don't bear any premium with him. His policy, permitted to be carried out, will give us security and peace. Let us sustain him, and insist that everybody sustain him. You will see his policy only in its effects, and it will come upon some of our people like a peal of thunder from a cloudless sky. I refer to those who don't want to live in a free State, or who refuse to obey the laws and respect the civil authority.

I apprehend that we will have an efficient Militia. Those who cannot be trusted with guns will still be militia, and will not think it hard if, instead of being required to shoot their friends, the rebels, they should be detailed to the pioneer corps, the engineer corps, or the sappers and miners, and be armed with axes or spades. We will want block houses, stockades and forts all around the State, and in all exposed places. Roads and bridges are to be made for military purposes, perhaps; and I do not know but the militia might be called on to assist to complete some of our railroads, as a military necessity. We may lose some of our exceedingly *estimable* citizens who love slavery and civil war better than peace and prosperity. But I don't know where they can go. It is dangerous to be a traitor everywhere now, and there is no security for Slavery on this continent to-day, nor henceforth forever.

There are counties in this State where the large majority of the people make no effort to enforce the laws, or to render secure the lives and property of their loyal neighbors. It may be necessary to have a military force in such counties, and if so, the circumstances justifying it, that county will have to pay the troops stationed there. I tell them that the loyal men among them are not to be compelled to flee their homes. They shall be protected, and those who do not attempt to assist in putting down lawlessness shall pay for it.

In Free Missouri we intend that every man shall have something to do, and when a man is found doing nothing, we will ascertain whether he comes under the first section of the act concerning vagrants. I don't mean to *sell* these fellows who are loafers one day and bushwhackers the next. I don't believe any person could be found to invest in such chattels; but I hope the Legislature will annex another and greater punishment to vagrancy, so as to make the law a terror not only to evil doers who are taken in the act, but also to those who cannot give a good account of themselves, and have no visible means of support, useful occupation or known abiding place.

Soon the white-winged angel of peace will hover over Missouri, and, rising up in her greatness, she will beckon on Arkansas and "our sister slave States," to share with her the glorious destiny of Free America. One by one they will wheel into line beneath the flag that waves only over the free, and the land of Washington will shine forth in perfect freedom. The star of her glory will rise up to the zenith of its splendor, and, defying alike domestic feuds, civil discord, treasonable conspiracies or foreign aggressions, the genius of the re-United States of America, like the star which wise men beheld in the east, will, with the broad seal of eternal endurance stamped on her front, be the beacon light to lead the people of the whole earth to the shrine of Liberty, and teach them to worship with America, and rejoice in her blessed freedom.

PROCLAMATION OF FREEDOM

It having pleased Divine Providence to inspire to righteous action the sovereign people of Missouri, who, through their delegates in Convention assembled, with proper legal authority and solemnity, have this day ordained:

"That hereafter, in this State, there shall be neither slavery nor involuntary servitude, except in punishment of crime, whereof the party shall have been duly convicted; and all persons held to service or labor as slaves, are hereby declared free:"

Now, therefore, by authority of the Supreme Executive power vested in me by the Constitution of Missouri, I, Thomas C. Fletcher, Governor of the State of Missouri, do proclaim that henceforth and forever no person within the jurisdiction of this State shall be subject to any abridgement of liberty, except such as the law prescribe for the common good, or know any master but God.

Comments on Southern Unionist Pamphlets
Not Selected for Inclusion

I HAVE CHOSEN TO LIST and comment on twenty-two pamphlets that were not chosen for inclusion in this volume. So little has been written on the southern unionist leaders or on the way they expressed their views and concerns that I wanted to give the reader a larger sense of their significance. These pamphlets constitute a rich source of information and are important documents in their own right. They complement the ones included herein and provide further understanding of the issues that so concerned the southern unionist pamphleteers. Like those I selected to include, these pamphlets reveal the central preoccupations of a leadership class worried about the nature of governance during that disruptive war.

1. Lewis W. Powell, *Speech on Executive Usurpation* (Washington, D.C.: Congressional Globe Office, 1861).

A committed Kentucky unionist, Senator Powell spoke on July 11, 1861, to warn President Lincoln about aggressive use of force against the Confederacy. Of course, Powell was speaking to Kentucky unionists who at that time probably wanted to let the Confederates go in peace. Powell would change his views. But, like other slave state unionists who wanted the nation restored, he feared untoward coercion could unsettle his supporters.

2. William H. Collins, *Third Address to the People of Maryland* (Baltimore: James Young, 1861).

Speaking in Baltimore on September 2, 1861, to a unionist audience, Collins, a lawyer, equated loyalty to Maryland with loyalty to a reunited Union. In explaining the faulty logic of secession, he hoped to encourage citizens of neutral border slave states to support the northern war effort.

Collins affirmed that the Confederate government could in no way defend the rights and property of Marylanders, and that only the Federal government could.

3. Joseph Segar, *Letter to a Friend in Virginia* (Washington, D.C.: William H. Moore, 1862).

Segar read this letter to the Union Association of Alexandria on November 3, 1861. He then had it printed as a pamphlet to circulate in the border area of Virginia, and especially to his constituents in eastern Virginia. Originally sent to a relative in Virginia, Segar's letter explained why he supported the Union against the Confederacy. He used what became the stock argument of unionists who opposed the right of secession, denouncing secession as treason to the established government. Most troubling for Segar, southerners had defied the duly elected representative government and had behaved in a lawless manner. The result had been that even more slaves were lost through warfare than through any northern actions. He clinched his argument for why he chose to stay in the Union by saying a minority had forced secession on the majority of Virginians. For Segar, Virginia had become the "theatre of a devastating war," a border war that sapped resources and turned people against one another.

4. William A. Graham, *Speech on the Ordinance Concerning Test Oaths and Sedition* (Raleigh: W. W. Holden, 1862).

In a bitter speech of December 7, 1861, before the North Carolina convention, Graham spoke against the Confederate congress's demand for an oath of loyalty to the Confederacy. Although he would later join the Confederate congress, Graham voted against most war measures and insisted on his right of free expression and free press. He claimed that a free republican government did not need to abuse its citizens by demanding an oath of fealty. Was the Confederacy formed, queried Graham, to force its people into subjugation? "Let us not give just cause of offense to the people, by showing a distrust of that elevated patriotism and unanimity with which they are sustaining their country in this her hour of trial" (28). (Graham belongs to a category of Confederate supporters that is not represented in this volume. However, his plea against the divisive test oath reveals much about neutrality and unionism in his state of North Carolina.)

5. Andrew Johnson, *Speech on the Expulsion of Mr. Bright* (Washington, D.C.: Congressional Globe Office, 1862).

Johnson, perhaps the most famous southern unionist figure represented in this volume, gave a number of speeches in Congress and in the border northern states before he became military governor of Tennessee. Many of them were turned into pamphlets and widely distributed, even into Tennessee. This one, delivered in the U.S. Senate in January 1862, is typical of his violent outbursts and vigorous hostility toward Confederate authorities. Its subject was the expulsion of Indiana senator Jesse Bright for his prosouthern pronouncements. A former friend of Bright's, Johnson now believed that the Union government needed to present a united front, especially to its worried southern supporters. "The people of my state," said Johnson, "downtrodden and oppressed by the iron heel of southern despotism, appeal to you for protection" (9). Bright, he believed, stood in the way of the Federal government's desire to go all out to save the people of Tennessee, and Johnson had to stop him.

6. B. Gratz Brown, *Freedom for Missouri* (St. Joseph, Mo.: Weekly New Era, 1862).

From Washington, Senator Brown of Missouri wrote to praise the newest exponent of antislavery thinking, the *Weekly New Era*, published at St. Joseph. He repeated his arguments against slavery and insisted Missouri would have more people and be wealthier and more industrious if slaves had never been brought to the state. Although Brown found colonization one means to confront the racial issues surrounding abolition, he called upon the citizenry to support the freed people as equal opponents of the Confederate slave powers.

7. William G. Brownlow, *Irreligious Character of the Rebellion* (New York: Young Men's Christian Association, 1862).

In his Cooper Institute address of May 1862, "Parson" Brownlow added to his efforts to convince northerners to help liberate the loyal citizens of east Tennessee. His mode of operation this time was to chastise the Confederacy for its claims that the Lord supported its efforts. Rather, he argued, God favored the Federal government. Just look, he said, at the number of Union victories in 1862. Besides, the Confederates were a "mess of corruption," as infighting, drunkenness, and gambling prevailed even in Richmond. Did anyone, asked Brownlow, want to see this way of life perpetrated on the loyal unionists?

8. Robert J. Breckinridge, *Two Speeches on the State of the Country* (Cincinnati: Press of E. Morgan and Co., 1862).

In these addresses delivered in Ohio, the Kentucky preacher and editor of the unionist *Danville Review* continued to argue for a northern invasion of the middle South. Not only did he want to liberate Tennessee and Mississippi, but he knew that in the process Kentucky would also be freed from Confederate guerrilla invasion. Ohio, Indiana, and Illinois, he said, had saved Kentucky from the Confederacy. Its young men also could liberate the oppressed unionists of the mid-South.

9. Joseph Segar, *Vindication of the Union* (Washington, D.C.: W. H. Moore, 1862).

At a unionist meeting in his home district of Portsmouth, Virginia, Congressman Segar praised his constituents for their sacrifices in behalf of restoration of the Union. To his friends, North and South, he described how the Confederate forces had destroyed the commerce of coastal Virginia. Rather than protect slavery, said Segar, the Confederacy had placed it in jeopardy. But Segar also linked his own plight with that of his unionist constituents. He had been called a traitor by the Confederacy, and his life, he claimed, was in danger. Joining his actions with those of an earlier generation of loyal Virginians, Segar sought to show that his constituents were in the company of Washington, Madison, and Marshall.

10. Kelian V. Whaley, *Speech on a Bill to Provide for the Admission of West Virginia into the Union as a State* (Washington, D.C.: Hammell and Co., 1862).

Free state congressman Whaley spoke eloquently before Congress on the reasons for making western Virginia a separate state. The pamphlet was widely circulated among his western Virginia constituents to stir them to support statehood. His main point was that the people of western Virginia had long been discriminated against by the rest of Virginia, a bastion of the Confederacy. For Whaley, the desire to create West Virginia had begun forty years earlier when the east had deprived the people of equal representation, and the greatest wrong had been the east's use of the three-fifths clause to blackmail the west into supporting slavery. But most of all there should be a new state, Whaley said, because the people of the west, despite repeated attacks, had remained loyal to the Union. As to Virginia, "possibly we might forgive the bloodshed, the robberies, the imprisonments, which they have so ruthlessly inflicted upon us; but it is not possible for them to become worthy of such forgiveness, or capable of such forbearance" (7).

11. Andrew Jackson Hamilton, *Speech on the Condition of the South under Rebel Rule, and the Necessity of Early Relief to the Union Men of Western Texas* (New York: A. P. Warburton, 1862).

Hamilton spoke before the National War Committee of New York at the Cooper Institute on October 3, 1862. His pamphlet was said to influence northerners to aid southern unionists, and to have an impact on the unionists of New Orleans and east Texas. Hamilton emphasized that the majority of Texans had opposed secession and had been duped into supporting the Confederate war but now were eager to rejoin the Union. He also harped on the Confederate leaders' purpose in creating a new political system, one in which the nondemocratic slaveholding minority coerced the majority. In short, for Hamilton, what was at stake in the Civil War was the very existence of democratic society.

12. Lorenzo Sherwood, *The Slaveholders' Rebellion against Democratic Institutions* (New York: C. S. Westcott and Co., 1862).

A former Texas state legislator and native New Yorker, Sherwood had been forced to flee Texas after the war started. At Champlain, New York, he spoke of his experiences, and especially of his knowledge of a vast antidemocratic conspiracy by the leaders of the Confederacy. Since a majority of southerners believed in free labor and democracy, the North had to pursue the war to victory to free them. Sherwood warned that if the South succeeded, those who believed in democracy would be subverted and forced to support an aristocracy. The aristocracy would expand and the North would be engulfed. He then discussed the strength of the unionists in each southern state, to show northerners that a vigorous pursuit of the war would encourage the unionists to reclaim the government from the Confederate aristocrats. Sherwood's refrain to the North and to southern unionists alike was "be not discouraged." He concluded, "when the Union army goes to Texas, it will find a friend's country. This is my prophecy, for I know the people, and their attachment to free government, too well to be mistaken. Be not discouraged" (6).

13. Joseph Segar, *Speech on the Bill to Form the New State of West Virginia* (Washington, D.C.: W. H. Moore, 1862).

One who asked for careful political analysis of the plight of southern unionists was Virginia's loyal eastern congressman Joseph Segar, who, on December 10, 1862, addressed his fellow congressmen about his fears over the creation of the state of West Virginia. Segar's worries no doubt reflected those of his constituents in the Norfolk area, to whom the speech was circulated as a pamphlet. It was true, he said, that he wanted Virginia's Confederates to suffer for what they had done to the unionists. He wondered, however, whether a separate state of West Virginia would harm the restored government of Virginia and make things even worse for his constituents, because it could divide the unionists. "What," he said, "is to become of the people of the eastern shore . . . and those of York and Elizabeth City and other counties, who propose shortly to adopt the Wheeling government?" (5). Those counties would be set adrift, ignored by the Federal government, and that would allow the rebels to institute a reign of terror that would turn government anarchic. "Let us remain one and united, so that when the Union shall be reconstituted, we shall be once more a band of brothers" (7).

14. Andrew Jackson Hamilton, *Speech* (Boston: Press of T. R. Marvin and Son, 1863).

In this impassioned speech delivered at Faneuil Hall on April 18, 1863, Hamilton endorsed the abolition of slavery. To his northern allies he wanted to show the connection between their vigorous pursuit of the war and the southern unionists' support for the end of slavery. Hamilton also related his fellow Texans' love of democracy with their opposition to the slave-power antidemocratic conspiracy. Then, Hamilton turned to what he perceived to be the results of a Union military victory. Naturally the proslave aristocratic Confederates must be forever kept from postwar public office. But the loyal southerners, those who had come to oppose slavery, he said, were the rightful heirs of the reunited democratic government.

15. Charles Daniel Drake, *Camp Jackson: Its History and Significance* (St. Louis: Missouri Democrat Office, 1863).

Drake spoke in Union-controlled St. Louis on May 11, 1863, addressing all the state's loyal unionists about their victory over the state's secessionists. He reminded his fellow unionists of their need for vigilance against the state's Confederates, warning them that the pro-Confederates had used military force to try to remove Missouri from the Union and would use force again. Camp Jackson, a Federal military base, had become a symbol of unionism, just as abolition, said Drake, would unite Missouri's loyalists behind the union cause.

16. Hamilton Rowan Gamble, *Message to the Missouri State Convention* (Jefferson City: J. P. Ament, 1863).

The governor spoke to the state's leaders on June 15, 1863, on what he deemed a most difficult and controversial issue, the abolition of slavery in the state and the means to compensate unionist slave owners. He acknowledged that he had always believed that free labor was a better system than slavery, but that he had expected slavery to whither away gradually as slaves gave way to free labor. The necessity of winning the war, of striking the Confederacy at its heart, however, had forced him to favor immediate abolition. The need for proper compensation from the state government had made him decide that, rather than offer a scheme for payment, he would leave any action to the convention and the legislature. Gamble acknowledged that many Missouri unionists, such as Charles D. Drake, demanded uncompensated abolition, and that moderates favored some payment. (See Drake's attack on Gamble in this volume.) Caught in a dilemma of how to hold the antisecessionists together, at the end of his pamphlet Gamble resigned as governor.

17. Andrew Jackson Hamilton, *Letter to the President of the United States* (New York: Loyal Publication Society, 1863).

On July 28, 1863, fearing some loss of desire on the part of northerners to end slavery in the Confederate states, Texas governor-in-exile Hamilton wrote in support of the president's position on making ex-slaves citizens. He reminded the president that the ex-slaves were fighting and dying to restore the Union, and that made them citizens in fact. Southern unionists, he insisted, made up a majority of the South, and they would lead the government in a reunited republic. To allow slavery to continue in a restored nation would put the slaveholders back in power and support the continuation of the forced suffering of the southern masses. For those who worried about the future of race relations, Hamilton, who opposed forced colonization, argued that for the short term the paucity of white labor in the South required that ex-slaves be included in the workforce. When an adequate supply of white labor existed, "it is certain, that the black race will begin to desire a home and a government exclusively their own" (14).

18. William Alexander, *Elements of Discord in Secessia* (New York: Loyal Publication Society, 1863).

A northerner who had long lived in Texas, Alexander had been forced to flee his home when the war began and came to New York. Desirous of showing northerners the weaknesses in the Confederate governing system, Alexander hoped also to influence southern unionists to renew their resistance. He described the failure of the Confederate authorities to protect the people and charged that every promise made about the new nation had failed. The economy was in a state of disarray, the government could not feed the people, and the army was failing even to defend them. To make matters worse, Alexander claimed, many wealthy secessionists had taken their wealth to Europe, having given up on the future of the Confederate government.

19. Jacob Cooper, *The Loyalty Demanded by the Present Crisis* (Danville, Ky.: Moore, Wilstack, and Keys and Co., 1864).

Reprinted as a pamphlet and circulated widely in the upper South, Cooper's article was originally published in the *Danville Review* of March 1864. A professor at Centre College and a Presbyterian minister, Cooper wrote of his support for the Union cause and in favor of the actions of President Lincoln. He contrasted the evil Jefferson Davis with Lincoln and the movement to end slavery. At last, he said, the border slave states would give up that labor system which had so limited the opportunities of free white labor. Sacrifices to save the Union, even to the extent of punishing treason, were what was required. To his fellow Kentuckians, Cooper stated that there was no middle ground; one supported either the nation or a separate Confederacy. Therefore, to criticize what the Federal government had to do to restore the Union was to favor the Confederacy.

20. Peter G. Van Winkle, *Speech on the Reorganization of Virginia and the Admission of West Virginia* (Washington, D.C.: Gibson Brothers, 1864).

On April 21, 1864, the new U.S. Senator from West Virginia, Peter Van Winkle, spoke of the costs of loyalty to the Union for the people of the border slave states. Some had seen friends and even relatives turn to the Confederates, and that had wrenched families apart. Others who were loyal to the Union had their fidelity questioned time and again by northerners and even other border state leaders. Van Winkle commented specifically about Gov. Francis Pierpont of the restored state of Virginia, whose loyalty he defended on the floor of Congress. Even after West Virginia had been formed, he said, others questioned whether it should be allowed to continue as a separate state once the war had concluded. The political mess that had at one time created three Virginias, Van Winkle acknowledged, could trouble any loyalist. But the Pierpont and West Virginia governments should be recognized by all who worked to restore the Union. At that late date, to have to recall the history of the events of separation and to recount the loses of his people infuriated Van Winkle and indicated that sometimes so-called allies could be true enemies. And then, to question whether West Virginians and Pierpont's people would go along with the proposed Thirteenth Amendment guaranteeing the end of slavery was the final insult. For Van Winkle, the abolition of slavery was the best means to a restored Union, and that was what he and others had committed themselves to. But, he concluded, "as to the political and social status of the recent slaves it is only wise to await the development of events" (31). (Even at the last, Van Winkle and others fudged on just what the end of slavery meant. Speaking in a national forum, with his constituents reading his every word, he had to appease unionists who feared the effect of the end of slavery on their region.)

21. Bryan Tyson, *Object of the Administration in Prosecuting the War* (Washington, D.C.: McGill and Witherow, 1864).

Like Van Winkle, fearful of the administration's purpose in abolishing slavery, Tyson wrote this pamphlet under the auspices of the National Democratic Executive Committee. It circulated widely among northern Democrats, and his friends delivered copies to Virginia and North Carolina. In it, Tyson accused the Republican administration of prosecuting the war more to end slavery than to restore the Union. Tyson pointed out that many southern unionists were frustrated over the mingling of the slave issue with reunion. Some even questioned whether they could remain loyal to the Union. In North Carolina, he claimed, the Republicans wreaked havoc on the Union cause. Thus the upcoming presidential election was of utmost importance for him and other southern unionists. If his allies the Democrats won in 1864, then the Union with slavery would be restored. If the Republicans prevailed, then the war would go on for four more years. The southern unionists would continue to be victims, both of Confederates and of Republicans. In order to gain sympathy for his cause, Tyson described at length how Confederates slaughtered North Carolina unionists, even women and children. He wondered how long the unionists could survive those attacks.

22. Charles D. Drake, *Speech before the National Union Association* (Cincinnati: n.p., 1864).

In his speech of October 1, 1864, Drake of Missouri took exception with Tyson and other proslavery southern unionists. He urged northerners to reelect President Lincoln and border slave state unionists to support the abolition of slavery. Both events, claimed Drake, would hasten the end of the war and lead to the restoration of the Union. With peace, the bloodshed, especially the horrors of internal civil war in the slave states, would come to an end. The so-called Peace Democrats, he insisted, only prolonged the war and the devastation heaped upon southern loyalists.

Comments on Immediate Postwar
Southern Unionist Pamphlets

THIS LISTING OF PAMPHLETS from the immediate postwar years by former slave state unionists gives some indication of their continued loyalties. Alas, the plight of many of those unionists who stayed in the defeated Confederacy was horrendous. Their northern allies, and even some of their unionist friends, deserted a number of them. But many of those former unionists showed the courage of their convictions and thus in their actions revealed the dangers of having been on the winning side in the war. These pamphlets capture their desire for a lasting peace and to lead the new state governments. I have chosen to discuss the published efforts of ten of them in what should be called "pamphlets on the end game."

1. Robert Collier, *The Right Way for Restoring the Late Rebel States to the Federal Union* (Petersburg: A. F. Crutchfield and Co., 1865).

Written sometime in May 1865, this pamphlet had the goal of placing former unionists in authority in postwar Virginia. Collier explained to northerners and to Virginians that some of those who had been killed fighting for the Confederacy actually had been unionists. They had been forced into the war, being surrounded by enemies everywhere. Conversely, those who had remained loyal to the Union during the war "were not false to the South." Thus, the original Confederates should stand aside and make way for loyalists of all stripes to lead the movement to restore Virginia to the Union.

2. Francis H. Pierpont, *To the People of Virginia* (Washington, D.C.: McGill and Witherow, 1865).

In a speech of May 19, 1865, Restored state governor Pierpont of Virginia laid claim to his right to govern the state during Reconstruction. He described the secessionist leaders as "selfish" politicians who must be disfranchised. Pierpont argued that Virginia unionists had no government in 1861, so they had to create one for their own protection. Therefore, despite the indisputable fact that only a minority of the people had voted for him, many of whom now lived in West Virginia, his election had been valid. Although there was a difference of opinion among the state's union men on whether ex-Confederates could serve in office, he rejected any request for their gaining representation. Simply, he led the duly elected government and he would govern. (Soon, the Union general in command of Virginia would depose Pierpont, thus putting an end to that most loyal government in exile.)

In addition to wanting to establish stable government, Pierpont also wanted to restore civil life in the state. He discussed how a new banking system would have to be established, that a fund had to be raised to reopen the public school system, and that destroyed businesses would need help. He also demanded that slavery once and for all be abolished in the new state constitution. Since ex-slave labor was so important to getting the economy running again, Pierpont offered a plan for protection of those workers. The state would have to enforce a mutually agreed upon payment for labor. But a restored society above all "presumed that those who have contributed to bring the terrible strife and calamity on the State and nation, must see, by their misguided conduct, that their counsels will not be acceptable in the councils of the State or the administration of its Laws" (12). (Alas, Pierpont did not have his way.)

3. Rev. John Caldwell, *Slavery and Southern Methodism* (Newman, Ga.: printed for the author, 1865).

The author of the antiwar novel *The Thurstons of the Old Palmetto State* (1861), Rev. John Caldwell had chosen to remain in Georgia, despite threats to his person, to minister to his flock during the war. In the preface to this pamphlet of one of his sermons, Caldwell described how church members walked out when he preached on God's hostility to slave society. In hopes that the citizens of early postwar Newman would reconcile themselves to defeat and to the end of slavery, the minister once again took up the cause of peaceful reunion. But he now announced that he no longer could help them, and that he was leaving Georgia. (Thus were committed unionists lost to the postwar South.)

4. Joseph Segar, *Address on the War, the Union, and the Restoration of Peace* (Richmond: Richmond Republic, 1865).

Speaking in June 1865, at the Monumental Hotel in Richmond, Congressman Segar told of how the war for the Union had sapped all of his energy. This former defender of slavery had come to speak, he said, in favor of reconciliation of Virginians to the end of slavery. He accordingly asked them to pay fair wages to ex-slaves who worked for them. Segar also praised the Pierpont government and asked his audience to support the governor. Francis Pierpont, he said, had led the unionist state legislature to reenfranchise many who had supported the Confederacy, for the sake of harmony. (In that gesture Pierpont surely contributed to the political climate that would bring down both him and Segar.)

5. Albert W. Bishop, *An Oration Delivered at Fayetteville, Arkansas* (New York: Baker and Godwin, 1865).

The southern author of *Loyalty on the Frontier* (1863) spoke to a large audience in Fayetteville on the Fourth of July, 1865, to memorialize the suffering of Arkansas's loyalists. After recounting sadly the course of Arkansas into the Confederacy, Bishop derided the jubilation of early Confederate military victories. His real purpose, however, was to heap praise on those who had fought and sacrificed to restore the Union. Bishop insisted that Arkansas loyalists had been elected to bring the state back into the Union, but that the Federal congress had not accepted them as leaders. This was in part because those unionists had been careful about offering the freed people suffrage rights. "Revolutions beget great changes," he said, "and not infrequently the movers in them, by intemperate action, defeat the cause they labor to subserve" (10).

6. R. King Cutler, *Address to the Citizens of the State of Louisiana* (New Orleans: Rea's Steam Job Printing Office, 1865).

During August 1865, Senator Cutler, a former unionist, spoke to his constituents about Congress's refusal to seat him. He urged them not to despair and to continue to support the state constitution of 1864 as the best means of gaining readmission to the Union. He praised his ally Dostie and attacked his opponent Durant. But Cutler opposed the vote for Louisiana's ex-slaves out of fear that neither the state's former unionists nor President Andrew Johnson would support it. (In that way he played into the hands of the radicals in Congress who insisted that Louisiana's former unionists had joined the ex-Confederates.) Distraught at the turn of events, Cutler could only urge his fellow loyalists to support the Federal Union by refusing to vote any ex-Confederates into office.

7. Joshua Hill, *Letter on the Election of U.S. Senators* (Washington, D.C.: n.p., 1866).

Hill here replied to fellow Georgians who had sent former Confederate vice president Alexander H. Stephens to the U.S. Senate in 1866. Hill stated that despite his seeming neutrality in the war, unlike Stephens he had done nothing to hurt the Union cause. Indeed, Hill's aim was to protect his unionist credentials and gain the support of Georgia's former loyalists. He did not want former secessionists to win the peace and control Georgia's future. Hill bemoaned the decline of support for former unionists, and he predicted, all too correctly, that men like himself would fade from history while Georgia's Confederate heroes would become the leaders of a restored government. The Union, said he, will "become a phantom."

8. Anthony P. Dostie, *Address Delivered before the Republican Association of New Orleans* (New Orleans: published for the author, 1866).

In this pamphlet, delivered and printed just a month before his murder in July 1866, Dostie asked his fellow former southern unionists to cry out against restoring ex-Confederates to public trust and office. Those ex-Confederates, he said, threatened the very lives of the former loyalists. Dostie insisted President Andrew Johnson had brought those leaders back to power so they could restore slavery. For him, the war was not over, and the only way to keep out the ex-Confederates was to send even more Federal troops into the state, and particularly to New Orleans. To his audience and to history the future martyr proclaimed: "Let Andrew Johnson beware of treachery in himself, lest he call down the vengeance of betrayed millions" (9).

9. Alexander H. H. Stuart, *The Recent Revolution: Its Causes and Consequences, and the Duties and Responsibilities Which It Has Imposed on the People, and Especially the Young Men of the South* (Richmond: Printed at the Examiner Job Office, 1866).

Choosing as his topic the duties of the future generation of Virginia leaders, the former unionist sympathizer from the valley spoke on June 29, 1866, to students at the University of Virginia. Like former unionists, Stuart tried to explain what had caused the Civil War so that he could look in depth at its consequences. Having remained neutral in wartime, Stuart warned that if all Virginians did not unite, they would be overwhelmed by hostile outsiders. He acknowledge that former unionists had been correct in their positions, but he asked them to forget past wrongs and give up their cause. The pressures of peace, he said, overwhelmed the union cause and consigned their efforts to the dustbin of history. (In that way, history soon would manage to lump most southerners together.)

10. John Pool, *Address to the People of North Carolina* (Raleigh: North Carolina Standard Book and Job Office, 1867).

In November 1864, as a member of the North Carolina legislature, the self-declared unionist John Pool had called for the state to negotiate a separate peace with the Union. In 1867 he wanted to correct any impression that he had ever been anything but a unionist. To show his unionist credentials, Pool recounted the harrowing experiences of wartime North Carolina loyalists. His purpose in 1867 was to unite once again the peace activists of 1864 to drive former Confederates out of North Carolina politics. (Of course, unity with the peace opportunists would put diehard unionists in a minority position and thus lose the peace they had hoped for. That such a coalition made good politics was not the point. The unionist cause would now be forgotten as the Pool peace advocates would become the only voice in opposition to the former secessionists. Thus, another way was discovered to make unionism disappear from North Carolina and from former slave state history.)

Index

Abolitionists, Northern: southern unionist opposition to, 73, 84, 85, 189–90, 219; southern unionist support for, 226, 249, 255, 264, 370; and war policies, 97
Adams, John, 2, 370
Allen, Henry W., Governor, 353
American Revolution, 2, 3

Banks, Nathaniel P., General: as commander in New Orleans, 342, 343, 345, 347, 350–51, 352, 354, 355, 356, 357, 365
Bates, Edward, 293
Beauregard, P. G. T., General, 17, 25, 214, 362
Belmont, Battle of, 130, 203
Benjamin, Judah P., 212, 213
Bill of attainder, 87–88, 92
Blair, Jacob B., 325
Blair, Montgomery, 229
Bragg, Braxton, General, 6, 208, 251
Breckinridge, John C.: as C.S. general, 40; in U.S. Senate, 16, 18, 19, 22, 24, 25; mentioned 4, 5
Breckinridge, Robert J., 4, 16, 17, 27, 375
Bright, James, 85, 375
Brown, Albert Gallatin, 65, 213
Brown, Joseph E., 79
Brown, William G., 325
Browning, Orville Hickman, 83
Brownlow, William G., 5, 7, 105, 119, 375
Buchanan, James, 20, 21, 29, 39, 40
Buell, Don Carlos, General, 115
Burnside, Ambrose, General, 98

Bushwhackers, 153
Butler, Benjamin, General: in Louisiana, 363; policies in Norfolk, 273, 278, 279, 281, 282, 285, 286, 287, 290; mentioned, 291, 292, 295, 297, 298, 299, 302, 303
Butternuts, 277

Calhoun, John C., 18, 70, 72, 77, 109, 123, 124, 316
Carlile, John S., 82, 83, 276
Carroll, Anna Ella, 4, 16
Chase, Salmon P., 49, 291
Class appeal, 75, 78–79, 80, 103, 245–46, 258, 267, 270
Clay, Henry, 18, 110, 316, 317
Clayton, Philip, 269
Clemens, Jeremiah, 4, 7, 330
Clements, Andrew J., 309
Colonization of former slaves, 86, 220, 235, 271
Confederate government: corruption in, 6; failure of domestic policies of, 129–31, 145, 239–43, 331, 332, 334, 380
Conscript Law, Confederate, 129, 140, 145, 258, 331
Copperheads, 151, 226, 227, 232, 278, 302, 316
"Cotton is King," 5, 133, 193, 240, 241, 265, 335
Crittenden Compromise, 19, 20
Crittenden, John J., 99

Danville Quarterly Review, 27, 380